NOLO *Your Legal Companion*

"In Nolo you can trust." —THE NEW YORK TIMES

OUR MISSION
Make the law as simple as possible, saving you time, money and headaches.

Whether you have a simple question or a complex problem, turn to us at:

NOLO.COM

Your all-in-one legal resource

Need quick information about wills, patents, adoptions, starting a business—or anything else that's affected by the law? **Nolo.com** features free articles in our Nolopedia, legal updates, resources and all of our books, software, forrms and online applications.

NOLO NOW

Make your legal documents online

Creating a legal document has never been easier or more cost-effective! Create an online will or trust, form an LLC, or file a Provisional Patent Application! Check it out at **http://nolonow.nolo.com.**

NOLO'S LAWYER DIRECTORY

Meet your new attorney

If you want advice from a qualified attorney, turn to Nolo's Lawyer Directory—the only directory that lets you see hundreds of in-depth attorney profiles so you can pick the one that's right for you. Find it at **http://lawyers.nolo.com.**

ALWAYS UP TO DATE

Sign up for **NOLO'S LEGAL UPDATER**

Old law is bad law. We'll email you when we publish an updated edition of this book—sign up for this free service at **nolo.com/legalupdater**.

Find the latest updates at **NOLO.COM**

Recognizing that the law can change, we post legal updates during the life of this edition at **nolo.com/updates**.

Is this edition the newest? **ASK US!**

To make sure that this is the most recent edition available, just give us a call at **800-728-3555**.

(Please note that we cannot offer legal advice.)

A partnership between American Library Association and FINRA Investor Education Foundation

FINRA is proud to support the American Library Association

Please note

We believe accurate, plain-English legal information should help you solve many of your own legal problems. But this text is not a substitute for personalized advice from a knowledgeable lawyer. If you want the help of a trained professional—and we'll always point out situations in which we think that's a good idea—consult an attorney licensed to practice in your state.

12th edition

How to Buy a House in California

by Ralph Warner, Ira Serkes, & George Devine

edited by Alayna Schroeder

TWELFTH EDITION JANUARY 2009

Editor ALAYNA SCHROEDER

Cover Design JALEH DOANE

Proofreading ROBERT WELLS

Index MEDEA MINNICH

Printing CONSOLIDATED PRINTERS, INC.

Warner, Ralph E.

How to buy a house in California / by Ralph Warner, Ira Serkes & George Devine ; edited by Ilona Bray & Alayna Schroeder. -- 12th ed.

p. cm.

ISBN-13: 978-1-4133-0923-2 (pbk.)

ISBN-10: 1-4133-0923-2 (pbk.)

1. House buying--California. 2. Residential real estate--Purchasing--California. 3. Mortgages--California. 4. Housing--California--Finance. 5. Real estate business--California. I. Serkes, Ira, 1949- II. Devine, George, 1941- III. Title.

HD266.C2W37 2009

643'.1209794--dc22

2008031468

Quantity sales: For information on bulk purchases or corporate premium sales, please contact the Special Sales Department. For academic sales or textbook adoptions, ask for Academic Sales. Call 800-955-4775 or write to Nolo, 950 Parker Street, Berkeley, CA 94710.

Acknowledgments

Collecting and organizing the material for this book turned out to be a daunting task, one that might have defeated us had it not been for the enthusiastic help of Nolo legal editors Ilona Bray, Mary Randolph, Alayna Schroeder, and Marcia Stewart.

Special thanks to Mike Mansel, Certified Insurance Counselor, local insurance specialist, for keeping the book's material on the ever-changing insurance market up-to-date. Also thanks to Gwen Hoople of Holmgren and Associates (www.mortgageholmgren.com), who helped update and improve our advice on mortgage funding.

Tim Devaney also was a central figure in developing this work. A fine geographer and writer, he contributed much of the original research and writing in Appendix A, Welcome to California.

A number of real estate professionals contributed their good ideas and constructive criticisms. Recognizing that they don't necessarily agree with some of our conclusions or points of emphasis, many thanks to John Murphy, Guy Berry, John Pinto, Terry Moerler, Rob Bader, Judy Cranston, Shel Givens, Elizabeth Hughes, Donald Pearman, author of *The Termite Report;* Martin Reutinger, Temmy Walker, Gene Fama, Robert Jackson, and Judy Rydell.

Our heartfelt thanks to all those house buyers who shared their purchase experiences with us. Many of their stories appear throughout the book, though sometimes slightly edited and with fictitious names. Contributors (and general reviewers) include Mack Babitt, Mike and Carmella Boschetti, Valerie Brown, David Cole, Steve Elias, Jo and Don Gallo, Mary Glaeser, Rose Green, Barry Gustin, Ann Heron, Barbara Hodovan, Wendy Lewis, Jackie and Tony Mancuso, Ken Norwood, Mary Randolph, Barbara Kate Repa, and Ed Shelton.

Thanks, too, to Twila Slesnick, Ph.D., Enrolled Agent, for information on borrowing against retirement plans; Michael Cohen, Berkeley-based loan broker with Schnell Investment Company; Sue Giesberg of the California Attorney General's Office; L. Ann Wieseltier, E.A., for tax information; David Meyers, Real Estate Editor of the *Los Angeles Times;* Susan Tubbesing, Executive Director of the Earthquake Engineering Research Institute in Oakland, Dick Callahan of Callahan Insurance, and mortgage specialist Eryn Ramirez of NBT Realty; and Brian Moggan, Senior Loan Officer at Union Trust Mortgage Services, Inc.

Special thanks to Terri Hearsh, whose creative book design, financial savvy, and cheerful nature made a tremendous difference to this book.

Finally, the work of several prominent real estate writers especially inspired us, including Peter G. Miller, Jack Reed, and Leigh Robinson, and the late Robert Bruss.

Dedications

To Carol Serkes, who showed me how to buy a home when I'd only known how to acquire houses.

To Snidely and Gouger, furry felines and now just beloved memories, who kept me company in the wee hours of the night and helped give birth to the book by sleeping on the manuscript whenever possible; and Lucy The Cat who diligently helped in the revisions on previous editions, plopping herself on my chest whenever I'd lie down on the sofa.

To those of you willing to open your mind to new ideas, especially when your friends tell you that you're dreaming. At 20, I had my entire life planned; at 40, I had no idea what opportunities lay ahead! I'm now within experimental error of 60 (Yikes—I hope 60 is the new 30!). The day after Thanksgiving a few years ago, Puddy Maximus, our cat, strolled away—we did all we could to find her, but she seems to have adopted a new family. It was time to give another fur person a new home, and so Baby T came into our lives.

So our four-legged children continue to rule the roost, the garden is blooming, a 15" Mac Book Pro is our tool of choice, and we continue to live a wonderful life in Berkeley, California, the center of the universe.

Thanks to John & Ellen Pinto, pioneers and experts in the field of Buyer Brokerage. John and Ellen have also set the standard for living La Dolce Vita.

And thanks to Al Gore for inventing The Internet. Without it, I would have never been able to create berkeleyhomes.com and berkeleyblogcast.com.

—Ira Serkes

To my wife Joanne, son George, dedicated Realtor®-Associates Joseph G. and Annemarie D. Kurpinsky, and grandson, Joseph Gerard Kurpinky, Jr., in addition to my students and colleagues in the School of Business and Managment at the University of San Francisco.

—George Devine

Table of Contents

Your Legal Companion to Buying a Home in California

Buying a house should be fun. A good house not only provides shelter, warmth, and a place to lay your head, it has the potential to "come to life" and be a true friend to you and your family.

Unfortunately, locating an affordable house that suits your needs isn't always easy. And even if you find your dream house, that's only the first step to making it yours: You must still bargain with the seller for favorable terms, arrange for a good deal on a mortgage, have the house inspected for physical defects, and make decisions regarding dozens of other potentially daunting issues.

This book gives you the information you need to understand how California houses are financed, inspected, and, finally, purchased. If you've previously purchased a house in another part of the country, the lessons you've learned may be helpful—or may be misleading. While the fundamentals of home sales are similar nationwide, California's fast growth and geographic diversity have resulted in many unique and surprising home-sale customs. Some of these even vary regionally within the state of California.

Buying a house can be exciting but also anxiety-producing. Most people must face and overcome a number of worries. Maybe you're worried you won't be able to afford a decent house, or you'll pay too much. Or perhaps you wonder whether your bad credit will keep you from getting a loan, whether you'll be taken advantage of by aggressive real estate salespeople, or that you'll hit hard times and be foreclosed on.

Fortunately, this book will help you educate yourself about the process, and overcome those fears. But first, you must commit yourself to doing three things:

1. **Understand all the important aspects of the purchase process.** That's what this book is all about—giving you a thorough, practical discussion of the steps necessary to find and purchase a California house. We recommend reading this whole book, so you understand the entire process, step by step. Armed with this information, you can take informed action on dozens of matters, such as finding a suitable agent, deciding how big a down payment you can afford, choosing the best mortgage, and arranging for an inspection that will truly reveal hidden problems.
2. **Be patient.** By learning all the house-buying basics, you can plan carefully so that at each stage of the purchase process—and the sale of your old house, if you have one—you will have time on your side. Being relaxed while others are anxious and hurrying is often the key to saving a lot of money.

3. **Trust yourself.** The traditional approach to buying a house is to trust brokers, agents, mortgage lenders, and other "experts" to protect your interests. While many good, helpful people work in real estate, even the good ones must navigate potential conflicts of interest that are part of the purchase process. No one knows how to meet your needs better than you do.

Whether you're looking for a luxury beachfront home in Southern California, a bungalow in the San Francisco Bay Area, or an affordable new build in Fresno, this book shows you how to buy a house in California.

CHAPTER

1

Describe Your Dream Home

You Know the House You Want to Buy

This book is full of practical, up-to-date information about the financial realities, legal rules, and real estate industry customs involved in purchasing a California house. Two crucial things, however, no book can tell you: the location and type of house you want to live in. No matter how many experts you consult or how many opinions you get, you and only you are qualified to describe your dream house and ideal neighborhood.

Given your family's needs, tastes, and finances, you probably already have a good idea of the type of house you want to buy. Because this is true, we skip the typical first chapter in many home buyers' books, in which the author compares such things as the joys of living on a dusty road in outer suburbia to the convenience of living in a townhouse in a major city. If you haven't already thought these things though, you may need to do some critical self-evaluation before beginning your home search.

SKIP AHEAD

Already found the house you want to purchase and are mainly interested in the ins and outs of financing? Skip the rest of this chapter and move on to Chapter 2, How Much House Can You Afford?

Don't Be Talked Into Buying the Wrong House

In today's high-priced market, most buyers face an affordability gap between the house they'd like to buy and the one they can afford. Without an organized house-buying approach, there is a good chance you'll be talked into compromising on the wrong house by friends, relatives, a real estate agent, or even yourself.

"Not me, I know my own mind," you say. "Don't be too sure," we reply. Every day, confident and knowledgeable home seekers become so anxious and disoriented that they leap into a deal they later come to regret, sometimes bitterly.

Here is our method to ensure that you buy a house you'll enjoy living in, even if it means you must make some compromises:

- Firmly establish your priorities before you look at a house.
- Insist that any house you offer to buy meets at least your most important priorities.
- Do this even if, in buying a house that meets your top priorities, you must compromise in other areas.

In the following sections, we help you consider a range of house features, establish your priorities, and compare potential houses.

If your priorities are clearly set in advance, you're likely to know when to compromise on less-important features. If they aren't, you may become so frazzled by the house-purchase process that you buy a house that lacks the basic features that motivated you to buy in the first place.

Tips on Searching New Places

Perhaps you've heard it said that choosing a house's location wisely is as important as picking a good house. In a state the size of California, it's a vast understatement to say you have a lot of locations to choose from. To help you think about specific California areas, we include Appendix A, Welcome to California.

Despite the title, Welcome to California isn't meant only for newcomers to the state. Whether you're a San Franciscan moving closer to a San Ramon job, a New Yorker relocating to Los Angeles, or simply someone unfamiliar with certain California areas, you'll find a wealth of information. In addition, in Chapter 5 we discuss working with a local real estate agent to get essential information on neighborhoods.

But there's still no substitute for your own legwork. Ask your friends and colleagues, walk and drive around neighborhoods, talk to local residents, read local newspapers, check the library's community resources files, visit the local planning department, and do whatever else will help you get a better sense of a neighborhood or city.

Identify Your Ideal House Profile

When looking for a house, it's easy to become overwhelmed by the array of choices, from size to style to floor plan and fixtures. Then, there's the issue of location—houses come in all sorts of neighborhoods, school districts, and potential hazard zones (fire, earthquake, and flood, to name a few). And, of course, price and purchase terms are crucial considerations for most home buyers. To cope with all these and at least a dozen other relevant variables, it's essential to establish your priorities in advance and stick to them.

The first step is to identify house features most important to you by completing our Ideal House Profile, which lists all major categories such as upper price limit, number and type of rooms, and location. A sample is shown below, and a tearout copy is included in Appendix D.

If you're buying with another person, prepare your list of priorities together, so that each person's strong likes and dislikes are respected.

TIP

Getting price and financing information. Most people will have an upper limit on the house they can afford to buy and the maximum down payment they can make. If you need advice on these issues, be sure to read Chapters 2, 4, and 8 before completing the Ideal House Profile.

Must Haves: Mandatory Priorities

Use the Ideal House Profile to identify the essential features you're looking for (must have) in a house, such as a particular city or neighborhood. Since price is an obvious consideration for most people, fill in the top section first. For example, under *Upper price limit* you might note $600,000, with a *Maximum down payment* of $60,000. Then fill in the rest of the form.

If you have two kids, you might note that three bedrooms, excellent public schools, and a street with lots of children are "must haves." If you plan to live in the house after retirement, a minimal number of stairs and short distances to shops and services may be "must haves."

TIP

Pay close attention to the *School needs* category. If you have children, buying a great house at a great price in a lousy school district may mean years of paying for private schools. By contrast, paying a little more for a good house in an excellent school district may be a bargain in the long run. And if you plan to move in a few years, it will be easier to sell a house in a good school district, because that feature is important to many potential buyers. See Appendix A, Welcome to California, for advice on checking out schools.

Hope to Have: Secondary Priorities

Once you've compiled your list of "must haves," jot down features that you'd like but aren't crucial to your decision of whether to buy. For example, under *Type of yard and grounds,* you might note patio and flat back yard in the "Hope to Have" column. Or under *Number and type of rooms,* you might list finished basement or master bedroom with bath.

Take a second look at your "Must Have" column. If you're typical, you may wonder how you will ever afford a house with the features you've listed. Don't despair—at least, not until you understand the strategies (discussed in Chapter 3) to help you buy an affordable house. For now, you might need to change a couple of "must haves" to "hope to haves."

Absolute No Ways

Be sure to list your "absolute no ways" (you will not buy a house that has any of these features) at the bottom of the Ideal House Profile. Avoiding things you'll always hate—such as a house in a flood zone, poor school district, or high-crime area—can be even more important than finding a house that contains all your mandatory priorities.

If you're moving into a new-house development or condominium, be sure to check into covenants, conditions, and restrictions (CC&Rs), which may be quite detailed and restrictive on everything from the color of your house to your landscaping. (CC&Rs are discussed in more detail in Chapter 7.)

Once you've completed your Ideal House Profile, you're ready to create a House Priorities Worksheet, which will help you see how each house stacks up with your priorities.

Create a House Priorities Worksheet

Now it's time to use the information collected in your Ideal House Profile to create a House Priorities Worksheet for each house you visit.

Start by making several copies of the worksheet (which appears below) to allow for mistakes or the eventual scaling back of your priority list if it turns out you can't

Ideal House Profile

Upper price limit: $1,000,000
Maximum down payment: $200,000
Special financing needs: N/A

	Must Have	Hope to Have
Neighborhood or location:		
Northern Berkeley	✓	
Oxford Street		✓
School needs:		
Berkeley High School	✓	
Desired neighborhood features:		
Quiet street with little traffic	✓	
Walking distance to Solano Avenue	✓	
Neighborhood association		✓
Lots of trees		✓
Length of commute:		
Maximum of 15 minutes drive to Berkeley office	✓	
Access to public transportation:		
Walking distance to S.F. express buses	✓	
Size of house:		
Minimum 1,800 square feet	✓	
Number and type of rooms:		
3 bedrooms/2 baths	✓	
Modern kitchen	✓	
Family room for kids		✓
Eat-in kitchen or breakfast nook		✓
Condition, age, and type of house:		
Good shape, less than 100 years old	✓	
Type of yard and grounds:		
Fenced-in yard	✓	
Private yard		✓
Other desired features:		
Easy parking	✓	
Lots of lights		✓

Absolute no ways:
House in an active or potential slide zone

afford all the features you would like. Then, enter relevant information on a master copy of the House Priorities Worksheet under each major category—"Must have," "Hope to have," and "Absolute no ways." A sample is shown below, and a tearout copy is included in Appendix D.

Once you have completed your House Priorities Worksheet to your (and your partner's) satisfaction, make several copies (or install the form on your laptop computer if you'll be taking it househunting). Take the worksheet with you each time you visit a house.

For each house you see, fill in the top of the House Priorities Worksheet. Enter the address, asking price, name and phone number of the contact person (listing agent or seller, if it's a For Sale By Owner), and date you saw the house. As you walk around each house and talk to the owner or agent, enter a checkmark if the house has a desirable or undesirable feature. Also, make notes next to a particular feature if it can be changed to meet your needs (for example, an okay kitchen that could be modernized for $25,000).

Add comments at the bottom, such as "potential undeveloped lot next door" or "neighbors seem very friendly." If you look at a lot of houses, taking notes such as these will help make sure you don't forget important information.

You should seriously consider only those houses with all or most of your "must haves" and none of your "no ways." If you visit a nice, reasonably priced house that doesn't come close to matching your list and can't be easily changed to do so, say no. Take the time to find a more suitable house; you'll be glad you did.

Watch Out for Staged Homes

House "staging" is now a regular practice in home sales. The right paint, furniture, music, and smells can create illusions that would make Martha Stewart and Houdini jealous. The point is to optimize the charms of a house while distracting potential buyers from its flaws.

So if you visit a house that just reeks of charm—look behind, above, and below. Imagine it empty, or with your own furniture.

TIP

Set up a good filing system. As the list of houses you look at grows, keep track of the information you collect. Failing to adopt a good system may lead to revisiting houses you've already seen and rejected or making decisions based on half-remembered facts. For each house that seems like a possible prospect, make a file that includes a completed House Priorities Worksheet, the information materials provided when you toured the home, the Multiple Listing Service information, ads, and your notes. Or, if you are more digitally inclined, use your computer to set up a simple database with key details on each house you visit. (For advice, see "Organizing Your House Search" in Chapter 6.)

House Priorities Worksheet

Date visited: September 15, 2008 Price: $ 950,000

Address: 5 Marin Way, Berkeley

Contact: Jo Tulare, Berkeley Homes Phone #: 525-5555

Must have:

- ✓ North Berkeley neighborhood
- ✓ Berkeley High School
- ☐ Quiet street with little traffic
- ✓ Walking distance to Solano Avenue
- ✓ Maximum of 15 minutes drive to Berkeley office
- ✓ Walking distance to S.F. express buses
- ✓ Minimum 1,800 square feet
- ✓ 3 bedrooms/2 baths
- ☐ Modern kitchen
- ✓ Good shape, less than 100 years old
- ☐ Fenced-in yard
- ✓ Easy parking

Hope to have:

- ☐ Oxford or Spruce Street
- ✓ Neighborhood association
- ✓ Lots of trees
- ☐ Family room for kids
- ✓ Eat-in kitchen or breakfast nook
- ☐ Private yard
- ✓ Lots of light
- ☐

Absolute no ways:

- ☐ House in an active or potential slide-zone
- ☐
- ☐

Comments about the particular house:

This house is terrific! It will probably have several bidders, and go for an amount over our budget, but well worth the price. Street is pretty busy, but the house and location meet most of our needs. Neighbors seem very nice. Go for it!

Prepare a House Comparison Worksheet

If, like many people, you look at a considerable number of houses over an extended period of time—or even in the space of a week—you may soon have trouble distinguishing or comparing their features. That's where our House Comparison Worksheet comes in.

Across the top of the form, list the addresses of the three or four houses you like best. In the left column, fill in your list of priorities and "no ways" from your Ideal House Profile and House Priorities Worksheet. Then put a checkmark on the line under each house that has that feature to allow for a quick comparison.

A sample is shown below, and a tearout copy is included in Appendix D.

True Story

Ellen: How Not to Buy a House

I was a first-time purchaser on a relatively tight budget when I set out to buy an older, attached row house in San Francisco. I wanted two bedrooms, no (or a very small) yard, proximity to a downtown bus route, and walking access to a neighborhood market and bookstore. I looked for many months at houses that were completely unsuitable, far too expensive, or, with depressing regularity, both. So I broadened my search by reading the classifieds in the Sunday paper. When I saw that prices were more reasonable in the suburbs, I spent a sunny Sunday afternoon browsing in Contra Costa County.

At the first open house I visited, I met an energetic real estate agent who spun a wonderful word picture of the joys of suburban life: lots of sun, room for a tomato garden, and friendly neighbors. She showed me a split-level house with an apple tree in full bloom in my price range. Almost before I realized what I was doing, I signed on the bottom line.

That was the fun part. Soon I was getting up at 6:00 a.m., driving to the train station, and standing for the 40-minute ride to San Francisco. My fantasy about the joy of suburban life was just that. It's hard to believe now, but I seemed to have temporarily overlooked the fact that I'm allergic to direct sun, detest tomatoes, and moved out of the suburbs to get away from overly involved neighbors.

Fortunately, I sold the house six months later, at a small profit. I went in with a friend and together we bought a house in San Francisco that meets my needs perfectly.

House Comparison Worksheet

House 1 257 Loving Avenue, Berkeley

House 2 1415 Gaylord Street, Berkeley

House 3 999 Spruce Street, Berkeley

House 4 5 Marin Way, Berkeley

	1	2	3	4
Must have:				
North Berkeley neighborhood	✓	✓	✓	✓
Berkeley High School	✓	✓	✓	✓
Quiet street with little traffic	✓	✓		
Walking distance to Solano Avenue		✓	✓	✓
Maximum of 15 minutes drive to Berkeley office	✓		✓	✓
Walking distance to S.F. express buses	✓			✓
Minimum 1,800 square feet	✓	✓		✓
3 bedrooms/2 baths	✓	✓		✓
Modern kitchen			✓	
Good shape, less than 100 years old		✓		✓
Fenced-in yard	✓	✓	✓	
Easy parking			✓	✓
Hope to have:				
Oxford or Spruce Street		✓		
Neighborhood association		✓	✓	
Lots of trees	✓		✓	✓
Family room for kids	✓			
Eat-in kitchen or breakfast nook	✓	✓	✓	
Private yard	✓	✓	✓	
Lots of light		✓	✓	✓
Absolute no ways:				
House in an active or potential slide zone	✓	✓	✓	

CHAPTER

2

How Much House Can You Afford?

It's essential to determine how much you can afford to pay before you look for a house—first off, for your own planning and peace of mind. Crunching a few numbers is also important, however, to help you be either cautious when lenders offer you higher loans than you should realistically take on, or assertive with lenders who don't realize that you're a better credit risk than your records show.

SKIP AHEAD

If money is no object or you already know how much house you can afford, skip this chapter.

Most readers will find this chapter useful in two ways:

- to help you determine your price range—before you go house hunting, and
- to explain some of the techniques experienced mortgage brokers use to help borrowers qualify for a loan from a bank, savings and loan, or other lender.

The Basics of Determining Housing Affordability

As a broad generalization, most people can afford to purchase a house worth about three times their total (gross) annual income, assuming a 20% down payment and a moderate amount of other long-term debts. With no other debts, they can afford a house worth up to four or five times their annual income.

A much more accurate way to determine how much house you can afford is to compare your monthly carrying costs plus your monthly payments on other long-term debts to your gross (total) monthly income. Carrying costs are the money needed to make a monthly payment (both principal and interest) plus one-twelfth of the yearly bill for property taxes and homeowner's insurance. In real estate industry jargon, monthly carrying costs are often referred to as PITI (pronounced "pity"), which stands for principal, interest, taxes, and insurance.

Assuming you have a decent credit score, lenders traditionally want your regular monthly payments to be less than 36% of your gross monthly income. (Your credit score is a numerical measure that reflects how well you've managed credit in the past.) The lower your other monthly debts, the more of your 36% can be applied to your mortgage costs.

Using these percentages, if your monthly income is $4,000, you should not pay more than $1,440 (0.36 x $4,000) toward your debts. This is called the "debt-to-income ratio."

But there are really no hard and fast rules when it comes to determining the ratio of debt to income a lender will accept. Lenders follow general guidelines but will adjust them when it suits their interests. If your profile is extremely attractive to a lender, perhaps because you have a particularly high credit score, it may make an exception and approve

How Credit Scores Affect Loan Qualification

When reviewing loan applications and making financing decisions, lenders check a prospective home buyer's credit report. The lenders typically request that the credit agency reporting your file—probably one of three main repositories, Equifax, Experian, or TransUnion—provide your credit or FICO score.

This score is a statistical summary of the information in your credit report. It's calculated using an elaborate computerized scoring model that takes into account your history of paying bills on time, the level of outstanding debts, how long you've had credit, your credit limit, the number of inquiries for your credit report (too many can lower score), and the number of credit cards and the types of credit you have. These screening models don't consider your race, gender, marital status, age, or neighborhood.

California law (Civil Code § 1785.10) requires credit reporting agencies to provide consumers (upon request) with their scores and related information. Credit scores range from 300 to 850. The higher your credit score, the better. If you routinely pay your bills late or have a poor credit history, expect a lower score. A lender may either reject your loan application or insist on a large down payment or a higher interest rate. Because your credit history is so important, be sure to check your credit report and clean up your file or fix errors, as discussed below.

For more information on credit scores, check out www.myfico.com.

your loan even if your debt-to-income ratio falls outside its guidelines. Some lenders will accept a higher debt-to-income ratio if you'll take a less-attractive loan, such as one with a higher-than-market interest rate or higher-than-usual points. (Points are an up-front loan fee figured as a percentage of the loan, discussed in Chapter 8.)

Prepare a Family Financial Statement

The first step to determine the purchase price you can afford is to prepare a family financial statement, which includes:

- your monthly income
- your monthly expenses, and
- your net worth (your assets minus your liabilities).

We use the word "family" as shorthand for the economic unit that will buy a house. For our purposes, an unmarried couple or a single person is just as much a family as a married couple with ten kids.

CAUTION

This statement is for you, not your lender. No matter how much debt a lender ultimately says you can handle, the purpose of this statement is to help you develop your own realistic picture of what this debt will mean for your monthly cash flow. The information you collect will help you fill out your loan application, but you won't give this statement directly to the lender. That means that now is not the time to exaggerate your income or underestimate your expenses—you'll only be fooling yourself.

Preparing a family financial statement begins the process of learning how much house you can afford—in terms of both the down payment and monthly mortgage payments. And if you haven't been preapproved for a mortgage loan (see "Get Loan Preapproval," below) when you make a purchase offer, a financial statement can be extremely useful in convincing the seller that you're a serious bidder. This may be crucial, especially if there's more than one prospective buyer. The person who can convince the seller that he or she is financially able to swing the deal often prevails, even without the highest offer.

Below is a sample family financial statement. A tearout copy of the statement itself is in Appendix D, along with instructions for filling it out. Make several photocopies (and fill out the form in pencil) so you'll have a clean copy if you make errors or your financial status changes. If you need more space when filling out any section, include an attachment. Do this work carefully. It will be very useful when you complete a mortgage loan application. (See Chapter 13.)

How Much Down Payment Will You Make?

Generally speaking, the larger the percentage of the total price of a house you can put down, the easier it will be for you to qualify for a mortgage.

As we discuss below, the monthly mortgage payment (plus taxes and insurance) is the major factor in determining the purchase price of the house you can afford. And with a higher down payment, those payments are lower. A lender's financial interests are better protected: If you default on your mortgage (which is less likely anyway, because the payment is more affordable), a lender has more room to sell the property and recover its investment.

For now, you need down payment money. How much do you have by way of liquid and nonliquid assets? If you have a house or other property you plan to sell, estimate what you're likely to receive after subtracting costs of sale. If necessary, think about other ways to reasonably raise cash. Can you liquidate other assets or get a gift or loan from a relative or friend? (These and other money-raising techniques are discussed in Chapter 4.)

Once you've calculated the total amount of your liquid assets, you can do a quick and dirty calculation of how much home you can afford. Start by assuming that you'll pour all these assets into the down payment, and run through the various down payment percentage possibilities (5%, 10%, 15%, or 20%). For example, if you've got $30,000 in assets, that would work as a 5% down payment on a $600,000 home; a 10% down payment on a $300,000 home; a 15% down payment on a $200,000 home; and a 20% down payment on a $150,000 home.

But, as we said, these calculations are quick and dirty—you'll never be able to pour all your liquid assets into the down payment, because this would leave you nothing for closing costs and financial reserves. Closing costs can vary from approximately 2% to 5% of the purchase price. And, lenders will

Family Financial Statement

	Borrower	Coborrower
Name and address:		
Home phone number:		
Email address:		
Employer's name & address:		
Work phone number:		

WORKSHEET 1: INCOME AND EXPENSES

	Borrower ($)	Coborrower ($)	Total ($)
I. INCOME			
A. Monthly gross income			
1. Employment			
2. Public benefits			
3. Dividends			
4. Royalties			
5. Interest & other investment income			
6. Other (specify):			
B. Total monthly gross income			
II. MONTHLY EXPENSES			
A. Nonhousing			
1. Child care			
2. Clothing & personal expenses			
3. Food			
4. Insurance (auto, life, medical, & dental)			
5. Medical & dental care (not insurance)			
6. Taxes (nonhousing)			
7. Education			
8. Transportation			
9. Other (specify):			
B. Current housing			
1. Mortgage payment or rent			
2. Taxes			
3. Insurance			
4. Utilities			
C. Total monthly expenses			

WORKSHEET 2: ASSETS AND LIABILITIES

I. ASSETS (Cash or Market Value)	Borrower ($)	Coborrower ($)	Total ($)
A. Cash & cash equivalents			
1. Cash			
2. Deposits (list):			
B. Marketable securities			
1. Stocks & bonds (bid price)			
2. Other securities			
3. Mutual funds			
4. Life insurance			
5. Other (specify):			
C. Total cash & marketable securities			
D. Nonliquid assets			
1. Real estate			
2. Retirement funds			
3. Business			
4. Motor vehicles			
5. Other (specify):			
E. Total nonliquid assets			
F. Total all assets			
II. LIABILITIES			
A. Debts			
1. Real estate loans			
2. Student loans			
3. Motor vehicle loans			
4. Child or spousal support			
5. Personal loans			
6. Credit cards (specify):			
7. Other (specify):			
B. Total liabilities			
III. NET WORTH (Total assets minus total liabilities)			

want to see that you have at least two to three months of reserve money left over after you've bought the house, so they may insist on a lower down payment to achieve this. (However, reserve money doesn't have to be liquid; it can also be in the form of retirement money.) The result is that you'll need to fiddle with the figures a bit to figure out a realistic combination of down payment, closing costs, and home price, as illustrated in the example below.

> **EXAMPLE:** Brad and William want to buy a house. They pool all their available cash and come up with $45,000 in their checking and savings accounts, as well as ample money in retirement accounts (to be used as their financial reserves). They divide $45,000 by 10% to come up with $450,000. They've been told that closing costs will be about 3% of the purchase price, which in this case equals $13,500. Paying these costs would reduce their assets from $45,000 to $31,500. Continuing with the assumption that they'll put 10% down, their down payment of $31,500 will allow them to buy a house for about $315,000. Brad and William know they'll never be able to find a house for that price in the neighborhood they're looking in, so they try the numbers again, this time with 5%.
>
> They divide $45,000 by 5% to come up with $900,000. However, that seems like more debt than Brad and William can possibly handle. So, they approach the problem from a slightly different angle. They've been seeing houses that would suit their needs in the $550,000 selling price range. Closing costs on such a home, at 3%, would be about $16,500. That would leave them $28,500 in cash reserves—which is 5% of $570,000 (again, divide $28,500 by 0.05). Brad and William have just figured out that they have enough money to put 5% down on a purchase price in the $550,000 to $570,000 range, and have enough left for the closing costs. They'll use their retirement money as their financial reserve.

But remember, in addition to the down payment, you must be able to afford the monthly mortgage, insurance, and property tax payments. If your income is relatively low, you may have to increase your down payment to 25%–30% of the price of a house to bring down the monthly payments. If, however, you have both a good income and enough money set aside for a larger-than-required down payment, you have a choice: You can put more money into the down payment or invest it elsewhere. We discuss your options in Chapter 4.

Once you've completed your family financial statement and done the basic calculations described above, you should have a good sense of how expensive a house you can realistically hope to buy.

Estimate the Mortgage Interest Rate You'll Likely Pay

The next step in arriving at your monthly mortgage is to determine the interest rate you'll pay on a mortgage. This is important because, over the life of your mortgage, you will probably pay much more in interest than you will in principal. A relatively small difference in your interest rate will amount to a big difference in your total debt, and hence the amount of your monthly payments. The table below illustrates the differences by interest rate and mortgage term, using the example of a $100,000 mortgage.

Monthly and Total Payments on a $100,000 Fixed Rate Mortgage

	15-year period		30-year period	
Interest Rate (%)	**Mo. pmt.**	**Total pmts.**	**Mo. pmt.**	**Total pmts.**
5.0	790.80	142,344	536.83	193,259
5.5	817.09	147,076	567.79	204,404
6.0	843.86	151,895	599.56	215,842
6.5	871.11	156,799	632.07	227,544
7.0	898.83	161,789	665.30	239,509
7.5	927.01	166,862	699.21	251,717
8.0	955.65	172,017	733.76	264,155
8.5	984.74	177,253	768.91	276,809
9.0	1,014.27	182,569	804.62	298,664
9.5	1,044.22	187,960	840.85	302,708
10.0	1,074.61	193,430	877.57	315,926
10.5	1,105.40	198,972	914.74	329,306
11.0	1,136.60	204,588	952.32	342,836

Because different mortgage types carry different interest rates, start by deciding the mortgage type you want. If you haven't yet decided, read Chapters 8–12 for a thorough review of mortgage options.

Calculate How Much House You Can Afford

When you have a pretty good idea of the size of your down payment and the interest rate you expect to pay, you can calculate how much house you can afford.

The easiest way to do that is to use an online calculator, like those listed below. These calculators use your income and debts, along with the basic terms of the mortgage you expect or hope to get, to determine how much you can afford to borrow.

If you'd rather do the calculation yourself, follow the steps below.

1. **Estimate the amount you need to borrow.** First, you'll have to estimate the purchase price for the home you hope to buy. Reduce that by the amount of the down payment you expect to make. That's the amount you'll need to borrow.
2. **Estimate your monthly mortgage payment.** Begin by estimating the mortgage interest rate you expect to pay, based on up-to-date rate information in the Sunday paper or online. (See Chapter 13 for a discussion of gathering information on mortgage rates.) Then, using the Amortization Chart below, find the corresponding mortgage factor. Multiply this number by the number of thousands you'll need to borrow. The result is your estimated monthly principal and interest payment.

3. **Estimate insurance and property taxes.** Add the following factors together: homeowners' insurance (expect to pay $800 to $2,000 per year) and property taxes (approximately 1.2% to 1.8% of the purchase prize). Divide that number by 12 to calculate a monthly cost for insurance and taxes.
4. **Estimate other house-related expenses.** If you're making a down payment of less than 20% and you're not taking out two mortgages, estimate monthly payments for private mortgage insurance or PMI. (See Chapter 4 for more information on PMI.) Also, if you expect to pay fees to a homeowners' association, estimate that monthly fee. Add these numbers together.
5. **Calculate your other fixed monthly debt.** This should include any other monthly debt you have, such as a car loan, student loan, or credit card debt. Add these monthly debt obligations together.
6. **Add items 2–5.** These are your monthly expenses.
7. **Estimate lender qualification.** Generally, lenders will allow your monthly mortgage obligation to be between 0.28 and 0.36 of your gross monthly income (the fewer your debts, and the higher your credit score, the higher the number you use can be).
8. **Divide item 6 by item 7.** That number is the amount of monthly gross income you'll need to get the loan that you want. You can multiply that number by 12 to calculate the yearly gross income you'll need to qualify.

Amortization Chart

Mortgage Principal & Interest Payment Factors (Per $1,000)

Interest rates (%)	15-year mortgage	30-year mortgage
5.00	7.91	5.37
5.25	8.04	5.52
5.50	8.17	5.68
5.75	8.30	5.84
6.00	8.44	6.00
6.25	8.57	6.16
6.50	8.71	6.32
6.75	8.85	6.49
7.00	8.99	6.65
7.25	9.13	6.82
7.50	9.27	6.99
7.75	9.41	7.16
8.00	9.56	7.34
8.25	9.70	7.51
8.50	9.85	7.69
8.75	9.99	7.87
9.00	10.14	8.05
9.25	10.29	8.23
9.50	10.44	8.41
9.75	10.59	8.59
10.00	10.75	8.78
10.25	10.90	8.96
10.50	11.05	9.15
10.75	11.21	9.33
11.00	11.37	9.52

Online Mortgage and Financial Calculators

If you hate making calculations, you can quickly run the numbers yourself using one of the many financial calculators available on the Internet. Dozens of websites offer calculators to help you determine monthly payments on different-sized mortgages and how much house you can afford. All calculators are not created equal, so sample different ones until you find the calculator that gives you the information you're looking for in the format you prefer.

WEBSITE RESOURCE

Nolo's website has a variety of real estate calculators to help you, at www.nolo.com/calculators. A few others that appear to have staying power are www.homes.com, www.mortgage-net.com/calculators, www.quickenloans.com, and www.mortgage-calc.com.

Tips on Improving Your Financial Profile

Bringing your housing costs and monthly debts within the generally acceptable debt-to-income range of 28%–36% should allow you to finance a house. Many people will find, however, that it will require more than 36% of their monthly income to make house payments and pay their other debts. If you fit this description, here are some ways to bring yourself within the acceptable range.

Pay Off Debts

The best way to improve your debt-to-income ratio is to pay off some debts. Not only will this reduce your total monthly payments and thus, in the eyes of lenders, leave more of your income to be used for mortgage payments, it will also result in other savings.

First, because the interest rates on consumer debts (such as credit cards) are almost always higher than the rate on mortgage debts, paying off the first type to qualify for more of the second can result in substantial savings. And second, because the interest paid on consumer debts is not tax-deductible, while the interest portion of your mortgage is fully tax-deductible, you qualify for another substantial saving. For example, if you're in the 28% federal tax bracket and 9.3% state bracket, 34.7% of all interest you pay on your mortgage is subtracted from your taxable income. (This takes into account the fact that state income taxes are a deductible item on your federal tax return. For more on the tax deductibility of mortgage interest, see Chapter 4.)

Be sure to check with your lender before deciding which (and how much) of your debts to pay off. You don't want to improve your ratio and then discover you've wiped out a significant part of your down payment. If you do end up short for the down payment, consider selling some of your possessions or tapping friends or relatives for help (discussed below).

Convert Assets to Cash

If you need a few thousand extra dollars to pay off debts or increase your down payment, look for it in your garage, basement, or attic. If you're like most people, you may have many saleable items you don't really need. If you sell them and use the cash to either pay off other debts or increase your down payment, your financial picture can look significantly better.

Also look at your investments as a source of cash. Consider cashing in whole life insurance policies (if the cash value is significantly high) or withdrawing money from a retirement account or plan.

TIP

Keep records to show "source of funds." Lenders may suspect that any new savings with a less than two- to three-month history is really a loan.

Emphasize Imminent Income Raises

Lenders commonly require proof that you've been employed, without interruption, for the last two years or so. Exceptions, however, may be made in rare and compelling cases.

For example, if you have just graduated from college, and have started a new, salaried position within your field of expertise, a lender may waive the minimum employment requirement. If you worked part-time within the field you're studying, or worked as an intern, it will help to add that to your employment record on the application.

If future raises are given at the discretion of your employer, consider discussing your house purchase with your boss. If the boss believes that your future with the company is bright, he or she may commit to a pay raise now or, in some cases, even arrange for your employer to make you a loan at a lower-than-market rate of interest.

If You Work for Yourself, Show a Profit or Make a Big Down Payment

Millions of Americans work for themselves, or supplement their income by operating a small business on the side. Few of these businesses show large taxable profits; rather, most owners take advantage of the Internal Revenue Code rules which make it reasonably easy for small business owners to minimize their taxable earnings. Unfortunately, when a small business owner wishes to borrow money, doing everything legally possible to minimize income for tax purposes is likely to come back to haunt you.

Typically, a small business owner will try to convince a lender that the $28,000 of taxable income reported to the IRS was really closer to $50,000, if deductible business expenses such as transportation, meals, a home work space, depreciation, contributions to an IRA or Keogh plan, self-employment tax, contributions to medical insurance, and entertaining are added back in. But this may be difficult to do. Lenders have heard it all before, and although they may privately acknowledge that an applicant's financial situation is likely to be better than reported to the IRS, they won't normally lend money in this situation unless the buyer can make a down payment of 25% or more. With a high down payment (and excellent credit rating), a borrower may qualify to purchase within accepted debt-to-income ratios even with relatively modest taxable income.

Normally, however, to qualify for a mortgage if your business shows an artificially low profit, you'll need to report a larger taxable profit. If your business really is quite profitable, this should take only a year or two. Instead of writing off every possible personal expense as a business expense while paying yourself a low salary, raise your pay, and treat more expenses as personal. You'll pay more federal income tax, but once you qualify for a mortgage loan, you can cut it back by deducting your mortgage interest and property tax payments.

TIP

In rare cases, you may not have to prove your income. In the past, lenders liberally offered "stated income loans." To get one, you simply told the lender your annual income, without tax returns or pay stubs to back it up. In exchange, you'd pay a higher interest rate. You may still be able to get one of these loans, but don't count on it. In recent years, these "liar loans" have become less common because some borrowers were using them to artificially inflate their income, qualifying for large mortgages they later defaulted on. This made lenders nervous, and means that if you truly need a stated income loan, you'll have a harder time finding one.

Borrow From Friends or Family

We discuss ways to raise money from family and friends in Chapter 12, Private Mortgages. For purposes of showing that you're able to make a solid down payment, you'll need an outright gift, or a loan that doesn't need to be paid back for a considerable period of time, and you may need to get it into your bank account a few months (usually three) prior to loan approval. This is called "seasoning" the funds. A lender wants you to have the money necessary to qualify, not to create another debt that will compete for repayment with your mortgage.

A gift made at the time you're purchasing a house requires documentation that it is a gift, not a loan. (See Chapter 4 for more on gifts.)

Check Your Credit Rating and Clean Up Your File

Your credit report, specifically your credit score, will affect the type and amount of mortgage loan lenders offer you. (See "How Credit Scores Affect Loan Qualification," above.)

Prospective buyers should check their credit files kept by credit reporting agencies (also called credit bureaus) before applying for a loan. Unfortunately, credit files often contain out-of-date or just plain wrong information. Sometimes they confuse names, addresses, Social Security numbers, or employers. If you have a common name (say John Brown), don't be shocked if you find information in your credit file on other John Browns, or John Brownes, or Jon

Browns. Obviously, you don't want this incorrect information given to prospective lenders, especially if the person you're being confused with is in worse financial shape than you are.

A few credit problems doesn't mean you'll never get a loan. It may mean that you'll have to pay a higher interest rate or make a larger down payment. Talk to your mortgage broker—it's the best way to find out how or if you'll qualify for a loan.

How to Get a Copy of Your Credit Report

You can get a free copy of your credit report once a year from each of the three major credit bureaus, which adds up to three free reports per year if you time things right.

You can request your report on the Internet (www.annualcreditreport.com), by phone (877-322-8228), or by mail (Annual Credit Report Request Service, P.O. Box 105283, Atlanta, GA 30348-5283). If you request service by mail, you'll need to include a request form (available on the above website).

You can also contact any of the three major national credit bureaus directly, either to request a copy of your report or ask other report-related questions:

- Equifax, 800-685-1111; www.equifax.com
- Experian, 888-397-3742, www.experian.com
- TransUnion, 877-322-8228, www.transunion.com.

If you need to request more than one credit report per company in the course of a year, you may need to pay, usually no more than $13 apiece.

You are also entitled to a copy of your credit report for free, however, if:

- You have been denied credit because of information in your credit file. You must request your copy within 60 days of being denied credit.
- You are unemployed and planning to apply for a job within 60 days following your request for your credit report.
- You receive public assistance.
- You believe your credit file contains errors due to someone's fraud, such as opening up accounts by using your name or Social Security number.

How to Correct Errors in Your Credit File

If you find any wrong information, take steps to correct the errors. You have the right to insist that the credit bureau verify any wrong, inaccurate, or out-of-date information. Once the credit bureau receives your request, it has 30 days to reinvestigate and tell you its findings. If you need a faster answer, tell them. Items that can't be verified must be removed.

Typical problems include:

- You're a self-employed carpenter, yet your file says you work as a TV repairperson or, worse, are unemployed.
- You're listed as owing a debt that's been repaid.
- A department store bill you owed eight years ago is still listed as outstanding. A credit bureau cannot keep information on file for more than seven years—with

one exception: Bankruptcies may be listed for ten years.

If the credit reporting agency insists on retaining inaccurate, wrong, or outdated information, or lists a debt you refused to pay because of a legitimate dispute with the creditor, you have the right to place a brief statement in your file giving your version of the situation.

How to Clean Up Your Credit

If the information in your file is accurate but unfavorable, your best strategy is to clean up your credit before seriously trying to purchase a house. Here are some tips:

- **Remove delinquencies.** Fully pay off small debts ($500 or less). For larger accounts, contact the creditor and attempt to work out a payment plan so that you're no longer listed as delinquent. Then stay current on the account.

  Some creditors you've owed for a while may accept less than the total amount owed "as payment in full." A creditor who has given up on collecting may jump at a lump sum payment of two-thirds of what's due. If so, make sure the creditor acknowledges in writing that you've satisfied the debt in full. If the creditor has a court judgment, make sure a "satisfaction of judgment" is filed with the court that issued the judgment. Show the satisfaction of judgment to the credit reporting agency. Be aware that a bank creditor that waives $600 or more must report your "savings" to the IRS. The IRS considers it income to you, and you may have to pay income taxes on it.
- **As a last resort, get professional assistance.** If you owe several creditors varying sums and can't figure out how much to pay whom, you might contact a nonprofit credit advisory group such as Consumer Credit Counseling Services (CCCS). To find the nearest CCCS office, call 800-388-2227 or check the national website at www.nfcc.org, which will link you to local office websites. Be warned, however: There are many different consumer credit counseling organizations, and not all are created equal. Some charge high fees for little service. To find out more about consumer credit counseling, visit the National Consumer Law Center at www.nclc.org.
- **Rebuild your credit.** If you've suffered a major financial setback in the past few years (repossessed automobile, judgment against you for a large debt, foreclosed home, or bankruptcy), you'll need to rebuild your credit, unless a creditworthy person will cosign your mortgage loan, you have cash, or you can borrow from friends or family.

It normally takes two to three years to rebuild your credit. Here are some steps to do so:

1. **Create a budget.** Most of the information you need is in your Family Financial Statement. Compare your monthly income to your total monthly expenses. If your expenses exceed your income, commit to some spending reductions and stick to them.

2. **Get a secured credit card.** Many banks will give you a credit card and a line of credit if you first deposit money into a savings account or certificate of deposit. The line of credit can be up to 150% of the amount you deposit. Use the credit card, and keep absolutely up-to-date on payments. A major drawback with these cards is that the interest rate often nears 20%. To avoid piling up new debts, use the card to charge items that you would have purchased anyway, and pay it off in full each month. After a year or two, banks and other large creditors will likely grant you a higher credit limit and drop the savings account requirement.
3. **Borrow from a bank.** Requesting between $1,500 and $5,000, take out a personal loan. To qualify, you may need a cosigner. Make your monthly payment on time, and your credit will improve rapidly.

   If you have enough cash to handle more than one loan payment, deposit the loan you received from the first bank in a second bank, again turning in the passbook in exchange for a loan. Now your credit report shows that two banks have extended you loans.
4. **Obtain a revolving credit card.** Many department stores and gasoline companies will issue credit cards with low lines of credit to almost anyone. Even though you've had a major financial setback, before long you're likely to receive offers for store or gas company credit cards in the mail. Accept one or two and charge small amounts for items you need, paying bills promptly.

   Note: Strategies 2, 3, and 4 are also useful for someone who has never used credit and needs to build a credit history.
5. **Work with a local creditor.** Purchase an item that you really need (such as furniture or possibly a car) on credit. Even if you have a poor credit history, many local businesses will work with you to set up a payment schedule, but be prepared to make a large deposit (up to 30%), pay a high rate of interest, or find someone to cosign your loan.

RESOURCE

For additional information on credit files and rebuilding credit after a financial setback: See *Credit Repair,* by Robin Leonard and John Lamb (Nolo).

Get a Cosigner

If you have enough money for a down payment and monthly payments but are considered a poor credit risk because you went bankrupt or for some other reason, consider asking a relative or friend to cosign the loan. Some lenders will require that a cosigner be a blood relative, if not an actual occupant of your home.

While a cosigner doesn't "clean up" your credit rating, he or she brings his or her own, which is presumably much better than yours, which means it should be easier for you to qualify for a loan.

A drawback with cosigning is that if you default, the cosigner will legally be obligated to pay any difference between what the property fetches in a foreclosure sale and what you owe the lender. If you make a good-sized down payment, this shouldn't be much of a risk. If you default, the house is likely to be sold for enough to pay off the mortgage without obligating the cosigner.

Don't ask anyone to cosign who doesn't fully understand the risks being taken and who isn't financially solvent enough to handle a possible loss. Chapter 12 discusses the precautions to take against death or disability of the borrower to protect a person who lends a friend or relative money to buy a house. That discussion also applies to cosigners.

At the other end of the financial spectrum, some buyers find that their cosigners expect to be compensated for any increases in the property's value. Make sure you and your cosigner come to an agreement on this issue before signing—preferably in writing.

CAUTION

Exaggerating or listing bogus information on your loan application won't help anything. A lender can and will check the accuracy of your application. Your falsifications will very likely be discovered and held against you.

Get Loan Preapproval

As an essential step toward purchasing a good house at a reasonable price, it's important to be preapproved for a loan. This means a lender has actually done a credit check on you and evaluated your financial situation, rather than simply relied on your own statement about your income and debts. Preapproval means that the lender would actually fund the loan, pending an appraisal of the property, title report, and purchase contract.

Get a preapproval letter as soon as you start househunting. Sellers who are anxious to sell (the best kind, from your perspective) often accept offers from purchasers who can close quickly (that is, have already arranged financing and have a preapproval letter), even if they don't make the highest offer. A seller who has had earlier deals fall through because of a buyer's financing problems is especially likely to accept an offer, even a low one, backed by a loan preapproval.

TIP

Get a preapproval letter for the exact amount of your bid. When you bid for a home, ask your lender to prepare a new letter stating that you are preapproved for the amount you are offering—no need to tell the seller that you can actually pay more if you wish.

For preapproval, your lender will ask you to pull together various documents, which usually include:

- pay stubs for the last two pay periods
- last two years' tax returns and W-2 forms
- proof of nonsalary income such as rental income or alimony
- three months of bank statements for every account you have (all pages)
- proof of assets such as pension funds, stocks, or life insurance

- source of your down payment, including documentation for any gift funds involved
- names, addresses, and phone numbers of employers for the last two years, and
- names, addresses, and phone numbers of landlords for the last two years.

If you are completing the application yourself, complete every section of the application. Don't leave any blanks. If an item doesn't apply, write "not applicable" or "N/A."

The lender will review and approve your file, subject to some conditions such as, but not limited to, an acceptable property appraisal, a copy of your purchase contract, and clear title to the property. Your loan officer will review the lender conditions with you to make sure that you will be able to satisfy the lender's requests.

Prequalification Versus Preapproval

Once you've completed your financial statement, a lender or loan broker can prepare a prequalification letter saying that loan approval for a specified amount is *likely* based on your income and credit history. Unlike preapproval, prequalification is not a commitment by the lender to lend you that amount, or to lend you money at all. Prequalifying will just help you determine how much you're able to borrow and how much you'll need for a down payment and closing costs. However, unless you're in a very slow market, with lots more sellers than buyers, you'll want to do more than prequalify for a loan—you will want to be preapproved for a specific loan amount. Your offer will be more attractive because the seller will know ahead of time that you'll be able to afford the purchase.

CHAPTER

3

Narrowing the Affordability Gap: How to Afford Buying a House

SKIP AHEAD

No money worries. Those few readers with enough money to purchase the house of their dreams and no inclination to bargain hunt can safely skip this chapter. The other 95% should stick around and learn how to overcome the affordability gap.

Why California Houses Are Expensive

The concept of the affordability gap is simple—many house buyers can't afford to buy their ideal house. Some can't afford any house at all. The gap, while particularly acute in urban coastal areas of California, exists all over the state, for several reasons:

- In the past generation, millions of baby boomers have entered their prime house-buying years, creating heavy demand.
- Historically, more people have tended to move to California than leave it (though this has reversed with recent economic downturns).
- Rising construction and lumber costs and, in many areas, restrictive government regulations and taxes, have made it expensive, and sometimes even impossible, to build new housing.
- Recently, interest rates have been at historic lows, and for a period of time many creative financial strategies were available, allowing more people to enter the real estate market. This has increased demand, driving prices upward. Though this trend has leveled somewhat as many overextended buyers have recently defaulted on their loans, it has still contributed significantly to the growth of demand in recent years.
- Even in a down economy, houses are looked upon as a sound investment.

California House Prices

In May 2008, the median sales price of an existing California single-family detached house was $384,840, according to the California Association of Realtors®. The median price is the middle point of all sales prices, meaning that one-half of all houses sold for more than $384,840 and one-half sold for less. This is different from the average, which is considerably higher (because high-priced luxury homes pull the average up).

In much of the San Francisco Bay Area and Southern California, the median sales price was considerably higher, reaching $1 million or more in wealthy communities such as Beverly Hills, Palos Verdes Estates, and Manhattan Beach.

WEBSITE RESOURCE

For median prices of California houses, see the California Association of Realtors® website at www.car.org. Click the "Newsstand" or the "Economics" area.

Fortunately, as this chapter shows, there are many creative ways Californians have found to beat affordability problems—such as using equity in a starter house to finance a more expensive one later, having relatives or friends help with the down payment, buying a fixer-upper (substituting sweat equity for capital), and getting the seller to finance part of the purchase by taking back a second mortgage. All told, these approaches allow tens of thousands of people to buy a house who otherwise couldn't.

Don't Buy a House at All—Rent and Invest Elsewhere

Not everyone should strive to overcome the affordability gap to purchase a house. If you're happy renting and think you'll continue to be for years, there's little point in stretching your finances to the breaking point. In fact, if you live in an area where monthly rents are less than mortgage payments on the same house would be, renting might be a good strategy.

There are many advantages to renting: You don't tie up a lot of money in home equity and improvements, and someone else worries about (and pays for) property maintenance, repairs, insurance, and taxes. In addition, putting all your savings toward a house leaves you with no financial cushion to fall back on in case of an emergency.

A principal advantage of renting is that money not tied up in down payments and improvements can be invested in ways that may produce a better long-term return than a house will. Of course, this depends on interest rates and the housing market at the time you buy and sell. In the early 2000s, people watching their stock portfolios evaporate turned to houses as a more reliable investment. On the other hand, in recent years home buyers in many areas have seen home prices stagnate or fall.

The major disadvantage of renting is that your entire monthly payment vanishes. With home ownership, part of each mortgage payment goes toward equity in your home. The remainder (interest), along with local property taxes, is deductible from your income taxes. People in higher tax brackets obviously have the most to gain (in terms of the largest tax break) by buying a house versus renting.

So, what's the bottom line? Is it better to buy or rent? Too many variables make it impossible to produce a definitive answer. Below are a few factors to consider which, depending on your circumstances, may tip the balance one way or the other:

- **The shorter the time you plan to stay put, the more financially advantageous it is to rent.** People who buy and sell often incur transactional costs, such as real estate commissions and closing costs. Commonly, a buyer must own a house for at least three to five years, and sometimes longer, for its increase in value to cover these costs.
- **It's a lot easier to move from a rental unit than from a house.** With a house you own, you can't just give the landlord notice and pick up and leave.

- **Renters have no protection against rent increases beyond the term of their rental agreement or lease.** The exception, of course, is if you live in a rent-controlled area. If you have a fixed rate mortgage, your loan payments remain constant.
- **Rent payments are often less than mortgage payments for the same house.** In fact, they are usually a lot less than the total monthly cost of owning a house, even after the tax benefits of owning are factored in. This is true for both less-expensive digs and luxury property.
- **A house forces you to be a disciplined investor.** If you're not good at saving and investing money, buying a house is a good way for you to build up a financial nest egg, especially as compared to renting and spending your excess money.

RESOURCE

Rent versus buy: online calculators. Real estate websites often have useful information to help with your "rent versus buy" decision. See www.realtor.com, which has several useful calculators that will help you determine whether it makes more sense financially to buy or rent a home. You can find a calculator at www.nolo.com/calculators, or through online mortgage brokers such as E-Loan, www.eloan.com, discussed in Chapter 13.

Fix Up the House You Already Own

If you own a house and plan to sell it to purchase a more expensive one in the same area, consider remodeling rather than selling. You often get more for your money, and possibly a better location, by fixing up and adding on to your existing house than by moving up. And better yet, you avoid moving to a house that may be many miles from your job, your friends, or your children's school. Indeed, land prices are so high in some cities, such as Santa Monica, that they dwarf the cost of construction to the point that buyers commonly purchase modest houses on desirable lots only to tear them down and build afresh.

There are several other economic advantages to staying put and spending a large sum to redo your house. For one, you save the transactional costs of selling your existing house and closing on a new one.

However, it's easy to underestimate remodeling costs. In figuring out how much it would cost to fix up and perhaps add on to your existing house, don't take shortcuts. Make a detailed plan and cost it out carefully. Here's how to think about the cost of remodeling as compared with the cost of moving.

Moving

- Figure out how much cash you would net for your existing house by subtracting what you owe from its likely sales price.
- From this amount, subtract around 8% of the sales price for real estate commissions and other sales costs.
- Now add any money you've saved for housing. The total is the amount you can put down toward the purchase of a new house.

- Now estimate how much you'll need to pay for a suitable new house.
- Add 5% for your share of closing costs and moving expenses.
- Add remodeling costs, if any.

Remodeling

- Estimate the cost of hiring an architect experienced in house remodeling to draw the plans you need.
- Get a hard-eyed contractor's estimate for work you decide on.
- Add 10%–20% to the estimate to cover things you haven't considered and inevitable cost overruns.
- Add these costs to what you already owe on your house plus any costs of temporarily moving out and renting another place while remodeling, if that will be necessary.
- Consider how much you've saved to pay for remodeling or moving. You'll have to borrow any difference between what you have and what you need. If mortgage interest rates have gone down since you bought your house, often the cheapest way to borrow is to get a short-term construction loan and then, when the work is done, refinance the entire loan and your mortgage together. If interest rates have risen, however, keep your original mortgage and take out a second mortgage to refinance the construction.
- Finally, estimate how much the house will be worth in its remodeled condition. Ask local real estate agents and appraisers for their opinions on the house's current value and estimated value after remodeling.

Now ask yourself some big questions. How do the out-of-pocket costs of moving versus remodeling compare? And when the work is done, how much will each house be worth? If the cost of fixing your existing house is only 20%–30% of the purchase price of the new house, you're probably better off staying put.

It's not usually financially wise to remodel an existing house if any of the following are true:

- You plan to sell the house in a year or two. Although remodeling will increase the house's value, and you'll get more when you sell it, you're unlikely to get enough more to pay for your investment and trouble. In short, your improvements will benefit the next owner, not you.
- You live in a marginal area, and your renovated house will be substantially bigger and nicer than its neighbors. It's always hard to get full value when selling the best house on the block.
- The work you plan won't substantially increase your house's sales price. Remodeled kitchens, bathrooms, and extra bedrooms tend to increase the value of the house by 75%–100% of what the remodeling work costs. On the other hand, swimming pools and spas often increase the value by only 50% of what they cost to install—and can sometimes decrease a house's value, because they create maintenance and liability insurance costs. Improvements to the foundation, roof, wiring, or plumbing often result in an even

smaller increase in house value, as purchasers assume they should be in good shape to begin with.

RESOURCE

Online resources on remodeling. Everything you need to know about remodeling—from choosing a contractor to setting a budget to design ideas—can be found at ImproveNet at www.improvenet.com. Also see www.nari.org, the website of the National Association of the Remodeling Industry. And the website of *Remodeling* magazine, at www.remodeling.hw.net, offers an annual "Cost vs. Value Report," analyzing which home remodeling projects lead to the greatest rises in property value.

Strategies for Buying an Affordable House

One obvious way to beat the affordability gap is to find a good house at a comparatively reasonable price. Beating the odds and buying real property on favorable terms is possible because the residential real estate market is a highly imperfect one. A big reason is that there's no central mechanism, as is the case with a stock exchange or commodity market, to carry out transactions and set published prices on the half-million existing California houses and 100,000 new ones that are sold every year on local real estate markets.

Not only are there great differences among houses offered for sale, but the sellers and buyers, who often have little prior experience with real estate, have vastly different family situations, tastes, and even prejudices. For example, the house at 111 Maple St. may be offered for sale by a retired financial planner determined to get top value, while a similar house at 112 Maple may be offered for fast sale by a divorcing couple or an out-of-town seller who has just inherited it. Sometimes, homes sell to the first person who makes an offer, especially if the owner likes the person, without exposing the home to the entire real estate market.

Below we'll discuss 18 strategies to narrow the affordability gap. Most are practical in today's market. A few have less merit but are included because potential home buyers often ask about them. Some of these strategies won't be relevant to you, but skim through them to see if you find one that helps put an affordable home within reach.

What You Can Afford Relates to Your Financing

The focus of this chapter is on how to purchase a good house for 10%–20% below what many others will pay. A major consideration to being able to do this is how you finance the purchase—covered in the following chapters:

- Raising Money for Your Down Payment (Chapter 4)
- Financing Your House: An Overview (Chapter 8)
- Fixed Rate Mortgages (Chapter 9)
- Adjustable Rate Mortgages (Chapter 10)
- Government-Assisted Loans (Chapter 11)
- Private Mortgages (Chapter 12), and
- Obtaining a Mortgage (Chapter 13).

Don't Buy Until You've Saved More Money

First-time purchasers often ask whether it's better to buy a less-than-perfect house now or to save like mad for a few years to afford a better one later. Traditionally, the answer has been "buy now." In California, house prices have tended to increase faster than savings.

However, this general advice to buy now doesn't apply to everyone or to every time period. In recent years, prices in parts of California have dropped significantly and it's unclear how much further they could fall. If you believe that house prices in the area you are interested in are currently too high and are going to level off or drop, you may do better by saving your money and waiting a few years.

TIP

If you're a first-time buyer, calculate an extra tax break. Thanks to the Housing and Economic Recovery Act of 2008, first-time buyers are entitled to a tax credit of 10% of the purchase price up to $7,500. The credit starts to phase out when your income reaches $75,000 if single or $150,000 if married, and it must be repaid—6.67% each year for 15 years. Essentially an interest-free loan, it is still helpful in the first year, when it will reduce your tax liability significantly.

Move to a More Affordable Part of the State

There's no better strategy to buying an affordable house than moving from an area with high housing costs to an area where houses cost far less. A house that would cost $750,000 in a posh suburb of Los Angeles or San Francisco would sell for much less in some communities near Bakersfield or Sacramento.

However, unless you work at home or for an employer that pays the same wages no matter where the location (such as the state or federal government), you will probably make less money in low cost areas. But the ratio of your earnings to local house prices is what's important to comparing the affordability of housing in different areas. For example, if you can make 60% of your Orange County salary in Merced, but comparable houses cost 35% as much, your ability to buy a nice house has increased greatly.

Buy a Less Desirable House Than You Really Want

People caught in an affordability squeeze typically must scale down their new-house wish list. A good percentage fall into three broad categories:

- Buy a marginal house in a desirable area.
- Buy a desirable house in a marginal area.
- If you face a severe affordability gap, buy a marginal house in a marginal area.

How Leverage Can Work for You

A main reason why, in an up market, it's possible to trade up to a better house quickly is that investing in a house gives you a unique chance to make a big gain on a small investment. For example, if you buy a house for $400,000, putting $80,000 down and taking a $320,000 mortgage, and a few years later the house goes up in value 20%, you've doubled your $80,000 investment. Pros call this being "highly leveraged." If you put the same $80,000 into a government bond earning 6%, it would take you nearly 12 years to achieve the same result.

Of course, the flip side to being highly leveraged is that if the value of the property drops, your investment can be quickly wiped out. In the example above, if the property's value dropped 20%, the entire $80,000 would be gone.

Buy a Marginal House in a Desirable Area

In older residential areas, where houses were typically built one by one or in small groups, house size, construction techniques, and lot size often vary significantly. On the same block, house prices can differ by a hundred thousand dollars or more. This means that bargains can, and do, pop up where you might not expect to find them, particularly in older neighborhoods.

Here are some houses that seem undesirable but can be greatly improved at modest expense:

- **Houses with ugly exteriors but pleasant interiors.** You'd be amazed at the number of prospective buyers who won't even get out of the car to enter a truly homely house.
- **Houses on busy streets that can be "turned around" to focus on a backyard.** For example, you might spruce up the back by adding a deck or patio.
- **Houses with run-down interiors that need a lot of elbow grease and creative tinkering.** Not only is paint cheap, but replacing wallpaper, linoleum, formica, and light fixtures can normally be done at a reasonable cost.
- **Houses that can be screened from a busy street or other undesirable outdoor feature.** If there's room (and zoning rules allow you) to build a stout redwood fence or plant a thick, tall hedge, you can often block the problem from view. Street noise can often be reduced by walls, fences, and certain types of vegetation. (See, for example, *Sunset* magazine's *Landscaping for Privacy: Hedges, Fences, Arbors.*)

Buy a Desirable House in a Marginal Area

One good way to maximize gain in the short term is to buy a good house in an up-and-coming area that will appreciate quickly after purchase. We don't have a sure-fire technique for spotting a marginal area about to improve. (If we did, this book would cost a lot more than it does!) But we can give you a few useful hints:

- **Avoid the worst neighborhoods.** Prices in desperately poor areas with high crime rates may improve eventually, but not as soon as you'd like; in the meantime, you face the day-to-day reality of living in a dangerous environment.

- **Avoid marginal areas on the immediate periphery of the worst neighborhoods.** As long as the blighted area is there, the marginal area is unlikely to improve much.
- **Look for areas that have been substantially devalued by something no longer, or soon to be no longer, an issue.** For example, house values are likely to be depressed by the proximity of a large, loud, and filthy factory, cannery, or railroad spur-line. If the offending feature is about to close and the surrounding area is otherwise desirable, you may have found a terrific place to buy.
- **Look for blighted areas where a few hardy middle-class pioneers have already settled.** Once these pioneers begin turning things around, small businesses often follow, restaurants and cafes open, and then, seemingly overnight, individuals and developers buy and transform the dilapidated housing stock in the area. If you think you have a good idea about such an area, check with local planning departments. Applications for building permits and plans can tell you a lot about future prospects for a particular area.
- **Look for lower-priced areas touching on more desirable ones.** Many affluent California cities have one or more poorer cousins nearby. Areas particularly likely to improve are pockets of larger old houses.
- **Look for affordable areas where transportation, especially public transportation, is good or will improve soon.** Much of California is already experiencing almost terminal traffic gridlock. The

True Story

Problem Houses in Good Areas Can Be a Bargain

Our friend Tim, a savvy real estate professional, recently conducted an experiment. He blindfolded Kim, an experienced agent, and drove her to a house for sale, telling her only that it was located in a particular upscale neighborhood. When Kim entered the house, Tim removed her blindfold and asked her to look around, but not to open the blinds covering the front windows. After ten minutes, Kim was asked how much the house was worth. She replied that if the house didn't have any major structural problems, she'd guess it would sell for about $525,000.

When Tim told her the actual asking price—$410,000—Kim was flabbergasted. She then opened the blinds and saw that the house was on a busy local street. Even so, she continued to maintain that the house was underpriced.

The point should be readily understood—problem houses in nice neighborhoods are often underpriced, even when a reasonable amount is subtracted to compensate for the problem.

result is that older residential areas convenient to rail or ferry systems are almost sure to increase in value faster than the average residential area.

- **Look for affordable areas within excellent school districts.** It's sometimes possible to find a pocket of affordable housing in an upscale school district.

TIP

Think twice before buying a nice house in a poor school district. Because house prices (and their chances of appreciating comparatively quickly in the future) are always affected by the quality of local schools, even people without children should think twice about buying where schools are poor, because values will not appreciate as much.

- **Pay attention to where immigrants are locating.** Property values in many previously depressed areas have jumped substantially as large numbers of new Americans locate there.

Buy a Marginal House in a Marginal Area

There's not much positive to say about buying a relatively undesirable house in a bad neighborhood, even though you can do this comparatively cheaply. We purposely de-emphasize this approach, both because of immediate problems (high crime and run-down public and private services) and because property values in very poor areas usually appreciate far more slowly than in other neighborhoods. But as with any general rule, there are exceptions. Again, as mentioned, the most obvious is an area where large numbers of immigrants move in and quickly change the neighborhood's character. Another involves areas with an extremely desirable location that the city or private developers have already targeted for improvement. For example, plans to build a new ballpark or convention center in an area are often a tip-off that other major changes for the better are likely to follow.

Buy a Fixer-Upper

The era when a dilapidated house in a reasonably decent area could be purchased dirt cheap and fixed up at a moderate cost is past. The demand for this type of house has risen steadily for at least the last two decades, resulting in comparatively high prices for remaining fixer-uppers in all but the most undesirable neighborhoods. Part of the reason is that buying distressed houses, fixing them up quickly, and reselling at a profit is a profitable business for many small contractors, which means house buyers face professional competition.

While most fixer-uppers are no longer great deals, they still cost less than a comparable house in good shape. Ask your real estate agent about special loans available from the Federal Housing Administration for fixer-uppers. (See Chapter 11.) Also, consider purchasing a foreclosed property, which will often be a fixer-upper. (See "Buy a House Subject to Foreclosure," below.)

When you consider the time, effort, and cost of finding and renovating a house, however, a fixer-upper is unlikely to be a bargain. Indeed, many fixer-uppers sell above their fair market value when you take a hard-eyed approach to the real costs of repair. This is especially true for lower-priced houses, where it will be hard to recover the costs of major repairs in a subsequent sale. Fixer-upper bargains are more likely to be found in higher price ranges, where affluent buyers tend to look for houses already in good condition.

TIP

How to judge whether a fixer-upper is a good deal. If you're seriously interested in a particular fixer-upper, hire a reliable remodeling contractor to check it out carefully and give you an estimate of needed renovation costs. If the total cost of the rehabilitated house is 90% or more of the cost of a comparable house in good shape, keep looking. By the time you factor in the trouble you'll go through and the likelihood of cost overruns, you won't save anything.

How to Find an Ugly Duckling

Bargain hunters who want to find a reasonably priced ugly duckling and turn it into a swan don't always know where to look. Look for ads or write-ups that say "not a drive-by," "a diamond in the rough," "has potential," or "needs TLC."

Buy a Small House and Add On Later

If you find a small house on a relatively large lot priced comparable to, or only slightly above, similar houses on ordinary-sized lots, you pay little or nothing for the extra land. In addition to the added privacy and room to play and garden, you normally have the space to enlarge the house any time you can afford to hire a contractor or have the time to do the work yourself.

True Story

Monica and Dave: Building Additions

Monica and Dave knew they wanted a three-bedroom, two-bath house in the Berkeley-Oakland area for a maximum of $575,000. They also dreamed of a large deck for weekend lounging and parties. But after 18 months of looking at nearly 200 houses, they had not found anything even marginally decent in their price range. So they took a new approach—they looked at smaller houses with expansion potential.

Within weeks, they found a house in North Berkeley with only two bedrooms and one bath (and no deck). At $525,000, the price was right. Best of all, the backyard was deep enough to leave plenty of room to add on to the back. After checking carefully and assuring themselves it was feasible to add on a bedroom later, they said yes. They quickly added a second bathroom (using a space that had been a closet/hallway) and a large deck. After five years, their new equity allowed them to qualify for a home equity loan to add a second-story master bedroom.

Even if the lot isn't that large, consider buying a smaller house with remodeling potential and adding a second-story addition. Of course, check first to be sure that local zoning laws allow the changes you want to make.

Buy a House at a Probate Sale

Probate sales occur when a homeowner dies leaving property to be divided among inheritors, or to be sold to pay debts or taxes. The sale is handled by the executor of the homeowner's will (or a court-appointed administrator if there is no will). It is often supervised by the probate court judge, through a bidding process. The highest bidder gets the property. Some probate sales are handled directly by the executor of an estate without going through the court bidding process.

Occasionally it's possible to buy a house at an estate or probate sale for substantially less than the current market rate. The time and uncertainty involved in bidding discourages many potential buyers from participating. Less buyer competition can mean a lower-than-market price. Also, the cost of bidding (you will likely be required to include a cashier's check for 10% of the price you're offering) discourages people from making casual bids.

The down side is that probate sales aren't subject to disclosure laws (discussed in Chapter 19), so while agents must legally disclose all pertinent facts, many probate-sold houses are sold "as is." Your bid made in court cannot contain financing, inspection, or other contingencies.

How a Court-Supervised Probate Sale Works

Here are the basic steps in a court-supervised probate house sale:

- The house is advertised for sale in a newspaper (often a legal or fairly obscure one) published in the county in which the property is located and, if listed with a broker, in a Multiple Listing Service.
- An appraisal value is established.
- Bids are accepted by a certain date.
- During the court procedure, higher bids are accepted. A cashier's check may be required with each bid. The first higher bid (called an "overbid") must exceed the original highest bid by at least 10% of the first $10,000, plus 5% of the balance. For example, the first overbid on a $100,000 offer must be $105,500:

10% of $10,000	=	$ 1,000
5% of $90,000	=	4,500
		$ 5,500

- An alternate formula that will get you the same result is 5% of the offer price plus $500.
- Subsequent overbids are allowed in amounts set by the probate judge. For example, the judge might require that each new bid exceed the previous one by $1,000.
- The highest bid, if it is at least 90% of the property's court-appraised value, is accepted.
- Purchase of the property is normally financed in the same way as any other purchase.

If you're considering buying a house at a probate sale, here's some advice for getting the best deal:

- **Hook up with a knowledgeable broker or salesperson who knows the ropes of probate sales.** There are a few in every community.
- **If you plan to bid at a court-supervised probate sale, line up a highly trustworthy and thorough inspector.** Have the inspector check out any house before the court confirmation procedure. (See Chapter 19 for details on inspections.)
- **Find a house that has been appraised too low.** This may be less difficult than you imagine, since a good percentage of houses subject to probate sales are run down. (Chapter 15 discusses how to evaluate sales prices.)
- **For court-supervised sales, consider holding off on your bid until the court procedure begins and the first round of bids are in.** (See "How a Court-Supervised Probate Sale Works," above.) At some probate sales, many bids are placed by investors hoping to pick up a house very cheaply and quickly resell it for a profit. If you can figure out what professional investors will offer and bid just a little higher, you can sometimes save a bundle. Call the probate court clerk (it's part of your county's superior court) for a list of probate sales on the court calendar. Then check out the property carefully. If it looks like the buyer got a great price, inspect the property, line up your financing, and hope to overbid them at the court confirmation. Contact

True Story

Bill and Eileen: Lender Flexibility Can Mean Greater Savings

We bought our home for $300,000, in effect putting only $30,000 (10%) down, but paying no mortgage insurance or other higher costs normally associated with making a low down payment. We did it like this:

The house had originally been listed at $338,000, but was reduced in two stages to $308,000, in part because an inspection report said that the house needed $40,000 of work, and in part because houses were selling slowly that fall. The seller had already moved to Texas and was anxious to unload the house. He quickly accepted our $300,000 offer, with 20% down, requiring him to credit us with $30,000 to partially compensate for the repairs. Our lender didn't require that the work be done before sale, because the appraisal showed that we didn't overpay, even without the repair work and credit.

The day after the sale closed, we picked up our $30,000 escrow credit check from the title company. This meant we had only $30,000 invested in the house. We used the escrow credit money to remodel the house. In the process, we fixed the serious problems in the inspection report but skipped the nonessential ones, and used the extra money to sand floors, move a wall, and reface cabinets. Now, a few years later, our lovely, extensively remodeled house is worth over $400,000.

the attorney handling the estate for the date and time of the confirmation hearing.

Buy a House With a Structural Problem

California law strictly requires that a seller and agent disclose all known problems with a house, using detailed forms entitled "Real Estate Transfer Disclosure Statement" and "Natural Hazard Disclosure Statement." (Copies are in Chapter 19.) In addition (as discussed in Chapter 19), most buyers and lenders insist on careful prepurchase inspections before the sale. As a result, many California houses are inspected two or three times.

Recently, fear of lawsuits for failing to disclose house defects has resulted in some inspectors exaggerating flaws and generally emphasizing the negative. This makes some houses far more difficult to sell than was the case ten years ago. If buyer interest dries up (as it often does when a house has a long list of problems), the asking price of a house will almost surely drop, sometimes precipitously. The house is likely to be perceived by local agents as being stale (hard to sell at any price), and thus it will be shown to fewer prospective purchasers. Before long, the price may be lowered again, creating a bargain despite the physical problems.

CAUTION

It is often difficult to get loans that include funds for major repairs or renovations. Your best bet is to find a portfolio lender (see Chapter 2) with more flexible policies. To do this, you'll probably need the help of a fairly sophisticated mortgage broker who knows local lending practices well. (See Chapter 13.)

Buy a House Subject to Foreclosure

Foreclosure normally begins when a homeowner misses several mortgage payments and receives a notice of default. During the three months following, the homeowner can make the back payments and cure the default. If he or she does not pay up, the house proceeds to foreclosure. For some people, purchasing a house subject to a foreclosure is a way to buy a house for less than its appraised value.

Home foreclosures aren't usually advertised through the online Multiple Listing Service (MLS) or other normal channels. The best place to check on your own is through websites such as www.realtytrac.com, though you have to pay a weekly membership fee to get anything more than bare-bones details of the listings. Another membership-based service, which contains listings of government foreclosures, is www.hudworks.com.

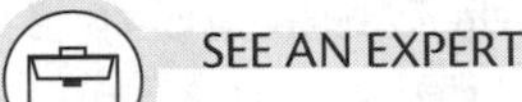

SEE AN EXPERT

In all stages, it's usually best to hook up with a real estate agent who knows the foreclosure ropes. Many foreclosure markets are dominated by savvy investors, and you'll be at a disadvantage if you aren't represented by someone familiar with the process.

The three broad approaches to buying a house subject to foreclosure are:

1. **Purchase from the owner during the three-month period before the foreclosure sale.** During the three-month period following default the owner may want to sell the property to avoid foreclosure and severe credit damage. At this point, some owners are delighted to sell for little or nothing more than they owe to the lenders, because they've given up hope of keeping the house. In some cases, the owner may even sell the house for less than is owed on the mortgage—this is called a "short sale," and requires the lender's approval.
2. **Purchase at the foreclosure sale.** If no one brings the mortgage current or buys the house before the sale, the trustee holds a foreclosure sale and sells the house to the highest bidder. The trustee opens the bidding at the amount of the outstanding mortgage being foreclosed. Potential buyers (often investors) attend the sale or auction with cash or a cashier's check in hand for a little more than the amount they plan to bid (to allow for a small increase). This up-front cash requirement eliminates casual bidders from foreclosure sales.
3. **Purchase after the foreclosure sale if no one bids.** If no one bids at the sale, the foreclosing mortgage holder gets the property back. In recent years, savings and loans and other lenders have ended up with a fair number of houses this way, most of which they want to sell quickly, even if it means taking a loss. (These properties are often called REOs, for "Real Estate-Owned.") Some lenders sell the properties themselves (often with favorable prices and low down payments); the better properties, however, are commonly turned over to real estate brokers, who try to sell them as they would any other house. Even so, the fact that the foreclosed house wasn't prepared for sale by an owner, and thus may be in less than perfect shape, often means there are bargains to be had.

Before purchasing a home through a private or government foreclosure sale, ask these questions:

- **Is the house worth significantly less than you would have to bid to get it on the open market?** If not, don't bother. (See Chapter 15 for how to assess the value of a house.)
- **Are there major problems with the house or property?** Like probate sales, foreclosure sales are an exception to California Civil Code § 1102 requiring sellers to disclose all known problems. Many foreclosed properties are sold "as is," so (if possible) be sure to arrange your own thorough inspection for any structural, mold, or pest control problems before you commit to a purchase. In fact, mold problems have been the cause of some recent foreclosures: Homeowners find themselves in situations where the mold remediation would cost tens or hundreds of thousands of dollars and the insurance company won't pay a cent—so the only choice they can afford is to hand their keys to the bank.

- **Are you taking clear title?** (Title is the history of ownership; see Chapter 18 for more information.) The owner may have had other financial problems, and creditors may have placed liens on the house. Normally, these are paid off or wiped out during the foreclosure process, but before agreeing to buy the house, you'll want to be sure all liens really have been removed.
- **Are there tenants living in the house?** If so, make sure they're gone when you get the house. The last thing you want to do is evict a tenant who doesn't want to leave. If you're buying in a rent controlled area, however, you may have to buy subject to "tenants' rights." Although as an owner you are entitled to live in your house, you may very well have to assert this right by evicting the existing tenants after you purchase. If so, we suggest *The California Landlord's Law Book: Evictions,* by David Brown (Nolo).

RESOURCE

Foreclosures:

- *The Complete Idiot's Guide to Buying Foreclosures,* by Bobbi Dempsey and Todd Beitler (Alpha).
- *The Smart Money Guide to Bargain Homes: How to Find and Buy Foreclosures,* by James Wiedemer (Dearborn Financial Publishing).
- *Big Money in Real Estate Foreclosures,* by Ted Thomas (Wiley).
- *How to Find Hidden Real Estate Bargains,* by Robert Irwin (McGraw-Hill Trade).

Government Foreclosure

If the distressed house had financing guaranteed by the U.S. Department of Veterans Affairs or insured by the Federal Housing Administration (of the U.S. Department of Housing and Urban Development), bidding at a foreclosure sale must follow the agency's rules (typically sealed bids submitted by mail). Buyers frequently must go through a time-consuming and bureaucratic process before the sale is final. But don't let this scare you—government agencies often have good-sized inventories of foreclosed properties and will sometimes offer bargain prices, low down payments, and attractive financing deals to move them.

A real estate agent experienced with government foreclosures can help you locate and buy these types of houses. Government-foreclosed properties are often advertised in local newspapers. For more information, contact the U.S. Department of Veterans Affairs or Department of Housing and Urban Development. (For addresses and websites, see Chapter 11, Government-Assisted Loans.)

Make Multiple Backup Offers

If you are patient and flexible, you may be able to buy a house at a substantial discount by placing low backup offers on houses for which the seller has already accepted a higher offer. In doing this, you're gambling on three things: that the first offer will fall through (we estimate this happens about 10%–20% of the time, usually because of inspection or financing contingencies), that the seller hasn't already arranged for a backup offer, and that the seller will accept your backup offer rather than put the house back on the market.

Here are some basic rules to follow in making backup offers:

- **Learn the local market.** Remember, it's no bargain to buy a house for 10% less than either the asking price or the amount of the first offer if its price was 15% too high in the first place.
- **Adopt a bidding strategy.** For example, some buyers decide to bid about 5%–10% lower than a house's fair value (not the asking price). If you bid lower than this, you probably won't be taken seriously.
- **Make all backup offers contingent on your subsequent right to approve, should the seller accept.** Reserving a right of approval is essential if you make more than one backup offer; otherwise, if two or more are accepted simultaneously, you may find yourself in a legal mess and may lose any deposit you've made.

Buy a "Shared Equity" House With Someone You'll Live With

Equity sharing is a fancy term for buying a house with someone other than a spouse. The attraction of equity sharing is that two or more people with pooled resources can buy more house than each can alone. It goes without saying that if you own and live in a house with others, you'd better be personally compatible. Equity sharing tends to be most popular among unmarried couples, although it's also reasonably common with friends and relatives not in romantic relationships. Although many equity-sharing couples live lives similar to married couples, their legal property-ownership arrangements are bound to be different, since California's marital property laws do not apply to them.

Regardless of whether the equity sharers are a couple or not, they should have a written contract. It should spell out the percentage of the house each person owns; who pays how much each month for the mortgage, taxes, insurance, and other costs; what happens if the household breaks up or an owner dies; as well as a number of other practical ownership issues. We discuss a few of these issues in Chapter 20, but to draw up an equity-sharing contract, you'll need additional information. (See "Resources: Writing shared equity contracts," below.)

RESOURCE

Writing shared equity contracts: Nolo publishes the following books to help equity sharers cope with owning property together:

- *Living Together: A Legal Guide for Unmarried Couples,* by Ralph Warner, Toni Ihara, and Frederick Hertz, contains several sample house purchasing contracts for unmarried couples.
- *A Legal Guide for Lesbian & Gay Couples,* by Hayden Curry, Frederick Hertz, and Emily Doskow, contains sample contracts similar to those in *Living Together* but adapted to

address the special concerns of lesbian and gay couples and groups buying together.

- *Deeds for California Real Estate,* by Mary Randolph, discusses the different ways of taking title to and transferring real property in California.

Buy a "Shared Equity" House With Only One Owner (You) Living on the Property

Equity sharing between a resident owner and an investor is often touted as a good solution for people with affordability problems. The idea is for a nonresident investor to put up a chunk of the down payment in exchange for a share of profits when the house is sold.

Equity sharing is not the best way for one person to help another buy a house. From the house purchaser's point of view, it's usually better to simply borrow the money and own the entire property. Similarly, equity sharing is often a poor idea for the investor. When a house is viewed as an investment by a lender and as a home by its occupant, the potential conflicts are huge. What if the resident wants to make improvements that will enhance the house's livability but which won't increase its market value? What if the nonresident wants his money back, but the resident doesn't want to sell and can't afford to pay the nonresident his share? Or, even more serious from the investor's point of view, what if the resident owner ceases making payments and refuses to vacate the house? Yes, a written contract can and should deal with these and many other similar questions, but, contract or not, the possibilities for future conflict are considerable.

If, despite these warnings, you want to pursue equity sharing with a nonresident because you've got no other way to raise enough money for a down payment, it may make the most sense to buy with someone who is not a relative or friend, so as to establish that it's clearly a business deal. A good real estate agent should be familiar with programs in your area that bring buyers and investors together.

Typically, the investor supplies all or most of the down payment while the buyer lives in the house, maintains it, and pays all or most of the mortgage, insurance, and tax payments. At an agreed-upon date, the home buyer refinances and pays the investor the down payment plus a specified share of the appreciation. A clear, written agreement is necessary to cover the following:

- the use of the home
- the amount of the initial investment and the percentage of ownership
- buy-out provisions
- the amount and type of insurance to carry, and allocation of the proceeds should the house be damaged or destroyed (for example, by fire)
- the responsibility for daily costs and capital improvements, and
- the details of any sale or refinance (such as time, price, and profit splits).

CAUTION

Take tax rules seriously. It's crucial that the buyer and investor clearly understand tax laws regarding shared equity arrangements. Consult your tax attorney or accountant for advice on your particular situation.

RESOURCE

Equity sharing:

- *The New Home Buying Strategy: Solve Your Cash Crunch With Team Buying Power,* by Marilyn D. Sullivan (Venture 2000 Publishers), contains sample contracts, useful tax information, and tips on how to make an equity sharing transaction work for both the investor and the resident owner.
- Another good book on equity sharing is *The Home Equity Sharing Manual,* by David A. Sirkin (John Wiley & Sons).

Rent Out Part of the House

One way to overcome affordability problems is to increase monthly income by renting out a room. Renting out a room in an urban area may bring in $800 per month or more, which is $9,600 a year. This increased income may not only help you pay the mortgage, it may also help you qualify for a larger loan amount because your debt-to-income ratio will decrease.

Renting also offers tax advantages. A homeowner can deduct only property taxes and mortgage interest on her income taxes, while a rental owner can also deduct business expenses, such as repairs and utilities, and take depreciation on the portion of the home that is rented out.

If you're seriously considering renting out a room or two as part of your house-financing strategy, you'll need to do some homework. Start by finding out how much rent you can reasonably charge—that is, what local tenants pay for similar space.

True Story

Deborah, Doug, and Rose: The Joy of Living Near Grandma

Deborah and Doug have a two-year-old daughter. Both artists, they wanted at least 1,500 square feet to accommodate their family and need for studio space. Here's how they bridged their affordability gap:

"We wanted to stay in our long-time neighborhood, but, unfortunately, couldn't afford it. Then we heard about a place right around the corner that sounded great—except that it was more expensive and larger than we needed.

"Deborah's mother, Rose, provided an unexpected solution. She offered to help us with the down payment and monthly mortgage payments in exchange for living in one of the units. We quickly struck a two-thirds–one-third financial split. Our family took the three-bedroom unit on the top floor and converted the bottom-floor unit into a home for Rose and the middle unit into a fantastic studio space. We now have our ideal house at a price we can afford, while still retaining our privacy. But the best part is the special relationship between our daughter and her grandma. We wouldn't miss it for the world."

Then check with your financial institution or loan broker to be sure they'll let you count the expected rent as part of your monthly income.

Buy a Duplex, Triplex, or House With an In-Law Unit

Another approach to increase income is to buy a duplex or triplex, then live in one unit while renting out the others. A variant of this approach is to buy a large house with a separate, smaller "in-law" unit.

However, there's considerable competition for these types of houses, which means prices are often marked up to the point that rental income is entirely eaten up by the extra monthly costs of the larger mortgage.

Your goal is to find a house selling for little more than if the second (or third) unit wasn't there. The more unconventional the second unit, the more likely you are to be able to accomplish this. For example, if an "in-law" unit is tucked under a hillside house with access down a driveway and around two trees and a rosebush (as opposed to being attached to your unit, with a door facing the street), the real estate market may undervalue it.

CAUTION

Make sure an extra unit is legal. Especially if an extra living space looks homemade, demand to see necessary permits. If they don't exist, you run the risk that the city or county will close down the unit—or make you fix it—because it doesn't comply with building codes. If there are no permits, don't pay any more for the property than you would if the extra unit didn't exist.

True Story

Author Ira Serkes's Purchase of a Small Berkeley Multiunit Building

"When I first got interested in real estate, I couldn't afford a single-family home. Instead, I looked for a small apartment building where I could live in one unit and have rental income from the others subsidize the mortgage. I originally looked at triplexes but ended up buying a fixer-upper seven-plex. My family invested with the down payment and shared the appreciation. For the next five years, I lived in one of the units. With the help of some tenants, I renovated each apartment as it became vacant. As the value of the building went up, I borrowed against it and used the money for a down payment on another small building.

"My successes inspired a friend of mine to begin investing with me. Now I own a nice house and a number of investment properties, whose monthly rents are helping put my nieces through college. And the best fringe benefit of buying this small apartment building is it was where I met my wife, best friend, and business partner Carol! She rented an apartment from me, I broke my rule about going out with a renter, and the rest was history!"

Lease a House You Can't Afford Now With an Option to Buy Later

A lease option is a contract where an owner leases her house (usually from one to three years) to a tenant for a specific monthly rent (which may be scheduled to increase during the contract term) and gives the tenant the right to buy the house for a price established in advance. The tenant pays some money for the option—a lump sum payment at the start of the contract or periodic payments (all nonrefundable). Depending on the contract, the potential buyer normally can exercise the option to purchase at any time during the lease period or at a date specified.

> **EXAMPLE:** Ted and Jane lease Robin's house for $1,700 per month for two years. In addition, they pay Robin $4,000 for the option to purchase the house for $380,000 at any time during the two years. If Ted and Jane decide to buy, the $4,000 will be credited against the purchase price; if not, Robin keeps it.

This example is deliberately made simple to give you the general idea. Most lease option deals are more complicated. For example, the house purchase price might be a fixed dollar amount, plus an amount tied to any increase in the Consumer Price Index. Or, instead of an up-front option fee, the rent might be set at a higher-than-normal amount, with part, or all, of the extra applied to the purchase price if the option to purchase is ever exercised.

TIP

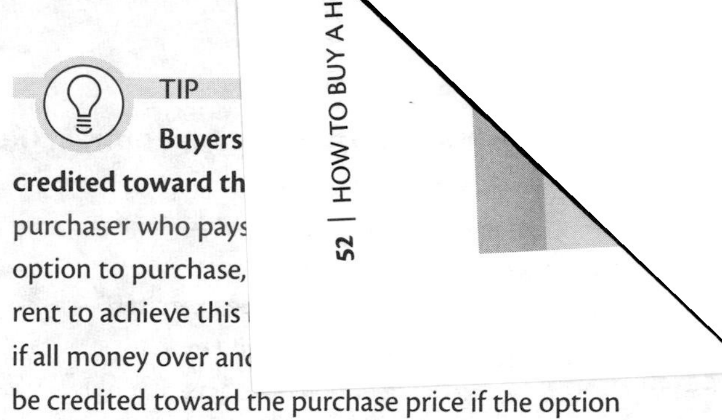

Buyers
credited toward th
purchaser who pays
option to purchase,
rent to achieve this
if all money over anc
be credited toward the purchase price if the option is exercised.

A potential buyer who chooses a lease option will get to move into a home without having to come up with a down payment or financing. It also gives the potential buyer time to clean up any credit problems and to see if he or she can handle the house's maintenance and repair costs and other issues. Even better, it allows the luxury of waiting to see if the value of the house reaches or surpasses the amount of the option price before deciding whether to purchase. If the value does increase, the house will be easier to finance, as the buyer will already have equity (the difference between the sales price and the then-current market value).

Lease options can often fairly easily be arranged in colder markets or when the house is a hard one to sell—don't be afraid to ask, especially if the house has been on the market for awhile.

Here's what to look for:

- An owner having trouble selling the house at the asking price.
- An owner who needs to move now, but who, for tax reasons, doesn't want the profit on the sale to be taxed in the

Lease Option Contract (Renter-Buyer's Perspective)

A lease option contract should address the following:

- **When the option can be exercised.** flexibility about when you exercise it. Avoid lease option contracts that only allow you to exercise your option under very restrictive circumstances—for example, for one week at the end of the second and fourth year.
- **The purchase price if you exercise the option.** It's far better to have it fixed at the start of the lease period, even if an increase for inflation is built in, not set by an appraisal at the time you exercise the option to purchase.
- **How much of the rent or upfront option payment will be applied toward the down payment or purchase price if the option is exercised.**
- **Exactly how you can exercise the option.** Written notice sent by certified mail is a good approach.
- **Whether the seller will help you finance the house by taking back a second mortgage, and if so, the details.**
- **An inspection of the house.** It is best to have the house thoroughly inspected before the lease option is signed to determine what repairs are needed.
- **Assignability.** If you choose not to exercise your option, you want to be able to sell that right to someone else, if possible, for cash or a share of the house's equity.
- **Any other significant terms of the purchase.**

CAUTION

Beware of termination clauses. Avoid any clause in a lease option contract that ends your option if you fail to perform your duties under the rental agreement in a timely manner. Such a clause could let the owner end the option contract if you're late with the rent, even once. Instead, you want a clause that lets you exercise the option to buy if your rent is paid up at the time you choose to exercise the option.

In addition, make sure the lease option contract is notarized and recorded at the County Recorder's Office. This will ensure that your right to purchase will appear on any title search, meaning the owner can't duplicitously sell the house out from under you without your knowledge.

Finally, unless you're experienced in this field, have the contract checked by someone who is. For sample lease option contracts, see "Resources on lease options," below.

current fiscal year. Often owners about to retire and enter a lower tax bracket fit this description.

- An owner for whom the initial option fee and/or higher-than-normal rent means an excellent short-run return—perhaps filling a house that would have otherwise remained vacant until it sold.
- An owner who hopes you won't exercise the option, giving the owner a premium rent (or up-front option fee payment) while keeping the house.

RESOURCE

Lease options: *For Sale by Owner in California,* by George Devine (Nolo), includes a sample lease option contract.

Buy a Condominium

Many California condos are priced temptingly low when compared to houses. A condominium (condo) owner owns the unit outright plus an undivided share of common areas (halls, parking areas, roof, plumbing, yard, deck, and the like). To maintain these areas, owners usually must pay fees to a condominium association, in addition to local property taxes assessed on each unit. Condos include a number of restrictions on how the property can be used, such as the type of landscaping you can do or the number or weight of pets you can own. These restrictions are spelled out in a document called the covenants, conditions, and restrictions (CC&Rs).

Condos come in all shapes and sizes, from duplexes to high-rises, and there can be good reasons for buying one. Many people appreciate the decreased maintenance that comes with having some areas held in common. Particularly if you're considering buying in a city or other area where there's limited land on which to build, a condo may be a very good choice.

Although historically condos haven't appreciated in value as fast as single-family homes, this has been changing, especially in areas where real estate is in short supply, or areas that attract many first-time home buyers or retirees.

Buy a Town House

Town houses—usually single-family houses with common walls—have surged in popularity in California because they're relatively inexpensive. And well they should be; they save on land, because common walls and roofs are cheap to build. With most town houses, you hold legal title to your house and the land it's on. You must pay real estate taxes even though you and your neighbors sit on the same piece of land and share common walls.

Town houses may be a better investment than condos. One reason for this is that many town houses, unlike most condos, are two-story, which means they physically look somewhat like single-family houses; condos, which often contain many units, often physically look more like apartment units. Because many people prefer the size and scale of a house (regardless of form of ownership), town houses are a bit more likely than condos to increase in value.

Does this mean that town houses are as good an investment as small detached starter houses are? On the whole, with exceptions for particularly desirable projects, usually not. Most people prefer living in a house that doesn't share walls with its neighbor. Still, if you can't afford a nice starter house in a decent area, an affordable town house may be a better choice than buying a run-down, detached house in a marginal neighborhood.

Buy Into a Cohousing or Cooperative Arrangement

Another increasingly popular way to find an affordable house is to enter into a cooperative arrangement with others. This usually involves finding or building an apartment building or a series of town houses or small units with shared common areas such as walkways, gardens, or children's play areas. In legal terms, the possible arrangements run the gamut, from condominium-type ownership, in which each buyer purchases his own mortgage ("cohousing"), to cooperatives, in which all share a "blanket" mortgage.

A cohousing community is often conceived of, designed, and developed by the people who will live in it. They are not guaranteed to be low cost. However, their emphasis on compact living units with shared resources such as common kitchen and dining areas, walkways, gardens, parking areas, and laundry facilities means that some savings are possible.

For more information on cohousing or similar forms of intentional communities, as well as architects and developers, contact:

- Abraham Paiss & Associates, Boulder, Colorado-based consultants specializing in startup cohousing groups, at 303-413-8066, www.abrahampaiss.com.
- Cohousing Resources, LLC, Langley, Washington-based development consultants, 360-321-7850, www.cohousingresources.com.
- Fellowship for Intentional Community, in Rutledge, Missouri, 660-883-5545, www.ic.org. You might enjoy their *Communities Directory,* which contains descriptions of over 700 communities in the United States and abroad.
- CoHousing Partners, 241 Commercial Street, Nevada City, CA 95959, 530-478-1970, www.cohousingpartners.com.
- The Cohousing Association of the United States, 22833 Bothell-Everett Highway, Bothell, WA 98021, 314-754-5828, www.cohousing.org.
- Wonderland Hill Development Company, 4676 Broadway, Boulder, CO 80304, 303-449-3232, www.whdc.com.

Unlike cohousing, housing cooperatives are normally set up as corporations. These corporations can either be private or nonprofit. The nonprofit arrangement is referred to as a "limited equity housing cooperative" or "LEHC."

People who want to live in a housing cooperative buy in as shareholders. Shareholders don't own individual units, but their shares entitle them to a proprietary lease on a specific unit. During their ownership, each buyer also pays a monthly carrying charge to cover the mortgage, insurance, and other expenses. If the cooperative will provide housing for low- and moderate-income people, public subsidies can be obtained to help with these carrying charges. In private cooperatives, individual members arrange private financing of their share purchases.

Limited equity housing cooperatives are more highly structured, since they're governed by California law. (Health & Safety Code § 33007.5 and Bus. and Prof. Code § 11003.4.) To qualify for entry into an LEHC, you'll need to meet eligibility criteria set by the cooperative (which may or may not include proving that you're low income). You'll also need to get lucky—these cooperatives are being developed only as quickly as nonprofit developers can find land or buildings at low cost, which is no simple matter for anyone in California. Still, the developers sometimes persuade the previous property owners to sell at a below-market price, which translates into savings for the shareholders. And there's nothing to stop you from forming your own nonprofit group to create a cooperative—in fact, some disgruntled tenants have used this method to take control of their living space, by getting together and buying out the landlord of their complex.

While limited equity housing cooperatives are affordable to buy into, the law creates

True Story

Ken Norwood: Strawberries, Consensus, and Low Monthly Fees.

In the late 1980s, the tenants of our 20-unit property in Berkeley got tired of watching the place go to pot. The tenants decided to organize a cooperative and buy the property. They arranged a private bridge loan for the purchase, which gave them four years to go through the process of organizing as a nonprofit, meet other state requirements, and get long-term financing.

I was interested in cooperative housing and was actually providing architectural services to the group, while renting a room somewhere else. When a unit came open, the group actually loaned me part of the initial purchase price, and I've been happily living here ever since.

Now the property is in great shape—we've just torn up some asphalt to make room for five more fruit trees. We've got four or five green-thumbers, and they voluntarily tend to the strawberries, chard, tomatoes, flowers, and trees around the property. Two common rooms and a roof deck are used for our monthly potluck meetings as well as for parties, exercise (we invested in weight machines), and free laundry. Our monthly meetings are consensus-based. We make decisions on how best to improve the property—such as our planned seismic work and attic insulation—and choose new owners. Sellers get a 4% increase over the amount they paid in. And, best of all, our monthly fees are far less than most people in Berkeley pay for rent.

a catch when you sell. You'll receive only a little more than your purchase price back, plus interest (a maximum of 10% per year), regardless of the property's current market value. That allows your unit to be resold at an affordable price, but it prevents you from following the traditional path of building equity in a starter home and working your way up as property values increase. Still, if your primary goal is to find a decent place to live with comparatively low up-front and monthly payments, an LEHC may be a good choice. And if your monthly payments are low enough, you'll have an opportunity to save—and invest—money that you might not have had if you'd been renting.

To find out more about cooperative housing arrangements, contact your city or county building departments or do a Web search for "limited equity housing," "cooperative housing," or "affordable housing."

RESOURCE

Our search turned up the following organizations that help create or find this type of housing option:

- National Association of Housing Cooperatives, in Washington, DC, at 202-737-0797, www.coophousing.org.
- Northern California Land Trust, in Berkeley, California, at 510-548-7878, www.nclt.org.
- Rural Community Assistance Corporation, in West Sacramento, California, at 916-447-2854, www.rcac.org.
- Shared Living Resource Center, in Berkeley, California, at 510-548-6608.

RESOURCE

The following books offer information on shared living alternatives, designs, and lifestyles:

- *Cohousing: A Contemporary Approach to Housing Ourselves,* by Kathryn McCamant, Charles Durrett (Contributor), and Ellen Hertzman (Ten Speed Press)
- *The Cohousing Handbook: Building a Place for Community,* by Chris ScottHanson and Kelly ScottHanson (New Society Publishers)
- *Rebuilding Community in America: Housing for Ecological Living, Personal Empowerment, and the New Extended Family,* by Ken Norwood and Kathleen Smith (Shared Living Resource Center).

Buy a House at an Auction

In parts of California where the real estate market has been particularly slow, sellers try to attract buyer interest by auctioning houses. Many auctions are of new houses in situations where developers need to raise quick cash to pay lenders. Foreclosed properties are also sometimes sold at auction.

As a general rule, buying at an auction won't get you a good deal. It should go almost without saying that amateurs (home buyers) rarely beat pros (homesellers familiar with auction procedures and investors who regularly buy at auctions) at their own game. This is especially true when you understand that the seller will take steps to be sure that the house won't sell at a rock-bottom price, including:

- setting a floor price—a price below which the house won't be sold
- advertising extensively—to be sure to collect a crowd
- hiring a professional auctioneer skilled at loosening up the crowd and building auction fever, and
- although it's illegal, sometimes planting shills in the audience to bid up the price.

If auctions are held in your area, a better strategy than actually bidding at the auction is to compare the prices for houses sold at auction with those of houses sold in the normal way. (You may need to attend a few auctions to get this information.) Just learning which sellers are motivated to sell is extremely valuable. And if you like what you see at the auction and the seller has other houses to sell (which is common with developers), stop by on a weekday near the end of the month and offer to buy for slightly less than the auction price. Or make a list of sellers with similar properties not being auctioned, and offer to buy for a little less than the auction price.

If despite this advice you decide to bid at auction, follow these basic rules:

- Research how much comparable houses are selling for in the same area—if you don't know the local market well, you're almost sure to get taken. (See Chapter 15 for how to find out comparable sales prices.)
- Attend several auctions without your checkbook (or paying a bidding fee)

True Story

Anne and Frank: We Bought a Great House at an Auction

We bought a nice house 13 years ago for $200,000 and recently sold it for $450,000. Because we both have fairly good jobs, we had the down payment and the income necessary to move up.

We wanted to live in Marin County and heard that some new luxury houses that had originally been listed at $900,000 had proved unsaleable and were being auctioned with a floor bid requirement of $625,000. We were there for the first sale, but didn't bid. The house went for $710,000, which we figured was too high. On the second and third house to be auctioned, we noticed that one person (let's call him Ollie) who bid at the first sale was bidding again, but each time dropped out at the last minute.

We smelled a rat (a shill) but didn't say anything. We wanted the fourth house and bid several times, until the price was $650,000. Then, when Ollie bid higher, we objected and said we were going to call the District Attorney's Consumer Fraud Unit and the State Real Estate Department and file a complaint. Ollie immediately disappeared, and we got a great house at a good price.

to get the hang of how they work. You can also get a sense of how auctions work by checking a Web search engine for "real estate auctions."

- Research deposit requirements and financing options before you commit yourself to buying property at an auction.
- Ask for brochures that describe the property, and read all the fine print.
- Check out the house's physical condition before buying. Real estate auction companies must disclose known structural problems and defects of property (excluding foreclosures). (See Chapter 19 for details on state disclosure law and inspections.)
- Be sure you're taking clear title to the property. (See Chapter 18 for details.)
- Don't pay more than 10% above the minimum or "floor price," or 70%–75% of the original asking price.
- Get help researching.
- Decide in advance how much you'll pay, and don't bid a penny more.
- If there is lots of bidding on a particular house, drop out fast—if you get into a bidding war, you'll surely pay too much.

CHAPTER

4

Raising Money for Your Down Payment

Let's start with the basics. Down payments are usually discussed as a percentage of a house's purchase price, not a specific dollar figure. A 20% down payment is 20% of the price you pay for the house, such as $60,000 on a $300,000 house. In addition, lenders often use the real estate industry jargon "loan-to-value ratio" (LTV) in referring to the down payment required. A mortgage with an LTV of 90% requires only 10% down, an LTV of 80% requires 20% down, and so on.

The down payment amount depends on the interplay of many factors, including:

- your savings from all sources
- your monthly income
- the house's purchase price
- the type of mortgage you choose
- your credit history, and
- the size of the mortgage.

SKIP AHEAD

If you're relatively affluent and will put 20% or more down: You can skip most of this chapter, except for "How Much Should Your Down Payment Be?" It discusses the pros and cons of making a big down payment.

Assisted No and Low Down Payment Plans

The Federal Housing Administration, U.S. Department of Veterans Affairs, California Housing Finance Agency, and Cal-Vet program and a few California municipalities offer either no down payment or low down payment mortgage plans. Down payment and eligibility rules for these programs are discussed in Chapter 11, Government-Assisted Loans. Also, ask banks and other private lenders about any low down payment plans available to low- and moderate-income buyers with good credit.

Conventional Lenders' No Down Payment Loans

Some lenders offer loans for up to 100% of the home purchase price to qualified buyers. Usually these loans are split into two, with an 80% first loan and a 20% second loan. These loans usually come at a higher-than-average cost. The lender may charge high interest rates on both loans or more than is normal in points. Many of these loans also contain prepayment penalties.

These loans were very common a few years ago, but are less so now. As values across the state have dropped, lenders have been stuck with foreclosed properties that are worth less than the mortgages against them. Making sure borrowers have sufficient equity—20% or more—ensures the lender will get what's it's owed in a foreclosure.

Five and Ten Percent Down Payment Mortgages

Some lenders offer mortgages to people who put 5% or 10% down, assuming the buyer has enough income to make the monthly payments within the lender's debt-to-income guidelines.

If you're really strapped for cash, ask your lender about low down payment plans such as FannieNeighbors and the Community Home Buyer's Program. Many California lenders offer these Fannie Mae mortgage plans, which feature a 5% down payment (even 1% in some cases) and flexible qualifying guidelines. FannieNeighbors is a revitalization program, available to buyers who purchase a home within designated central cities or eligible census tracts. The Community Home Buyer's Program is available for loans outside of these designated areas. Both programs, however, are limited to home buyers whose income is 100% or less of the area median income.

RESOURCE

For more information, contact Fannie Mae at 800-7FANNIE or check out the website, www.fanniemae.com.

If you take out a very low down payment loan, be ready to pay a slightly higher interest rate and loan fee (points) and show that you have an excellent credit history. In addition, be prepared to purchase private mortgage insurance (PMI), discussed below.

Private Mortgage Insurance

Private mortgage insurance (PMI) policies are designed to reimburse your mortgage lender up to a certain amount if you default on your loan and the foreclosure sale price is less than the amount you owe the lender (the mortgage and the costs of sale).

Today, most California lenders require PMI on loans where the borrower makes a down payment of less than 20%. PMI typically protects lenders for 20%–25% of the purchase price of the house, usually more than enough to make good any loss resulting from foreclosure and resale.

The Cost of PMI

Traditionally, PMI policies cost more the first year (initial policy) and less in subsequent years (renewal policy). Recently, however, many mortgage insurance companies have offered PMI with an even monthly payment plan and with no up-front deposit of the first year's premium. In this case, the buyer pays only the first two months' payments to close escrow. These policies are usually pegged at 0.52% of the loan amount.

> **EXAMPLE:** A buyer of a $400,000 house pays two months' PMI payment at the close of escrow, or $347 (two months out of the annual payment, or 0.52% of $400,000), divided by 12 and multiplied by 2.

TIP

For mortgages on your primary residence taken out between 2007 and 2010, PMI is tax deductible. The deduction starts to fade out when your family income reaches $100,000, disappearing completely beyond $109,000.

Comparing PMI Policies

Some PMI policies are better consumer deals than others. Here's what to look for.

Premium rates. Although you can't choose your own PMI company, you can choose your lender and, if all else is equal, borrow from a lender offering PMI with lower rates.

Impound account. PMI policies also require that you set up an impound account, to pay the lender (or organization that services the loan) the cost of the premium. The lender in turn pays your property taxes and homeowner's insurance. These impound accounts result in your paying for taxes and insurance before you need to, thus losing the interest you'd earn if you kept that money in the bank. Even worse, some lenders require that you pay up to a year's worth of PMI into the impound account when the house purchase closes, thus increasing your up-front costs. And you still pay an amount monthly.

If you're required to set up an impound account, monitor it carefully. In the past, some borrowers have faced significant hassles because the lender forgot to pay the taxes and insurance, with the buyers unfairly receiving a negative credit rating as a result.

How to Drop PMI

Except for some government loans, California law allows you to drop PMI once your loan is no more than 75% of either the original purchase price (so long as its value hasn't dropped) or the current fair market value of the house and you meet the following requirements (Civil Code § 2954.7):

- The house was purchased after January 1, 1991.
- You own and live in a one- to four-unit residential building.
- You pay at least two years of PMI premiums.
- You are up-to-date on mortgage payments.
- You have not been more than 30 days overdue on any mortgage payment during the previous two years.
- You make a written request to the lender based on an appraisal you paid for, by an appraiser chosen by the lender.

If you meet the above conditions and your loan was made after January 1, 1998, the PMI should be automatically canceled—that is, you should not need to take the initiative and request PMI cancellation (Civil Code § 2954.12). There are some exceptions to this law—ask your lender for details.

If your loan is sold to Fannie Mae or Freddie Mac (see Chapter 8), your lender must agree to drop PMI once your equity reaches 20% and you've made timely payments for at least 12 months.

How Much Should Your Down Payment Be?

If you can afford to make a large down payment, should you? Consider the following factors in support of it:

- **The larger your down payment, the lower your monthly payments.** It feels good to have adequate money each month for other expenditures.

- **The larger your down payment, the less it will cost you to borrow.** For example, if you put 20% down on a $300,000 house and borrow $240,000 at 6% for 30 years, you'll pay $278,019 in interest over the life of the loan. If, however, you put 40% down and borrow $180,000 at 5.5%, you'll pay $187,932 in interest.
- **Lenders won't require private mortgage insurance (PMI) if you make a down payment of 20% or more.**
- **It's easier to get a good loan.** With a large down payment, the lender knows you're unlikely to default, and, even if you do, the house can almost surely be resold for enough to cover the mortgage.
- **A large down payment is like forced savings.** Money tied up in a house can't be spent on frivolous things. But it may be available if you need it in an emergency, by refinancing the house or taking a home equity loan.
- **A large down payment and a short-term mortgage mean you are likely to own your house well before you retire** (or even before your kids go off to college). Many people sensibly want to pay off their mortgage before they retire (when their income is likely to decrease) or have to pay college tuition.

But there are also reasons not to make a big down payment, even if you can afford to:

- **By making a smaller down payment, you can buy a more expensive house than if you make a larger down payment.** (This assumes you qualify for the monthly mortgage payments.)
- **You'll have more cash available for closing costs, loan fees, and "new house" expenses like moving and redecorating.**
- **The interest portion of your mortgage is tax deductible.** Unlike other debts, you can deduct the annual interest paid on mortgage loans up to $1 million from your federal and California income tax returns. This figure is for married couples who file a joint income tax return; you can deduct up to $500,000 if you're single. See IRS Publication 936, *Home Mortgage Interest Deduction*, available from the IRS at 800-829-1040 or www.irs.gov.
- **You can invest the money.** Whether you'll earn more doing this than it costs you to borrow the money with a large mortgage depends on your rate of investment return.
- **You have money available for other needs.** If you tie all your money up with a big down payment, you may find yourself having to borrow it back on a home equity loan (usually at a higher interest rate than the first mortgage) if you want to remodel the house, put your kids through college, or whatever else. And interest paid on a home equity loan is only deductible on your federal income tax for loans up to $100,000. If you need to borrow more, there is no deduction.
- **If your house appreciates, you'll receive a higher return on your investment with a lower down payment.** For example, if you put 20% down and took out a loan for the balance at 10% interest,

and the house appreciated 8%, your return on your original investment would be 40%. If you put 10% down, by contrast, your return on that same house would be 80%.

Why Does Everyone Seem to Have an Equity Line of Credit?

Equity lines of credit that are secured by one's home have become very popular of late—and no wonder, as their interest rate is tied to the federal Prime Rate Index, which has reached record lows in the past few years. That makes an equity line one of the cheapest forms of credit available to borrowers, even though many borrowers pay a small margin above the prime rate.

Does that mean you should plan on taking out an equity line? Not necessarily. Most home equity lines of credit are adjustable rate loans. If the federal Prime Rate increases, borrowers can expect their payments to go up in lockstep fashion.

Using Equity in an Existing House as a Down Payment on a New One

Trading up is an integral part of home buying. You buy a starter house, wait for it to appreciate, sell it, and use the profit for the down payment on a nicer house. If the California real estate market is strong in the next decade, it may take two or three sales to get your dream house.

In a rising real estate market, trading up to raise down payment money works better than saving money or making other investments, because it allows you to maximize your investment leverage. For example, if you put $20,000 down on a $200,000 house (borrowing $180,000) and the house jumps to $300,000, you've made $100,000 with a $20,000 investment. By contrast, if you deposited the same $20,000 in an unleveraged investment, such as stock or art, and it goes up the same 50%, you'd end up with $30,000.

Using a Gift to Help With the Down Payment

If you're fortunate enough to receive a gift of part or all of the money you need for a down payment, you're in great shape—your monthly payments will be lower, and the amount of house you can afford will be higher than if you borrow for the down payment. As a practical matter, the gift is probably going to have to come from a close family member—the lender involved in the deal won't trust that recent gifts from distant family members or friends are not secret loans.

Often parents and grandparents will help when it comes to buying a house. Gifts up to $12,000 per year per person (2008 figure—it's indexed to go up with inflation) can be given gift-tax-free. This means, for example, that every year your mother and father can give you and your spouse $48,000 total without having to file a gift tax return.

If a gift will exceed the gift tax exclusion, the gift giver will have to file a gift tax return

Get a Gift Letter

If you're lucky enough to receive gift money well in advance of applying for a loan, and three months of your bank statements reflect this extra money, you're in good shape and don't need to ask what a gift letter is. (The lender views money that has been in your account for three months or more as "seasoned," that is, it's been sitting there long enough to be treated as your own.)

If, on the other hand, a large deposit shows up in your bank account closer to the time you apply for a loan, the lender is going to question where that money came from. The lender may suspect that the money was meant to be a loan—for example, from a sympathetic friend—rather than an outright gift. You'll need to allay the lender's concerns by providing a written document stating that the money was indeed a gift, with no expectation of reimbursement.

A sample gift letter is below. The letter should specify the amount of the gift and the type of property for which it will be used. Most important, the letter should say that the money need not be repaid. In addition, if money has not yet been transferred, be prepared to document that it's available by providing the name of the savings or securities institution where it's kept, the account number, and a signed statement giving the mortgage lender authority to verify the information.

Date ________________

To Whom It May Concern:

I/We ________________________ intend to make a GIFT of ________________ to (recipient(s)) ________________, my/our (relationship) ____________, to be applied toward the purchase of property located at: ________________

________________________________.

There is no repayment expected or implied in this gift, either in the form of cash or by future services, and no lien will be filed by me/us against the property.

The SOURCE of this GIFT is: __________

____

____

Signature of Donor(s)

____

Print or Type Name of Donor(s)

____

Address of Donor(s): Street, City, and State

____

Telephone Number of Donor(s)

ATTACHMENTS:

1. Evidence of Donor(s)' ability to provide funds

2. Evidence of receipt of funds by Borrower

with the IRS—but, thanks to legislation passed in 2001, there's a good chance he or she won't have to pay gift taxes at all, ever. That's because computing the gift tax debt is now put off until the giver's death—at which time the first $1 million of his or her total gifts given will be exempt from tax. The result is that only the wealthiest of people, who give away more than $1 million over their lifetime, will need to give a second thought to gift tax debt.

However, the estate tax is in flux—it's scheduled to be repealed in 2010, but return in 2011, unless Congress votes to extend the repeal. The upshot is that if your benefactor expects to die before 2010 and leave more than $2 million behind, his or her gift to you may help reduce estate taxes—but if not, you needn't mention estate taxes as an incentive to making the gift. For more information, see the Wills & Estate Planning section of Nolo's website at www.nolo.com.

RESOURCE

Giving gifts. For detailed information on estate and gift taxes, see *Plan Your Estate*, by Denis Clifford (Nolo).

Borrowing Down Payment Money From a Relative or Friend

Another way to raise money for a down payment is to borrow it from someone you know.

While it's not as advantageous as a gift (since you'll have to pay it back and it will affect your debt-to-income ratio), it can help if:

- **You're short for the down payment, but have a relatively high monthly income.** If lenders conclude that you have enough income to pay a first mortgage and another loan, they may let you borrow some of the down payment. Most lenders will usually require that at least 5% of the purchase price come from your own funds.
- **The person lending you money for the down payment will accept no, or very low, payments for several years.** If you don't need to make payments, your debt burden won't increase. Understanding this, a relative or friend may forgive payments for a few years. If these loan payments are eliminated or substantially reduced for three to eight years, the house will likely have risen in value; you can then refinance the mortgage and pay off the down payment loan. (We discuss this strategy in Chapter 12, Private Mortgages.)

CAUTION

Before arranging for a loan for the down payment, check with your lender or loan broker. (Loan brokers are discussed in Chapter 13.) There are many ways to structure down payment loans, and you want to be sure that your plan will be approved by the lender. In general, the loan must be at least pegged at "market" interest for a minimum of five years.

Is It a Gift or a Loan? Sometimes It Pays to Be Vague

Some people are tempted to ask for a loan from a friend or relative but tell the lender it's a gift when applying for a mortgage. This scenario may be superficially attractive, but it's technically fraud. While it's unlikely you'd be prosecuted, it's nevertheless a poor idea to obtain a loan under false pretenses.

But, fortunately, you can legally treat money as a gift, as far as a lender is concerned, while reserving the right to repay your benefactor if necessary. For example, if your parents advance you money but worry that circumstances might cause them to need it later, your response might be that you'll do your best to help if they run into problems. As long as there's no written loan agreement and your statement is one of intent (not a promise), the money qualifies as a gift.

Borrowing From Your 401(k) Plan

An excellent source of down payment money is a loan against your 401(k) plan. Check with your employer or the plan administrator to see whether your plan allows for loans. If it does, the maximum loan amount under the law is the lesser of one-half of your vested balance in the plan or $50,000 (unless you have less than $20,000 in the account, in which case you can borrow the amount of your vested balance, but no more than $10,000). Other conditions—including the maximum term, the minimum loan amount, the interest rate, and applicable loan fees—are set by your employer. Any loan must be repaid, with interest, in a "reasonable amount of time," although the Tax Code doesn't define "reasonable."

Be sure to find out what happens if you leave the company before fully repaying a loan from your 401(k) plan. If the loan would become due immediately upon your departure, income tax and penalties may apply to the outstanding balance. But, you may be able to avoid all this hassle by repaying the loan before you leave.

Borrowing against your 401(k) plan has several advantages:

True Story

Juan and Yolanda: Getting Help From Customers of the Family Business

We immigrated to the U.S. from Mexico 15 years ago and started a small landscaping business. Last year, in our mid-30s with two kids, we really wanted to buy our small house. Although we had saved $15,000 for a down payment, we needed another $10,000 to close the deal. With no deep-pocket relatives or friends to call on, we decided to approach our half-dozen best customers to ask if they would be willing to pay in advance for gardening services for the coming year. Most said yes, with the result that we raised the needed money in a few days.

- By borrowing against your own plan, you are receiving the interest payments.
- The loan fees are usually lower than a bank would charge.
- There's less paperwork than is usually required in getting a bank loan.

Are You Having Too Many Tax Dollars Withheld?

Many people have more of their income tax withheld than is necessary. Some enjoy getting the large refund at the end of the tax year, others want the IRS to protect them from their own spending habits. If you're having too much of your income withheld, ask your employer to adjust the amount to a more realistic level (by filling out a new W-4 form). That way you'll be able to use the money now, instead of letting the feds play with it until next April.

Tapping Into Your IRA

You can now withdraw up to $10,000 penalty-free from an individual retirement account (IRA) for a down payment to purchase your first principal residence. (However, you may have to pay income tax on the withdrawal, and you might have less time than you'd like within which to return it to the IRA if you decide not to use it.) This $10,000 is a lifetime limit—and it must be used within 120 days of the date you receive it.

The law defines a first-time homeowner as someone who hasn't owned a house for the past two years. If a couple is buying a home, both must be first-time homeowners. Ask your tax accountant for more information, or contact the IRS at 800-829-1040 or see their website at www.irs.gov.

Sharing Equity

One way to enlist the help of family or friends, or even an investor, is to give up a share of the ownership of your house in exchange for a cash contribution. We discuss this approach in Chapter 3.

Getting a Second Mortgage From the Seller

As you should understand by now, a principal function of a down payment is to bridge the gap between what you can borrow and the purchase price of the house. If a lender will lend $350,000 on a $400,000 house, you can make up the balance with a down payment of $50,000. There are other ways as well. One is to get the seller or a private investor to take a second mortgage for some or all of the $50,000.

EXAMPLE: Ralph wants to buy a house but has saved only $12,000 and has no friends or relatives to borrow from. He has an excellent salary with good prospects of earning more, so he looks for a seller who will accept a second mortgage instead of a cash down payment. Ralph finds Mimi, who is anxious to sell him her $290,000 house.

She still owes $250,000 on her adjustable rate mortgage, which can be assumed by a qualified purchaser.

Mimi offers Ralph a six-year second mortgage at 10% interest to cover the $40,000 difference between her $250,000 loan, which he'll assume, and the sale price. Because making payments on this second mortgage would increase Ralph's debt-to-income ratio to a level most lenders won't approve, Mimi agrees to a flexible payment schedule with no payments for three years and interest only for the three following. At the end of six years, Ralph will owe Mimi the balance in the form of a large balloon payment. If the property has gone up in value, he can refinance the mortgage and pay Mimi her balance.

The lender, who must approve Ralph assuming the mortgage, likes most of the deal. He demands, however, that Ralph put 10% (or $29,000) down; Mimi's second mortgage is reduced to $11,000. To comply, Ralph uses his savings and sells his new car, which fortunately was paid for.

In addition to reducing the down payment, a second mortgage may eliminate the need for PMI, if it keeps the primary mortgage below 80% of the home's value.

You should also consider the down sides of second mortgages:

- **Second mortgage interest rates are often higher than first mortgage interest rates.** That's because the mortgage holder carries greater risk, and if you default, will only get paid after the primary mortgage holder.
- **Most sellers want cash when they sell a house, not a note from the buyer.** Thus, it's not easy to locate a very desirable property that can be financed this way.
- **A short-term second mortgage with low payments may have a lump sum (balloon payment) at the end.** If the house is fairly priced, house prices increase, and interest rates don't go through the roof, you shouldn't have trouble refinancing the first mortgage to pay the balloon payment. But if refinancing proves impossible, you'll need another way to raise the cash (or face foreclosure), unless your second mortgage lets you either gradually increase payments or delay the payment date if you can't refinance when it first comes due.

For more on second mortgages and seller financing, see Chapter 12.

Balloon Payments and Second Mortgages

A balloon payment is the balance owed at the end of a loan term when the loan is not fully paid off. To help buyers qualify for loans, a loan may be amortized (calculated) as though the buyer had 30 years to pay it off when, in fact, the buyer may have a few years—five or seven years is common. The payments are kept artificially low, and, at the end of the five or seven years, the buyer must pay off the balance in a balloon payment.

Secure Your Loan Using Stock as Collateral

Before you decide to cash in all your stocks to make a large down payment, see if it makes better financial sense to keep the stocks—and use them to secure your home loan instead. Here's why: When you sell stocks, you'll have to pay taxes on any appreciation, and you also lose the benefit of what can be an appreciating asset—or the hope that it will someday pull out of its current trough. Ask your lender to review different options—you may be better off keeping your stock and putting 10% down (obtaining an 80/10/10 loan) rather than selling your stock and putting 20% down.

CHAPTER

5

Working With Real Estate Professionals

This chapter focuses on how California home buyers can work with real estate agents and brokers to find a good house. It also discusses the pros and cons of buying a house without professional help. If you do hire a real estate professional, we recommend you take the following steps, in order:

- Complete your Ideal House Profile in Chapter 1.
- Decide how much you can afford to pay after reading Chapter 2.
- Estimate what it will cost to buy the type of house you want in the area you want by checking prices of recently sold comparable houses. The information in Chapter 15 will help you do this.
- Decide what legal relationship you want to establish with a real estate professional, after reading this chapter.
- Find a good real estate professional. We discuss how to do this in "Finding a Good Agent," below.

Advantages and Disadvantages of Working With a Real Estate Professional

Before describing the different ways you can work with a real estate professional, here are some of the pluses and minuses to consider.

Advantages of Working With a Real Estate Professional

Access to the market through the Multiple Listing Service (MLS) and allied computer services. The MLS database lists most homes currently on the market. A real estate agent who participates in this service (as most do) will usually share this information with buyers. The agent can also supply a price list of recently sold homes. Together, these lists provide a good overview of the housing market. While you can find some of the information on your own, a real estate professional will have details that aren't publicly available.

Access to a broker's in-house listings. A salesperson employed by a large or well-connected firm will know about houses listed for sale with that firm before they are widely advertised.

Legwork. An energetic salesperson should do lots of house searching for you. This includes going to open houses held for real estate professionals (and often closed to the public), as well as personally checking out all listed houses that seem to meet your criteria.

Business experience. An outstanding real estate salesperson will have successfully completed many transactions. His or her experience may be valuable in helping your house purchase run smoothly. The salesperson's negotiating skills may also help you get the best price and terms.

Knowledge of related professionals. A good salesperson will be one source of referrals to other important professionals like inspectors, title and escrow companies, and loan brokers.

No cost to the buyer. Under the typical contractual arrangement, the seller pays the commission, and the services of the real estate salesperson are free to the buyer.

Real Estate People Defined

Before getting help from someone in the California real estate business, it helps to know who the players are.

Agent or Salesperson. One of the foot soldiers of the real estate business who shows houses, holds open houses, and does most of the other nitty-gritty tasks involved in selling real estate. An agent or salesperson (the terms are used interchangeably) must have a license from the state and must be supervised by a licensed real estate broker.

Broker. A broker may legally represent either the seller or buyer. While brokers (except buyer's brokers) almost always receive compensation from sellers, they owe the highest legal duty (fiduciary duty) to whomever they have agreed in writing to represent (seller and/or buyer). A fiduciary duty is one of utmost care, integrity, honesty, and loyalty, like that of a doctor to a patient. A broker can legally supervise one or more agents and must have two years of full-time experience as a real estate agent or salesperson, pass a state licensing exam, and (like a salesperson) complete a continuing education requirement every four years.

Buyer's Agent (or Broker). An agent (as described above) chosen by the buyer to help find a house. The agent owes a legal duty of trust to the buyer but is typically paid a commission by the seller.

Dual Agent (or Broker). A dual agent is paid by the seller but, at least in legal theory, represents both buyer and seller. This legal arrangement must be confirmed in writing by the buyer, seller, and agent.

Listing Agent. An agent or broker who simply lists the seller's house for sale and markets it for the seller. Unless the listing agent signs a Dual Agency Agreement, he or she represents only the seller.

Real Estate Professional. A term used to include either a real estate broker or a real estate salesperson or agent.

Realtor®. A real estate broker who belongs to the National Association of Realtors®, a business trade group. (An agent or salesperson may also belong.) There are corresponding state associations (California Association of Realtors®) and local Boards of Realtors®; the latter usually operate Multiple Listing Services (MLSs).

Subagent. Another general term for the broker or salesperson who helps a buyer find a house. Unless all parties agree in writing that the subagent exclusively represents the buyer or is a dual agent, he or she is legally a subagent of the seller's broker (the person the seller retains to list the house) and owes a legal duty of trust to the seller, not the buyer. Put slightly differently, although a subagent may work with the buyer and never even meet the seller, his or her legal duty as the seller's subagent is to the seller, who pays the commission, not to the buyer. This arrangement is uncommon.

Disadvantages of Working With a Real Estate Professional

Most real estate professionals are conscientious and honest, but real estate has its share of people who are incompetent or only care about their own self-interest. Because it's a relatively easy field to enter, minimally trained newcomers can have a huge financial impact, and it makes sense to watch out for the bad apples. These bad apples are often late for meetings, are uninterested in showing you houses, take several days to return your phone calls, and make you wonder why they're in the profession at all.

Even though your salesperson has a legal duty to fairly represent your interests (unless he or she represents the seller exclusively as a "seller's agent"), this agent has a more basic conflict of interest. Unless you've agreed to pay by the hour, the agent won't get paid until you buy a home, and the amount of payment depends on the price of the house you buy.

Here are some ways the agent's self-interest (desire to be paid) can manifest itself to your disadvantage, particularly if your agent is a bit of a bad apple:

- The salesperson may try to convince you that a house is worth more than it really is because:
  - If you bid high, you're more likely to get the house and the salesperson will get the commission with the least amount of legwork.
  - The salesperson's commission is a percentage of the sales price; the more you pay, the higher the commission.
  - If the salesperson owes a legal duty of trust (fiduciary duty) to the seller, he or she is legally obligated to protect the seller's interest by maximizing the price. This is true if the salesperson is legally a seller's agent rather than a buyer's agent or a dual agent.
- The salesperson may downplay the shortcomings of a particular home or neighborhood, be it size, commute time, or quality of local schools, in an effort to get you to say yes and hence earn the salesperson a commission.
- The salesperson may show you a long list of unsuitable houses if he or she doesn't know of any houses that meet your specifications at a price you can afford. Rather than admit it, some (especially inexperienced ones) will drag you over half the county muttering something like, "I know this isn't your cup of tea, but I want you to get a feel for the market." The agent is hoping that if he or she wears you out, you'll eventually purchase one of the houses.
- The agent may lack the experience or ethics to best represent the buyer's interest. In unusual situations, the agent may even try to pressure you into buying by misrepresenting the facts (for example, implying that you need to offer the full asking price because of competition that doesn't exist) or withholding material information (not telling you the roof leaks). Sometimes these tactics are subtle, such as, "This place is such a bargain; I'd buy it myself if I could."

Our recommendation: When you evaluate the suitability of a house, don't rely principally on the advice of a person with a major financial stake in your buying it. Take the responsibility to make your own informed choices; among other things, be knowledgeable about the house-buying process, your ideal affordable house and neighborhood, your financing needs and options, your legal rights and the local zoning laws if you're planning to remodel, and how to evaluate comparable prices.

True Story

Barbara Kate and Ray: Touring with Traci

Tired of paying too much rent for too little space in our San Francisco apartment, we began to ponder buying. When we became more serious, we met with Traci, an agent at a large real estate firm. Traci led us to a plush conference room, then through an elaborate list of considerations designed to elicit a Wish List for Our Ideal Home.

"Naive," proclaimed Traci, scanning our list: two bedrooms, good sunlight, lots of closet space, perhaps a little space for a garden, under a half million dollars. "But I'll see what I can find—in this price range." She added a final admonition: "I only work with people I really, really like."

Apparently, Traci really, really liked us—she phoned at seven the next morning with three houses for us to see that very evening. The space in all three was mostly taken up by the kitchen—the one room we confirmed restaurant-goers hadn't even thought of including on the Wish List. None of them had a second bedroom—our number-one priority.

Two nights later, an excited Traci phoned at 11:50 with an exclusive news flash. A nearby two-bedroom owned by her coworker was going on sale the next day. "I've got the keys. I can tour you through right now, before anyone else sees it. I have already prepared the paperwork. I think we can close on this one," whispered Traci. We declined the offer of the midnight ride; the house was still for sale six months later. A week later, Traci had pegged Barbara Kate as the softer sell and suggested that "just the girls" go look at houses. She tracked Barbara Kate down at home, where she was in bed with pneumonia, unwilling and unable to make any girlish outing. But Traci was undaunted. She phoned back that afternoon with a weather report promising a warming of five degrees and "a blanket for you in the trunk."

Two weeks later Traci called, having found our "dream house": two bedrooms, good sunlight, good neighborhood. She never mentioned it had only one small closet—in the pantry. Outside, post-tour, Traci became adamant. "What can I do to get you to buy that place?" she asked, with a Rumpelstiltskin-like stomp for punctuation.

It was our sixth tour with Traci. It was our last. We're still paying too much rent for too little space. But it beats the alternative.

How Brokers and Agents Are Paid

Real estate agents work on commission and get paid only after your home search is over, the contract negotiated and all its terms fulfilled, the loan funded, and the deed recorded.

Most listing brokers get sellers to pay a commission of 5%–7% of the sales price. "Discount" brokers typically charge 4%. However, an increasing number of clients are successfully arguing for lower commissions, pointing out that buyers are doing much of the house-finding legwork—such as scouting out homes using the Internet and visiting them without the agent.

Because most real estate transactions involve two brokers—the one producing the buyer and the one helping the seller—the commission is divided, usually 50-50 between the two brokerage offices. That's $7,500–$10,500 per office on a $300,000 house. Within each office, the salesperson who handled the transaction gets a share, often 50%. In that case, on a $300,000 sale, the salesperson earns a $3,750–$5,250 commission before expenses, which include wear and tear on a car, gas, phone, and the like. The salesperson must sell a considerable number of houses in a year to make a decent living and is under relentless pressure to "close deals."

Still, great agents go out of their way to make sure you get the house for the best price and terms. They know that if they save you $10,000 on the purchase price, after splitting commissions this way it will only affect the size of their check by a few hundred dollars. Knowing you'll refer others to them, and possibly be a repeat customer, is more important than that little bit of extra cash.

Work With a Real Estate Professional Paid by the Seller

Normally, the seller pays the commission of the real estate salesperson who helps the buyer locate the seller's house. Even though the salesperson you work with is typically paid out of the seller's brokerage commission, that doesn't necessarily mean he or she legally represents the seller. Recognizing potential conflicts, California law requires salespeople who help buyers find houses to alert them in writing that they have three different options:

- **Buyer's agent.** The salesperson you work with legally represents you exclusively.
- **Dual agent.** The salesperson you work with legally represents both you and the seller.
- **Seller's agent.** The salesperson you work with legally represents the seller exclusively.

These three choices are outlined in the "Disclosure Regarding Real Estate Agency

Relationships" form you'll be asked to sign as soon as you start working with an agent. You and the seller will confirm your relationships with your agents in the purchase contract as described in Chapter 16 (Clause 16).

Buyer's Agent (Your Best Choice)

A buyer's agent has "a fiduciary duty of the utmost care, integrity, honesty, and loyalty" to you. Your real estate professional rejects any legal duty of care to the seller (called "subagency" in real estate speak) and represents you exclusively. Can you legally insist on this? Unfortunately, no, not if the seller is paying the commission. You can ask, but the seller and the real estate agent helping you must agree—and they may have already committed to another arrangement. However, if you're separately paying your agent, that agent is yours alone. Also, with a little searching, you can find agents (usually independent ones, not working with a firm) who dedicate their services to acting as buyer's agents and can normally count on being paid a commission by the seller. Also, practically speaking, if you cannot get all concerned to agree to the buyer's agent option, they should, at the very least, agree to the dual agent option. After all, you have considerable clout as the one who proposes to buy the house.

Dual Agent (Your Second-Best Choice)

Here the real estate professional is paid by the seller, but represents both the buyer and seller in a house sale and owes the same legal duty of fair conduct to each. Are you in a good legal situation under dual agency? In theory, yes: A dual agent cannot disclose to the seller (without your written permission) that you are willing to pay more than the offering price; conversely, a dual agent cannot tell you if the seller is willing to accept less than the asking price.

A dual agency situation can arise if you've entered into an agency relationship with a real estate agent and subsequently look at a house listed with that agent's company—even if the listing agent is not your agent and works in a different branch office of the company. Your agent should disclose immediately if a property you're interested in is listed by his or her company. Dual agency should only be entered into under a written agreement signed by both buyer and seller.

It's still better, however, to work with a real estate professional as a buyer's agent than a dual agent (often preferred by large brokerage companies that want to sell houses buyers have listed with them and to do so can't solely represent the buyer), because dual agency can mean divided loyalties.

Seller's Agent (A Poor Choice)

Run, don't walk, from this agency relationship where the seller pays "your" agent's commission, and "your" agent legally represents the seller. This is the way it was in the old days (and still is in most states), and some real estate offices still push it. Why is this such a poor choice? Because "your" real estate agent is legally the subagent of the seller and owes a fiduciary duty of honesty, integrity, and loyalty to the seller, not to you. Specifically, if you make a low offer but the agent knows you will go higher or will pay for repair work, the agent should tell the seller.

The only time you might have to accept the seller's agent option is if you're buying a new home in a development, where all transactions are handled by the developer's sales force directly or by a broker who represents the developer/seller. Chapter 7 discusses using a real estate agent when purchasing a new home.

EXAMPLE: Connie lists her home for sale using Acme Real Estate Associates. Troy, a potential buyer, works with a salesperson from Basic Realty, which represents sellers exclusively. Basic Realty locates Connie's house for Troy. Even though the Basic salesperson has been showing Troy houses for months and has never met Connie, the Basic salesperson is the legal subagent of Connie. This means that while he must act fairly and with good faith toward Troy, he owes the highest duty of trust to Connie. If he knows that Connie needs to sell her house in a hurry and that she'd accept a lower offer than Troy makes, he can't tell Troy this, even though he's been working with Troy for months. Conversely, if he knows Troy will pay more than his first offer, or accept the house "as is" even though it needs $25,000 worth of pest control work, he can, and should, tell Connie.

Hire and Pay a Buyer's Agent

Brokers who market their services directly to buyers are called "buyer's agents" or "exclusive buyer's agents." They owe a fiduciary duty to the buyer, not the seller. They are paid a commission from the buyer, usually a percentage of the purchase price. The buyer's agent agrees to offset his or her fee by the amount the seller offers through the MLS. The arrangement between the buyer and the buyer's agent is often laid out in a written agreement entitled a "Buyer's Listing Agreement" or "Exclusive Authorization to Locate Property (Buyer-Broker Agreement)."

Before California law was changed in the late 1980s to make agency relationships clearer, salespeople who helped buyers find houses were almost always the legal representatives (subagents) of the seller. This led to the types of conflicts of interest discussed above. It also led to some buyers preferring to hire and pay for a buyer's broker. Today, the law has been changed and there is much less reason for a buyer to agree to pay his or her own broker.

One major disadvantage to hiring a buyer's agent is that, in many contracts, the agent gets a commission on any house you purchase during the term of the contract, whether the agent finds it or not. If you consider a buyer's agent, ask that this condition be limited to the area where the buyer's agent specializes—or be eliminated altogether. You'll have an especially strong argument if you plan to look in two different geographical areas—one with the help of a buyer's agent and the other on your own.

Oversight by California Department of Real Estate

Real estate salespeople (agents) and brokers are licensed by the California Department of Real Estate (DRE). Under Business and Professions Code § 10176-7 and DRE regulations, the DRE may suspend or revoke an agent's license for fraudulent or dishonest acts such as:

- making a substantial misrepresentation, such as failing to make a legally required disclosure about a property (see Chapter 19)
- making a false promise that is likely to influence, persuade, or induce
- acting for more than one party to a transaction without the knowledge and consent of all the parties
- commingling money entrusted to the agent with his or her own money
- making a secret profit
- acting fraudulently, negligently, or incompetently
- as a broker, failing to reasonably supervise an agent.

To file a complaint or find out whether action has been taken to restrict, suspend, or revoke a license, contact the nearest DRE office. Unfortunately, the DRE won't mediate complaints or order that money be refunded or unfair contracts be canceled. Also, it won't tell you whether any complaints have been filed against a broker or salesperson, or if disciplinary action is pending. Despite these shortcomings, it still pays to complain to the DRE if you believe you've been treated in an illegal or unethical manner.

You can reach the DRE at 916-227-0864 or visit their website—for example, to access real estate license suspensions and revocations—at www.dre.ca.gov. The DRE's website also includes contact information, updated information on real estate laws and regulations, frequently asked real estate questions, and links to other useful real estate sites.

Hire an Agent by the Hour

A few agents market their services directly to potential buyers at an hourly fee. They commonly charge between $50 and $250 per hour, with a typical house purchaser using between 20 and 50 hours of time.

Most of these arrangements are with licensed real estate brokers, particularly those who operate independently of large brokerage companies. A salesperson (agent) can legally provide advice by the hour, but only with the permission of an employing broker.

Advantages of Hiring an Agent by the Hour

The advantages of hiring an agent by the hour are:

Sample Hourly Fee Agreement

This agreement is made between ________________________________ (Buyer) and ________________________________ (Agent) on (date), concerning the contemplated purchase by Buyer of real property generally described in the Buyer's Ideal House Profile, which is attached. [*You created this Profile in Chapter 1. A copy should be marked Attachment A and stapled to this agreement.*]

1. Buyer agrees to retain Agent as a consultant on an hourly fee basis to assist Buyer in his or her attempt to locate and purchase property described in Buyer's Ideal House Profile. The terms of this agreement shall be as follows:
   A. "Agent" shall mean the licensed real estate broker or agent named above, acting directly as the employing broker of record or through an agent employed under the Broker's license.
   B. Buyer is retaining Agent as an independent contractor and not as an employee.
   C. Agent is a member of a local Multiple Listing Service (MLS); Agent will share with Buyer nonconfidential information from any Multiple Listing Service to which Agent has access as a participating member concerning properties fitting the description in Buyer's Ideal House Profile.
   D. Buyer and Agent agree that Agent shall assist Buyer, to the extent requested by Buyer, in completing offer and counteroffer forms, arranging financing, dealing with escrow procedures, and completing other paperwork pertaining to the real property purchase. This advice shall not include legal or tax advice.
2. Agent shall charge Buyer for consultation services at the rate of $ ________ per hour. Agent's services shall not exceed ________ hours for the contemplated purchase unless the parties mutually agree in writing. Buyer shall pay no commission to Agent; Agent will accept no commission from any Seller from whom Buyer buys.

READ, UNDERSTOOD, AND AGREED TO BY:

Buyer: ________________________________ Date: ____________

Buyer: ________________________________ Date: ____________

Agent: ________________________________ Date: ____________

Supervising Broker: ________________________ Date: ____________

- You get expert help with no built-in conflict of interest, because the agent has no financial stake in whether or not you buy a house.
- You get easy access to market information such as the Multiple Listing Service.

Disadvantages of Hiring an Agent by the Hour

The primary disadvantages of hiring an agent by the hour are:

- You may have trouble locating an outstanding agent by the hour; few experienced agents go this route because more money can be made on commission, and they don't want to take on all potential liability for their involvement with the real estate purchase agreement without proportional compensation.
- You pay for the hours you use, whether or not you buy a house.
- You must do a lot of legwork yourself; it's normally too expensive to pay a person by the hour to look for a house for you.
- An unscrupulous agent may try to "run up the meter" by selling you more time than you need. While this isn't a major concern, it can happen.

Hiring an agent by the hour is cost-effective only if you do most of the grunt work inherent in finding a house, deciding on the offer amount, and negotiating with the seller yourself.

Buy a House Yourself With No Professional Help

Some people enjoy looking for a house alone, feeling that professionals get in the way. If you have the time, you can find and purchase a house without an agent. Be prepared for a lot of details: finding a home that meets your needs and budget, making an offer, negotiating a contract, carrying out inspections and disclosures, and handling the closing.

Routine offer and acceptance forms, along with details on filling them out, are in this book. And there are many useful resources available online to help you buy a house—from checking out comparable sales prices to finding a good inspector. Only in rare situations will serious legal problems develop, and then you'll need a lawyer, not an agent.

Finding a Good Agent

As you read this, a veritable herd of real estate agents are trying to find you—the ready, willing, and able buyer. Almost half a million Californians are licensed real estate salespeople or brokers, and most are under-employed (though the best ones may be quite busy). So the problem isn't finding someone to work with, but finding someone you *want* to work with. The best way to do this is through recommendations from people who've purchased a house in the last few years and whose judgment you trust. (Sellers may give you a good steer, too, but agents who primarily work with sellers have somewhat different skills from those who work with buyers.)

Another possible source for obtaining recommendations is from local title companies. Call two or three title companies to find out who they say the best buyer's agents are.

After collecting the names of several agents, arrange to talk to each before making a decision. While you can always get rid of an agent you don't like, it's better to find someone good in the first place.

RESOURCE

Check out websites of individual real estate agents. More and more real estate agents operate their own websites. These give you a good sense of the real estate agent's listings and the services he or she provides. At the risk of being a bit biased, we suggest you see the website of one of the authors of this book, Ira Serkes. The Serkes Berkeley Real Estate Search Engine at www.berkeleyhomes.com is a good example of a consumer-friendly site with lots of useful information on local listings (often with photographs), and helpful details and maps on individual neighborhoods.

If you can't find the website of a particular agent, check the California Association of Realtors website, www.car.org, which includes a directory of California Realtors. Other websites with directories of real estate agents include Realty Locator, www.realtylocator.com; the National Association of Realtors' site, www.realtor.com; and HomeGain, www.homegain.com.

What to Look for in a Real Estate Agent

The agent or broker you choose should (ideally at least) have the following qualities:

- integrity
- dedication and availability to clients
- good rapport with other agents
- experience in the type of services you need
- knowledge of the area you want to live in, and
- sensitivity to your taste and needs.

True Story

Referrals Mean a Lot

Coauthor Ira Serkes, a Berkeley Realtor whose business is over 50% referral, puts it this way:

"Many real estate agents take a long-term approach. We want our buyers to be satisfied customers, so we try to negotiate the best price possible. If we can save the buyer $5,000 we'll do it, even if that means we earn $150 less in commission. We look upon that $150 as our investment in our future. We know that when clients are happy with our service, they will refer friends, family, and neighbors who want to buy or sell a house. The long-term value of a referral business is much more important than receiving a few hundred dollars more on one sale."

While the first trait, integrity, needs little elaboration, here are a few words about the other characteristics you should look for in a real estate agent.

Dedication and availability to clients. Because it's fairly easy to get a real estate license, many dabble in it for a few months or years, often part time, and become discouraged and move on. You don't want to be the guinea pig on which one of these neophytes practices. On the other hand, some agents so overbook themselves with clients that you won't get the time or attention you deserve. Make sure you select an agent with the skills, knowledge, and time necessary to represent you properly. See "Tough Questions to Ask Real Estate Agents and Brokers," below.

Good rapport with other agents. Although you want an experienced agent, you don't want one who's racked up a history of unpleasant dealings with sellers' agents. Ask other real estate professionals about a particular agent to see what his or her reputation is.

Experience in the type of services you need. If you're a first-time home buyer you'll probably need more patient guidance, especially with financing issues, than will someone who has owned several houses. If you're looking for a new tract house or a condominium (read Chapter 7 carefully), you may need more specialized help.

Knowledge of the area. Be sure the agent is extremely knowledgeable about the city, county, or, better yet, neighborhood you want to live in.

Sensitivity to your tastes and needs. While it's not essential that you and your real estate agent agree on everything (you're not marrying the person, after all), it certainly helps if you and the agent have compatible tastes or the agent is sensitive to yours.

RESOURCE

More information on advanced real estate training. These organizations can provide information on and referrals to different real estate specialists:

- **Certified Residential Specialist.** Call the Council of Residential Specialists at 800-462-8841, or check their website at www.crs.com.
- **Accredited Buyer Representatives.** Call the Real Estate Buyer's Agent Council at 800-648-6224, or check their website at www.rebac.net.

One way to get an idea about how well an agent understands the sort of house you want is to provide the agent with a copy of your Ideal House Profile and then ask him or her to show you a few houses. If what you see looks pretty decent (don't expect miracles on the first day), you're probably on the right track. If the agent immediately and repeatedly shows you houses that you simply wouldn't live in, end the relationship politely but firmly.

How to Help a Real Estate Agent Help You

While you're checking out real estate agents, keep in mind that they'll surely be assessing

Tough Questions to Ask Real Estate Agents and Brokers

Here are some questions to ask when interviewing real estate salespeople:

- How long have you been in real estate? How long in this area?
- Are you a licensed real estate broker or an agent?
- Are you full time? If yes, for how long?
- How many buyers have you personally found houses for in the past year? How does this compare with other real estate salespeople in the area?
- Can you give me the names and phone numbers of satisfied customers, or testimonial letters?
- Have you completed any nationally sponsored advanced real estate training programs offering professional designations, such as Graduate Realtor Institute (GRI); Certified Residential Specialist (CRS); Accredited Buyer Representative (ABR); or Certified Relocation Professional (CRP)? (While advanced training doesn't guarantee that an agent will do a good job, typically people who invest time and money in courses take their profession seriously.)
- What systems do you use to make sure all transaction details are completed in a timely manner? (Ask to see sample transaction logs the agent uses to document communications—phone, mail, fax, email, in-person—with house buyers and sellers. Also, ask to see checklists of house-buying details from financing through closing.)
- Do you have the MLS as well as comparable sales information and contracts online? If yes, how will this help you find the right house for me? Do you use other online services that might help me?
- How will we keep in touch? Will you email me home information and updates, preferably daily? Do you have a voicemail system where I can leave detailed messages?
- Do you keep an up-to-date list of lenders, inspectors, roofers, painters, contractors, and other service providers you have personally used and can recommend?
- Can you provide me with a CMA (comparative market analysis) of my home against nearby homes?

you. The agent will want to know whether you:

- Are highly motivated to buy, or are just a "Looky-Lou" (real estate slang for a person who makes a hobby out of looking at houses and is, essentially, a waste of time).
- Can realistically afford to buy a decent house.
- Are reasonably sensible and considerate. An experienced real estate professional knows how miserable it is to work with people who are demanding and rude. If you come across this way, most will back off.

To alleviate an agent's understandable concerns, and show you're really serious about house hunting, here are some tips for your first meeting:

- Give the agent a copy of your Ideal House Profile. (See Chapter 1.)
- Give the agent an idea of your price range and a copy of your financial statement or, even better, a letter from a lender stating that you are preapproved for a mortgage up to a designated amount. (See Chapter 2.)
- Explain why you want to purchase a house in the near future.
- Treat the agent in a businesslike way. This should allay fears that you're demanding, complaining, or neurotic.

True Story

Amy and Bruce: Other People's Agents

We found our real estate agent, Kate, through the grapevine of friends and coworkers. We were happy with the choice; she was knowledgeable, efficient, and cooperative, never pushy. We felt comfortable knowing she was looking out for our interests.

We came to feel very differently about the seller's agent, Bob. The annoyances were minor at first. He was always late for meetings. The papers he prepared were sloppy and full of mistakes. He didn't tell our agent that another prospective buyer was making a bid the same day we did, then claimed he'd left a phone message. (Kate rechecked her tape; he hadn't.) The last straw was when Bob's failure to relay messages about key points to the sellers nearly made the deal fall through.

By this time, the sellers weren't happy with Bob, either, but they didn't fire him, and we couldn't. Luckily, we could go around him. We went to the broker Bob worked for and told her that from then on, we would either speak to the sellers directly or communicate through her, not Bob. From that point on, we got reliable information—and soon we got the house.

How Not to Find an Agent

Here is some advice on how not to find an agent.

Avoid asking an agent where you live now to make a referral in the new area (unless the agent actually knows an experienced colleague there). An agent who receives a referral from someone else in the business is expected to compensate the referrer with a percentage of his or her commission. Some salespeople are overanxious to make referrals and may steer you to someone they met once at a real estate conference or otherwise know only casually. Other salespeople are required to go through their relocation department and can't recommend the best agent for you.

Don't choose an agent just because they're with a nationally advertised chain. Most offices of a nationally advertised chain are individually owned and operated, and pay a franchise fee to the national organization. While the national organization may establish some operational standards and provide a degree of training and support, a local branch is no better than its particular owner and staff.

Don't pick someone from the yellow pages, the Internet, a newspaper ad, or a direct mail flyer. As in any business, the best salespeople get plenty of word-of-mouth referrals.

Don't seek referrals from the Better Business Bureau or local Board of Realtors. They either won't make a referral or will simply send you to the next name on their list.

Don't work with someone you meet at an open house, unless and until you thoroughly check the person out. Some real estate salespeople offer to keep houses open for other agents precisely because they're short of business and looking for clients. While you may meet a wonderful agent this way, you can usually do better by getting recommendations from people you trust.

Don't work with someone just because he or she is your first contact when you phone or visit a real estate office. Agents take turns handling cold calls and greeting walk-ins; you'll end up with the person "on the floor" when you call or walk through the door. Many real estate offices have "client protection" policies, meaning that you "belong" to the first agent you happened to talk to or who showed you a house. Obviously, the agent is the only person protected by this sort of arrangement, so if you're treated as if you were the property of someone you don't even know, leave.

CAUTION

Check real estate licenses. Make sure your real estate agent's license has not been suspended or revoked. Call the nearest office of the California Department of Real Estate or check the DRE website, www.dre.ca.gov.

Getting Rid of a Broker or Agent You Don't Like

Suppose you realize that your relationship with a real estate professional isn't working. Perhaps the agent repeatedly shows you houses you hate or doesn't show you enough houses. Or maybe you discover that the agent isn't as ethical or careful as you'd like—he or she dismisses your legitimate concerns about the physical condition of the property or pushes you toward a particular lender even though you suspect there are cheaper alternatives. Even if the agent simply doesn't return your phone calls promptly, you may want to work with someone else.

In short, because your home is probably the biggest purchase you'll ever make, you should be very satisfied with your agent. If you're not, don't hesitate to switch. Your agent is a business colleague, not a personal friend. To keep things simple, just make sure you end the relationship before the agent starts negotiating a purchase for you.

Here is how to legally end a relationship with a particular broker or agent:

- If you're working with an agent in a relationship where the seller pays the commission, you need only notify the agent that you no longer want to work together. This is true whether you've signed a Disclosure Regarding Real Estate Agency Relationships form or not. That's it.
- If you've hired an agent by the hour, pay for the services you've used and end the relationship. If you precommitted to a set number of hours and haven't used them, pay only for what you've used. The agent may demand payment for the rest. If so, point out that the agent has a legal duty to try to earn other income in the remaining hours and to subtract that income from what you owe (this is called "mitigating damages"). You may eventually decide to make a small settlement, but don't be in a hurry or pay for time you haven't used.
- If you've hired a buyer's agent to whom you've agreed to pay a commission, there are three ways to end the relationship:
  - If you're unhappy with the agent before you locate a house, simply write a letter terminating the relationship, and don't look at any other houses the agent tries to show you. Even if the contract states that you're bound to work with the agent for a longer period, the letter should legally put you in the clear.
  - If you've found a house you want to buy with the help of the agent, you're legally (and ethically) bound to honor the terms of the contract. In short, pay the agent the commission; he or she has earned it.
  - If you locate a house on your own but it's during the term of the buyer-broker contract that calls for the agent to get a commission on any house you buy, and you haven't written the agent to terminate the contract, you technically owe the agent a fee. Should you grit your teeth and pay it? Consider the fairness of the situation. If the agent did a lot of work for you but didn't happen to locate the house you bought, you owe the money and should pay it if that's what the contract says.

But don't pay a large chunk of money to someone who has done nothing to earn it. If you refuse to pay because you received no services, the agent must sue you to collect. This costs time, money, and good will. Few agents want it known publicly that they sued a buyer because the agent didn't do his or her job. Also, before you're actually sued, you'll probably have a chance to settle the dispute for a smaller amount. If you do, get a release of all claims when you make your payment. (See *101 Law Forms for Personal Use,* by Robin Leonard and Ralph Warner (Nolo), for forms.)

When You're Really Thrilled With Your Agent

Buyers often wonder if it's okay to "do something" for their agents. The best thing to do is refer the agent to your friends, coworkers, and relatives. In addition, consider buying the agent a gift. Some people we know bought their agent the finest bottle of Napa wine they could afford. Another couple we know gave their agent some books on topics of interest to him. Another gave a $500 cash bonus. (The deal was a mess—the agent was a savior.)

Use your imagination.

CHAPTER

6

How to Find a House

In Chapter 1, you did an important part of identifying what you want by creating your Ideal House Profile. Now you need to devise a plan to find a house that matches it as closely as possible. Your first task is to pay close attention to your time and financial constraints. For example, the house search of a well-paid executive with money in the bank, who needs to relocate over the summer so her kids' schooling won't be interrupted, differs tremendously from that of a sporadically employed foreign language translator who likes his apartment but eventually wants to buy a modest place with a small down payment.

The Best Time to Look for Houses

When you look at houses may be out of your control. A major event in your life such as a new job or need to move your children before the start of school means you must find a new house quickly. For those people with the luxury of timing their purchase, however, here are a few hints:

- House prices often jump in the spring, absent some major external factor, such as a recession.
- Historically, mid-November through the end of February is a slow time for the housing market.
- Bad news, such as job layoffs, can temporarily depress a local real estate market. However, house prices often bounce back fast. The big Bay Area earthquake of 1989 is an example; bargains were to be had in some affected areas for a few weeks, but they didn't last long.
- When interest rates are low, there's often more competition for housing.

Where to Look for Houses

There are lots of places you may find your new home. Here are some of the best places to get started.

Check the Classified Ads

All California newspapers publish real estate classifieds, usually on Sundays. Reading them will help you learn the real estate market, and spot new listings and price reductions.

If you see a new listing, especially a For Sale By Owner (FSBO), drive by on Saturday. If you like it, don't be afraid to knock on the door or call to arrange an early showing. It's okay to be a little assertive with FSBOs—after all, the seller is probably at least as anxious to sell as you are to buy.

If the home is listed with a real estate agent, however, and you're already working with an agent, don't disturb the owner or call on signs or ads yourself. Ask your agent to call for you. You may jeopardize your representation by talking directly to the seller's agent or asking him or her to show you the home. The seller's agent may even expect to handle the sale for you or ask for part of your agent's commission.

Organizing Your House Search

Set up a file folder on each house that seems like a prospect. Include a completed House Priorities Worksheet; the information sheet provided at the open house; the Multiple Listing Service information; ads; and your notes. This may seem like overkill, but as the number of houses you look at grows, it will become the best way to keep track of details.

Set up a simple spreadsheet for each house, with columns for the street address and city, price, number of bedrooms and baths, date, comments, or whatever else is important to you. Here's an example:

Address	6938 San Lorenzo	411 Solano Avenue	169 Colusa Avenue
City	Berkeley	Albany	Kensington
Price	$950,000	$750,000	$850,000
Number of bedrooms	3	2	3
Number of bathrooms	1	1	2
Date seen	2/14/09	2/21/09	1/22/09
Comments	Nice home with lots of light	Fixer-upper, but big yard	$14,000 termite report!

You can sort the list by price, date, city, address, or other variable.

House Hunting Tips

Here's advice from seasoned house hunters:

- Measure your largest pieces of furniture and musical instruments, and take these measurements with you.
- Pace yourself; don't try to see more than six to nine houses in a day. Also, try to visit a few in the evening after work.
- Make copies of a local street map or visit www.mapquest.com and plot the open house locations to save driving time.
- Come equipped with your own home hunter's kit: a notebook, pen or pencil, calculator, tape measure, graph paper, your House Priorities Worksheet (Chapter 1), and a digital camera or video recorder. (But ask the agent or house owner for permission before using it.)
- If you're interested in the house, fill out the worksheet carefully. Take notes on the layout, condition of major appliances and fixtures, and problems such as stains on the ceiling or cracks in the basement. Use the tape measure to check that the room's dimensions are the same as on the listing sheet and big enough for your needs.
- Don't let the current decor unduly influence you. Remember, the uglier it is, the more likely you are to buy for a lower price. Think creatively about what can be changed.

How to Translate Ads

Anyone who makes a living in the real estate world learns to translate the exaggerated language of classified ads into down-to-earth English. Because most house purchasers aren't around the business long enough to develop this arcane (and only momentarily useful) skill, here is a humorous glossary of some of the most common real estate business euphemisms.

Convenient to shopping. For a month before Christmas, your front lawn will become a parking lot.

Cozy. Rooms are the size of closets; closets don't exist.

Fixer-upper or handyman special. Nothing that an experienced four-person construction crew couldn't fix in nine months.

Fruit trees. Impossible to say anything better.

Half-bath. A small closet contains a 60-year-old toilet located three inches from a basin half the size of a teacup.

Low-maintenance yard. Half-dead Bermuda grass interspersed by an occasional patch of pastel-colored gravel.

Modern kitchen. The rest of the house looks like the birthplace of Abe Lincoln.

Needs tender loving care. Last owner was a recluse with a dozen incontinent dogs.

Not a drive-by. So ugly you have to be dragged by the ear.

Off the beaten path. A bloodhound couldn't find it.

Priced to sell. No one was interested at a higher price.

Quaint. Need you ask?

Starter house. If your alternative is to live in a city shelter, it will look good; otherwise, keep looking.

Water view. Subject to flooding at high tide.

Visit Sunday Open Houses

To really get the feel of the market, visit some open houses. Don't be terribly selective at first; your goal is to broadly orient yourself as to general market conditions and current price levels, not to buy the first or second house you see.

CAUTION

While you're looking at open houses, real estate agents are looking at you. Agents view open houses as a way to find more clients, not just to sell property. Be prepared for agents to ask your name and phone number so they can contact you later. Just say no, unless you really do like the person and will take the time to check him or her out. While it's possible to connect with a good agent at an open house, there are better ways, discussed in Chapter 5.

TIP

The sellers may also be looking you over. Open houses are an opportunity for you to make a good impression on the seller—which may tip the balance your way in a bidding situation. Not all sellers attend, but they could be there incognito. Dress respectably, and if you're with someone, keep your comments about the house positive. (You can sneer at their choice of linoleum when you're back in your car.) If there are any tenants who will be staying, try to chat them up—tenants have been known to lobby sellers in favor of a particular future landlord.

Gain Access to the Multiple Listing Service

Local Boards of Realtors for most areas of California publish the Multiple Listing Service (MLS), which lists most houses for sale. Listings usually include the price, the address, and a photo of the house; the number and type of rooms; the size of the lot; and other features included, such as the kitchen appliances.

Real estate agents also publish comparable sales data, containing most houses sold through the MLS during the previous three months, arranged by city or neighborhood, each with the original asking price and the selling price.

Until recently, real estate professionals associated with a local Board of Realtors had a monopoly on MLS and comparable sales information. Unless you worked with a salesperson associated with a member broker, you'd have to do without.

The situation has changed dramatically in the past few years, with most MLS information now available online, as described below.

Don't Be a Victim of Illegal Discrimination

Illegal discrimination is the refusal to show property to someone, allow them to make an offer to purchase, or accept an offer from them on the basis of age (except in qualifying for senior citizen housing), ancestry, color, creed, gender, having children, marital status, national origin, physical or mental disability, race, religion, or sexual orientation.

This list is illustrative only. Under California law, any arbitrary or prejudicial action based on a person's personal characteristics such as geographical origin, physical attributes, or personal beliefs could be considered illegal. Thus, if a seller refused to sell to someone with good credit simply because he or she was a member of a particular political party, the seller could be in trouble.

If you believe you've been discriminated against, file a complaint with the California Department of Fair Employment and Housing within 60 days. (Check the Government Pages of your phone book for the nearest office, call 800-233-3212, or check their website at www.dfeh.ca.gov.) You may also want to see a lawyer who handles this type of work.

If you prove the discrimination and the property is still available, you're entitled to buy it for the fair market value and you're eligible to receive substantial damages under California Civil Code § 52. If it's not still for sale, the seller must pay you damages.

Sample MLS Listing

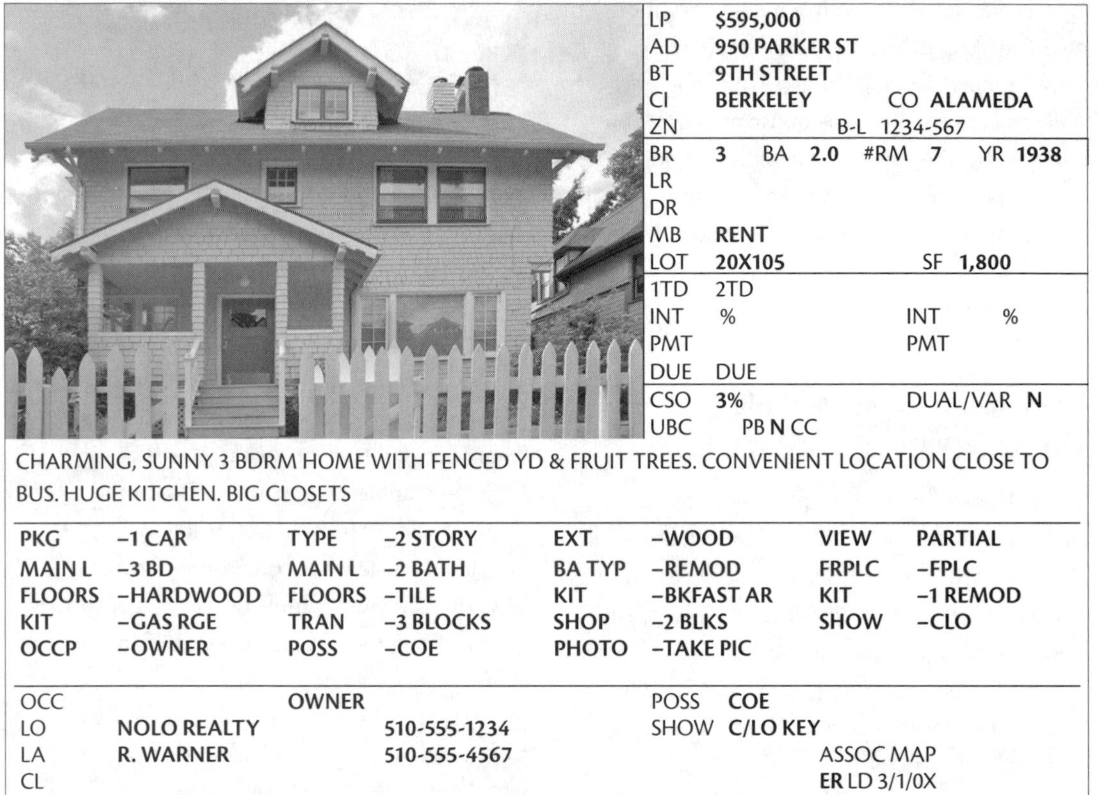

LP	**$595,000**						
AD	**950 PARKER ST**						
BT	**9TH STREET**						
CI	**BERKELEY**			CO	**ALAMEDA**		
ZN	B-L 1234-567						
BR	**3**	BA	**2.0**	#RM	**7**	YR	**1938**
LR							
DR							
MB	**RENT**						
LOT	**20X105**			SF	**1,800**		
1TD	2TD						
INT	%			INT	%		
PMT				PMT			
DUE	DUE						
CSO	**3%**			DUAL/VAR	**N**		
UBC	PB **N** CC						

CHARMING, SUNNY 3 BDRM HOME WITH FENCED YD & FRUIT TREES. CONVENIENT LOCATION CLOSE TO BUS. HUGE KITCHEN. BIG CLOSETS

PKG	**–1 CAR**	TYPE	**–2 STORY**	EXT	**–WOOD**	VIEW	**PARTIAL**
MAIN L	**–3 BD**	MAIN L	**–2 BATH**	BA TYP	**–REMOD**	FRPLC	**–FPLC**
FLOORS	**–HARDWOOD**	FLOORS	**–TILE**	KIT	**–BKFAST AR**	KIT	**–1 REMOD**
KIT	**–GAS RGE**	TRAN	**–3 BLOCKS**	SHOP	**–2 BLKS**	SHOW	**–CLO**
OCCP	**–OWNER**	POSS	**–COE**	PHOTO	**–TAKE PIC**		

OCC		OWNER		POSS **COE**	
LO	**NOLO REALTY**		**510-555-1234**	SHOW **C/LO KEY**	
LA	**R. WARNER**		**510-555-4567**		ASSOC MAP
CL					**ER** LD 3/1/0X

Find Homes on the Internet

Probably the most powerful tool home buyers have for finding prospective homes with minimal work is the Internet. Many sites will display photos or virtual tours, which may be all you need to determine whether the house is worth a visit.

Here are the best sites for house listings on the Internet.

Real estate sections of local newspapers. If you live in a major metropolitan area such as San Francisco or San Diego, online newspaper classifieds are a good bet. On most websites, you can browse all the listings or customize your search by typing in your criteria, such as price range, location, and number of bedrooms and baths. Go to the website of your local paper and see if it has a similar section—most large metropolitan papers do, and even smaller communities may too.

The California Living Network (CLN), at http://ca.realtor.com. The CLN provides real estate listing information from nearly every MLS in California. Sponsored by the California Association of Realtors®, the CLN includes the property address, price, number of bedrooms and baths, a list of basic amenities such as a fireplace or view, and a brief description of the house. Photos are often included. CLN also provides local community and school information and a forum for your real estate questions and answers. The CLN also has a Spanish-language equivalent, at www.sucasa.net, and a Multilingual Directory of Realtors to assist non-English-speaking home buyers.

Coldwell Banker's site, www.californiamoves.com. This site includes all home listings posted on Northern California's MLS, whether or not the seller is represented by Coldwell Banker (they've got reciprocity agreements).

Realtor.com, at www.realtor.com (sponsored by the National Association of Realtors®), and MSN's Real Estate, at http://realestate.msn.com. These national sites provide lists of homes for sale throughout the country, including some areas of California. Most of the listings will probably be found in the CLN, but additional features on these sites, such as handy maps to locate the neighborhood of a specific home and useful links to real estate websites, are nice features.

The National Association of Home Builders' site, www.move.com. This provides a listing of new homes and developments in major metropolitan areas of California.

The Owners' Network at www.owners.com. This is the site to see for homes sold without a broker.

Craigslist.org. This is an excellent source for homes listed by real estate professionals or owners. Listings are broken down by major metropolitan area.

Websites sponsored by local real estate brokers. Don't forget this valuable way to check out homes for sale. Some of the best include detailed photographs and downloadable flyers with extensive information on the property for sale and its surrounding neighborhood. Coauthor Ira Serkes's website, for example, at www.berkeleyhomes.com, offers a direct link to the MLS where you can search for San Francisco or East Bay homes.

Once you identify a house that looks interesting, you can give your real estate agent the MLS number or property address. Your agent can send you any additional information that's available and schedule an appointment for homes you want to see in person. If you're not working with an agent, you can call the listing agent directly (or the owner, if it's FSBO).

Use an Agent With Good Skills

If you work with an agent, find one with good computer skills who will check new listings on the computer several times a day and email you new information as soon as it comes out. Some real estate professionals, such as coauthor Ira Serkes, create customized websites allowing clients to view detailed information on the latest house prospects. To save time sifting though new listings, an agent can create a computer code to correspond to your specific needs (such as price, location, and number of bedrooms) and enter it into the computer. Any new listing that matches the code will be tagged by the computer, providing speedy access to the relevant new listings. (Computer-savvy real estate professionals can link property addresses to digitized maps and then print out a customized tour map for their buyers.) In addition to providing up-to-date sales listings, real estate agents can access a wealth of other data for their clients via their computers:

- the date a particular property was bought and for what price, plus property taxes, legal information, and details on the neighborhood
- comparable sales data in bar chart form, with each property's address, asking price, and final selling price, a format that is much easier to use than pages and pages of printout
- information on properties that never sold and were taken off the market, in which case you might approach the owners with a new offer, and
- loan origination and mortgage rate comparison programs to speed up loan qualification.

Real estate agents don't have a monopoly on these services, however. As discussed throughout this book, many of these online services are available to consumers. However, real estate agents and brokers normally have access to houses before they're opened to the public.

Enlist the Help of Personal Contacts

If you know people who live or work near where you want to buy, ask them to become house scouts. When people plan to move, friends, neighbors, and business associates almost always know about it before a house is put on the market.

Approach your friends and acquaintances in a formal, structured way. You want them to understand that you're seriously requesting their assistance, not just fantasizing about owning a new home. Here is how to do it:

- Prepare a cover letter or email containing a brief—perhaps humorous—description of exactly what you want your scouts to do. Generally, this should encourage your scouts to spread the word about your needs and, of course, to call you immediately if they spot a likely house, especially if they hear about it before it goes on the market. Attach your Ideal House Profile.
- Send your letter and worksheet to friends and fairly close acquaintances. Include local businesspeople with whom you have a friendly relationship. Doctors, lawyers, dentists, and insurance brokers may also be good sources of information. They routinely have advance information about impending moves.
- If your house search turns out to be prolonged, contact your scouts with periodic progress reports and reminders that you need help.

Do Your Own House Scouting

In addition to enlisting the help of friends, you can do much looking on your own.

Sample House Scout Letter

Dear Friends:

We have a problem and need your help!

We've been house hunting for months, but without much luck. We're looking for a 3- or 4-bedroom home in Piedmont or the Montclair district of Oakland. Our lender tells us we can pay up to $1,200,000.

It's important that the house be light and airy, with a private backyard that is (or can be) closed in for our old hound, Faithful Fred. We've attached a sheet listing the most important attributes of our ideal house.

Do you know of anyone thinking of selling? Can you help in one or more of the following ways?

- Keep your eyes open for suitable houses already on the market.
- Look for For Sale By Owner houses that we might otherwise miss. (These don't appear in real estate listings and are often hard to find.)
- Tell your friends, neighbors, and business associates—they'll probably hear about a house from someone moving long before it's listed with a broker.
- Tell doctors, dentists, lawyers, and other service providers, who are often the first to know when people plan to move.

If you hear about or spot a house that seems even remotely likely, give us a call pronto, at 555-4377.

Thanks for your help.

Dennis and Ellen Olson

P.S. As soon as we move in, we plan to throw the best 60s Motown dance party you've ever been to for all our house scouts. And whoever tips us off about the house we buy will be promptly invited to dinner for four at your choice of Chez Panisse in Berkeley or Masa's in San Francisco.

True Story

Paul and Barbara: Our House Scouts Came Through!

After the birth of our second child, we searched for a bigger house in our general area for almost a year, to no avail.

One technique we used was to tell as many people as possible about our search. One day a friend went for her annual teeth cleaning and her dentist mentioned that he was retiring in about six months and moving out of town. Our scout asked if he and his wife planned to sell their home, which they did. She mentioned us to the dentist and then relayed his invitation for us to call and set up an appointment to look at his house. We did, and loved it.

We suggested to the dentist and his wife that if we could agree on the price, we could jointly handle the entire sale without real estate agents. They named a moderately high, but fair, price, and we said yes. It turned out, however, that they had promised to list the house with a real estate broker friend. They wanted to honor that promise, and so they paid her a 3% commission in exchange for helping with the contract, inspections, and closing.

We not only got a great house, we got a great deal. If we hadn't heard about the house and it was put on the market months later, the combination of fast-rising local prices and the need to pay an additional $15,000 in real estate commissions would have increased the price by $50,000 or more, effectively putting it out of our price range.

Canvass Neighborhoods

While it may be a little aggressive for some tastes, we know people who have found houses simply by notifying every owner in the area of their interest in their neighborhood. If you have the time, the best way to do this is to hand carry a flyer door to door and hang signs on notice boards in laundromats and grocery stores.

Another possibility is to mail a friendly letter containing your house specifications to everyone in a particular area after getting the names and addresses from a "reverse directory," available at the public library or at www.reversephonedirectory.com. This type of directory is organized by street address and phone number rather than by last name.

Look for Houses That May Soon Be on the Market

Driving around neighborhoods and looking for run-down houses (peeling paint or weeds in the front yard, no curtains in the window) is one way to find houses that may soon be for sale. For many reasons (foreclosure, ill health, divorce), run-down properties, especially rentals, are often available for purchase, even though they aren't formally listed. If you locate a likely house, ask neighbors if they know whether the house is for sale and the name and phone number of the owner. You can also find the owner's name at the County Assessor's or Recorder's Office, from a local title or escrow company, or using the reverse phone directory described above.

How to Research Property Ownership

Property ownership data collected from tax assessor's records is available from many cities and counties and at most title companies.

The data, often available online, is usually organized by property address, owner's last name, assessor's parcel number, or map corresponding to assessor's parcel number to simplify retrieval.

If you look up properties by address, you'll find the owner's name and where his or her tax bill is sent (probably where he or she lives), the parcel number, and deed of trust recording information. One way to use the information is to pick several streets where you want to live and scan the records for the names of owners who don't live on the premises (out-of-town or out-of-state owners are best). They may be the most motivated to sell, and to sell at a good price. Ask the title company to print the owner's addresses onto 8½" x 11" paper so you can photocopy them directly onto mailing labels.

Advertise for Sellers

Why not let sellers find you by placing a classified ad listing your requirements? Especially if you need help with financing and want the seller to take back a second mortgage, or if you are looking for a house with very particular characteristics (for example, wheelchair accessibility or within one block of public transit), placing your own ad may be an efficient way to narrow down the possibilities.

How to Approach an Owner You Don't Know

The reason you want to know about houses that may soon be for sale is to contact the owner, preview the house, and, if you like it, make an offer before it's listed. This is often easier said than done. Many people, especially those moving because of health, financial, or marital problems, aren't likely to appreciate an aggressive potential buyer.

It's best to approach a potential seller as politely and nonaggressively as possible. If you have a mutual friend (perhaps a house scout), ask that person to introduce you. If this isn't possible, write the owner a friendly note (use a nice card), saying you've heard he or she might be moving and, if so, would he or she be willing to show you the house. Follow up with a phone call a few days later. If you meet with resistance, back off.

If you get to see a house, and you like it, you'll naturally want to know how much the seller wants. It's fine to ask, but don't be pushy. The seller may not have thought about it, and if he or she thinks you're trying to "steal" the home, you'll probably never hear from him or her again. Do mention that if a sale can be conducted without brokers (or with one broker who gets a 2%–3% commission instead of the customary 5%–7%, or who works by the hour), the seller will save a good bit of money.

Enlist More Than One Agent

Another house search strategy is to notify all brokerage companies in your area of your needs, rather than to work with one agent. While not always practical—the best agents will work only exclusively with a buyer in one area—you may want to give it a try. Mail each real estate company your Ideal House Profile. Include a cover letter stating your price range and asking any agent to call you if he or she knows of any property that fits. Emphasize that you don't want to be called about houses that don't closely conform.

Be clear about your existing relationship with real estate salespeople. If you're already working closely with an agent, say so. In this situation, only salespeople who represent sellers will contact you. If you aren't already working closely with a salesperson, all agents knowing of houses that fit your needs may contact you, as they're eligible for a commission if you buy.

Find Foreclosures, Probate Sales, and Lease Option Properties

In Chapter 3, we discuss finding properties subject to foreclosure and probate sale, and houses you may be able to lease option.

Shop via TV

In most urban areas, anyone with a TV can shop for a house via video classified advertising programs. Some programs feature still photographs of the interiors and exteriors of homes. Others are more elaborate video productions that show not only the house, but a bit of the neighborhood as well.

True Story

June and Marty: Persistence Paid Off

Our search started in August; by January we'd seen 100 houses and were too tired to look at any more, even if it meant moving to a motel.

To get a bit of order in our lives, we listed (in alphabetical order by street) *all* the houses we'd seen. We included comments on each house—price, area, amenities—and sent the list to 30 real estate offices in our area, with a cover letter stating what we were looking for. The list let them know what we'd already seen and why each house wasn't suitable. We asked any agent or broker who knew of a house that met our needs to contact us.

Apparently, few agents wanted to work with finicky buyers like us, as only one responded. He told us he knew of three houses that might be suitable. He was right. We made offers on two, and one was accepted. Our experience convinced us that half the battle of finding a good house is to find an agent who really understands the client's needs.

Unfortunately, the huge downside to video real estate shopping is that most programs are only a half-hour or hour, which means they show relatively few houses. Once you eliminate houses in areas and price ranges you aren't interested in, there often isn't much left. Also, because putting a house on TV is costly, the houses shown tend to be high-priced.

Finding a House When You're New to an Area

If you're completely unfamiliar with the area you're moving to, you're at an obvious, and serious, disadvantage—you don't have the basic information normally considered essential to locating a good house, in a congenial location, at a fair price. While a good salesperson can show you the best homes in your price range in different neighborhoods, it will take some time to figure out which communities you'll feel most comfortable in. Getting a real sense of what houses are worth may also be difficult, but a good market analysis can help. Chapter 15 explains how to find the prices of comparable houses.

Some brokers train their agents to be "relocation specialists." While they can't know your personal desires, they have thorough knowledge of schools, community services, and neighborhood features, and if you're clear about what you want, they should be able to answer your questions or send written information such as local maps and home price information.

If you're in a hurry, a sensible alternative to trying to find a house right away is to leave your furniture in storage and rent a furnished place until you have a sense of your new turf. Sure, this means moving twice, but it's better than paying too much for a house in an uncongenial area that you may have difficulty reselling when you want to move, which is likely to be soon.

Talk to friends, coworkers, shopkeepers, homeowners, and anyone else familiar with where you're moving to before settling on a geographic area. If possible, take advantage of the valuable information available from online services. Emphasize the personal by telling them who you are and what you like. You want to know the specific towns and neighborhoods where you'd fit in. In our view, it's more important to live in such an area than in the perfect house.

Online Help With Community and Neighborhood Information

Fortunately, there are many useful websites that will help with your relocation decisions—whether you need to check into home listings, prices, local real estate agents, neighborhoods, schools, or jobs. To check out city, community, and neighborhood information such as schools, housing costs, demographics, crime rates, and jobs visit the California state Web page (www.state.ca.us) and Sperling's Best Places (www.bestplaces.net). (See Appendix A, Welcome to California, and Appendix B, Real Estate Websites, for more resources on specific topics.)

HomeFair, www.homefair.com, has useful calculators to help you decide where to live based on home prices, schools, crime, salaries, transportation, demographics, and community services. Realtor.com, at www.realtor.com, has a useful feature called "Neighborhood Tour" that helps you identify communities that meet your preferences as to house type, size, age, and price range, as well as neighborhood demographics, schools, and crime rates.

Finding a Newly Built House

We discuss new houses in Chapter 7. One point worthy of mention here is that to get a good deal on a new house, you need to understand and follow the market for some time. New housing developments, and new sections of old developments, are continually coming on the market. The best tend to sell quickly; the worst hang on for months. It's extremely difficult to accurately judge the new house market in a weekend, or even a week. The best approach is to follow it for some time, making a careful list of all new projects in the geographical area that interests you.

CHAPTER

7

New Houses, Developments, and Condominiums

If a new house is definitely not for you, skip this chapter. But if you're open to buying a new house, read on for common problems and pitfalls and for suggestions on ways you can save time, aggravation, and money. Also, while much of this chapter focuses on new houses, there's lots of useful advice for people buying a condominium or a property governed by a homeowners' association and CC&Rs.

Pitfalls and Pluses of Buying a New House

Buying a newly built house in California usually means purchasing in a tract development. There are some disadvantages to this, including:

- **Your choice is limited to relatively few models.** Most developers have a few floor plans to choose from, and while you can usually customize features like cabinets or light fixtures, you'll be limited to the available configurations.
- **You may have to deal with a slick sales rep.** Home developers tend to have commissioned sales representatives trained in carefully orchestrated sales techniques designed to make as much money as possible. (We use the terms seller, builder, and developer interchangeably in this chapter to refer to the person, or company representative, who has built the houses and is trying to sell you one.)
- **You'll be lured to the development based on a seemingly impossible low price.** Then you'll be shown model houses which are typically loaded with expensive extras.
- **Many developers make their profit by selling you add-ons and upgrades.** These are commonly overpriced; other developers price their houses high to start with and will resist calling in their workers to install anything extra.
- **You'll get discount financing and extra features only if houses are selling slowly.** But the seller will charge you top dollar, with no extras, if the market is hot.
- **You'll be asked to sign a contract written primarily to benefit the seller.** The contract will typically be handed to you on a take-it-or-leave-it basis, with little opportunity to negotiate over most terms.

New House Contracts: Special Considerations

As we mention in Chapter 16, you can use our contract when buying a new house. But you will want to complete it very carefully, to allow for homeowners' association membership, optional add-ons, and warranties. You may also want to obtain and review copies of documents relating to the construction of the house. Other clauses unique to new houses relate to developer delays, deposits on optional items, and development and improvement plans in undeveloped areas.

- **Once you place your order, you have little control over when your house is delivered.** The exception, of course, is if you buy a model already in inventory.
- **If the house turns out to be a lemon, getting problems fixed is extremely difficult.** Getting your money back is next to impossible.
- **The price is seldom negotiable.** When it comes to price, the sellers usually adopt a "take it or leave it" approach. This doesn't mean you shouldn't attempt negotiation, especially if the home seems overpriced—but your most likely bargain is to get the seller to include additional amenities at the same price.

Does this mean you should forget about buying a new house? No. New houses often have many advantages over comparable older houses, such as:

- **Price.** In areas where land is still relatively affordable, many developments are built on large chunks of land, meaning a low per-house land cost. In addition, because many houses are built at once, building supplies are purchased in bulk, bringing construction costs down. In addition, when new houses don't sell, developers are often under pressure from lenders to raise money quickly, sometimes by slashing prices.
- **Amenities.** Many new house developments include pools, tennis courts, golf courses, and meeting rooms. This is great, as long as any user fees are reasonable. Check to be sure.
- **Less immediate maintenance and fix-up work.** Since everything is new, you should spend less time and money on repairs or improvements, at least in the early years.
- **Lower utility bills.** New homes are usually more energy efficient than older homes, (but, ask the builder to estimate the gas and electric bills).
- **Restrictive rules.** "Covenants, Conditions, and Restrictions" (CC&Rs) regulate many aspects of community life, especially the look of yards, driveways, and exteriors. If you appreciate order, this will be an advantage.

Choose the Developer, Then the House

The most important factor in buying a new house is not what you buy (that is, the particular model), but rather whom you buy from. You want a solid house, delivered on time, from a quality builder who stands behind his or her work.

Usually a few developers build in a particular locale, and their reputations are well known. To check out a particular builder, talk to:

- **Existing owners in the development you're considering (or in a recently completed development by the same builder).** If they like or hate the developer, you probably will, too. The homeowners' associations will be an especially good source of information because they often hear about, and sometimes coordinate, complaints from buyers. Also check out postings on homeowner-run websites such as www.hadd.com (Homeowners Against Deficient Dwellings) and www.hobb.org (Homeowners for Better Building.) And see the consumer satisfaction survey on the website of J.D. Power and Associates, at www.jdpower.com.

- **An experienced contractor.** Have your contractor look at other houses the developer is building. It's hard to tell a lot about how good the construction techniques were on a finished model; it's much easier if someone with experience can get access to a house as it's being built.
- **County planning or building office staff who deal with local developers.** For the best results, ask your questions positively. "Do Brady and Jones finish their projects on time, with few complaints?" will probably be answered candidly, while "Is it true Brady and Jones is a real schlock outfit?" might not be.
- **Real estate agents who've worked in the area for some time.** While agents won't usually deal directly with new house sales, they will likely have handled the resale of other houses built by the same developer and will know developers' reputations.
- **The Contractors State License Board (CSLB) for any complaints filed against the developer.** You can reach the CSLB at 800-321-CSLB, or check their website at www.cslb.ca.gov. The CSLB will tell you only about complaints that have been fully investigated and referred for legal action. Remember, however, that the lack of complaints doesn't necessarily say anything positive about the builder.

True Story

Marcia and Drew: Boy, Were We Naive

We visited a model home; we liked it and the financing the builder offered. We told the salesperson we had some design changes in mind and were assured that the developer was fair and flexible and would work everything out as we went along. We took him at his word and signed on the dotted line. Within a few days, problems began. For one, we wanted to eliminate some completely nonfunctional pillars in the living room. The builder said "no way." We then asked for different bathroom countertops and offered to pay the extra. Again, we got no cooperation and had to hire an outside contractor to remove the countertop and install the one we wanted. Whatever we requested turned out to be either impossible or prohibitively expensive. When we asked to see the original salesperson who had promised us "total cooperation," we learned that he was now working as a scuba diving instructor in Hawaii.

I guess you can say we learned the hard way. Next time, we'll be better prepared.

TIP

Green building is a growing trend. If you're looking for a house that was built without excessive waste, is energy efficient (perhaps even solar powered), and uses less water than the typical home, then look for one built by a green builder. You don't need to take the builder's word for his or her environmental concern—there's a certification process, developed by the Building Industry Institute (BII). For more information on the BII standards, see www.thebii.org. To search for builders who've met these standards, see www.greenbuilder.com.

RESOURCE

Look for new houses online. For details on new home developments throughout California, check out specialized new-home websites such as www.move.com and www.newhomeguide.com. The former website, sponsored by the National Association of Home Builders, allows you to search new houses by city, price range, minimum number of bedrooms and baths and size of the home, move-in date, or other variables such as gated or adult community. You can view floor plans, elevations, color photos, and sometimes virtual tours, and check for details on amenities such as pools or tennis courts. If you want to focus on a particular area, such as San Francisco, you can easily see all new homes available in participating developments. Move.com includes new home developments in the Central Valley, Los Angeles, Riverside, Sacramento, San Diego, San Francisco, and other areas of California.

Of course, don't forget to check other online sources of homes for sale, as discussed in Chapter 6.

Using a Real Estate Agent or Broker

Chapter 5 discusses the legal and practical issues of working with a real estate broker or salesperson. Unfortunately, those rules don't always apply when purchasing a new house:

- Developers don't want to pay a commission to a real estate salesperson, so they hire their own sales staff (who only represent them). Not surprisingly, local real estate people, knowing they won't earn a commission, won't show these houses and may even bad-mouth an entire development in an effort to divert you to houses where commissions are being paid.
- Developers with slow-selling projects may cooperate with local real estate salespeople. This can extend to offering prizes and other come-ons to the salesperson who brings in the most potential buyers. Thus, you may be dragged to completely unsuitable developments for the sole (but unstated) purpose of qualifying the salesperson for a drawing for a trip to Mexico.
- Some developers cooperate with agents under their own (often unusual and not widely published) rules. For example, a developer might not pay a commission if you first visit without your agent, even if your agent is involved in every subsequent step of the purchase; but the developer would pay one if your agent was with you when you first registered. Knowing this, the agent with whom you are working is economically motivated to steer you away from any

such tracts you've visited on your own and toward one with rules that will result in a commission if you buy.

If you want professional help negotiating the purchase of a new house, hire an agent familiar with the local new housing scene for a fee before you sign a contract.

If the developer won't pay the commission, you can get a break in the sales price, or provide upgrades such as higher quality carpet, if he or she doesn't have to pay a real estate agent's commission.

Find Out How Many Houses or Condos Are Owner-Occupied

When you're considering a house in a new development or a condominium, find out early on what percentage of the units are owner-occupied. The higher the percentage, in general, the better maintained is the development or building. Owners have more at stake (resale value of their property) than do renters, who are more transient.

This information may also affect your ability to get a competitive loan from a conventional lender. If you are buying in a new development, lenders often require at least 50% owner occupancy before granting a loan. In a condominium building, many lenders make loans only where two-thirds or more of the owners occupy their units. If you don't qualify for a loan as a result of low owner occupancy in a new development, you may need to arrange financing with a developer, perhaps on less-favorable terms. In a condo, you may still be able to borrow from a conventional lender, but you may have to put down 20%–30%.

Financing a New House

The discussions on how to determine how much house you can afford (Chapter 2) and the various ways to finance your purchase (Chapters 8 through 13) apply to buying new, as well as existing, houses. A few noteworthy differences, however, exist.

Help Arranging a Loan

Often, developers of new housing will help you locate financing by referring you to a local bank or savings and loan that has already appraised the property, or to a loan broker. As discussed in Chapter 13, a lender will check your creditworthiness and appraise the house to see if it's worth what you agree to pay. For new houses, however, a lender often does a blanket appraisal of all development houses and agrees to approve loans for creditworthy borrowers up to a set amount. If you borrow from one of these lenders, no new appraisal will be necessary.

A developer cannot, however, insist that you accept financing through this network. This is important to remember if the developer pressures you to use its lender or offers incentives to accept a loan with a higher-than-normal interest rate or fees. Such practices have been the subject of consumer complaints, including cases in which the developer secretly offset the supposed discount incentives by raising the house's base price. To get the best deal on a loan, be sure to comparison shop.

Government Housing Programs

Some builders may have their developments qualified for special government loan programs such as the California Housing Financing Agency. For more on this, see Chapter 11, Government-Assisted Loans.

Buydowns and Other Direct Financing Subsidies

In slow markets, developers may increase buyer affordability through a "buydown" of the mortgage. Stripped of jargon, this means the developer pays a part of your monthly mortgage for a set period of time. For example, if you find a house with $1,200 in monthly carrying costs, and you have $300 a month of other debts, you'll need a family income of at least $4,550 per month to qualify. If the builder pays $150 a month toward your mortgage for five years, you'll only need a gross income of $4,100 a month to qualify. (This assumes a debt-to-income ratio of 33%. Most lenders want this ratio to be between 28% and 36%.)

More commonly, the builder will buy down your mortgage by subsidizing the interest rate you pay. One way is through the 3/2/1 subsidy, where the developer subsidizes part of your mortgage for three years, decreasing the subsidy each year. The table below shows how a buydown for a $100,000, 30-year loan at a fixed rate of 10% might work.

Why would a developer buy down your mortgage? When sales are slow, unsold inventory accumulates. Developers must continue to pay interest on the money borrowed to finance construction. Selling a house, even if it means helping pay your mortgage to do it, reduces this burden. Sure, it reduces the developer's profit as compared to selling all houses with no subsidy, but when this isn't possible, profits (albeit lower ones) depend on selling homes.

How a Builder Buydown Works

	Your Interest Rate	Your Payment	Mortgage Subsidy From Full 10% Fixed Rate
Year 1	7%	$665.30	24%
Year 2	8%	$733.76	16%
Year 3	9%	$804.62	8%
Years 4–30	10%	$877.57	(none)

If you do not need the lower payment that a buydown would give you, consider bargaining for something else instead, just as you might when buying a new car for cash while dealers are offering low interest rates. For example, you might offer to purchase for a lower price, thereby lowering the down payment, or ask for extra features such as a deck or better-quality light fixtures at no extra cost. In short, the buydown is a tip-off that the market is soft and you have room to bargain for a better deal.

Another reason for substituting a lower price for the buydown is that many buydowns take back many of the benefits they claim to provide—they give you a mortgage that has a higher-than-market interest rate after the buydown period is exhausted.

If you can choose between a buydown of your mortgage and a significantly lower price, a reduced price (resulting in a smaller mortgage) will normally save you more if you plan to own the house for a long time. If you intend to own the house for only a few years, however, a short-term mortgage buydown is probably better, as you'll pay less during this period. (To help with the calculations, use one of the online mortgage calculators listed in Chapter 2.)

Optional Add-Ons and Upgrades

Many developers advertise their houses at comparatively low prices to get you to come out and have a look. The moment you become seriously interested, the price goes up as the developer tries to sell you high-profit extras, such as added features (an extra fireplace, personal spa, or home office), upgrades (replace sliding doors with French doors, or tile countertops with granite), or design changes (greenhouse windows or security and alarm systems).

Buying extras and upgrades may enable you to semi-custom-design your home at a reasonable price. Many buyers appreciate a wide choice of kitchen cabinets, floor coverings, air conditioning systems, windows, skylights, and sprinkler systems. You may even be able to add on a room or two at a reasonable cost. But before you get too carried away, pull out your Ideal House Profile (Chapter 1). What do you really need to add to meet your needs, and how much will it cost? Use this figure to compare one new house to the next.

Be sure you investigate all payment options. Typically, some upgrades must be paid for up front, while others can be added to the price of the house and paid for over time—obviously a much more affordable option if you're on a budget. If you do agree to pay a substantial amount of extra cash, make sure the funds are deposited in an escrow account, to be released when the work is done.

CAUTION

Negotiate refunds on optional items. If you cancel your contract, some builders will not refund the deposits you paid for optional items. If you plan lots of expensive upgrades, try to negotiate the right to a full (or at least partial) refund if the options (for example, a new security system) haven't been bought or installed. Or negotiate the right to keep any optional items that you've paid for and that haven't been permanently installed.

Upgrades can add 5%–20% or more to the cost of a new home. To get the most for your money, follow these steps:

1. **Make sure prices are fair.** Steer clear of developers who deliberately use poor-quality materials in highly visible spots in their models, almost forcing you to upgrade to overpriced substitutes. Always confirm, in writing, what you are getting at what price, and whether the developer will allow you to make

changes on your own and give you an allowance for materials and labor not used (kitchen cabinets, floor coverings). This can commonly be an issue if you don't like the developer's standard kitchen cabinets, floor coverings, or bathroom fixtures, or the optional upgrades the developer offers, and want to separately purchase and install these items yourself.

To double-check the prices of extras, visit consumer-oriented showrooms, do-it-yourself home stores, and home improvement shops. Also check home improvement magazines.

2. **Negotiate the cost of extras.** Don't be shy about negotiating over the price of extras, even if the developer tells you they're etched in marble. In fact, negotiating over extras is often easier than negotiating over the purchase price. Consider asking for one free extra for every two you buy. For example, if you pay top dollar for a stainless steel refrigerator, tile, and kitchen cabinets, ask the developer to install a better stove at no charge. This is particularly reasonable if the developer does not credit you with the cost of an original item (a plastic countertop) when you upgrade. Also, as mentioned in our discussion of price above, don't be afraid to ask for the right to purchase and install extras or upgrades on your own. If you're considering adding an expensive option such as an oak staircase, built-in window seats, or a deck, you may get a better deal from an outside contractor.
3. **Inspect model houses carefully.** Be sure that the linoleum, tile, rugs, and kitchen cabinets are of good quality, and that they're the ones you'll get if you buy a house. Many new house contracts

True Story

Helen: How I Got the Carpet I Wanted

I bought a new house in El Sobrante that came with low-quality carpeting. The developer offered two better grades, but I didn't like either—they were overpriced and still not really top grade. Thus, my offer to purchase was contingent on the developer installing the carpeting of my choice, at no charge. He balked, but I pointed out that he was planning to install carpet anyway, so what was the difference? He finally agreed and also agreed to give me the carpeting that came with the house. (Why I had to bargain for this is a real mystery, as, of course, I'd paid for it.) At any rate, I purchased my own carpet at a local warehouse for $3,800 and had it delivered. The developer installed it. I then sold the original carpet through a classified ad for $1,500. Not only did I save several hundred dollars over the cost of upgrading to the developer's supposedly top-quality carpet, I also got the carpet I wanted.

Clues to Good Construction and Amenities

The more you pay for a house, the more—and better-quality—amenities you should expect. Here are some things to look for.

Air conditioning. If you live in a hot area, be sure the central air conditioning is adequate. In many tracts in the Central Valley, air conditioning units that supposedly meet minimum standards don't do the job.

Building site. Review a copy of the soils and engineering report, which the builder should have available, and the Transfer Disclosure Statement and the Natural Hazard Disclosure Statement. (See Chapter 19.) You are obviously not interested in buying a house that is likely to flood or slide off a hill, or that is built in immediate proximity to an earthquake fault. If you think the report is incorrect—that is, it says the soil is in better condition than it appears—or fear the consequences of earthquake or flood, check U.S. Geological Survey maps for soil stability and earthquake and flood zones. Federal or state agencies should have these and other impartial information.

Carpets and drapes. Look for good quality. Poor-quality carpets and drapes are often an indication that the house itself is poorly built.

Electrical outlets. You'll want at least four outlets per room, with plenty of phone, cable TV, and computer jacks.

Energy efficiency. Insulation is measured by an "R" factor. In cool areas of California, look for a development that exceeds R19. Good insulation now will save you enormous heating bills later. Make sure the air conditioning and heating systems are the most efficient.

Entryways. Are the front and back porches covered? Stepping directly into the rain is a nuisance, but eliminating porches saves developers a few dollars.

Floors. The best, but most expensive, floors are hardwood or ceramic tile. Make sure any plywood floor has two layers.

Foundation. Poured concrete is superior to concrete block.

Inside doors. It's usually worth paying extra for solid core doors if they don't come with the house.

Kitchen cabinets. If you're paying top dollar, you want hardwood cabinets, not plywood. Again, this is a good tip-off as to whether you're dealing with a quality developer.

Soundproofing. Make sure you won't hear neighbors or highway noise. In developments where houses are only a few feet apart, or if you're on a busy street, this is particularly important. If some houses in the development are already occupied, check this out with the occupants.

Yard. An underground watering system is a good sign that the builder is committed to quality. Given a choice, it's more efficient and convenient, and it's often less expensive, to install an underground watering system before the yard is graded. Also, starting a lawn from sod is normally better than starting from seed.

contain a clause saying that the model's features are not necessarily the features you'll receive—you are guaranteed only the functional equivalent of what you see, which will almost always be different and will cost the builder far less. If you suspect this problem, shop elsewhere, or make a list of the precise features you're concerned about (include makes and models) and include it in your contract.

CAUTION

Know what you're buying. Model homes will almost always have the best of everything, including mirrored closet doors designed to make the rooms seem larger. Don't be fooled into expecting that your home will have the same details. If in doubt, get your understanding in writing or included as a contingency in your purchase contract. And be sure to look at an "unfinished" model, to see exactly what you're buying.

4. **Take care of the essentials before negotiating the flashy add-ons.** Investing in essentials (a fenced yard, wiring for high-speed Internet, or extra office space) tends to add more to the resale value of a home than investing in other add-ons (a hot tub, wine cellar, or home theater). Whatever you do, don't buy the builder's model with all the upgrades unless you get it at a huge discount. Recouping the cost of all the extras at resale is likely to be impossible—resale buyers tend to be far less excited than original owners about add-ons.

5. **Get it in writing.** When dealing with a developer's sales representative, get all promises as to what will be done, and when, in writing. If you haven't yet signed the purchase contract, make sure it includes all agreed-upon changes. If the developer's contract allows him or her to install appliances or use materials different from those in the model, establish exactly what you will get and when. If you've already signed the contract, and you later negotiate for changes, write them down in a separate document.

   Developers often resist writing things down, wanting you to rely on oral promises. ("Sure, the deck will be built by March 1.") Oral commitments are notoriously unreliable and, in practice, almost impossible to enforce.

Below is an example of what a supplementary written agreement should cover.

Choosing Your Lot

In some popular new housing developments, you will need to select a lot before your house is built. Sometimes you must choose before any house has been built. This can be tricky, as many builders won't even allow buyers on site for insurance reasons. And even if they will, it can be hard to make an accurate assessment as to what the area will ultimately look like, especially if it's full of earthmovers and construction equipment. Still, if you take your time and really study the developer's maps, paying particular attention to the elevation of various parcels

Sample Supplementary Agreement

February 1, 2009

On January 12, 2009, Alex Stevens, Sales Manager for ABC HomeCrafters, presented me with a contract to purchase the house at 8 Warden Crescent. After a discussion, I agreed to sign this contract with the following conditions:

- ABC HomeCrafters agrees to install a drainage system along the rear property line, according to the specifications set out in Attachment A to this agreement, and a redwood deck with railing behind the kitchen, according to the specifications set out in Attachment B. In exchange, I agree to pay $11,000 above the amount agreed to in the purchase contract dated January 17, 2009. Payment will be made by March 10, 2009.
- Work on the drainage system and deck, plus all landscaping called for in the purchase contract, will be completed on or before November 1, 2009. If any work is not completed by this date, we agree that the money to cover the cost will remain in escrow until the work is completed.

2/1/09 — Date

Patricia Nelson (signature)
Patricia Nelson

2/1/09 — Date

Alex Stevens (signature)
Alex Stevens, for ABC HomeCrafters

and to traffic-flow patterns, you should get a pretty good picture of what a particular house will be like when the development is complete. Here are some things you will want to consider:

- **Privacy.** Study the elevation of the lot. Will passersby on the street, or neighbors, be able to look into your windows? If so, will they be viewing rooms where you want privacy?
- **Driveway.** Will you have a clear view down the street? It's dangerous to pull out into the middle of a blind curve.
- **Noise.** A lot at the end of a cul-de-sac will be quieter than one on a main access road, especially if you're on a hill or a corner. Also look at how close you'll be to the house next door. Many developments jam numerous houses close together.
- **Flooding.** Lots on the tops and sides of hills are usually dry. Lots at the bottom are often more prone to flooding, especially if they're near a stream.
- **Geology.** It is impossible to see below the surface of a lot, and most geologic testing is prohibitively expensive. But in a new development, you can ask to see geologic reports that must be done to obtain building permits.

Getting a good lot at a good price is often a matter of timing. The best locations in each price range usually go first. Most developers offer waiting lists for popular locations where houses are under construction. In deciding whether to take an okay lot in a section now being built or to wait and hope for a better location in the next section, consider the following:

- Salespeople who receive a full commission if you buy now—as opposed to a small cut if you put down a deposit on a house that won't be built for a while—will sometimes overpraise existing lots and emphasize possible difficulties and delays in connection with sections where future building will occur. If, however, you state that you'll buy in the yet-unbuilt area or not at all, these difficulties are likely to quickly evaporate.
- Developers often, but not always, build the more desirable sections of a tract first. This excites buyers' interest and moves in many people quickly, creating a positive atmosphere for later sales.
- In large developments where new sections open periodically, the longer you wait, the more choice you'll have. This strategy may cost you dearly, however, if the development is popular, because the developer may then mark up prices for newly built houses, and the resale price of existing houses will likely also increase.
- Sales in yet-to-be-completed sections of developments often fall through, and good houses may reappear on sales lists, sometimes just before closing. So, if you can commit quickly, you may save time and money by staying in touch with a developer and being ready to move fast when a good deal presents itself.

If you're buying a lot in an undeveloped area, be sure you get the developer's written confirmation of promised improvements, such as sidewalks and parks.

Restrictions on the Use of Your Property: CC&Rs

Many new house developments and community associations such as condominiums include, as part of the deed to the property, a number of restrictions on how the property can be used and the responsibilities of the homeowners. These are called covenants, conditions, and restrictions (CC&Rs). CC&Rs commonly limit the color or colors you can paint your house (often brown or gray), the color of the curtains or blinds visible from the street (usually white), and even the type of front yard landscaping you can do.

Some developments have so many restrictions that it's almost as if your house is part of a common park, over which you have little say. For example, with some CC&Rs, you don't have the right to cut your lawn, plant a tree, or tend flowers; instead, you pay a monthly fee to a gardening company that does the work. Typical CC&Rs in condos have additional restrictions such as limits on the placement of television satellite dishes and the banning of some home-based businesses.

CC&Rs in California may not, however, prohibit owners from keeping at least one pet—unless, however, the homeowners' association's bylaws were adopted before this law took effect in 2001. That leaves plenty of developments that prohibit pets or limit their number and poundage.

Getting relief from overly restrictive CC&Rs after you move in isn't usually easy. You'll likely have to submit an application (with fee) for a variance, get your neighbors' permission, and possibly go through a formal hearing at which you may not succeed. And if you want to make a structural change, such as enlarging a window, building a fence, or adding a room, you'll likely need formal permission from the association in addition to complying with city zoning rules.

Role of Homeowners' Associations

Some CC&Rs—especially with condos—put costly decision-making rights in the hands of a homeowners' association. These associations can assess mandatory fees for common property maintenance, which can get expensive in older housing developments requiring upkeep, or in upscale areas with a pool, golf course, or other recreational facilities. Many associations in housing developments let their boards raise regular assessments up to 20% per year and levy additional special assessments, for a new roof or other capital improvement, with no membership vote. Ask how much these assessments have been raised in recent years.

In some housing developments, homeowners' associations are well run and enhance living conditions. Many residents, especially those who buy in an effort to build equity and move on, appreciate the fact that most associations are very sensitive to making decisions which will enhance the value of the properties.

Unfortunately, however, some associations are poorly run. Often the majority of residents aren't interested in management details, which can mean a small group of activists gains control and imposes restrictive and sometimes expensive rules and policies. These can lead to bitter squabbles, where neighbors fight each other, using the association as their arena, and splinter groups war with boards of directors. A mismanaged or underfinanced association can go bankrupt and lose assets such as cash reserves.

Avoiding Disputes With the Homeowners' Association

Don't discount the possibility that all sorts of problems may happen in a development you buy into. A 2001 study by Sentinel Fair Housing (a nonprofit), for example, found that foreclosure actions by homeowners' associations—the ultimate sign that the relationship between association and homeowner has collapsed—accounted for 17% of all foreclosure actions across five California counties. More telling yet, the amounts being foreclosed over were relatively minor—an average of $2,557, as compared to an average in other foreclosure cases of $190,000. In other words, these weren't cases where the homeowner had failed to pay the mortgage, but more often where they had failed or refused to make assessment payments and in many cases had been punished with additional fines or collection costs. Also realize that many disputes will simmer along without getting to a foreclosure action, and that, in many cases, it's the homeowner who sues the association. In fact, experts estimate that 75% of all California homeowners' associations are embroiled in some sort of legal dispute. To minimize lawsuits, state law requires homeowners' associations and their members to attempt arbitration or mediation when there is a dispute over who should do what according to the CC&Rs. (Civil Code § 1354.)

True Story

Steve and Catherine: Study Your CC&Rs

After burning out looking at overpriced quaint old houses, we decided to check out new ones. We found the ideal house in a beautiful development in Sonoma County. And the price was right, too. "What's wrong?" we asked ourselves.

We didn't have to wait long for the answer. "Here are your CC&Rs," the sales agent said as she handed us a package about an inch thick. Arrgg. No way will I live in a place governed by dozens of rules and a homeowners' association. Case closed.

But wait. Why did we like this house? It was near a school, and our son had about five years to go before he graduated from high school. Then we could move to our dream rural hilltop. In truth, we were very interested in enhancing short-term property values. Suddenly, the CC&Rs looked quite different. By preserving the attractive character of the development, the CC&Rs might be our friend, not our enemy.

So, with some trepidation, we bought. Surprise! Over four years later, we're still happy with how the CC&Rs work. They provide a framework for resolving minor neighbor disputes and have set maintenance standards that keep our community looking spiffy. So far, we've not been set upon by power-hungry CC&R enforcers. And as we hoped, property values are soaring.

Does the Association Have Adequate Reserves?

In condominiums, the money in reserves must cover repairs to all common spaces: roof, garage, and the like. While a $50 or $200 per month homeowner's fee may seem steep when added to your mortgage, insurance, and taxes, you are better off with a fee that's too high, not too low. Low fees often equal inadequate reserves. When something needs repair, and the reserves are too low, the owners must pay. Usually the association authorizes the repair and bills the owners through a special assessment. If your co-owner(s) don't have the money, you may have to pay their share or face a lawsuit or other collection efforts by whoever did the repairs.

How to Check Out a Development or Condo

While development or condo living is not for everyone, many people like the idea that rules govern the conduct of their neighbors and are happy to obey the rules themselves. If you now live in an area where people fix their cars in the driveway until midnight, and the house on one side of you hasn't been painted in 15 years and the one on the other side is bright purple, a little order may be welcome. If so, you'll want to investigate further. Here are some tips:

- Get a copy of the CC&Rs and relevant documents that govern any development or condo you're interested in. Many listing agents selling condos will not give out CC&Rs until you have submitted an offer—with a contingency that the CC&Rs are okay, of course. But CC&Rs are public documents, which you can get by visiting the County Recorder's Office. It is harder to get bylaws and minutes of association meetings before making an offer. But after the offer is accepted, you should firmly ask for them. If anyone hesitates to hand them over, there may be information they don't want you to learn.

- Read the CC&Rs carefully and decide whether the rules are compatible with your lifestyle. If you don't understand something in the CC&Rs, ask for more information and seek legal advice if necessary.
- Knock on a few doors. If you find a friendly neighbor politely ask what he or she likes the most and least about the community. Ask how long he or she has lived there, and whether there have been any arguments between the owners and the association during that time.
- Check the membership fees and assessments and how easy it is for the board to increase these amounts. Review past budgets and the history and amount of fee and assessment increases. Also, find out how much money is in the reserve account. If you know the roof needs to be replaced in one year for $500,000 and the association has only $100,000 in reserve, you could be facing a shocking special assessment soon after you buy. But the association must, by law, disclose to you before you buy whether there are plans for special assessments or whether they are contemplating any legal actions.
- Find out how much parking is available, whether there's an extra charge, and where and how parking spaces are assigned.
- Make sure the association has adequate liability and property insurance. Your mortgage lender or insurance agent may be willing to review the policy for you. But be aware the agent may have a financial interest in saying the insurance is inadequate and trying to sell you additional coverage for your own property or to cover the costs of unforeseen association expenses. Find out whether the development is involved in litigation. If the association is suing the developer, for example, you may have difficulty getting a loan.
- Seek as much information as possible concerning the physical condition of the entire development and the financial position of the homeowners' association, and any pending litigation involving the development or association. State law requires associations and developments to give homeowners access to information about defects, along with a timeline for repairs. (Civil Code §§ 1375, 1375.1.) The law also compels sellers to inform buyers if the association is fighting a builder to make repairs and to provide a list of the association's demands. (Civil Code § 1368.) You should have a good general contractor (or an

accountant, depending on the situation) review all disclosures.

CAUTION

Don't expect your real estate agent to help with homeowner association disclosures. Real estate agents are not legally required to inspect areas off the site or public records regarding title to or use of the property. (*Padgett v. Phariss*, 54 Cal. App. 4th 1270 (1997).) (See Chapter 19 for more details on legally required disclosures.)

- If you ever plan to rent your house or condo, pay close attention to rules affecting tenants and your liability for their actions.
- If parts of the development have been occupied for a while, attend a homeowners' association meeting and talk with the officers. If that's not possible, ask to see the written minutes of recent association meetings and what the key issues are. Either way, you'll get a good sense of how the association works. Some associations enforce every rule with the enthusiasm of a Marine drill sergeant; others are run in a far more relaxed way.

(See Clause 10 of our offer form in Chapter 16, which requires your review and approval of items such as CC&Rs and homeowners' association budgets.)

RESOURCE

CC&Rs and homeowners' associations. Many homeowners' associations belong to organizations that publish a wide variety of useful materials. These include:

- **Executive Council of Home Owners (ECHO),** 1602 The Alameda, Suite 101, San Jose, CA 95126. 408-297-3246. www.echo-ca.org.
- **Community Associations Institute (CAI),** 225 Reinekers Lane, Suite 300, Alexandria, VA 22314. 703-548-8600. www.caionline.org.

CC&Rs and bylaws must conform to the California Corporations Code, §§ 5000 through 10014. You can find the Corporations Code in any law library and in the business or government section of many public libraries. (Also, see "How to Find a California Statute Online" in Appendix B.)

Dealing With Delays

If you agree to buy a house that isn't finished (or even started), you'll be asked to sign a very one-sided contract. You'll be given numerous deadlines (to make deposits, agree to design changes, get loan approval, and more, while the developer will have great leeway—even up to a year from the target date—to deliver the house.

Do what you can to change this. Most important, you want to establish some reasonable date at which you can cancel the contract and get all of your money back if the developer doesn't deliver your house. At some point, you should be entitled to walk away or assign your contract to another buyer. Again, get it in writing.

Developer delays can cause serious problems, especially with your mortgage loan. As discussed in Chapter 13, Obtaining a Mortgage, lenders normally won't lock in (guarantee) a particular interest rate for more than about 30 days, although you can sometimes get an extension if you pay a higher fee up front. Thus, if the closing on your new house is delayed several months at a time when interest rates are rising, you'll end up paying a higher rate and, in volatile economies, may no longer be eligible for the loan. If you have to cancel your contract because interest rates have jumped so much that you can't afford the house, you'll most likely have to forfeit your deposits to the builder. In this situation, try (in writing) to have the deposits returned to you. Or insist that your contract with the developer contain a financial penalty if the house isn't ready in time.

If you're a current homeowner, you also face the problem of selling your existing house so you can move into your new one when it's ready. When you aren't sure exactly when a new house will be ready, your best bet is to sell the old one with a contingency that allows you to either delay the closing on your old house or to continue to live in it (and pay rent) for as long as possible. If you have a choice, it's possibly better to delay the closing, because mortgage interest is deductible but rent is not. Also, you will be paying rent based on the purchaser's monthly carrying costs, which will almost always be higher than yours.

The buyer of your old house will probably want some limitation (say 60, 90, or 120 days) on your right to remain living there. If you must accept this, realize that you may find yourself living in a motel if completion of your new house is seriously delayed.

If you rent, especially if you have a month-to-month tenancy, you're in a better position. When your new house is ready, give your landlord 30 days' written notice of when you plan to move out. Even if you have a lease of a year or more, you're probably in pretty good shape. Although you're liable to pay the rent for the entire lease, your landlord is legally responsible to try to rerent your place and to subtract the new tenant's rent from what you owe. See *California Tenants' Rights,* by Janet Portman and David Brown (Nolo), for steps to take to assure that your landlord rerents a place promptly.

Inspect the House Before Closing

The biggest complaint of people who live in newly built developments involves the developer's failure to do all the things promised in the purchase contract in a timely fashion—such as installing small items like shower heads, cabinet hardware, and closet fixtures; repairing or replacing malfunctioning appliances, heaters, or air conditioners; or completing promised landscaping. Sometimes more serious problems occur, such as shoddy construction or the omission of a room in the plan.

The best way to protect yourself is to include a contingency in your contract allowing you to conduct inspections during specific phases of construction as well as before escrow closes. (See Clause 9 of our offer form in Chapter 16). You can then refuse to close escrow until everything is complete and to your satisfaction. Otherwise, once escrow closes and you take occupancy, the developer pockets the money and has little incentive to finish anything quickly or correctly.

To make sure you're getting the best-quality construction, hire professionals experienced in checking out new homes to inspect the site at key points in the building process, such as during the framing of walls, doors, and floors. While it will cost you extra, hiring professional inspectors is the best way to assure quality construction. *Your New House,* by Alan and Denise Fields (Windsor Peak Press), includes an excellent discussion on scheduling inspections during home construction.

You'll also want to hire a professional home inspector during the entire construction process and definitely before closing.

Most Common New Home Defects

Buying a new home may help you avoid termites, corroded wiring, and other defects that aging homes commonly develop. However, new homes can present their own array of problems—some of them quite serious. In fact, a 2004 *Consumer Reports* article cited estimates that 15% of all new homes are seriously defective. Careless and hurried work, particularly by unskilled laborers, is often the cause. Here are the areas to make particularly sure your inspector checks on:

- **Foundation and drainage.** Some builders skimp on materials, fail to install drains, or don't let the concrete dry enough before continuing with construction. The result can be cracks that allow water into your basement or crawl space. The grading of the surface around your home is also critical to the health of the foundation.
- **Paint.** Some builders save money by thinning the paint or by not applying enough coats. Add to that the streaks and splatters that can result from hurried work, and you've got a potential problem worth examining.
- **Framing.** The bones of a house are its wood framing. The inspector will need to check not only that all the beams and joists are in the right places, but that the initial drying and settling of the wood hasn't caused cracks in the gypsum or plaster drywall or sagging floors.
- **Leakage.** Around the roof and windows, faulty flashing (gutter protection), improper installation, or badly placed shingles can leave cracks for rainwater to enter, causing mold, rot, and insect infestation. Inside the walls, pipes can leak if they're not joined correctly or have been damaged during the completion of construction.

You should also do your own final inspection. Bring a tape measure, note pad, and pencil. Be as methodical as you can—open every cupboard door and window, turn on every faucet, and test every appliance.

Resist promises that if you'll move in now, the developer will fix all problems promptly. ("We'll install the washroom sinks the day they arrive, and start the landscaping as soon as the rainy season ends.") It's amazing how much work can be completed before closing, and how quickly "impossible to get" parts can appear if you refuse to close until everything is done.

But what if you're living in a motel (or will be soon) if you don't move in? If significant and costly work remains, insist that the necessary funds be placed in a trust account after escrow closes. Then ask for a written agreement providing that if the work is performed on time, the money will be released to the developer; but if it isn't, the funds go to you to hire someone else to do the work. If the developer refuses, at the least make a list of what needs to be done, assign a new completion date to each, and have it signed by the developer. (See the sample, below.)

Sample Agreement to Complete Work

Date: December 1, 2009

To: John Addison, Acme Development
From: Abigail Williams
Re: 11 Tulip Drive

On December 17, 2009, escrow is scheduled to close on the house I am planning to buy at 11 Tulip Drive. The price I am paying includes a high-quality sod lawn. In exchange for my promise to go ahead with the closing, Acme Development agrees to complete all yard grading and drainage work, and to install this lawn by March 15, 2010.

I'm sending you two signed copies of this memo. Please sign one on the "Agreed to by" line and return it to me by December 10, 2009.

Sincerely,
Abigail Williams
Abigail Williams

Agreed to by: ____________________________
John Addison, Sales Manager
Acme Development

RESOURCE

New construction defects. *Home and Condo Defects: A Consumer Guide to Faulty Construction*, by Thomas E. Miller and Rachel M. Miller (Seven Locks Press). Also see *Your New House*, by Alan and Denise Fields (Windsor Peak Press).

Guarantees and Warranties

You've probably heard horror stories about new houses that began to disintegrate the day the buyer moved in. This shouldn't be a problem if you buy from a reputable developer. To protect yourself further, ask if the developer provides any guarantees. Even better is a new-house warranty provided by third-party insurers.

Developer guarantees. Most developers give a one-year guarantee on new houses. The better guarantees include all workmanship and materials. In addition, appliances will be new and will come with their own warranties. Get all model and serial numbers and a copy of each appliance warranty.

One problem with developer guarantees is that you have only the developer's promise that a problem will be fixed. If the developer goes out of business, as many do, you're out of luck. Also, most developer guarantees are worded vaguely, guaranteeing "acceptable standards of workmanship and material." This is hard to enforce if a developer doesn't voluntarily stand behind his or her work.

Consumer Action Lines Might Help With Contractor Complaints

If you can't get a developer to make good on a new home guarantee or warranty, take your problem to a consumer action line. Offered by many radio and TV stations and newspapers, the best have volunteers who will look into your problem and, if they're convinced you've got a legitimate beef, will go to bat for you against the developer. If this fails and the problem costs less than $7,500 to correct, consider suing the developer in small claims court. See *Everybody's Guide to Small Claims Court in California*, by Ralph Warner (Nolo).

Insurance company warranties. Some developers purchase new-home warranty policies from independent insurance companies, which are far better than developer guarantees. Typical policies cover workmanship and materials for one year; plumbing; and electrical, heating, and air conditioning systems for two years. Less typically, but worth looking for, are policies that cover major structural defects for ten years. Definitions of defects in material and workmanship, and your rights, are spelled out in much more detail than in developer guarantees. And most third-party policies contain fair dispute resolution procedures if you're dissatisfied with an insurer's response to a claim.

If your developer doesn't—or won't—offer third-party insurance coverage, you can purchase your own house warranty. Be sure you're aware of all restrictions, deductible dollar limits of coverage, and dispute resolution procedures. (See Chapter 19 for more on home warranties.)

CHAPTER

8

Financing Your House: An Overview

SKIP AHEAD

If you've already arranged to finance your house, skip ahead to Chapter 14.

Let's start with the bold truth—arranging to finance a house can be disheartening. To qualify, you must normally come up with a good-sized chunk of cash for the down payment. Then you need to borrow a huge sum of money and make monthly payments for what seems like the rest of your life. And, finally, if you don't want to end up with a lousy deal, you must understand seemingly endless details about the variety of mortgages with different interest rates, up-front costs, and fine print terms.

Chapters 8 through 13 provide the basic information necessary to sensibly finance the purchase of a house. If you carefully read all our material before making important decisions, you'll be equipped to obtain a good mortgage at a competitive price.

How Mortgage Lenders Think

The more money you have for a down payment, the higher your personal income, and the lower your debts, the more mortgage options you'll have and the better deal you're likely to get. You'll be a likely candidate for a favorable mortgage loan if:

- **You make a large down payment.** People rarely default on their loans when they have a large personal stake in the property.
- **You do well financially and have limited long-term debts.** The affluent usually repay their loans, often ahead of time.
- **You have an excellent credit history.** People who have paid their bills on time for many years are likely to continue to do so. The reverse is also true.
- **The property is worth more than the loan amount.** The lender feels secure that if you default, the property can be sold for more than enough to repay the loan. Again, the reverse is also true.

Unfortunately, the less money you have to put down, the lower your income, and the greater your debts, the more likely you are to be stuck accepting a mortgage (if you can get one at all) with some undesirable features, such as a high interest rate, substantial points, private mortgage insurance, or a requirement that you get a coborrower.

Who Lends Mortgage Money?

Many entities, including banks, credit unions, and savings and loans make home loans. Large lenders tend to work statewide, while smaller ones specialize in narrower geographical areas, types of housing, or types of mortgages. Fortunately, because mortgage rates are widely published and available online (see Chapter 13), and many types of loans are standardized no matter who the lender is, comparative shopping is not difficult. Government-guaranteed loans (see Chapter 11) offered by the Federal Housing Administration (FHA) and the U.S. Department of Veterans Affairs (VA) are also options.

As you sift through all the financing details in the next five chapters, remember this important truth: There's no one universally desirable mortgage, only one that will help you buy the house you want with maximum efficiency at a minimum cost.

TIP

Don't overlook private financing. To bypass lender rules and restrictions, many home buyers borrow some or all mortgage money privately, that is, from parents, other relatives, and friends. (Chapter 12 covers private mortgages.)

Standardized Loans: Fannie Mae, Freddie Mac, and the Secondary Mortgage Market

Most financial institutions that lend money (banks, credit unions, savings and loans) don't keep most of the loans they make in their portfolio, but rather sell them to investors on the "secondary mortgage market." Several large institutions, including the Federal National Mortgage Association (FNMA or Fannie Mae) and Federal Home Loan Mortgage Corporation (FHLMC or Freddie Mac), buy a large portion of these mortgages.

But the secondary mortgage market buys only mortgages that conform to their financial qualification standards and rules regarding maximum size loan. (See Chapter 2.) The result is that most lenders follow these rules, and many mortgages are remarkably similar. For example, Fannie Mae and Freddie Mac buy no loans exceeding $625,500 in high-cost areas, and less in lower-cost areas. These limits change annually; to find the current limit where you live, visit www.fanniemae.com or www.freddiemac.com.

CAUTION

Conforming mortgages may look different soon. As of the printing of this book, the federal government had recently taken over the management of Fannie Mae and Freddie Mac. Whether the government will initiate any sweeping changes to Fannie and Freddie-backed mortgages is unclear. If they do, we'll update you at www.nolo.com.

If you need a mortgage larger than the limit where you're buying you probably need what's called a "jumbo" loan, which typically has a slightly higher interest rate than Fannie Mae or Freddie Mac loans. These loans are becoming less common and more difficult to get as government regulation of the mortgage industry increases. If you need a loan for more than the conforming loan limit where you live, you'll almost certainly want to work with a mortgage broker, who can help you figure out the best option.

RESOURCE

Online mortgage resources. For information on Fannie Mae and Freddie Mac loan limits and programs, check their websites at www.fanniemae.com (click on "Homeownership Resources") and www.freddiemac.com (select "Buying and Owning a Home").

Mortgage Types

Mortgages come in many varieties and are covered in the chapters that follow. Here's an overview.

Traditional Mortgages

There are two basic types of mortgages, and many permutations of these types.

Fixed Rate Mortgage. The interest rate and the amount you pay each month remain the same over the entire mortgage term. A number of variations are available, as explained in Chapter 9.

Adjustable Rate Mortgage (ARM). With an ARM, the interest rate is set for a fixed period, but then adjusts. Here are some of the most common types of ARMs:

- The traditional ARM, offered at an initial, "teaser" interest-rate, but with that rate very soon subject to monthly adjustments.
- Hybrid ARMs that start out as a fixed loan for a certain period of time—usually three, five, or seven years—then turn into a traditional ARM.
- ARMs that come with monthly payment options (negative amortization loans). For example, you have a choice each month of making a minimum payment; an interest-only payment; a payment that combines principal and interest; or a larger payment that allows you to pay off your loan in a shorter period of time. (You can switch payment options month to month.)

Creative Financing Techniques

If a traditional mortgage doesn't work for you, or if you need additional financing, there are other flexible strategies that may help you make your purchase. Although many of these strategies were commonly used just a few years ago, they're scarce now, due in part to the large number of borrowers who defaulted on these types of loans. Still, you may be able to find a lender that will agree to one of them.

Second mortgage. This is an additional loan (made by the seller or another lender) traditionally used when the first mortgage loan and down payment amount fall short of the total purchase price. (See Chapter 12.) However, there are a number of other reasons why you might take out a second mortgage. For example, if you are unable to make a down payment of 20% or more, most lenders will require you to pay private mortgage insurance (PMI). To avoid this, you may be able to take out a second mortgage to cover the difference between the amount of money you have for your down payment and the 80% first mortgage.

Another good use of the second mortgage is to reduce your interest rate if you'll need a very large loan. (Lenders tend to charge higher interest rates on the largest loans.) But by combining two smaller loans at lower interest rates, you may be able to get around this problem. Second mortgages are not as common today as they once were. Many secondary lenders worry that the value of the property you buy will drop, and because they're paid after the primary mortgage holder if you default, they won't get paid what they're owed.

Assumable mortgage. Qualified buyers can sometimes take over a seller's loan by assuming the seller's unpaid loan balance at the same terms that the seller had with the bank. Most fixed rate mortgages are not assumable, while some ARMs are. (See Chapters 9 and 10.)

Interest-only loans. Some lenders offer you the option of paying off only the interest you owe each month (without paying off any of the principal) for a certain number of years, usually five or ten. This can help you qualify for a larger mortgage than you might otherwise get, although it has some obvious disadvantages (namely that your underlying debt remains unchanged for years).

Mortgage buydowns. These are traditionally used as part of new house sales. (See Chapter 7.) The developer prepays part of the purchaser's mortgage payment for one or more years to make the purchase more affordable. Recently, some lenders have provided buydowns for fixed rate loans on existing houses.

Comparing Fixed Rate and Adjustable Rate Mortgages

Before shopping for a mortgage, you'll probably want to decide whether a fixed rate or an adjustable rate mortgage (ARM) is a better fit for your financial situation.

With a fixed rate mortgage, your interest rate is fixed for the life of the loan. That means your monthly payment is always the same, which can be good for home buyers who want to minimize their financial risk and are happy with the current interest rate. But the downside is that you're paying a premium for that certainty. Fixed-rate loans usually have higher interest rates than adjustable rate loans. (The higher rate is because lenders build in a cushion against the possibility of interest rates increasing while they're stuck with charging you the same old rate.)

Also, if interest rates drop, you're stuck with your fixed interest rate, while home-buyers with ARMs may actually see their interest rates drop. Of course, refinancing may be an option for you, but every new loan costs money to set up, and those costs may eat into the gains that you acquire with your new, lower-interest mortgage.

With adjustable rate loans, on the other hand, you need to be ready for a less-predictable series of payments. Some ARMs can change as early as the first month after your purchase, immediately increasing the interest rate. Most other ARMs protect you—and the lender—from wild ups and downs in interest rates by including percentage limits on these fluctuations, applied either every six months, yearly, or over the life of the loan. (These limits are somewhat misleadingly called "caps," even though they limit drops in your interest rates as well.) The classic ARM is attractive to people who need the initially low rate to afford a house and are prepared for the possibility of later rises in the interest rates.

Some ARMs let you start slowly, offering a rate that's fixed for the first three, five, or seven years and adjusts after that. These tend to start at lower interest rates than fixed rate mortgages. That makes them particularly attractive to borrowers who expect their personal or financial situation to change before the interest rate changes.

Rough-and-Ready Comparison of a Fixed Rate Mortgage and an Adjustable Rate Mortgage

Assume you're borrowing $250,000 for 30 years. Here's how the initial payments on a 4% adjustable rate mortgage and a 6.5% fixed rate compare:

6.5% Fixed	$ 1,580	
4% ARM	1,194	
	$ 386	difference each month

In this example, the fixed payment is 38% higher than the adjustable to start with. But this advantage won't last long. Assume the ARM is tied to a financial index that has an average interest rate of 4% over the next four years and that the lender collects a margin of 2.5% above this index interest rate. Assume also that the ARM can never increase more than six interest points (a life-of-the-loan cap). (Adjustable rate mortgage margins, indexes, and caps are all discussed in Chapter 10.) By the beginning of the second year, the interest rate on the ARM loan would be 6.5%, the same as the fixed rate.

If the index interest rate rises to the life-of-the-loan cap by the end of the four years (a full six interest points above the initial interest rate), the ARM owner would be paying 10% interest. A comparison would look like this:

6.5% Fixed	$ 1,580
10% ARM	$ 2,194

Nolo's website has calculators to help you choose between a fixed or adjustable loan. See www.nolo.com/calculators.

In California a Mortgage Is Really a Deed of Trust

When you borrow money to buy a home, the lender records a legal instrument at a county office. That instrument is called a deed of trust, not a mortgage. We use the term mortgage in this book, however, because it's the word in common use. Here's the technical difference: A deed of trust gives the trustee (often a title company) the right to sell your property, with no court approval, if you fail to pay the lender on time (default). By contrast, a mortgage normally involves only a borrower and a lender, and often requires more complicated judicial foreclosure proceeding if you default.

Here are common deed terms.

Beneficiary. Your lender is the beneficiary of the deed of trust; if you default and the trustee sells the house, it gets paid from the proceeds.

Promissory note. When you borrow, you sign this note promising to repay the loan over a set time period at certain terms. Normally, the note is secured by a deed of trust, in which you agree that the house itself is collateral (security) for repayment. If the note isn't repaid, the house can be sold and a portion of the proceeds used to pay off.

Trustee. If you default, the trustee's role is to sell the house and a portion of the proceeds used to pay what you still owe the lender.

Trustor. The trustor is the borrower—that's you. As trustor, you legally own the house but sign a deed of trust giving the trustee certain powers if you default on the loan.

Comparison of Adjustable Rate Mortgages, Option ARMs, and Fixed Rate Mortgages			
	Adjustable Rate Mortgages	**Option ARMs**	**Fixed Rate Mortgages**
Advantages	• Initially lower interest rates. • Initially lower monthly payments. • Possibility that interest rates will go down (should interest rates drop). • Possibility that, over the life of the loan, you'll end up paying less interest than if you'd chosen a fixed rate loan. • May be easier to qualify for than a fixed rate loan, or you may qualify to borrow more money. • Comes with a lifetime rate cap (the rate can't exceed a predetermined interest rate). • Possibly assumable by a qualified purchaser when you sell.	• The minimum monthly payment is very low. • Every month, you may choose between three or four payment options. • Flexibility that's great for people who do not have a steady flow of income, such as self-employed persons. • Possibility that, over the life of the loan, you'll end up paying less interest than if you'd chosen a fixed rate loan. • Possibly assumable by a qualified buyer when you sell. • Comes with a lifetime rate cap (the rate can't go up beyond a predetermined interest rate).	• Monthly payments don't change, even if interest rates rise. • You get the peace of mind of knowing exactly how much your total mortgage will cost.

Comparison of Adjustable Rate Mortgages, Option ARMs, and Fixed Rate Mortgages (cont'd)			
	Adjustable Rate Mortgages	**Option ARMs**	**Fixed Rate Mortgages**
Disadvantages	• If interest rates go up, your monthly payments will rise. • If you chose the ARM because your finances are extremely tight, higher monthly payments may force you to sell the house or go into foreclosure.	• If you choose the minimum monthly option, your payments may not cover the actual interest that accrues over the month, in which case you will be increasing the amount you owe. • Your minimum monthly payment will remain the same for 12 months at a time even if interest rates go down. • After the first five years, your loan balance will be reamortized over the remaining 25 years, meaning your payments will be adjusted based on the remaining loan principal. For example, if you deferred any interest, your loan balance will be larger than in the beginning and you'll have only 25 years instead of 30 years to pay it off.	• If interest rates go down, you may end up spending more than you would have over the life of the loan with an ARM (though the possibility of refinancing ameliorates this issue). • You'll be paying a premium on your interest rate to cover the lender's risk that interest rates will rise over the many years of the mortgage.

The Cost of Getting a Loan

Every mortgage comes with several fees. Here are the common ones.

- **General fees.** The lender typically charges loan application fees (around $675–$900) to cover the cost of processing your loan. And, if you make a low down payment, you'll likely be required to purchase private mortgage insurance, and prepay at least a couple of months' worth of premiums.

  The lender will also require that you pay fees to various third parties—including the appraiser who confirms the value of your house, the escrow company that acts as middleperson in the transaction, the title company that figures out whether the seller has the right to sell you the property free and clear, credit reporting companies, and the like.

  These so-called closing costs typically add up to as much as 2%–5% of your purchase price. The fees can be added to your down payment money and paid at closing, or they can be folded into your mortgage. (See Chapter 18 for a full description of closing costs.)

- **Points.** Many lenders also charge a loan fee in the form of "points." Each point is 1% of the loan principal. Points, too, can add up fast—1% of a mere $100,000 is already $1,000. Lenders like to charge points because it's often their main source of profit on your loan, especially if they immediately turn around and resell on the secondary market.

  Not all mortgages come with points. But by choosing to pay a point or more up front, you can usually "buy down" your interest rate, for an overall savings in the long term. For example, you might be offered a 30-year fixed rate loan of $500,000 with two points ($10,000) at 6.625% interest, or the same loan with no points at 7.125%. Let's run some numbers to see when paying points on this loan will start to save you money:

No points loan	7.125%	$3,368.59 monthly payment
Two points loan	6.625%	$3,201.55 monthly payment
Loan comparison		$167.04 monthly difference

  As you can see, the loan at two points allows you to pay $167.04 less every month at mortgage-payment time. To find out how long it will take you to recoup your $10,000 investment, simply divide it by $167.04. You'll see that it will take approximately 60 months (five years) until you've saved enough to equal your investment. After the 60 months, you're looking at pure savings.

  So before comparing points to interest, factor in how long you plan to own your house. The longer you live in your house (or pay on the mortgage), the better off you'll be paying more points up front in return for a lower interest rate.

CAUTION

The APR isn't all it's cracked up to be. You may have heard that the way to compare loans and points between lenders is to look at the Annual Percentage Rate, or APR. Unfortunately, the APR tends to be misleading, because it's oversimplified. The APR is the cost of taking out a loan, expressed as a percentage spread out over the life of the loan. All the costs associated with obtaining the particular loan (lenders fees, credit report, appraisal fee, and so on) are factored in to arrive at the percentage. The oversimplification comes in because the calculation assumes that the loan will not be paid off until the loan term ends, usually 30 years. Most people don't keep their mortgages that long. Also, not all lenders use the same approach when calculating the costs that go into their loans, so it's very hard to arrive at an apples-to-apples comparison.

You can compare various combinations of interest rates and points (assuming all other up-front fees are the same or nominal) on a 30-year fixed rate loan by using the table below to determine at what year the tradeoff between points and interest is about even. The table ("When to Pay Additional Points for a Lower Interest Rate") assumes the current interest rate, including the effect of points, is 8.75%. The results will not be appreciably different as long as interest rates are between 5% and 15%.

RESOURCE

Use an online mortgage calculator such as the ones available on Nolo's website at www.nolo.com/calculators to quickly compare various combinations of interest rates and points.

Refinancing: The Effect on Points and Interest Rates

Whether to opt for a loan with more points and a lower interest rate doesn't only depend on how long you'll own the house, but on how long you'll own the loan. Refinancing to get a better interest rate has the same effect as selling the house and buying another.

If interest rates are fairly high when you look for your initial loan, and you expect them to drop before long, you're a candidate to refinance soon. You'll want to shop for a loan with the fewest points, even if this means paying slightly higher interest.

RESOURCE

For calculators to help make refinancing decisions, see Nolo's website at www.nolo.com/calculators.

Which Mortgage Is Best for You?

With careful thought and planning, you can choose the best mortgage for your own individual needs. For now, try to keep an open mind. As mortgage broker Gwen Hoople advises, "Choose your mortgage only after all loan options available to you have been explained, and you've carefully weighed them against your own financial plans and needs." In the next five chapters, we'll give you lots of facts relevant to efficiently putting every piece in place. First,

When to Pay Additional Points for a Lower Interest Rate

Let's compare a fixed rate, 30-year mortgage at 8.25% interest and 2.5 points with one for the same amount at 8.75% and no points.

Step 1: Calculate the difference between the points on the two loans; here, it comes to 2.5 points (2.5 – 0).

Step 2: Calculate the difference between the interest rates; here, one mortgage charges 8.25% interest and the other 8.75%; the difference is 0.5% or ½%.

Step 3: Use the table to determine the number of years at which both loans are equal. (Look under the 2.5 column until you reach the ½% row. According to the table, if you are paying 2.5 more in points for a ½% lower interest rate, at 7.2 years both loans are about equal.

Conclusion: Using this example, if you plan to have the loan for more than 7.2 years (and not sell or refinance), it makes economic sense to pay the extra points to get the lower interest rate.

Interest Rate Reduction	Additional Points													
	0.25	**0.5**	**0.75**	**1.0**	**1.25**	**1.5**	**1.75**	**2.0**	**2.25**	**2.5**	**2.75**	**3.0**	**3.25**	**3.5**
⅛%	2.3 yrs.	5.3	10.0	23.5	**No matter how long you plan to have the loan, don't pay the extra points.**									
¼%	1.1	2.3	3.7	5.3	7.2	10.0	13.5	21.0						
⅜%	0.7	1.5	2.2	3.1	4.2	5.3	6.5	8.0	9.8	12.0	15.0	21.0		
½%	0.5	1.1	1.6	2.3	2.9	3.6	4.4	5.3	6.2	7.2	8.5	9.8	11.4	13.5
⅝%	0.4	0.8	1.3	1.8	2.3	2.8	3.3	3.9	4.6	5.3	6.0	6.8	7.7	8.7
¾%	0.3	0.7	1.1	1.4	1.8	2.3	2.7	3.2	3.6	4.1	4.7	5.2	5.9	6.5
⅞%	0.3	0.6	0.9	1.2	1.6	1.9	2.3	2.6	3.0	3.4	3.8	4.3	4.7	5.2
1%	0.3	0.5	0.8	1.1	1.3	1.6	2.0	2.3	2.6	2.9	3.3	3.6	4.0	4.4

however, ask yourself the following five questions. The answers will help guide you as you read on.

Tax Deductibility of Points

Points on a mortgage are tax deductible. The IRS allows buyers to deduct points paid for them by the home sellers—in addition to points buyers themselves pay for a mortgage. This IRS ruling is retroactive, starting with homes purchased in 1991.

For more information on the tax deductibility of points, call the IRS at 800-TAX-FORM or check their website at www.irs.gov.

How Much House Can You Afford?

Making the determination as to how much house you can afford is directly related to choosing a mortgage. The more you can easily afford a particular purchase (that is, your debt-to-income ratio is low), the more likely you can qualify for a good mortgage at a competitive interest rate. Chapter 2 gives detailed instructions on determining the maximum amount a lender will let you borrow to purchase a house, based on your income, down payment, and other factors. If you haven't yet done so, read Chapter 2 and complete the calculations.

Is Your Income Likely to Increase Soon?

If your income is modest now but likely to go up soon, you may be able to get a mortgage with smaller initial payments that will increase in the future. This will allow you to buy a more expensive house. One option is an ARM that is fixed for the first three, five, or seven years. This gives you short-term security and usually a lower interest rate, hopefully until your income increases. (You may even be able to get a loan in which you pay only interest during this period—but of course, that means you won't build any equity unless the value of the property goes up.) The downside is that if interest rates go way up later, when the loan becomes adjustable, your monthly payments could go higher than you had foreseen.

How Much Down Payment Can You Make?

The reality is that the less money you put down, the fewer lenders and loans you'll have to choose from, and the higher your mortgage payments will be. Loans with no down payment tend to charge higher interest rates than any other, and are extremely rare in any case. Most lenders will require at least a 3% down payment.

But it's most convenient if you can put down at least 20% of your loan. If not, you'll either have to pay private mortgage insurance (PMI) or take out two mortgages.

How Long Do You Plan to Own Your Home?

The length of time you plan to own your house is very relevant to choosing a mortgage. For example, if you intend to keep your home for five years, why not choose an ARM that is fixed for five years? That will give you a lower interest rate than a 30-year fixed rate loan, but you will still have the security of knowing exactly how much your payments will be for the next five years.

RESOURCE

Choosing a mortgage. *How to Save Thousands of Dollars on Your Home Mortgage,* by Randy Johnson (Wiley). Also see *All About Mortgages: Insider Tips to Finance the Home,* by Julie Garton-Good (Kaplan Publishing), and *106 Mortgage Secrets All Homebuyers Must Learn,* by Gary W. Eldred (Wiley).

If inflation becomes more of a danger, however, interest rates are likely to increase. In this situation, ARM interest rates will surely go higher, perhaps much higher, than those for fixed rate mortgages.

RESOURCE

Several useful websites cover market trends and forecasts on mortgage interest rates. One especially good one is sponsored by HSH Associates at www.hsh.com. Also see www.bankrate.com.

CHAPTER

9

Fixed Rate Mortgages

A generation ago, mortgage rules were simple—interest rates were fixed in advance and repayable in equal monthly installments over a term of 15 to 30 years. The mortgage lender, usually a bank or savings and loan on a downtown corner, required the purchaser to make a down payment of 20% or more and have steady income and a good credit rating. The fixed rate mortgage is the one that most closely resembles this old system.

Today there are many more mortgage options, including relatively new (and more affordable) types of fixed rate mortgages.

Should You Choose a Fixed Rate Mortgage If You Can Afford One?

Many people ask whether they should get a fixed rate mortgage if they can afford one. The answer is a qualified yes; a fixed rate mortgage is the safest bet if you plan to own the house for an extended period. A fixed rate mortgage offers two main advantages:

- The amount you must pay is established in advance and does not increase.
- You may save on interest costs. Even though many Adjustable Rate Mortgages (ARMs) offer a lower initial interest rate, the total interest paid on a fixed rate mortgage may be less than on an ARM if interest rates go up substantially and stay up for an extended period. This is because the interest rate on ARMs increases over a few years' time to a current market rate. If market rates go up, so do the interest rates on ARMs.

Monthly Payments for a $100,000 Fixed Rate Mortgage

This chart shows the variation among monthly payments for a 30-year, $100,000 fixed rate mortgage at different interest rates.

Interest Rate	Monthly Payment
5.0%	$537
5.5%	$568
6.0%	$600
6.5%	$632
7.0%	$665
7.5%	$699
8.0%	$734
8.5%	$769
9.0%	$805
9.5%	$841
10.0%	$878

You may want to forgo a fixed rate mortgage, however, if:

- **You'll be moving to another house or refinancing within three to four years.** If you're not planning on keeping your mortgage for a long time, you can usually find an ARM that will cost less in the short term. For example, if you plan to move within five years, a five-year hybrid ARM will have a low interest rate for five years, then adjust to a higher rate after that. You'll never pay the higher rate, because you'll move before it happens.

- **You believe that interest rates are likely to fall substantially (unlikely in the current market).** In this case, ARM rates will stay close to their initial level, or perhaps even drop. By contrast, if you have a fixed rate mortgage, you'll have to refinance to take advantage of lower rates.

Not All Fixed Rate Mortgages Are the Same: Down Payments, Points, Interest Rates, and Other Variables

Purchasing a good fixed rate mortgage involves comparing several features. In addition to interest rates, you need to consider:

- **Down payment.** In Chapter 4, we discussed the considerations in making a down payment within the generally required range of 5% to 20%. If you can readily put 20% down, doing so is probably advisable because it will eliminate the need to either take out two mortgages or pay private mortgage insurance (PMI). If you can't put 20% down, then do the best you can. (See Chapter 4 for tips on scraping together cash.)
- **Private mortgage insurance.** Buyers are commonly required to purchase private mortgage insurance (PMI) when the lender supplies more than 80% of the financing. PMI protects the lender if you fail to make your mortgage payments. The cost of the insurance gets added to your monthly mortgage payment. We discuss PMI at greater length in Chapter 4.
- **Points and interest rates.** Points are up-front charges made by a lender as a condition of lending money. One point equals 1% of a loan. In Chapter 8, we discuss the relationship of points to interest rates and show you how to determine how many points, if any, you should pay.
- **Prepayment penalties.** If you can avoid it, don't take a loan that has a prepayment penalty—a financial penalty for paying off your mortgage early. At some point you may want to sell your home, refinance, or prepay the mortgage, and a penalty may limit your ability to do so. If you can't avoid a prepayment penalty, at least read the loan papers carefully so that you know the time period during which the lender may charge you a prepayment penalty (many loans penalize you only during the first few years of the loan; three years is the legal maximum for loans of $250,000 or less, under California's Finance Code § 4973), the maximum charge for prepaying your mortgage, and the periods, if any, when prepayment may be made without a penalty.

Mortgages' Lengths and Payment Schedules

Not all mortgages last for 30 years; 15-year terms are also available. (Ten-, 20- and 40-year loans were once available but have now become quite rare.) And some mortgages play with the timing a bit—for example, charging you month by month as if it were a

30-year mortgage, but then, at the end of 15 years, requiring that you pay off the entire remaining loan in a "balloon" payment.

Short-Term Fixed Rate Mortgages Versus Prepaying Your Mortgage

Lenders commonly offer 15-year mortgages at more favorable interest rates than 30-year mortgages. That's because the faster the loan is paid off, the lower their risk of interest rates jumping (and eating up their profits) or buyers defaulting.

Even if the interest rate is low and you'll save money in the long run, the relatively large monthly payments of a shorter term mortgage will decrease your ability to take out other loans (for home improvements, a new car, and the like) or make other investments. You'll also be committed to high monthly payments, which may take quite a bite out of your income.

However, you will save significant interest over the long term. For example, with a $100,000 fixed rate loan at 6%, you'd have a higher monthly payment but pay nearly $64,000 less in interest with a 15-year mortgage. And that doesn't even account for the lower interest rate you're likely to pay.

But you can achieve the same savings and benefits by voluntarily paying more principal each month on a longer-term loan. The advantage of prepaying a long-term mortgage is its flexibility—you don't legally obligate yourself to the higher payment, so you can change your mind and pay less if need be.

Even prepaying a small amount per month makes a large difference in your total payments. For example, by paying an extra $50 per month on a 30-year, 8% fixed rate $100,000 mortgage, you'd repay the loan in 24 (not 30) years and save nearly $40,000 in interest. If you don't want to pay a little extra each month, consider making a yearly lump sum payment—perhaps when you receive your tax refund.

The Graduated Equity Mortgage (GEM)

The Graduated Equity Mortgage (GEM) is fairly rare these days. The loan is paid off sooner than the normal term by gradually increasing monthly payments according to a preset formula, such as 5% per year for five years, at which point the payments stabilize.

GEMs obligate you to make higher payments than you would otherwise have to make, but also substantially cut interest costs.

CAUTION

If you plan to prepay a mortgage, remember this rule: No matter how much extra you pay in one month, you still must make at least the regular payment the next month.

RESOURCE

How to calculate savings from prepaying your mortgage. *The Banker's Secret* is easy-to-use software that quickly calculates how much money and how many years you cut off a

mortgage by prepaying. A book is available with the same title. You can also use one of the financial calculators found on Nolo's website at www.nolo.com/calculators.

Weekly and Biweekly Mortgages

Some lenders offer fixed rate mortgages (and ARMs) that require weekly or biweekly (rather than monthly) payments. Others require an extra payment or two during each year. With these plans, you pay less interest over the life of the loan because the loan term is shortened and the lender gets the money sooner.

With biweekly mortgages, you make the equivalent of 13, not 12, monthly mortgage payments per year. On a 30-year, $100,000 fixed rate loan at 8%, your monthly payments are $734 and the total cost of the mortgage is $264,240. With a biweekly mortgage, you would pay $367 every two weeks and pay off your mortgage in a little less than 23 years at a cost of $217,998, saving over $46,000 in interest.

All this sounds good until you realize that most lenders charge an extra fee to handle this type of mortgage, which often cancels out any savings. (There are exceptions, though.) It's better to stick with a monthly payment plan, prepaying principal whenever you can.

Short-Term Fixed Rate Mortgages With Balloon Payments

Most people get a new mortgage within five to seven years because they either move or refinance. Recognizing this, lenders have begun to offer shorter-term mortgages. One of these is a five- or seven-year fixed rate mortgage with payments figured (amortized) as if the mortgage would last 30 years.

The five-year mortgage is sometimes called a 5/25 and the seven-year version a 7/23, with the first number referring to the original "known" interest rate period and the second number referring to the remainder of the 30-year term. At the end of the five- or seven-year period, you must pay off or refinance the remaining balance.

> **EXAMPLE:** Gina and Tony get a $400,000 5/25 fixed rate mortgage at 5%, with payments amortized over 30 years. Their monthly payments are $2,147 for 60 months. At the end of 60 months, they will still owe their lender $367,315, which they must pay off or refinance.

The advantage of choosing this type of mortgage over a conventional 30-year fixed rate mortgage is a significantly lower interest rate. Because the lender is tying up money for only a fraction of the 30-year period, interest rates may be as much as a half a point less. But you are taking a risk to get the lower interest rate. If interest rates are high when the balloon payment comes due, you will have to refinance at a higher rate or pay off a huge lump sum.

Most fixed rate mortgages with a balloon payment have a reset feature or a "conditional refi" (refinancing) with a 5% cap for the remainder of the term, which limits your risk. Check with the lender, and read disclosure material carefully, to understand how this feature works. Also, ask your lender about hybrid mortgages that don't have the balloon feature but convert to an ARM after a period. See Chapter 10 for a discussion of hybrid adjustable rate mortgages.

Most Fixed Rate Loans Aren't Assumable

Fixed rate loans in California (except government-guaranteed loans) are generally not assumable by a buyer. If you get a fixed rate loan and later sell your house, you must either pay it off and have the buyer take out a new loan or get the lender's permission for the buyer to assume yours. The latter rarely occurs, for obvious reasons: The buyer won't want the loan if it's above the current market rate, and the lender won't allow it to be assumed if it's below.

Two-Step Mortgages

A two-step mortgage has two fixed periods and one rate increase between them. Two-step mortgages are very similar to 5/25 or 7/23 mortgages but start at a slightly higher interest rate. After the original five- or seven-year period is up, there is a one-time adjustment based on an index like the National Mortgage Contract Rate, plus a margin (such as 2.25%). Then the two-step mortgage's interest rate remains stable for the 23- or 25-year balance, unless you move or refinance sooner. The advantage of a two-step over the reset 5/25 and 7/23 mortgages is that you are assured of a fully 30-year loan with no balloon payment.

Buydown Mortgages—The Seller Subsidizes Your Payments

A buydown mortgage (sometimes called a compressed buydown) usually works like this: The lender or seller subsidizes the mortgage for the first years of the loan by prepaying part of the mortgage interest. You can also arrange a buydown mortgage by paying more in initial points. Buydowns are most common when a new-house developer wants to move new houses that are selling slowly. (See Chapter 7.) Or, lenders sometimes offer a slightly lower initial interest rate to help you to qualify for a loan. The catch is that the lender will eventually come out ahead, by charging higher interest later.

CHAPTER

10

Adjustable Rate Mortgages

While adjustable rate mortgages, or "ARMs" may be a fine way to finance a home, especially if you're on a tight budget, they can be dangerous if you don't know exactly what you're getting. Fortunately, once ARM language is deciphered, obtaining a good one isn't too difficult. We'll show you how in this chapter, and in Chapter 13 we'll explain how to measure the true cost of a mortgage, adjusting for interest, margins, index, and finance charges.

When Should You Finance With an ARM?

Initial ARM interest rates are lower than fixed rate mortgages. However, the rate can change on a predetermined schedule such as monthly, semiannually, or annually. When it does, the new interest rate is tied to a current market rate (called an index) plus the lender's profit (called a margin). If market rates have increased since you first took out the loan, your loan payment will increase, too.

ARMs can be a good choice in either of the following cases:

- You need money for other purposes—say to start a small business—so having a lower initial monthly payment makes sense.
- You plan to move or refinance in the next three to five years. Because your initial ARM interest rate is lower than a fixed rate, an ARM is cheaper than a fixed rate loan for the first few years.

Don't Believe All the Ads

Many lenders heavily advertise low initial ARM rates—but before you get drawn in, realize that:

- The advertised start rates don't last long (usually six months).
- Discounted rates don't necessarily help with loan qualification, because your ability to handle the loan is usually analyzed using the first-year rate, not the discounted rate.
- The lender will probably get its money back by including less attractive ARM features in the fine print, such as higher periodic interest rate caps or negative amortization.

Loan and Payment Caps

The term "cap" sounds simple. If you have a 5% ARM with a 5% life-of-the-loan cap and a 2% one-year periodic cap, your mortgage can't go above 10% and can't increase to more than 7% after one year.

But caps aren't this straightforward. First, be aware that the "5% life-of-the-loan cap" refers to five percentage points, not a 5% increase. Five percentage points raise an interest rate of 5% to 10% during the life of a loan, a 100% increase.

Most ARMs also cap the maximum amount your interest rate can go up in a particular adjustment period (periodic caps) between one and two percentage points per year, often adjusted every six months.

ARM Terms Defined

Before getting an ARM, review the following mortgage terminology.

Adjustment period. The time that goes by before the interest rate or payment amount changes. Most loans have monthly, semiannual, or annual adjustment periods. Annual or semiannual are preferred; try to avoid monthly adjustment periods, if possible.

Caps. The term "cap" refers to two different concepts. One is how much your interest rate can go up or down over the term of your mortgage (life-of-the-loan cap). The other is how much it can go up or down at each adjustment period.

Life-of-the-loan cap (or overall cap). This is the maximum (usually five to six percentage points) that the interest rate can increase or decrease over the life of the loan. For example, if the interest rate starts at 4%, and the life-of-the-loan cap is six percentage points, your interest rate can never exceed 10%. (Although arithmetic dictates that your loan could decrease to –2%, ARM loans always include a floor provision, usually of 1%.)

Payment cap/negative amortization. A payment cap limits the dollar amount your monthly payment can change at each adjustment period, usually once a year by 7.5% of the previous payment; a $1,000 loan minimum payment can increase to $1,075 or decrease to $925. The term "payment cap" (as opposed to "periodic cap") is usually a clue that the loan has negative amortization. If your capped monthly payments don't cover the interest that accrues that month, the difference will be added to your loan balance, and your mortgage debt will increase, not decrease.

Periodic cap. This limits the amount the interest rate of an ARM can change at each adjustment period. With a periodic cap, your interest rate might go up as much as 1% every six months or 2% annually—with your payments increasing accordingly.

Index. A market-sensitive financial yardstick to which ARM interest rates are linked. An index computed by averaging rates over a fairly long term (such as 26 or 52 weeks) will move up or down more slowly than one tied to daily or weekly rates.

Margin. The factor or percentage a lender adds to your index interest rate to arrive at the interest rate you pay. Most initial interest rates are set at, or below, the index interest rate (with no margin added). This means that, subject to the periodic or payment caps, ARM interest rates will automatically rise in the first several years to reach the market rate, unless the index interest rate falls substantially during this period.

Fully indexed rate. An ARM's true base interest rate after all initial discounts are filtered out. The fully indexed rate is calculated by adding the margin to the index. If your loan is based on the COFI with a 2.5% margin, your fully indexed rate is 7.5% when the COFI is 5%.

For a loan with an initial rate of 5%, a one percentage annual point cap means the rate can rise to 6% in one year.

Negative Amortization, Deferred Interest, and Option ARMs

Who wouldn't be attracted by lenders' advertised promises of "low monthly payments!"? And there is some truth to these promises—the usual deal is that the lender will allow you to pay a monthly minimum amount, even if your rate adjusts upward. But the catch is that ignoring your interest rate doesn't make it go away. If your monthly payments don't cover the accrued interest, the amount you owe on your total mortgage will go up. We're talking about loans that contain what's called "negative amortization" and go by such names as Option ARMs, Deferred Interest Loans, Negative Amortization Loans, and Interest Advances. These loans were once very common but have become quite scarce because in recent years, many borrowers defaulted on them. Still, you may be offered such a loan, particularly if you are a good credit risk.

You'll normally have a choice of three or four options, explained to you on your monthly statement, and you can choose the option you wish. The normal options are as follows.

Option One: Minimum payment. This amount may or may not cover the amount of interest due each month. If the interest is higher than the minimum amount you pay, the difference is added to your loan balance. After a set period, usually 12 months, your payment may increase or decrease according to the payment cap.

Option Two: Interest-only payment. You may choose to pay only the interest owed. If you choose this, your loan balance will remain exactly the same as it was the prior month. How much interest will be due depends on the current interest rate (which adjusts).

Option Three: Principal and interest payment. With this option, you pay all the interest due plus some principal, so that your loan will be completely repaid (amortized) over the original term of the loan.

Option Four: Accelerated payment. You may also choose to make a larger than normal mortgage payment. It will be a combined principal and interest payment, based on the assumption that you will pay off the loan within 15 years.

The main benefit of an option ARM is greater payment flexibility and therefore more cash flow. You may want to invest your money in other things, such as a college fund for your child, a new business venture, or another property. Another benefit is that if interest rates drop, the monthly adjustment on a negative amortization ARM means that you'll feel the benefits sooner than people with more traditional loans.

The risks are very obvious. If you pay less than the interest due, you will add to your loan balance. While this may be an acceptable strategy to deal with a short-term need for money, it only works for so long. Most lenders "recast" these loans every five years, which means they recalculate your payments based on the current loan balance. If the total amount you owe has gotten too big (7% to 25% over the original loan amount), the lender will reamortize your loan and increase your payments to make sure that the new, larger balance can be paid off within the remaining years of the loan.

EXAMPLE: Susan and Harry take out a $400,000 loan. Their interest rate is 1% for the first month. After that, it's fully indexed at 3.995% (because the index is at 1.995% and their margin is 2%). Their lender gives them four payment options for two months:

Option 1: Minimum payment: $1,286.56

Option 2: Interest-only payment: $1,331.66

Option 3: Principal plus interest payment: $1,908.51

Option 4: 15-year amortization payment $2,957.75

If, in this second month, Susan and Harry make the minimum payment, they will add $45.10 to their principal balance. (You can calculate this yourself, by taking the interest-only payment of $1,331.66 and subtracting the minimum payment of $1,286.56.) As a result, next month their loan will rise to $400,045.10. Their minimum payment will remain the same (it's good for a total of 12 months), but options 2, 3, and 4 will adjust according to the new loan balance as well as the new interest-rate.

TIP

Don't be shy about asking for explanations. In the words of Gwen Hoople, a loan consultant with Holmgren and Associates, "If you don't understand something that your lender or loan broker is telling you, it's not because you're dumb. Ask for a fuller explanation in plain English—and if you still don't understand, then their explanation wasn't good enough. Don't sign your loan papers until you fully understand the terms of your loan."

CAUTION

Beware of lender interest shelving. Another ARM feature to watch out for is "shelving" (or "warehousing"). Although not as bad as negative amortization, it lets lenders recover interest rate increases above the periodic cap if interest rates subsequently go down. For example, if a periodic cap prevents interest rates from going up more than 1.75 points in the first year, but the index goes up three points, the amount between the cap and the index (which would have contributed to negative amortization were that allowed) is instead "shelved" by the lender and added on later if interest rates drop substantially. Currently, most ARMs don't have this feature, but check to be sure.

ARM Indexes and Margins

By now you understand that when interest rates go up, so do ARM payments. Different ARMs, however, are tied to different financial indexes, some of which fluctuate up or down more quickly than others.

Indexes that lenders often use include those tied to the rates paid on six-month or one-year U.S. Treasury Bills (called "T-bills"). Other common indexes use the rate at which U.S. T-bills are sold in Europe (LIBOR); the six-month Certificate of Deposit (CD) rate, which is based on a mixture of long- and short-term treasury securities called the "moving treasury average"; and the Cost of Funds (COFI) of the 11th Federal Home Loan Bank District.

Lenders don't simply lend you money at the interest rate of the index, which is only slightly above what they pay their own CD depositors. Instead, lenders tack on two to three interest points (called a margin) to cover their costs and to make a profit.

So your payments don't jump too quickly, you want an ARM tied to a financial index that is likely to fluctuate slowly. Look for a loan where the lender computes interest rates based on an average of the index calculated over a number of weeks, because it will take a while before a quick spurt in interest rates moves the average significantly higher. The most volatile indexes (and therefore the worst if interest rates spike up) are computed on a daily or weekly "spot basis." Sure, they can go down fast, too, but if you can't afford a big increase, they're not worth the risk. Historically, LIBOR rates have been the most volatile, while the COFI has been the least. T-bill and CD rates have fallen in between.

Don't get so caught up in the index that you forget to look at the margin, the number added to the index to arrive at the interest rate you are charged. In the current market, we believe that a margin of 2.5% to 2.75% (for a six-month ARM) is a fair deal, as is 2.625% to 2.875% for a one-year ARM; adding a larger margin isn't. This is because a small difference in the margin can translate into substantially higher loan costs. On a 30-year, $130,000 loan with a 2.5% margin and a 5% index, your interest rate will be 7.5% and your payments $909. With a 3% margin, your interest rate will be 8% and your payments $45 more per month and $19,440 more over the life of the loan.

Assumability

Most ARMs are written to allow creditworthy purchasers to assume them from the seller. After the interest rate discounts offered in the first few years are eliminated, ARMs track current interest rates, and lenders have nothing to lose by someone assuming your loan. In contrast, fixed rate mortgages (except those that are government-backed) are not normally assumable and usually must be paid off in full when a house is sold.

Should you make it a high priority to find an assumable loan? Most of the time, no. Many purchasers will want a fixed rate loan and won't want to assume your ARM. And even if they want an ARM, they will normally be able to get a new one at an initial rate lower than your current one. Only if interest rates skyrocket, as they did in the early 1980s, and you have an ARM with a fairly tight life-of-the-loan cap, will a subsequent purchaser want to assume it. This, of course, is because your ARM will then be cheaper than a new loan.

Prepayment Penalties

Most ARM loans written in California on single-family homes don't have a prepayment penalty. (Some zero-point ARMs have a three-year prepayment penalty for large prepayments, although some exemptions apply.) In fact, for certain loans under $250,000, California law prohibits lenders from assessing prepayment penalties after the first 36 months of the loan. (Finance Code § 4973.)

With no penalty, you can make an extra payment or increase your payment to reduce the amount of interest you pay. (Chapter 9 discusses the advantages of prepaying your mortgage.) Also, you can refinance your ARM without penalty.

Hybrid Adjustable Rate Mortgage

Some lenders offer a hybrid mortgage that features an initial fixed rate (often for three, five, seven, or even ten years) that later converts to an ARM. You get the security of fixed rate payments in the early years and risk paying more later, when, hopefully, you'll have more income or can refinance.

This mortgage is especially popular with people who don't expect to own their houses beyond the point when the conversion to an ARM occurs. Because of life's unexpected happenings, however, look carefully to see that once the loan turns into an ARM, it's a good-quality one. Specifically, check the caps, the index and margin used, and whether there's negative amortization. Some hybrid mortgages allow the lender to adjust upward at an unreasonably high rate of three points as opposed to a more typical one- to two-point interest rate increase cap. Fortunately, this is only a one-time increase at the time the loan goes from a fixed rate mortgage to an ARM. Thereafter, the frequency cap should be no more than 1% every six months or 2% every year.

Summing Up—What Good ARMs Look Like

When it comes to ARMs, we recommend that you get the best margin and index you can, and be skeptical about initial discounted rates. Look for an ARM that conforms to these guidelines:

- A margin that is as low as possible, such as 2.5% points for a six-month ARM or 2.75% points for a one-year ARM.
- An ARM tied to an index that will adjust for inflation relatively slowly, if you expect rates to increase. Again, historically, this has been most often the COFI. If possible (and it often isn't), avoid ARMs tied to much shorter periods.
- A periodic cap that limits interest rate increases to no more than two interest rate percentage points per year.
- Interest rates that can be changed only once a year or, if you can't find one of these (they are scarce), once every six months.
- A life-of-the-loan cap of six interest points.
- The right to prepay without penalty, and the right of a subsequent qualified buyer to assume your loan at the same interest rate you'd be paying, rather than the then-current market rate. These features are normal.

What to Ask When Choosing an ARM

If you're considering an ARM, here are the basic things you'll want to know before you commit:

- **Initial rate (start rate).** How long is your initial interest rate fixed for? For example, it may last one month, six months, one year, three years, five years, seven years, or ten years.
- **Index.** What index is your ARM's interest rate based on (for example, the LIBOR, COFI, CODI, or T-bill index)?
- **Margin.** What's the bank's profit margin—in other words, what percentage will your lender add (usually 2%, 2.25%, 3%, or more) to bring your interest rate above the index rate?
- **Periodic caps.** By how much could your interest rate go up or down, and how often does it adjust? (For example, it might change by 1%, 2%, or 5%, and this could happen every month, six months, or 12 months.)
- **Lifetime cap.** What is the lifetime maximum interest rate of your loan?

EXAMPLE: José and Sandra have a $200,000 loan with an initial interest rate of 5%, which is fixed for five years and then varies based on the LIBOR index plus a margin of 2.5%. The periodic cap is 5% for the first adjustment and 2% thereafter, occurring every 12 months. The lifetime cap is 5% above the initial start rate.

For the first five years, José and Sandra's monthly payment is $1,073.64. Then, their interest rate gets recalculated based on the latest LIBOR index, at 4.5%, to which the bank adds its 2.5% margin, bringing the interest Prate for the next 12 months from 5% to 7%. Their monthly mortgage payments go up to $1,330.60.

José and Sandra know their interest rate will never go higher than 10% (the 5% initial rate plus the 5% lifetime cap) and it will never go lower than the margin plus the index at the time of adjustment. They can also expect that every 12 months, a new interest rate will be recalculated based on the current index plus the margin—but with a limit of 2% in any direction (the periodic cap). So, even if, after the index's initial jump from 4.5% to 7%, it went up by 3% to 7.5%, their interest rate for the next 12 months would be capped at 9% (7% plus the periodic cap of 2%). If the index fell by 3%, their interest rate would go down from 7% to 5% (again because of the 2% periodic cap).

CHAPTER

11

Government-Assisted Loans

Four government-assisted mortgage programs (and some local financing programs) are available to help Californians buy homes. These are:

- U.S. Department of Veterans Affairs (VA)
- Federal Housing Administration (FHA)
- California Housing Finance Agency (CalHFA), and
- California Department of Veterans Affairs (Cal-Vet).

The CalHFA program primarily provides mortgage financing for first-time California house purchasers in designated areas, and for qualifying first-time buyers who wish to buy outside these areas. The Cal-Vet program provides low-down-payment mortgage loans to qualifying California veterans.

Veterans Affairs Loans

So-called "VA loans" are available to men and women who are now in the service and to veterans with an other-than-dishonorable discharge who meet specific eligibility rules, most of which relate to length of service. Certificates of Eligibility are available from a VA office, after you've submitted VA Form 26-1880, *Request For A Certificate of Eligibility For VA Home Loan Benefits.* The form is available on the VA website, www.va.gov.

However, the VA doesn't actually make mortgage loans, but guarantees part of the house loan you get from a bank, savings and loan, or other private lender. If you default, the VA pays the lender the amount guaranteed, and you in turn will owe the VA. The idea of VA loans is to give veterans home-financing opportunities with favorable loan terms and competitive rates of interest.

The VA itself doesn't set a maximum loan amount, but limits the amount of your loan that it will repay. The maximum amount the VA will guarantee depends on the county. In most counties, it's $417,000, but can go much higher in certain high cost areas. To find the limit in your county, visit www.homeloans.va.gov.

Maximum VA Guarantees

Size of Loan	Maximum Guarantees
$45,000 or less	50% of loan
$45,000–$144,000	40% of loan, up to $36,000
$144,000 or more	25% of loan

Also, the loan amount may not exceed the VA's Certificate of Reasonable Value (CRV), based on the VA's appraisal of the property.

RESOURCE

To find out whether your military service qualifies you for a VA loan, visit the VA website at www.homeloans.va.gov/elig2.htm.

In the following situations, the purchaser will need to come up with a cash down payment, in addition to the VA loan guarantee:

- The loan exceeds the guaranteed loan limit.
- The sales price of the house exceeds the VA's Certificate of Reasonable Value. All VA purchase contracts give the buyer the right to cancel the deal if the contract price exceeds the CRV.

The VA's guarantee effectively replaces the down payment. You still must repay the whole loan; the guarantee protects the lender against loss and makes it easier for veterans to get favorable loan terms. But you won't have to pay PMI.

Eligible VA borrowers must have a good credit history, prove that they've been employed for the last two years, and show that they've got enough cash to cover the down payment and closing costs. They must also demonstrate an ability to pay monthly carrying costs on the house, plus other monthly obligations, using approximately 41% or less of their monthly income. And, they must show that they plan to live in the house themselves (not rent it out, for example) within a reasonable period of time after closing the loan.

As a general rule, most mortgage companies make VA loans, but many banks and savings and loans don't. Contact a regional office of the VA for a list of lenders active in the program.

You must pay the VA an administrative fee for the loan, ranging from 1.25% to 3% of the total borrowed, depending upon the amount of the down payment; members of the Reserves and National Guard pay the highest fees. The interest rate is often slightly below the market rate, and the lender may try to compensate by requiring more points.

CAUTION

Don't procrastinate in applying. The VA warns that you should expect to wait four to six weeks for a decision on your application.

These loan benefits are reusable, though you have to pay off the first loan and sell the property to become newly eligible for full benefits. Even if you're buying a second property, however, you can take a second VA loan if you have any "leftover" from the first loan—that is, if you used only a portion of your earlier entitlement, or if the maximum loan amounts have risen since your last loan. You can also refinance with a new loan.

New Houses and VA Loans

For most loans for new houses, the VA inspects construction at various stages to ensure compliance with the approved plans. The builder must provide a one-year warranty that the house is built in conformity with the approved plans and specifications. If the builder provides an acceptable ten-year warranty, the VA may only require a final inspection. (See Chapter 7 for more on inspections of new houses.)

Assuming a VA Loan

You do not need to be a veteran to assume a VA loan on an existing house, as long as you are a creditworthy purchaser and meet VA standards. This means a fixed rate loan is assumable at its original interest rate, which can be a bargain if rates have increased.

The credit eligibility requirements for buyers seeking to assume VA loans are fairly strict. If a buyer assumes a VA loan, the veteran remains liable for the payments unless the VA approves the buyer and the assumption agreement and issues a release of liability. This release protects the seller in case the buyer (or any other future owner) defaults. The seller cannot, however, reuse the full eligibility until the old (now assumed) loan is fully paid off.

RESOURCE

The main VA phone number—which will lead you to a lot of prerecorded messages—is 800-827-1000. For general VA mortgage information, ask for VA Pamphlet 26-4, "VA-Guaranteed Home Loans for Veterans," and VA Pamphlet 26-6, "To the Homebuying Veteran." To get a Certificate of Eligibility, complete VA Form 26-1880, *Request for a Certificate of Eligibility.* Also ask for the list of participating lenders.

You can also check the VA's website (and download forms and pamphlets and get contact information for local VA offices) at www.va.gov. (Click "Benefits," then "Home Loans.")

Federal Housing Administration Financing

The Federal Housing Administration (an agency of the Department of Housing and Urban Development) insures loans made to U.S. citizens, permanent residents, and other noncitizens who have Social Security numbers and permission to work in the United States. You must meet financial qualification rules and pay an annual premium. Under its most popular program, if the buyer defaults and the lender forecloses, the FHA pays 100% of the amount insured.

This loan insurance lets qualified people buy affordable houses. You can use it for both fixed and adjustable rate loans. The major attraction of an FHA-insured loan is that it requires a low down payment, usually about 3.5%–5%. FHA also counts nontraditional sources of income when assessing your ability to make your monthly payments or down payment, including seasonal pay, regular overtime and bonus income, and money from a community savings club (a popular way of saving money in many minority communities). Qualified veterans may be eligible for a reduction in the minimum down payment.

The FHA loan limits vary by county and can go as high as $625,500 in some high-cost areas. Check with a regional FHA office or on the HUD website at www.hud.gov to find current rates in your area.

Like most government benefits, FHA loans have downsides:

- **Mortgage insurance.** If you'll be making a down payment of less than 20%, you'll probably have to pay for mortgage insurance (similar to, but not exactly the same as PMI). In 2009, you'll be charged an up-front premium of 1.5% of the loan amount, and a 0.5% annual fee thereafter. Unless Congress decides otherwise, after 2009 the program is "risk-based," meaning the better your credit, the lower your premium.
- **Condition of the property.** Fixer-uppers and properties needing significant repair won't qualify for the standard FHA loan program. If you want to buy a house in need of repair, any work

recommended by FHA appraisers or by a licensed pest control inspector must be done before the sale closes. Fixer-uppers might, however, qualify for the FHA's Rehabilitation Loan Program (Section 203(k)). The details of this program are beyond the scope of this book. Contact the FHA for more information.

- **Appraisals.** An FHA-approved appraiser must establish a fair market value for a house. FHA appraisers are strict, but reasonably fair. If the appraisal is less than what you pay for the house, the difference must be made up in cash, not by the FHA loan. A clause must be inserted in all sales contracts giving the buyer the right to cancel if the appraisal value is lower than the agreed-upon sales price.
- **General red tape.** It is often said that FHA loans are subject to inordinate bureaucratic snags and delays. But this isn't always true. In the hands of an experienced mortgage company or other FHA loan originator, FHA loans can be processed in about the same time as conventional loans.
- **Limits on seller-assisted down payments.** If buyers didn't have the requisite down payment for an FHA loan, they used to be able turn to the seller for assistance. The seller could essentially donate the money to the buyer (often, increasing the purchase price to make up for the "donation"), who could then qualify for the loan. These programs are now eliminated.

RESOURCE

You can also get information on FHA loans, or find a regional HUD office, by calling the FHA Mortgage Hotline at 800-HUDSFHA or by checking the FHA website at www.hud.gov.

California Housing Finance Agency Programs

The California Housing Finance Agency (CalHFA) provides mortgage financing for first-time home buyers or people who haven't owned a home in three years. You must be a U.S. citizen, permanent resident, or other qualified alien. CalHFA's various mortgage products include an interest-only and 40-year fixed rate loan, in addition to a conventional 30-year fixed rate loan, all available at below-market interest rates. You can make a low down payment or none at all. The "first-time" requirement is waived if you are purchasing in a designated "target area." The program is available for both existing homes and newly constructed homes.

Unlike the VA and FHA programs, CalHFA will help only if your income doesn't exceed certain limits established for the county where the house you want to buy is located. In fact, there are two levels of income limits: low income, which qualifies for a lower interest rate if the buyer has reasonable credit; and moderate income. For 2008, the low income limits range from $33,090 to $81,432 for a family of two buying an existing home, depending on what county you'll be living in—but check with CalHFA, as the limits change fairly rapidly. Moderate income limits range from $67,800 to $135,720 in the most expensive counties. Income limits are higher if you purchase in a "target area," and for families of three or more.

Because mortgage money comes from the sale of tax-exempt bonds, interest rates are lower than those offered by conventional lenders. Depending on the county, qualifying house prices are usually between $237,032 and $525,091, though they can go as high as $819,113 in targeted areas.

CalHFA requires that you have sufficient income to pay your closing costs and make payments. They recommend that you contact an approved CalHFA lender for an analysis of your personal situation.

RESOURCE

For up-to-date information about the CalHFA program and a list of approved lenders, call 877-922-5432, or check the CalHFA website at www.calhfa.ca.gov.

Cal-Vet Loans

The California Department of Veterans Affairs, through the Cal-Vet Loans Program, provides loans to qualified veterans who purchase homes within the state. Cal-Vet home loans are direct loans funded from the sale of tax-exempt bonds. No taxpayer revenue is used to fund this program.

Cal-Vet loans work a little differently from ordinary mortgage loans: Cal-Vet buys the property you select, then immediately sells it to you using a contract of sale. You make monthly payments directly to the department. It is set up as a 30-year loan, though you can pay it off sooner with no penalty. The department holds title to the property until you have paid in full.

TIP

You don't have to be a current California resident to get a Cal-Vet loan. It's okay if you're simply planning to buy a house in California. You will, however, need to start living in the house within 60 days of buying it and make it your primary residence. Nearly all veterans purchasing homes in California are now eligible, including those who served during peacetime or are serving currently.

RESOURCE

If you are a veteran and would like to know whether your military service qualifies you for a Cal-Vet loan, visit the Cal-Vet website at www.cdva.ca.gov (search for "eligibility").

Many borrowers can qualify for a no down payment loan. Other Cal-Vet home loan programs offer down payment options as low as 2%–3% of the purchase price. Single-family homes, condominiums, and manufactured homes on private land are currently eligible for loans of up to $521,250. The maximum loan amount is tied to the Fannie Mae conforming loan limit and can be expected to adjust annually. And you can add up to $5,000 to the loan for the cost of any solar heating equipment. Manufactured homes located in rental parks are eligible for loans of up to $125,000. Before you make any decisions based on these figures, however, double-check them at one of the Cal-Vet Home Loans district offices or on their website.

RESOURCE

For more information, call the California Department of Veteran's Affairs at 800-952-5626, or check out their website: www.cdva.ca.gov. Click "Home Loans."

The interest rate on Cal-Vet home loans is based on the continuing cost of bonds sold to fund the program. The interest rates are variable, not fixed. However, the initial interest rate is set at the time you submit your application, and subsequent rate increases are limited to 0.5% over the life of the loan. Your initial interest rate will depend on the particular funding source. In 2008, the rate was around 6.1%

You will also be charged a loan origination fee, currently set at 1% of the loan amount. If you will have less than 20% equity in the property, you will additionally need to pay a fee of 1.25%–3.35% of the loan amount to guaranty your loan.

What if the house you wish to buy costs more than the maximum Cal-Vet home loan (even after your down payment)? In this situation, you are free to seek a second mortgage from another lender to close the gap.

Cal-Vet also offers low down payment construction loans. The interest rate and terms will be the same as for a Cal-Vet loan on an existing home. You can use the loan both to buy the land and to build a home or to purchase a manufactured home to be placed on the land.

Municipal Financing Programs

Several California cities and counties offer various forms of financial assistance with down payments, primarily to first-time home buyers who are buying modestly priced properties. Often, these are the result of the city or county selling bonds for low "municipal rates" and passing the savings on to local purchasers. Call your city or county housing or planning office and inquire about any programs in your area. Programs come and go fairly quickly, because below-market-rate mortgage money tends to get committed very quickly. Here are some examples of municipal programs:

- Low-interest down payment loans and subsidies (in the form of second mortgages) to qualified first-time home buyers.
- Requirement that some local developers provide down-payment assistance as a condition of municipal approval of the project.
- Participation in the federal Mortgage Credit Certificate (MCC) program, which gives income-eligible, first-time home buyers who receive a certificate from a participating lender an IRS tax credit equal to 15% of the mortgage interest payments made on a home. This credit is in addition to standard tax deductions available to homeowners and, in effect, makes it easier to qualify

for mortgage loans by increasing a borrower's after-tax income. The MCC program is not available with bond-backed loans such as CalHFA or Cal-Vet but may be used with FHA, VA, and privately insured loans.

RESOURCE

Looking for more information? The federal Housing and Urban Development office maintains a Web list of California cities offering first-time homebuyer assistance programs. See www.hud.gov (search for "California Assistance Programs").

CHAPTER

12

Private Mortgages

Financial institutions and government programs are not the only sources for mortgage loans. A great deal of mortgage money is supplied by private sources—parents, other relatives, friends. Borrowing money privately is usually the most cost-efficient mortgage of all.

The three broad approaches to borrowing all or most of the money necessary to buy a house privately are:

- Borrow from friends or relatives.
- Borrow from the seller.
- Borrow from a noninstitutional private lender.

Advantages of Private Mortgages

The principal advantages of a private mortgage are:

- **Low interest.** Friends and relatives often charge 10%–30% less than conventional lenders.
- **Flexible repayment structures.** Private lenders may let you pay interest only, or less, for a few years, or otherwise customize your payment schedule.
- **No points or loan fees.** Institutional lenders normally charge thousands of dollars in up-front points and fees. You avoid these costs by borrowing money privately.
- **Easier qualifying.** Private lenders don't insist on a great credit score.
- **Saving on private mortgage insurance.** By borrowing privately, you avoid paying PMI, which lenders require if you borrow 80% or more of the purchase price. (See Chapter 4.)
- **Minimal red tape.** To borrow from an institutional lender, you must fill out an application form, provide verifying documentation, and wait for approval. The process is much simpler when you borrow privately.
- **No lender-required approval of house's physical condition.** Private lenders don't usually require that a house's defects be repaired before closing, as institutional lenders do.

Get a Loan From Friends or Relatives

To consider whether private financing, either in whole or part, will work for you, ask yourself two questions:

- Can a parent, grandparent, other relative, close friend, or business acquaintance afford to lend the money?
- Does that person trust you?

If the answer to both of these is "yes," follow up with two more:

- Of those people who can help, who is most likely to do so?
- Of those who can help, who tends to make reasonably conservative investments, such as bank CDs and money market funds, not speculative investments, such as stocks, commodities, or commercial real estate?

This last question is important, because people who invest conservatively are more likely to be interested in lending mortgage money at an interest rate higher than they get now. By contrast, people who invest aggressively in an effort to achieve larger returns won't be as impressed by the prospect of getting an interest rate a little better than a bank would pay (though they may lend anyway, for personal reasons).

If a relative or friend has the ability to help you, don't assume that he or she will. The hardest part about borrowing money is convincing the lender that the investment is safe.

CAUTION

Beware of imputed interest. The IRS assumes that mortgage lenders receive reasonable interest on every loan and assesses taxes accordingly. This is true even if the lender charges no interest or low interest to a family member or friend. The "imputed" interest rate charged for loans of more than $10,000 changes, but generally is between 4% and 9%. So even if your generous friend or relative charges you less, the IRS requires him or her to report interest income at that rate. If your friend doesn't and is audited, and the IRS discovers the omission (a very unlikely scenario), the IRS will readjust his or her income using the imputed interest rate and charge the tax owed on the readjusted income plus a penalty.

Approaching Friends, Relatives, and Other Private Lenders

As you prepare to approach someone you know about borrowing, start with the idea that you're not asking for charity. You're offering a business proposition: a loan at a fair rate of interest, secured by a first mortgage. Understand that trust is the key to getting any business deal to work.

If your relative or friend has the money to lend and knows you're trustworthy, chances are he or she will make a loan. If your relative or friend doesn't trust you—you've racked up large credit card bills, bounced checks, or even forgotten to return a lawn mower—he or she will probably back off quickly.

So, are potential lenders likely to trust you? If you can unequivocally say "yes," terrific. If it's "no," or "maybe, with coaxing," consider what you can do to improve their view of your reliability. If you currently owe money to a relative or friend, pay it back in full before proposing a new loan. If you were wild in your younger years but are now staid and responsible, make sure your parents spread the word to wealthy Uncle Harry before you show up on his doorstep asking to borrow $280,000.

Once you decide whom to ask, think carefully about how to raise the subject. Never surprise a potential lender by blurting out a request at a social event or other inappropriate occasion. Make an appointment, even if you see the person regularly and the formality seems odd. Give the person a general idea of what you want to talk about, but save the details. For example, you might say, "Grandpa, I'm trying to buy a house and I'm reviewing a number of ways to finance it. Can we sit down and talk soon?" If Grandpa never seems to find the time, you have your answer. If he says "How about Tuesday?" be on time and prepared to make an effective presentation.

True Story

Mort: My Good Friend Helped Me

Several years ago, Mort found a house he wanted to buy. Although he had enough money to make a good-sized down payment, he needed much more to finance the entire purchase. Upon hearing about the new house plan, Babette, his good friend, volunteered to lend Mort $200,000, to be repaid over 20 years, at a very competitive interest rate, secured by a first mortgage.

Why would Babette make this generous, unsolicited offer? Certainly, the trust and good regard accumulated over a 20-year friendship was important. Financial factors were also important. Babette had just retired and was living off the interest from her investments, and she wanted a higher rate of return on her money than she currently received from CDs.

They quickly struck a bargain. Mort got a fixed rate, 20-year loan at 6.5% (about 1.5% points lower than the going rate at the time) and saved close to $10,000 on the fees, and $170,435 in interest over the life of the loan (assuming he would have taken out a 30-year fixed rate loan). He also saved the hassle and time of filling out a loan application.

But what was in it for Babette? She got a 6.5% interest rate on her money at a time when CDs were paying 5%. She also got a first mortgage on the house. Should Mort default, Babette could easily foreclose, have the house sold, and recover the balance of her loan, plus the costs of sale.

Making an Effective Loan Presentation

Before approaching anyone for a loan, put together a businesslike proposal explaining:

- **How much you wish to borrow.** Be as specific as you can if you don't have a particular house in mind yet.
- **The interest rate you propose to pay.** It should normally be higher than what financial institutions currently pay their investors, and lower than what you'd pay an institutional lender. Find out what CDs pay and what fixed rate mortgages cost. Propose paying around half the difference. For example, if fixed rate mortgages cost 6% and banks pay 4% on CDs, you might propose paying 5%.
- **The loan terms you propose.** This should include the length of the mortgage and the amount of the monthly payments. Use the amortization table in Chapter 2 or an online mortgage calculator to come up with exact figures.
- **A copy of the family financial statement you prepared in Chapter 2.** This lists your sources of income, existing debts, and other financial information.
- **A copy of a recent credit report from a credit reporting agency.** In Chapter 2 we discuss how to get one.

- **An estimate of the purchase price of the house you want to buy.** As explained, this won't be exact unless you've already made an offer and had it accepted, but do your homework. Be ready to show the potential lender your Ideal House Profile from Chapter 1 and a fairly tight estimate for such a house. If the potential lender wants to make sure the house you find will be worth what you want to pay, offer to get it appraised prior to purchase.
- **How much you have available for a down payment.** If it's 20% or more, point out that you're investing more than enough of your own money to guarantee that the lender will have little risk of loss, even if you default. (Chapter 4 discusses down payments.)
- **Your debt-to-income ratio.** As discussed in Chapter 2, financial institutions have found that it's safest to lend to people whose monthly carrying costs don't exceed 28%–36% of their monthly income. Even though a friend or relative probably won't insist on rigid qualification rules, it can be very important to demonstrate that you'll have enough income to comfortably make the payments.

When you meet with the potential lender, present your proposal in general terms first. This gives the other person a chance to back off gracefully, if desired. If you sense this happening, say, "Thanks for listening," and change the subject. Remember that people have many reasons for not lending money—don't take "no" as a personal rejection.

If the person shows some interest, briefly present the details. Give the potential lender ample time to ask questions, and don't expect a decision on the spot. Be prepared to leave photocopies of all documents.

How a Large Down Payment Minimizes the Lender's Risk

If you miss payments, the mortgage holder or lender has the legal right to have the property sold through foreclosure. Proceeds (after the costs of sale are subtracted) go to the first mortgage holder. If you have more than one mortgage, the mortgages are numbered in the order in which they were recorded at the county recorder's office. The lower the number (first being the lowest), the more likely the mortgage holder will be paid if you default.

If the sale price doesn't cover the mortgage debt, the mortgage holder doesn't get all that is owed. For this reason, lenders want the house to be worth considerably more than what they lend. Even allowing for the fact that houses usually sell for relatively low prices at foreclosure sales, most lenders feel safe in lending 80% of appraised value, with the buyer making a 20% down payment.

Responding to a Proposed Lender's Questions and Concerns

First, and most important, if you plan to approach a relative who doesn't have much business savvy, consider whether the loan makes sense for that person. For example, if Aunt Muriel's health is such that she may need most of her money in the next few years, don't borrow from her, even if she'll lend it. She's better off having access to her money, even at a lower interest rate.

Often, friends or relatives will be concerned about what happens to their investment should you become ill or disabled and unable to pay them back, or if you (or another breadwinner) die. The lender fears being caught needing the mortgage repaid and having to foreclose on a distressed family member or friend to get it.

One way to deal with this concern is to purchase both life and disability insurance on yourself and any other cobuyer, and to keep the insurance in force until the loan is repaid. Term life insurance for younger people, particularly, will cost little. (With a life insurance policy, you'd make the friend or relative the beneficiary.)

A good disability policy that will pay a large proportion of your monthly salary should you be unable to work is more expensive, but worth it. Make sure your policy pays at least 60% (more is better) of what you would have received had you been able to work.

Finalizing the Loan

If your presentation is successful, and your friend or relative agrees to lend you the needed money, you need to prepare the paperwork. You can do this yourself, although given what's at stake, this wouldn't be a bad time to hire an attorney. Here's what's needed:

- A promissory note for the amount of the loan, including the rate of interest and repayment and other terms. *101 Law Forms for Personal Use,* by Ralph Warner and Robin Leonard (Nolo), contains promissory notes, and Nolo also offers electronic promissory notes at www.nolo.com.
- A mortgage or, to use the technically correct term, a deed of trust. A tear-out one, with instructions for its use, is in *Deeds for California Real Estate,* by Mary Randolph (Nolo). Or, as part of the closing process on the house you buy, simply pay the title (or escrow) company a modest fee to prepare and record a deed for you.

CAUTION

A promissory note is not enough. Some people skip the preparation and recording of a deed of trust, reasoning that a promissory note is enough. It isn't. The lender isn't fully protected—from either subsequent lenders or purchasers—unless a formal notice of the loan is recorded.

Shared Equity Transactions

If you're considering borrowing privately, you may also be open to purchasing a house with an investor. In this scenario, you ask a private investor to contribute toward the purchase and share equity in the house as a co-owner. When the house is ultimately sold, the investor will make a profit on his or her portion. For more information, see Chapter 3.

Second Mortgages—Financing by Sellers

In theory, if a seller has no immediate need for money, he or she can transfer his or her house to you and receive nothing in return but your promise to pay in the future, secured by a mortgage. In practice, however, because most sellers have no personal reason to help you, they will generally insist that your down payment and amount borrowed add up to the sales price. Still, some sellers will finance at least a portion of your purchase price themselves. In this situation, a conventional lender has usually agreed to lend you a substantial portion, and the seller provides a much smaller portion, say 10%, of the total secured by a second mortgage.

Here are some of the reasons a seller may provide a second mortgage:

- **To sell a house that has been on the market for a long time.** Taking back a second mortgage makes a house easier for a buyer to finance and, therefore, for the seller to sell.

  EXAMPLE: You have $33,000 for a down payment on a house listed at $380,000, and qualify for a mortgage of $324,000 from an institutional lender, leaving $28,000 necessary to complete the deal (allowing $5,000 for closing costs). Your seller is retired and living off investments. He agrees to take back a second mortgage for the remaining $28,000, at a competitive interest rate.

- **For tax reasons.** If the seller doesn't qualify for the exclusion of capital gains, he or she will owe taxes for the year of sale. (See Chapter 14 for more on tax laws.) The seller may benefit by receiving a portion of these profits in future years, particularly if he or she is retiring and expects an income drop to a lower tax bracket.
- **For investment.** Because second mortgages are riskier than firsts, it's sometimes considered reasonable for the buyer to pay a fairly high rate of interest. A seller may take back a second mortgage if you'll pay a higher rate of interest than banks do on CDs, short-term U.S. government securities, and money market funds.

Second Mortgages: A Buyer's Wish List

- A reasonable interest rate
- Low initial payments so as to not jeopardize first mortgage financing
- No prepayment penalty
- No balloon payment for at least five years, and the automatic right to extend the loan if it's impossible to refinance to pay the balloon in full on the due date
- The right to have a subsequent credit-worthy buyer assume the second mortgage.

Seller financing can be as flexible as the buyer and seller agree. Many sellers will accept promissory notes with variable payment structures or interest rates. You can have low interest rates in the first year or two, with increases later. Or you can provide for fixed monthly payments with a floating interest rate.

A serious problem with second mortgages is that the monthly payments on the second are likely to be so large that you no longer qualify for a first mortgage under standard debt-to-income ratios. After all, if you weren't having affordability problems in the first place, you could borrow more on a first mortgage and wouldn't need a second.

Fortunately, second mortgages can be structured to deal with this problem. For example, you may make very low monthly payments on the second mortgage for several years, paying off the entire balance with a large balloon payment at a specific future date (often three to ten years after the sale). Under optimum circumstances, the house's value and your income will have risen before the balloon payment is due, so you can refinance the first mortgage, using a portion to pay off the second.

To allow for the possibility that your income and the house's value may increase more slowly than expected, institutional lenders usually require that at least five years of interest-only payments pass before the balloon payment is due on the second mortgage. You should also insist on an option to extend if you can't refinance the first mortgage.

CAUTION

Don't overextend yourself. The need to arrange a second mortgage with a large balloon payment tells you that you're stretching your finances close to the breaking point and betting heavily on future property value appreciation to pull you through. Also, be aware that interest rates may increase substantially by the time the balloon payment is due and you need to refinance. Consider whether you're in danger of purchasing more house than you can reasonably afford.

CAUTION

Watch out for wraparound notes. Some sellers will offer a wraparound note ("wrap"), also known as an All Inclusive Trust Deed (AITD). It "wraps around" existing financing; you pay the seller, and he or she pays the other note holder.

Be wary! You're usually much better off paying the first mortgage holder directly, rather than risking that the seller won't make the payment. A seller offers a wrap because he or she receives a higher interest yield for the total loan than you would pay by negotiating the two mortgages separately.

EXAMPLE: Sally and Burt want to buy a $500,000 house and have $70,000 for a down payment. Their combined monthly income is $5,700. Unfortunately, the best deal they can get is an ARM for $400,000 at 7.5% for 30 years. They're $30,000 short.

They approach Patience, the seller, and propose that she take back a second mortgage for the $30,000. Because she needs to move fairly quickly and there are no other likely buyers, Patience agrees. She offers Sally and Burt a five-year interest-only second at 10% interest, which will result in payments of $333.33 per month. Unfortunately, Sally and Burt now no longer qualify for the first mortgage, as the monthly payments for the two mortgages exceed the institutional lender's debt-to-income ratio. They propose a seven-year second, with interest-only payments of 5% for the first two years. Beginning in the third year, the payments would increase 20% per year for five years. At the end of the seventh year, Sally and Burt would owe the balance in a balloon payment.

Second Mortgages—Financing by Private Parties Other Than the Seller

Sellers aren't the only people who can provide second mortgages. Relatives and friends can make second loans, and some private investors will as well. Loan brokers can bring prospective borrowers and prospective second mortgage lenders together for a fee. Finally, many commercial lenders make second mortgage loans.

Preparing a Second Mortgage

Step 1: Determine the terms of the second, including the dollar amount, length of the loan, interest rate, and repayment terms. Make sure the second mortgage doesn't include a prepayment penalty.

Step 2: Be sure the lending institution that will provide the first mortgage knows and approves of the terms and conditions of the second.

Step 3: Prepare the necessary paperwork—the buyer's promissory note for the amount of the second mortgage, containing all mortgage terms. Nolo's *For Sale by Owner in California*, by George Devine, includes a promissory note for a second mortgage. Relatively straightforward arrangements can be handled by the title or escrow company that is doing the closing. For more complicated mortgages, including those with an adjustable interest rate, you may need the help of an experienced real estate lawyer. In addition, the title or escrow company should prepare and record a second mortgage (a "deed of trust") at the county recorder's office.

Step 4: Make sure your purchase contract contains all the terms and conditions of the second mortgage (required by Civil Code §§ 2956 through 2967).

CHAPTER 13

Obtaining a Mortgage

The previous five chapters describe the kinds of mortgages available, and their pros and cons. You should have a good idea as to the type you want and can afford. Now it's time to actually get a mortgage, either on your own or with the help of a broker.

Assuming you're in decent financial shape (if you're not sure, refer back to Chapter 2), real money can be saved if you carefully shop for a mortgage. Everything else being equal, even a one-quarter percentage point difference in interest rates can mean savings of thousands of dollars over the life of a mortgage. To help you shop, this chapter will cover:

- where to get the latest information on mortgage rates and fees
- where to find useful information online
- how a good loan broker can help you
- how to work directly with mortgage lenders
- how to complete the loan application and get a speedy approval, and
- what to expect from the lender's home appraisal.

Gather Information on Mortgage Rates and Fees

Interest rates and mortgages change frequently—and often dramatically—and you need to be up-to-date. Fortunately, this need not be a daunting task, as mortgage interest tables are printed in the Sunday real estate sections of many metropolitan newspapers and are readily available online. These tables include current mortgage interest rates and points and fees charged by various lenders for different mortgages.

Advertisements for mortgage loans will give you a feel for the market and an approximate idea of where your interest rate should be, but take them with a grain of salt. They always presume "best case scenarios" to arrive at the lowest possible rate. Remember that interest rates change daily, sometimes even twice or more a day. By the time you see an interest rate advertised in the newspaper, it may already be history.

While mortgage interest tables include only a small percentage of the total mortgages on the market, they can give you a feel for the current price range, especially if you ignore the mortgages with the lowest rates, which are usually lower than what most buyers will be offered and serve more as advertising to attract customers. And remember, just because a low-interest loan is available, there's no guarantee that you'll qualify for it or that it has all the features you want.

Researching Mortgages Online

Many online services provide mortgage rate information. While these sites don't list all the loans available, they offer a great way to get a sense of market rates and terms.

Individual lenders provide mortgage rate information online as well as all kinds of advice for buying a home—from choosing a mortgage to negotiating closing costs. Simply search for the name of a specific financial institution. However, realize that many of them present only their standard mortgage

How to Compare Mortgage Rates by APR

In an attempt to allow buyers to compare loans, federal law (Regulation Z) requires all lenders to state the Annual Percentage Rate (APR) and to include fees and points. When these fees are figured in, the APR is usually 0.25% to 0.30% higher than the advertised rate for 30-year loans.

Assume you're considering a $100,000 loan at 6% for 30 years. If there were no loan fees, the APR would be 6%. If there are two points, the APR would be 6.18%, because you'd receive only $98,000 after the $2,000 in points was subtracted.

But even APR comparisons aren't perfect. Depending on how lenders write loans, identical packages can end up with slightly different APRs. In addition, APR comparisons assume you'll pay off the loan over its entire term, and thus amortize the fees and points over this period. But most people move or refinance sooner, with the result that a loan with lots of points may be more expensive than one with fewer points (and a higher interest rate), even though the APR is the same. Also, APR comparisons don't take into consideration the tax deduction you get on mortgage interest and points. Your loan will cost you more or less depending on your tax bracket. (To compare points and interest rates, see "The Cost of Getting a Loan" in Chapter 8.) APR discussions also omit closing and transaction costs, which can vary slightly.

plans and deliberately provide only enough information to get you to personally contact the lender.

Online real estate sections of your local newspapers also provide mortgage rate information on the Web. See, for example, the *L.A. Times* website at www.latimes.com/mortgage.

Other sites, such as HSH Associates, at www.hsh.com, publish mortgages and consumer loan information but do not make loans. The "Lender Showcase" area of hsh.com allows you to compare mortgage rates from financial institutions in a specific area. The site also includes all kinds of detailed mortgage information, including market forecasts and the latest ARM indexes.

Several websites have gone beyond providing basic mortgage rate information and actually allow you to compare rates from dozens of lenders, based on the amount, type, and length of mortgage you want. You can even prequalify and apply for a home loan online.

Other Internet mortgage loan sites include:

- www.bankrate.com
- www.e-loan.com
- www.infoloan.com
- www.indymac.com
- www.quickenloans.com
- www.interest.com
- www.realestate.msn.com
- www.lendingtree.com, and
- www.mortgagemarvel.com.

Name Your Price ... for a Mortgage?

Priceline, the service that lets you "name your price" on airline tickets, offers home mortgage bidding online at www.priceline.com. Purchasing a home is obviously a lot more expensive and complicated than buying an airline ticket—for example, it can be hard to be sure the bids you receive are really for identical loans. Even so, you may want to take a peek at this newest spin on finding a mortgage online.

Work With a Loan Broker

Another approach to looking for a loan (after doing your own preliminary work) is to hire a loan broker, a person who specializes in matching house buyers and appropriate mortgage lenders. Assuming you qualify financially, a savvy loan broker can find you a competitively priced mortgage that meets your needs.

Loan brokers must have a real estate broker's license (although someone who works for a broker needs only a salesperson's license). They usually receive two types of compensation:

- A commission from the lender that is a portion of the points you pay on your loan. If there are no points, the lender pays the broker and recoups this payment by charging you a higher interest rate.
- A processing fee, ranging from $200 to $500. Brokers may charge this fee up front or at the close of escrow.

The broker is legally required to tell you both the amount and source of his or her compensation—but that doesn't always mean they'll volunteer this information. Be prepared to ask for it if it's not readily disclosed on the Good Faith Estimate (explained in Chapter 18).

Financial institutions accommodate loan brokers because lenders want more loan business and will pay a middleperson a commission to get it. In addition, because loan brokers do much of the paper preparation work, they often save lenders time in loan transactions.

Advantages. Working with a loan broker has its pros and cons. On the positive side, it's often much easier and more effective than looking for the cheapest rates yourself. If you are a first-time home buyer or simply don't have the time to shop for mortgages, you'll appreciate the help a good loan broker can provide, such as:

- reviewing your financial profile and, if necessary, counseling you on steps to improve it before applying for a loan
- providing information about types of mortgages that meet your needs, comparing different mortgages, and translating difficult loan language
- identifying the financial institutions that offer the type of mortgage you want and are likely to qualify for
- helping you prepare the papers needed to apply for a loan (if you don't use a loan broker, you'll do this directly with the financial institution)
- acting as a buffer between you and the lender, clearing up problems such as an appraisal that's too low or a supporting

document that's inappropriate before the lender ever sees them, and

- talking to the loan officers on your behalf, to anticipate and solve any problems.

Disadvantages. The downsides of using loan brokers include:

- You must be sure that the person you work with is knowledgeable and trustworthy.
- Not all loan brokers handle government loans or work with all lenders.
- A few loan brokers have been known to prefer financial institutions that treat them well (pass on more points or offer attractive prizes or gifts) but don't necessarily offer you the lowest or best rates.
- Some lenders keep their best loans in-house. That means they are available only if you contact the lender directly—these loans are not made available to loan brokers.
- A few loan brokers (like some banks) use bait-and-switch advertising to recruit customers—that is, they claim they can arrange better loans at lower rates than is actually possible. You can minimize your risk by checking out mortgage rates and features before contacting a broker.

California has thousands of loan brokers; some work alone, others in fair-sized companies. To find a good one, ask friends, relatives, acquaintances, and your real estate agent for a recommendation. Then make a few phone calls and check out the referrals. Some loan brokers are known on the local grapevine to be more helpful, creative, and trustworthy than others.

If you have a problem with a loan broker or a bank loan department, you can file a complaint with the Department of Real Estate. The DRE website is www.dre.ca.gov.

Mortgage brokers are required by law to publish their license number and a telephone number where you can verify their license status. (California Business and Professions Code §§ 10235.5, 10236.4, and 10236.5.)

True Story

Antonio and Gretel: Working With a Loan Broker

We'd made an offer on a house that several other people wanted. We knew that to be considered seriously we needed to show the sellers we could afford the purchase. We'd heard that a particular bank was a quick qualifier for adjustable rate mortgages and charged no application fee for ARMs.

Sure enough, within a few days, for no cost, we were told we qualified for a loan. This satisfied the sellers, who accepted our offer (rejecting another attractive one because the people couldn't secure financing).

Now we had time to shop for a good loan. We went back to the "quick qualifier" bank and pointed out that their rates seemed to be on the high side. They said take it or leave it; we left. On the recommendation of friends, we called a local loan broker. Though this took some time, we came out of it with an excellent fixed rate loan.

Why Use a Loan Broker?

We asked Michael Cohen, a loan broker with Schnell Investment Company in Orinda, California, "Why use a loan broker?" Here's what he said:

"The main reasons are flexibility, service, and security. Any one lender has only a few products to offer. By contrast, a well-connected mortgage broker may place loans with 50–60 lenders, including large S&Ls, small local banks, or mortgage bankers representing insurance or pension fund investors.

"A loan broker has many program options, pricing trade-offs, and underwriting variations to offer. These may include access to swing loans, commercial and multifamily loans, and construction and 'rehab' loans. In addition, a good loan broker can counsel the borrower on loan qualification strategies and financing alternatives. The broker will also spot potential problems early on and suggest a way to resolve them. This may mean the difference between getting the loan or not.

"If one lender doesn't come through (despite the loan broker's advocacy efforts), the broker may be able to place the loan elsewhere. In these uncertain days when banks are combining into larger and more distant, faceless monoliths, working with an actual person may provide you with better service.

"One final word: The loan broker doesn't get paid by the lender unless the loan closes. Therefore, it's in the broker's enlightened self-interest to see that the loan is approved and the borrower is satisfied."

Interview Lenders

An alternative to working with a loan broker is to comparison shop for a loan on your own. Even if you plan to work with a loan broker, doing your own research helps you get the best deal and educates you about market conditions so you can work more efficiently with the broker.

One good way to mortgage shop is to interview several lenders. Start by identifying lenders offering loans appropriate for you, based on newspaper or online listings or ads or recommendations from your real estate agent or a friend, relative, or employer. If you regularly do business with a bank or other financial institution, it makes sense to include that bank if it offers reasonably competitive loans. Obtain all written material describing available mortgages from lenders you have identified as possibilities. To the extent possible, gather all information on the same day, so you can do an accurate comparison.

After reviewing the lenders' written material, make an appointment to meet a residential real estate loan officer or to speak with one on the telephone. If you, or a relative or close friend, own a business and have an ongoing relationship with a bank, ask for an introduction to a real estate loan officer. You may get some extra personal time and attention this way.

When you call to schedule an appointment or obtain information, be sure to verify that the lender offers the type of loan you want, in terms of rates, fees, and points.

A Comparison of Six Mortgages

By now, you may be completely overwhelmed by the chapters on mortgage financing, thinking, "I like the stability of a fixed rate mortgage, but the initial low cost of an ARM is tempting." Before finalizing your decision, compare six $150,000 mortgages through seven years (the typical length of time a homeowner keeps a mortgage). For information on margins, indexes, and life-of-the-loan caps, see Chapter 10.

As the chart shows, a 15-year fixed rate mortgage pays down the $150,000 balance the quickest. If you can't afford this loan's higher monthly payments, be comforted in knowing that in this example, the differences between the other mortgages are not that great. This will remain true regardless of changes in interest rates.

		Start of Mortgage		After 7 Years	
Mortgage type	Interest Rate	Annual % rate (APR)	Monthly payment	Total payment	Total paid on principal
30-year fixed	7.625%	7.925%	$1,062	$89,182	$12,002
15-year fixed	7.25	7.717	1,370	115,021	50,476
1-year ARM; after 1 year, rate increases with 2.625 margin, 3.5 index, 10.625% life-of-the-loan cap	4.625	4.853	772	99,765	11,552
3-year ARM; after 3 years, rate increases with 2.625 margin, 5.25 index, 11.875% life-of-the-loan cap	6.375	6.643	936	99,192	10,149
5-year ARM; after 3 years, rate increases with 2.625 margin, 5.25 index, 11.875% life-of-the-loan cap	7.25	7.540	1,024	91,586	11,142
Two-step; fixed for 7 years; changes to ARM with 2.25 index and 5.0 life-of-the-loan cap	7.125	7.412	1,011	84,889	13,016

When you visit or speak to a lender, your goals are to review the following materials with the loan officer:

- The various mortgage plans available, including the required down payment, APR, interest rate, points, loan origination fees, credit check charges, and appraisal fees. If you've read the written material, what the loan officer tells you should come as little surprise.
- The family financial statement you prepared in Chapter 2. Based on this or an online mortgage calculator, the loan officer should be able to give you a good idea of the type of mortgage you qualify for.
- All details important to you. For example, if you plan to make a low down payment, find out whether private mortgage insurance (PMI) is

required. If you're considering an ARM loan, ask about periodic caps, life-of-the-loan caps, negative amortization, and the like.

CAUTION

Shop around. Keep in mind that the financial institution you talk to first—or even second—may not be the cheapest or best for you. If a loan officer tries to thrust a loan into your hands, politely state that you still want to look at other loans. Be sure to ask whether the loan officer is paid any commission for mortgage loans. Some loan officers make a commission based on the number or dollar amount of loans they make; this may affect what loans they recommend.

Apply For and Get a Loan

Once you've made an offer on a house and have identified what seems to be the best mortgage for you, it's time to apply for a loan. We're assuming that you applied for preapproval before you made an offer on the house. If not, your loan approval will involve a few more steps, as you'll have to fill out an application form and pull together basic supporting documentation such as W-2s, tax returns, pay stubs, bank statements, retirement statements, and the like. After you've been preapproved and are in contract to buy a house, the lender will additionally require the following:

- A copy of the purchase contract for the house you are buying. (If you're using a real estate agent, the agent will give this directly to the mortgage broker or lender.)
- Preliminary Title Report. (The title company will ordinarily give this to the broker or lender.)
- Property appraisal report. (The appraiser will ordinarily give this to the broker or lender.)
- If you are also selling a house, the listing agreement or sales contract or the final HUD1 statement if your house is already sold. (HUD1 Statements are final settlement statements prepared by the escrow company handling sales transactions.)
- The original, signed copy of your gift letter, if applicable.

Despite the ads that tout "overnight approval," you should allow a reasonable period for approval (or denial) after you complete a loan application. Before final loan approval (called funding the loan), the lender must verify all your financial, employment, and credit information; arrange an appraisal of the property; and prepare the necessary paperwork. Normally, this process takes about two to three weeks, unless you have a high income and plan to make a substantial down payment, in which case approval should be faster. And, in times of high volume, the process may take about a month.

The timeline at the end of this chapter shows all the steps involved from loan application to close of escrow.

Tips for Speeding Up Loan Approval

Here are some tips for faster loan approval.

Don't wait until the last minute to collect financial and other documents. Particularly if you haven't yet been preapproved, you don't want the process to be held up while you sift through piles of paperwork.

Neatly complete every section of the application. Your broker may help you with this form. Don't leave any blanks! If some item doesn't apply, write "not applicable" or "N/A."

Tell the truth. Don't exaggerate your earnings or hide negative credit information—the lender will find out anyway. And, if so, this misrepresentation (or fraud) may automatically cancel your loan application.

Show you're creditworthy. If you're concerned that something on your application may work against you—for example, you have a job gap—write a simple letter of explanation.

Hand-deliver paperwork. To speed up the process, offer to hand-carry forms to your employer and banks, verifying your employment and deposit information.

Monitor the process. If you're under time pressure to close by a certain date, or have a limited time when interest rates are locked in, be sure to keep close tabs on the process. Make sure your loan officer has all the information needed to process your loan application. Keep in regular touch and document all phone and written communications with the lender.

Getting the Lender's Commitment

If a lender says that you qualify for a loan, ask for a "commitment" or "loan qualification" letter, stating the size and type of the loan and the interest rate you qualify for. The commitment letter may specify that certain conditions be met before final loan approval—for example, that you pay off a long-term debt or that the house appraises for at least the loan amount. As a precaution, don't remove financing contingencies from your offer (see Chapter 16) until these conditions have been met.

Locking in Interest Rates

It's important to understand that even a commitment letter isn't the same thing as a guarantee to borrow at a particular interest rate or particular terms. If interest rates go up, the lender will demand that you pay the higher amount, unless you've received a "lock-in" or "rate lock." If you haven't, and interest rates rise significantly, the lender could recalculate your debt-to-income ratio to see if you still qualify at the higher interest rate.

A rate lock is a guarantee by a lender to make a loan at a particular interest rate, even if the market changes. Most rate locks are good for about 21–30 days and usually apply to a specific house. (You can often arrange for a rate lock for longer, but you'll have to pay for it, usually in the form of higher points—as much as ⅕ to ⅜ of a point more.) One reason you'll have to pay more is that when a lender locks in a rate, it has made a commitment to deliver the loan to Freddie Mac, Fannie Mae, or another investor. If the lender doesn't deliver—that is, you don't buy the house—the lender still must pay a fee to the investor. Also, because of volatility in the market, Freddie Mac and Fannie Mae set a higher price on loans to be delivered later—for example, within 60 days versus ten days.

A rate lock is particularly valuable when the house is in escrow and you are on a tight budget, as it protects you from the possibility that a hike in interest rates will result in your no longer qualifying to make the purchase. If you are not worried about increasing rates, you'll probably want to skip obtaining a lock-in and hope rates go down so that you'll get the benefit of the lower rate.

CAUTION

Beware of strategies unscrupulous lenders may use to avoid meeting a rate lock. If your lender requires additional (and often very picky) documentation at the last minute—for example, details on a minor credit problem or more income data if you're self-employed—be leery. To avoid these kinds of delays, make sure all your information is complete when you apply for a loan. Get the rate lock agreement in writing. Keep in touch with the lender so you can head off any problems. Finally, file a complaint with a regulatory agency (see "Where to complain about problems with a loan application," below) if the deal threatens to come undone.

Get Your House Appraised

A few weeks after you apply for a loan, the lender will arrange for an appraisal of the property, to make sure it's worth the amount you want to borrow. The buyer typically pays a fee for the appraisal as part of the closing costs, usually $400 or more, depending upon the size and price of the house and property. Larger houses, houses with many units, and investment properties all tend to cost more to appraise. Some government loan programs, such as FHA, set their own appraisal procedures. (See Chapter 11.)

The appraiser may physically inspect the property inside and out and will estimate the value based on recent documented prices of comparable sales within a few blocks of the house, adjusting for differences in size and features among the properties.

If the appraisal comes in at or above the amount of money you need to borrow, and everything else checks out, your loan will be approved. There may be problems, however, if the appraisal comes in low. The lender doesn't want to risk a scenario in which it later forecloses on your property and comes up short because the property was worth less than its appraised amount. If the appraisal comes in below the asking price, make a list of the home's important features and gather together your research on recent sales prices of comparable homes, and give copies of these to the appraiser. If it still comes in too low, your next step is to get a copy of the appraisal; if you pay for the appraisal, the lender is legally obligated to give you a copy. If you've collected your own comparable sales data before determining your offer price (see Chapter 15), you should be able to justify a higher appraisal price to the lender. Consider asking for a second appraisal.

If you can't get a higher appraisal, you can either back out of the deal (assuming financing contingencies in your contract allow this), come up with more money for a down payment, get the seller to lower the price or take back a second mortgage (discussed in Chapter 12), or look for another lender.

A Hypothetical Timeline: From Loan Application to Close of Escrow

Let's assume you submitted an offer to purchase a home to a seller and it was accepted on January 1. The application process should proceed roughly as follows. We assume here that you'll seek a loan directly from an institutional lender; if you instead work with a mortgage broker, he or she will perform many of the duties of the lender identified below.

Range of Possible Dates	Action
January 2–3	You submit loan application; lender runs credit check immediately and reviews with you any negative information.
January 3–4	Day after running credit check, you submit pay stubs and year-end tax documents to lender, in addition to 6 months' worth of bank statements.
January 2–5	Within 72 hours of when you submitted your application, lender must send you loan disclosures (annual percentage rate and other information) and good faith estimates of closing costs.
January 10–18	One to two weeks after lender arranges for appraisal of property, it's completed.
January 12–February 4	Lender assembles a loan package. Loan underwriter compares loan package to lender's guidelines. If it fits, underwriter sends package to supervisor and others for approval. If it doesn't fit, but is in the ballpark, underwriter sends package to others for second opinion. If it totally fails to fit guidelines, loan is rejected or lender specifies conditions for approval.
January 13–February 6	Lender loan committee gives final approval, sometimes with certain conditions (such as to pay off a long-term debt).
January 14–February 9	One to three days after loan approved (or condition removed), lender prepares loan papers.
January 15–February 10	One day after lender prepares loan papers, escrow holder prepares final closing papers for you and seller.
January 16–February 11	One day after escrow holder prepares final closing papers, you and seller go to escrow holder to sign all papers.
January 17–February 13	One to two days after you and seller sign escrow papers, loan package is sent to lender for final review and funding check.
January 18–February 15	One to two days after loan package is sent to lender for final review and funding, a check is sent to escrow holder or local bank. (Closing may be delayed until check is deposited into local bank or otherwise clears.)
January 19–February 16	Escrow closes! Congratulations.

RESOURCE

Where to complain about problems with a loan application. If you have a problem with how your loan application was handled and can't work things out with the lender, document your concerns and be prepared to file a complaint with a regulatory agency. Where you complain depends upon the type of financial institution—for example, whether it's a state-chartered bank or a savings and loan. To find out where to complain, start with the Department of Real Estate. The DRE website is www.dre.ca.gov. Also, contact the Department of Consumer Affairs (800-952-5210 or www.dca.ca.gov). If you feel the lender discriminated against you in the loan application process, contact the Department of Fair Employment and Housing at 800-233-3212 or www.dfeh.ca.gov.

CHAPTER

14

Buying a House When You Already Own One

If you already own a home and plan to sell it before buying another, questions of timing inevitably arise. Is it better to sell your old house before buying a new one? Or vice versa?

If you sell first, you'll be under time pressure to find another house quickly. This is stressful, and you may overpay in an anxious effort not to lose out to another purchaser.

But buying a new house first and then scrambling to sell your old one is no fun, either—especially if you're trading up substantially and need to sell your old house for top dollar to make the down payment on the new one. Being under time constraints to close on the new house, you may accept a lower-than-optimum price on your old house to make a quick sale.

This chapter gives you constructive steps to minimize the psychological and financial down side of selling one house while buying another.

SKIP AHEAD

If you are a first-time buyer or can afford to own two houses at once (even if for just a short period) you can skip this chapter.

RESOURCE

Nolo's book for home sellers. *For Sale by Owner in California*, by George Devine (a coauthor of this book), provides practical, easy-to-use forms and the legal, financial, and real estate knowledge needed to sell your house—on your own or with the help of a broker.

True Story

Mary Advises: Listen to Grandpa

In selling my house and buying another, I remembered my grandfather saying always, "Buy low and sell high." To accomplish this, he explained, you must get time on your side. People pay top dollar when they're pressed for time and get a bargain when they can be patient.

So the question became, how could I apply Grandpa's advice to my situation? To avoid selling my house in a hurry in order to pay for a new one, I called my dad and asked for a short-term loan. He helped some. Next I called my uncles and a college roommate who has a knack with money. Together they agreed to advance me the rest of what I needed for a few months. Combined with my own savings, this let me make a very chunky down payment (55% of the purchase price) on a new house without the need to sell the old one. I then listed my existing house for sale at an aggressive price, perfectly prepared to have to wait for a while, and maybe even to take less. Instead, I immediately got a full price offer. I was so surprised, I almost forgot to say "yes." By preparing to be patient, I sold for about $25,000 more and bought for about $35,000 less than if I'd been in a hurry.

Check the Housing Market Carefully

Before you put your house on the market or commit to buying a new one, carefully investigate the sales prices of houses in the markets where you'll be selling and buying. Focus on whether the market is "hot" (favors sellers) or "cold" (favors buyers). Judging the relative temperature of the market is important to buyers and sellers and is crucial for people who are both. Your dual position lets you adopt a strategy of protecting yourself in your weaker role while letting your stronger role take care of itself.

CAUTION

Market conditions in California change frequently. Don't assume you know how to price your house, even if you bought it just last year.

Strategies in a Seller's Market

If sellers have the advantage in the communities where you both now own and plan to buy, selling your current house will likely be easier than buying a new one. Thus, you want to compete aggressively in purchasing a new house, while insisting on maximum flexibility as to the date you move out of your present house.

You can guarantee yourself this leeway by stipulating that the sale of your current house be contingent upon your finding and closing on a new one. When a buyer makes an offer on your house, include in your written counteroffer a provision spelling this out. Although few buyers will agree to an open-ended period, some will be so anxious to buy your house that they'll agree to delay the closing until you close on a new house or until a certain number of days pass, whichever comes first. In hot markets, buyers may even let the seller live rent-free in the home for two to four weeks.

Is the Market Hot or Cold?

Here's how to take the temperature of a particular housing market (see Chapter 15 for more details):

- If many more people want to buy than to sell, it's a hot, seller's market. Prices tend to rise (often quickly), and buyers must bid competitively (read: high) and have their financing lined up (and be preapproved) in advance.
- If sellers outnumber buyers the market is cold and favors buyers. Sellers often must court buyers by lowering prices and offering innovative financing packages. (See Chapter 12.) In new housing developments, sellers often offer to pay a portion of the buyer's monthly mortgage. (See Chapter 7.)

Because markets can change (sometimes very quickly), it's crucial to have current information. Pay careful attention to media reports on upward and downward trends in local real estate markets.

EXAMPLE: Roberta plans to sell her house. Both where she now lives and where she hopes to buy a home are hot (seller's) markets. She puts her current house on the market, making the sale contingent upon closing on her new house. A number of potential buyers surface, and the highest bidder is agreeable to waiting a reasonable time but balks at an open-ended contingency. Roberta agrees to move out either when she closes on another house or after 120 days pass from the closing on her present house, whichever occurs first.

Although she remains under a degree of time pressure, four months should be enough time to find a good new place, especially given that she got such a great price on the sale of her old one.

Strategies in a Buyer's Market

In a buyer's market, with lots of sellers, your position as a buyer is the stronger one. Consider protecting yourself by making your offer to buy contingent upon your selling your current house. A seller having a hard time finding a buyer is likely to accept this contingency, even though it means waiting.

Be ready for the seller to counter with a "wipe-out" or release clause. This lets the seller accept your offer, but keeps the house on the market, with the requirement that the seller give you written notice if he or she receives another offer and wants to accept it. Then, within 72 hours (or whatever length of time your agreement says), you must satisfy all contingencies and proceed with the purchase, or your offer is wiped out, and the seller can proceed with other offers.

In this situation, a wipe-out clause is not unreasonable, as the seller needs some way to get out of a deal if you never sell your house. We discuss wipe-out clauses in more detail in Chapter 18, After the Contract Is Signed.

EXAMPLE: Ronald and Phil would like to purchase a larger house than the one they already own, but houses are moving slowly. When they find a house they want to buy, they make their offer contingent upon their selling their old house. The seller accepts, but insists on including a 96-hour wipe-out clause, to take effect 30 days after the contract is signed. This means that once 30 days pass, the seller can accept other offers, contingent upon giving Ronald and Phil 96 hours' notice to satisfy (or eliminate) the requirement that they sell their existing house and go ahead with the deal.

Sometimes, the offer is made contingent upon arranging financing. This usually has the same effect as making your offer contingent on selling your present house. Unless you have large savings, a lender won't normally approve financing on a new purchase until the sale of the old house is made and the down payment money is in hand, or at least until the lender is confident that your present house is priced fairly and will sell soon.

Renting Your Own House

When you sell your house contingent upon moving into a new one, you have two options if you need more time to move.

Becoming a tenant. One option is to become a tenant in your old house. Here are a few hints on how to handle this:

- You and the new owner should sign a written rental agreement. A copy is available on the CD included with *The California Landlord's Law Book: Rights & Responsibilities*, by David Brown, Ralph Warner, and Janet Portman (Nolo). Modify the agreement to pay by the month but only require seven days' written notice to move, rather than the normal 30 days.
- Your daily rent should be the buyer's daily carrying costs (mortgage principal and interest, taxes, and insurance). This will be considerably higher than what you paid to live in that house (your old mortgage), but the interest you earn on the cash proceeds of the sale will offset this to a degree. In addition, it will probably be less than if you had to move to a temporary place, and it saves you the trouble of moving twice.

Delaying the closing. Another possible option is to put off the closing. As long as you are confident the buyer won't try to back out, this can make sense for two reasons. As an owner, you can deduct mortgage interest and property taxes; as a tenant, you can't. As a tenant, your rent will be figured at the new owner's higher costs. Of course, you will have a pile of money in the bank from the sale, but its true value won't equal your higher costs as a tenant.

Renting out your old house. Finally, if you're having a difficult time selling your house—and you must move into your new home right away—consider finding a tenant to rent your old house. Use the rent payments to cover your old mortgage and make your new purchase financially feasible. Try to make the rental temporary, and keep trying to sell your old house—assuming you anticipate a profit. Consult your tax adviser for tax consequences of renting out your old house. For advice on being a landlord, see *The California Landlord's Law Book: Rights & Responsibilities*, by David Brown, Ralph Warner, and Janet Portman (Nolo).

Save Money on Real Estate Commissions

If you're selling and buying in the same area, consider using the same real estate agent to sell your current house and buy a new one. If you do, you may well be able to save money on the typical 5%–7% commission sellers pay the listing agent, by negotiating a lower rate. Remember, even a 1% or 2% savings is a lot of money.

Bridge Financing: How to Briefly Own Two Houses

No matter how carefully you time things, you may not perfectly dovetail the sale of one house with the purchase of another. You may own no houses, in which case you'll have money in the bank and will need a temporary place to live, or you may own two houses at once. The following suggestions should help you pull this off:

- **Raise as much money as possible for the down payment on a new house.** If your savings, without the sale, put the second house within reach, maximize your cash, perhaps by charging living expenses or getting an advance from your employer. Although the interest on credit cards is high, you'll be able to pay bills off promptly when your existing house sells.
- **Borrow down payment money from family or friends.** Point out that you need help for only a short period, and offer a competitive interest rate. (In Chapters 4, Raising Money for Your Down Payment,

True Story

Jenny and Gregg: We Had to Act Fast

We found the house to buy so fast, we were late getting in gear to sell our existing house. We knew the sellers of the house we planned to buy wanted a quick, easy sale, and we would look good to them only as long as we appeared ready to close. If we tried to make the purchase contingent on our selling our existing house, they'd lose interest.

Instead, we agonized for a bit and said "yes." Immediately, we put our existing house on the market. Unfortunately, it was harder than we expected to sell at the high price we wanted. We faced the possibility of owning two houses at once. Rather than panic and sell our existing house cheap, we lined up a bridge loan from a bank but held off making the final commitment, which would have cost a lot in fees. We then lowered our asking price slightly, to awaken buyer interest. It worked. The house sold at a still-very-good price, in time for us to make the closings simultaneous. We may have done better if we took the bridge loan and held out for a higher price, but with two kids and two jobs, the last thing we wanted to worry about was owning two houses.

and 12, Private Mortgages, we discuss borrowing from private sources.)

- **Get an equity line of credit in advance.** For a small application fee and annual fee, you can arrange a line of credit to be ready if you need to draw on it. Most lenders won't ask why you need the line of credit, but if they do, they don't like hearing you're essentially looking for a bridge loan. Make sure there are no prepayment penalties if you sell your home.
- **Get a bridge loan from a financial institution.** If you have no other choice, you can normally borrow money from a financial institution to "bridge" the period between when you close on your new house and when you get your money from the sale of your old one. We say "no other choice" because bridge loans can be expensive. Lenders often charge a host of up-front points or fees for credit checks, appraisals, loan originations, and physical inspections. These can amount to 5%–15% of the amount borrowed. On $50,000, that's $2,500–$7,500. This wouldn't be unreasonable if you needed the money for a long time and spread the cost over many years. It's very expensive, however, if you need money for only a few months.

This is an area where a loan broker who specializes in matching house buyers and appropriate mortgage lenders should be able to help.

What to Look for When Shopping for a Bridge Loan

- The lender from whom you obtain your financing for your new house may offer you a less-expensive home equity bridge loan than other lenders. Ask about this possibility before committing to a long-term mortgage.
- When applying for a bridge loan, ask the lender to waive inspection and appraisal of your existing house. If the equity in that house is much larger than the bridge you need, the lender may do this. Also ask that the lender not charge points.
- If you purchased or refinanced your existing house only a few years ago, find your paperwork. Some lenders will accept a recent appraisal, physical inspection, or title report in lieu of charging you for new ones.
- If you don't know whether you'll need a home equity bridge loan until the last minute, see if you qualify for a standby personal line of credit. Although interest rates are higher than on a bridge loan (and nondeductible), up-front costs are minimal.
- Consider working with an experienced loan broker. (See Chapter 13 for tips on finding a good one.)

Tax Breaks for Selling Your Home

The 1997 Taxpayer Relief Act contained a big break for homeowners. If you sell your home, you may exclude up to $250,000 of your capital gain from tax. Joint owners may divide their gain and exclude up to $250,000 per person. For married couples filing jointly, the exclusion is $500,000.

The law (I.R.C. (Title 26) § 121) applies to sales after May 6, 1997. To claim the whole exclusion, you must have owned and lived in your residence an aggregate of at least two of five years before the sale, and it must be your main home, not a vacation or second home (this rule is called the "ownership and use" test). You can claim the exclusion once every two years.

Even if you haven't lived in your home a total of two years out of the last five, you are still eligible for a partial exclusion of capital gains if you sold because of a change in employment, health, or unforeseen circumstances. You get a portion of the exclusion, based on the portion of the two-year period you lived there. To calculate it, take the number of months you lived there before the sale and divide it by 24.

RESOURCE

More information on tax laws involving real estate transactions. Contact the IRS at 800-829-1040; or visit www.irs.gov. See IRS Publication 523, *Selling Your Home.*

California Property Tax Relief

As a result of the California initiative of the mid-1970s, Proposition 13, property taxes are levied on the assessed value as of March 1, 1975, or the purchase price at any later transfer date, with exceptions for certain intrafamily transfers—for example, between spouses or between parents and children. For people who've owned homes for many years, their values are comparatively low. When they sell that house and purchase another, however, they pay property taxes on the price of the house being bought, which is likely to be higher than the one being sold.

To help older and disabled people deal with this, California law lets owners over age 55 (only one spouse of a married couple need qualify), or owners who are severely or permanently disabled, who sell one house and purchase another within two years in the same county, transfer their old tax assessment rate to the new house. (Revenue and Tax Code § 69.5.) Transferring the tax assessment intercounty is possible if you move to a county that participates in the statewide transfer system. The county tax assessor can tell you whether or not your county participates.

To qualify for this tax break, the new house must be of equal or lesser value than the old house. Check with your county tax assessor to see if the law applies when you contemplate your transaction.

For information on state taxes, contact the Franchise Tax Board at 800-852-5711, or check their website at www.ftb.ca.gov.

CHAPTER

15

What Will You Offer?

This chapter assumes that you've found a house you like and have the financial resources to buy it. Now you must decide how much to offer and what other terms to include in your offer.

How a Contract Is Formed

A contract to transfer ownership requires that one party make a specific, written, legal offer to buy or sell a particular piece of property and the other person legally accept it in writing.

The first legally binding offer in a real estate sale is usually made in writing by the prospective buyer. Legally binding means that the offer is specific (lays out the price and other terms) and the seller has the opportunity to accept it in writing either before it is withdrawn or the time period for its acceptance runs out. The seller isn't obligated to accept, even if the offer is for the full asking price, as long as the refusal isn't motivated by an intent to discriminate. (He or she may be under pressure to sell with a full price offer, however, because the contract with the broker probably guarantees the broker a commission if the seller gets such an offer.)

Decide What You Will Offer

In putting together your actual offer, consider the following factors:

- the advertised price of the house
- what you can afford
- prices for comparable houses
- whether the local real estate market is hot or cold
- whether the house itself is hot or cold
- the seller's needs
- whether the house is uniquely valuable to you
- how much you're willing to pay, and
- nonmonetary ways of making your offer attractive.

Let's consider each in brief.

What Is the Advertised Price?

A seller's advertised price should be treated as only a rough estimate of what the seller would like to receive. Some sellers deliberately overprice, others ask for pretty close to what they hope to get, and those in the most competitive markets underprice their houses in the hope that potential buyers will compete and overbid.

In considering the list price of a house you're serious about, take the time to learn about the seller's personality. Here are a few of the more common seller profiles.

Optimistic Charlie. Arrogant and optimistic, he tends to believe that his house is especially valuable and is like to price it way above what comparable houses are selling for: as much as 30%–40% more, although 10%–25% is more typical. Unfortunately, some Optimistic Charlies are encouraged by brokers or agents so anxious to get the listing that they "romance" Charlie into believing that his house will fetch an inflated price. But FSBO (For Sale By Owner) sellers are also notoriously prone to this.

Straightforward William. William prices his house at exactly what he believes it's worth, not a dollar more, nor a dollar less. William may be stubborn if offered less than the asking price, but he may accommodate a buyer on other terms of the deal. For example, if a physical inspection turns up structural problems, William might agree to pay for $10,000 of needed work in the form of a credit in escrow if the buyer pays the asking price, rather than lower his asking price by $5,000.

Canny Cynthia. Cynthia deliberately underprices her house. Her plan is to excite a feeding frenzy among bargain hunters, who'll bid against each other so furiously that the winner will pay more than the house is worth. This strategy works best in hot real estate markets when competition is fierce. (See "Is the Local Real Estate Market Hot or Cold?" below.)

TIP

Don't be suckered by too low a price. It's tough not to get excited when a house comes on the market with a "too good to be true" price. But keep in mind that loads of other aspiring purchasers will spot the same bargain. Don't get into a bidding war that only the seller will win.

Is Underpricing Ethical?

Why would a home seller (or a real estate agent) ask less for a home than it's really worth? To attract more lookers, create excitement, and generate a bidding war, of course.

Frustrated would-be buyers sometimes consult lawyers, hoping to find that sellers are obligated to accept the first offer at the full asking price. They're not.

The present consensus within the real estate community seems to be that pricing a tad under the market to attract a slightly larger pool of buyers is not a big deal; it's when a home is deliberately listed significantly below its true market value (say, a $500,000 home is listed at $399,000) that something is not right. We believe that it's unethical for a seller to put a house on the market at a price they'd never accept. (These sellers can often be identified by the listing comment "Seller reserves the right to refuse all offers.") Your best recourse, however, is to know the market and not waste your time bidding list price for a deliberately underpriced house.

How Much Can You Afford?

Chapter 2 focuses on how to determine how much house you can afford, based on your income, savings, and nonhousing long-term debts. Once you know your maximum, lower the number a little, to allow for the following additional expenses:

Closing costs. Your share will be about 2%–5% of the purchase price. (See Chapter 18 for details.)

Moving expenses. The amount depends on how much stuff you have to move, how far you're moving it, and how much you'll do yourself. If you plan on hiring a mover, get an estimate and add about 25%.

Redecorating. Keep a few dollars to redecorate with. If the house you buy hasn't had a facelift recently, you'll probably want to paint it, at least.

Two months' mortgage payments. The lender will probably want to see that you have two or three months of mortgage payments in the bank, as a cushion in case anything goes wrong like you losing your job.

What Are Prices of Comparable Houses?

Before making an offer, you should know the recent selling prices of comparable houses. If you've been looking for only a short time, or in other areas, you have some research to do. If you're working with an experienced agent, he or she should be able to provide you with the information, preferably laid out in a handy spreadsheet.

Real estate appraisers have developed the following sensible guidelines to distinguish comparable houses from others:

- A comparable sale should have occurred within the last three to six months (the more recent, the better). If prices are fluctuating quickly, comps should be on sales within the last 30 to 60 days. In extremely volatile markets, you'll need to compare prices of houses where sales are still pending.
- A comparable sale should be for a house quite similar to the one you're interested in. Look for houses of similar age, in comparable locations, and with a similar number of rooms, square feet, and similar yard size. In the real world, however, comparisons often must be made between houses that are somewhat different. A physically comparable house a few blocks away might be in a better school district or have a great view, which will raise the property's value. The more difference between houses, the less valuable the comparison.
- A comparable sale should be within six to ten blocks of the house you want to buy. The boundaries should be adjusted if the neighborhood changes significantly in a shorter radius, for example, if a major freeway marks a border between two different residential areas.

Realtors®' Comp Information

Usually, the best comparable sales data are in a Board of Realtors® database for the geographical area where you're looking (accessible by your agent). The database will list the sales price of houses that sold recently. We discuss the Multiple Listing Service, comp databases, and other services offered by local Boards of Realtors® in Chapter 5.

How to Analyze Prices of Current Listings and Pending Sales

Houses pending sale (still in escrow) are listed in the Realtors' Multiple Listing database and are noted in appraisal reports—but the actual sales price is not listed until the transaction closes. To find out the prices of houses pending sale, your real estate agent may need to call the broker who represents the seller of the pending sale you're interested in.

The asking prices of homes still on the market can also provide guidance. Despite the fact that asking prices don't tell you what a house will eventually sell for, they can give you some idea of the range of market values in your area.

Property Profiles From Title Companies

If you can't get access to a comp database, ask a local title company for help. You can either provide them with the street addresses of comparable sales and they'll give you the prices, or ask them to print out information on all sales on certain named streets or map sectors. You can also get detailed information on specific property (a property profile). Property profiles are often free if you've done business with the title company or it thinks you may in the future.

Checking Deeds at the County Recorder's Office

Comparable sales information is also available at the county recorder's office. You need to know the street name or the name of the buyer (grantee) or seller (grantor) of a particular property. If you don't know either, you can find out the seller's name at the county assessor's office. You then look up the deed in either the grantor or the grantee index.

When you find the deed, note the documentary transfer tax, located in the upper right-hand corner. The basic documentary transfer tax is $1.10 per $1,000 of price, except in cities and counties with local surtaxes. The sales price is figured from this transfer tax. You can use this technique to find out how much the current owner of the property originally paid and when he bought the house.

CAUTION

The documentary transfer tax may not reflect the full price paid by the buyer. If the buyer assumed loans held by the seller, this amount won't be included.

Comparable Sales Prices Available Online

A few private companies now offer detailed comparable sales prices for many areas of California, based on information from county recorder's offices and property assessors, notably:

- Zillow, www.zillow.com
- SmartHomeBuy, www.smarthomebuy.com, and
- www.homeradar.com.

Zillow and homeradar are free. By entering your prospective new home's address on both websites, you can collect a fair amount of information, including an estimate of that house's value, each comparable house's address and location on an aerial photo, purchase price, year built, sales date, square footage, and numbers of bedrooms and bathrooms. In addition, SmartHomeBuy offers a free preliminary report that tells you your prospective home's assessed value and zoned use.

All of this information will help you decide which recently sold homes are truly comparable to the one in which you're interested, and how much a fair sales price would therefore be.

Is the Local Real Estate Market Hot or Cold?

To know whether the market you're in is hot or cold, you'll need to closely follow the local residential real estate market for an extended period. This involves visiting lots of houses and reading MLS and comparative sales listings. If you don't have time to get this "up to the elbows" sort of knowledge, consult with one or more experienced local real estate people.

To do your own temperature research, keep in mind these rules:

- If 25% or more of the houses sell within a week or ten days of being listed, the market is hot.
- If more than 40% of the houses listed sold for more than the listing price, the market is sizzling.
- If more than half of the houses were on the market a month or more before selling, and most sold for less than their listing price, the market is cool.
- If the supply of houses on the market is steadily increasing, sales are slow, and prices of the houses you're looking at have decreased more than once, the market is cold.

EXAMPLE: Thad falls in love with a house listed at $425,000, in a marginal neighborhood adjacent to a much nicer one. A comparable house in the upscale area sells for $575,000.

If houses are selling relatively slowly, and the house he wants has been on the market for a month or more, Thad can probably offer less, perhaps even much less, than the asking price. If houses are selling briskly, however, and the house he likes is new to the market (and reasonably priced, given the comparable sales data), he should offer close to the asking price. In a very hot market, he may even want to bid slightly more to preempt other offers and avoid a bidding war.

Another good long-term gauge of a market's temperature is the level of current mortgage interest rates. As rates jump substantially (usually one percentage point or more), most housing markets begin to cool—although just as rates begin to rise, people may rush to buy, hoping to lock in before rates climb even higher. Conversely, as rates drop, more people can afford houses, and the market perks up.

Chapter 17 includes several strategies for bidding on houses in a competitive market.

Is the House Itself Hot or Cold?

At least as important as determining the local housing market temperature is figuring out the "temperature" of the particular house you want to buy. For many reasons, a particular house may be more or less attractive (hotter or colder) than those surrounding it. Here are some questions to ask:

- **How long has the house been on the market?** If it's more than 30 days, you can probably buy it for less than the asking price.
- **Has the asking price dropped?** If it has been reduced once and it still hasn't sold (give it a month), the house is an icicle and may be ready for another reduction.
- **Does the house have serious structural problems requiring a hefty cash infusion?** If so, the house, even if otherwise attractive, may be hard to sell. If you have cash or can finance the purchase privately, the house may be yours. (See Chapter 3 for more on buying a house with structural problems.)
- **Has the seller, or perhaps the listing agent, tipped you off that a lower offer will be considered?** If you're told that the seller needs to sell quickly to close on a new house, because of a divorce or to move far away, you're almost surely being told to try a lower offer. Or, if a real estate agent says the seller "hopes to receive" a certain amount, the agent is saying that the seller is being unrealistic and that a lower offer will probably be accepted.
- **Has the seller set a cut-off date by which all offers must be made?** This can be a good indication that the house is hot, and you may have to bid aggressively to get it. But be careful—the seller and his agent may create a bidding war, or at least the appearance of one. A seller may state that "five offers will be made" (or that "many people are considering bidding"), when only one or two are serious.
- **Is the house an ugly duckling?** In a hot market, interest in an unattractive house is likely to be lukewarm; in a cool market, icy. If you find a dowdy place you know how to turn into a swan, keep your passion to yourself and bid relatively low. (Again, see Chapter 3 for more on buying a homely house.)
- **How eager is the seller to sell?** It's to your advantage to figure out where the seller is coming from. For example, if you see a house where the price has been reduced substantially after only one month on the market, chances are the owner is anxious to sell and may be willing to reduce the price further.
- **Is the house very expensive?** The biggest fluctuations in price occur at the luxury end of the market. Houses that sell for $3 million at the very top of a market can often be purchased for 30% to 50% less during the next recession. And, of course, the opposite is also true. The problem, of course, is that it's very difficult to accurately time economic cycles. As a general rule, avoid markets that have been going up for more than five years—but jump on those that have been going down for more than two.

What Are the Seller's Needs?

Historically, the real estate business is structured to keep buyer and seller at arm's length. Unfortunately, this tradition can work to your disadvantage. You want to be able to size up the seller and structure your offer and your negotiating strategy accordingly, but obviously you can't if you never meet.

Sometimes you can make friendly contact at an open house, if the seller is present. Follow up with a phone call (or a knock on the door) to ask a few questions that the agent wouldn't be expected to know the answer to. There's the danger that the seller will be annoyed. But if you're as pleasant as you are persistent, you may make contact and learn a lot.

Your agent may also be able to glean useful information by talking to the seller's agent, such as how much room there is to negotiate on price or other items. Also, you may gain valuable insights by chatting with the neighbors while legitimately checking out the neighborhood. If you have school-age children, talk to neighbors with kids about local schools. In casual conversation, they're likely to tell you why the seller is moving and lots of other useful information.

For example, sellers likely to want to close on the deal quickly, even if it means taking a lower price, include those who:

- have accepted a job in a different area
- have made an offer on another house contingent on selling the existing one
- are older people selling a long-time family home (sometimes with the help of a younger relative or friend)
- are families with small children, who have enough to think about without the disruptions of the home-marketing process
- are divorcing or going through other major life changes, such as a loss of a job or retirement
- have inherited a house they don't plan to live in, or
- need a new home because of an expanded family.

We are not advocating taking advantage of a seller in distress. But, nevertheless, it's only common sense to find out if a seller needs to close quickly. If so, you may find a good house for a very reasonable price.

Is the House Uniquely Valuable to You?

A house's worth on the market isn't necessarily the same as its worth to you. A modest house listed at a reasonable price, for example, may be a bargain if you have three kids, the house is in a city that has excellent public schools, and the lot is large enough to add on a couple of rooms. The same house, however, may be overpriced for a couple not planning to have children.

How Much Are You Willing to Pay?

Okay, now for the last and most important consideration. How much money do you really want to pay for the house? While tactical considerations (the temperature of the market, the seller's needs) are important, nothing should outweigh your own honest assessment of how much you are willing to fork over.

Going through this valuation process is particularly important in overheated markets where real estate agents are likely to urge you to increase your offer. Deciding in advance how much you'll spend and then sticking to your convictions can help you avoid overpaying.

CAUTION

Find out whether the house will be hard to insure before you bid high—or bid at all. Insuring a house with a history of problems, particularly from mold or water damage, has become surprisingly difficult. To find out what claims the seller and previous owner have made, request what's known as a "CLUE" report (Comprehensive Loss Underwriting Exchange) from the seller. These reports can also be obtained from www.propertyid.com (their website is difficult—best to call them, 800-626-0106), but you'll need the seller's written permission first.

Don't Stretch Your Finances Too Far

Many real estate people urge buyers to plow every possible dollar into a house. This can be a mistake, especially if you can afford a nice house that meets your needs but instead choose to pour a lot of money into a fancier one. Once you invest money in a house, it's very difficult and costly to try to get it back out.

Why are we cautious? Anyone familiar with the California housing market knows that family problems are commonly traced to paying too much for houses, leaving inadequate money for other needs. A devastating illness or loss of work means a large house payment will be almost impossible to make. People who refuse to stretch their finances to the limit, however, have money for other uses, including paying for the kids' private school and taking an occasional vacation.

True Story

Art: I Got a Bargain Without Being Too Greedy

I was on a tight budget when house hunting, and excited when a bargain surfaced. An acquaintance was moving out of the country and needed to sell his two-bedroom bungalow quickly. After visiting the house, and based on looking at dozens of houses in the area, I guessed that it was worth close to $425,000. The seller indicated he'd take about $385,000 for a quick sale.

Then I heard that another person was ready to make an offer. My spirits fell. I spoke to my dad, who had worked in real estate years before. His advice was not to be too greedy. "Bid a few thousand more than $385,000." I agonized about the exact amount and bid $392,000. I beat the other bidder by $4,000 and got a super house for the price.

Making the Final Price Decision

The moment of truth has arrived: It's time to look at the many personal and market factors we discussed and come up with a dollar amount that you think is appropriate. There's nothing scientific or absolute about these factors, and you'll ultimately have to decide whether to err on the side of underpaying, at the risk of losing the house—or overpaying, at the risk of paying more than you had to.

> **EXAMPLE:** After a long search, Randy and Lee find a house that meets all their needs. It lists for $310,000 but needs about $28,000 in repairs and fix-up work. They check comparable prices and conclude that if the house were in tip-top shape, it would sell for about $350,000. Though the local market is cold, they believe that the house is competitively priced and will probably sell quickly.
>
> Randy and Lee first lean toward offering the full $310,000, in the hope of preempting other bids, but after looking at how many houses are on the market, they decide to start much lower. They offer $278,800. Although this increases the chance that someone else may get the house, they reason there's only a slight chance of this happening given the structural problems and figure if they can buy the house for between $290,000–$295,000, they have made a good deal. If not, they'll just keep looking.

In a superheated market, submitting lowball offers could backfire. Finding that you've been outbid on house after house, all the while watching house prices spiral further up from what you can afford, is downright depressing. Choosing to bid high may shorten the time, energy, and other costs put into your home search.

Other Ways to Make Your Offer Attractive

Though price is usually the most important part of your offer, the seller will be considering other aspects of the deal as well. Some sellers have even been known to choose a lower-priced offer because it met their other needs. Below are some strategies for making the nonmonetary terms of your offer as appealing as possible; you'll learn more about some of these offer terms in subsequent chapters, which describe the offer contract in detail.

- **Schedule a speedy closing.** If you've got all your financing lined up and are prepared to throw yourself into following up on other parts of the deal such as inspections and appraisals, you may be able to offer a closing date that's a week or two earlier than the typical 30–45 days. That will be attractive to a seller who needs to get money out of the house quickly and move on.
- **Give sellers ample time to move out.** Not all sellers want the deal to be tied up in a hurry. If, for example, your seller still needs to find a new home, you might

offer a long closing period (60 days or more) or allow the seller to continue living in the home after the closing (for a low rent, or even free). If you offer a long closing period, however, make sure that your lender's commitment won't run out during this time.

- **Show good financing prospects.** You'll need to start by being clear about what type of loan you'll apply for and what interest rate you plan to pay, so that the seller can ascertain whether this is realistic in the current market. (The purchase contract we provide in the next chapter will help you with this.) In addition, a preapproval letter from a lender will help show the seller that your financing will go through. And the higher your down payment, the more confidence the seller will have that your loan will go through. Offering a higher-than-normal earnest money deposit (discussed in Chapter 16) can also be used to show the sellers that you're serious about the deal and have the cash to follow through.
- **Offer to pay incidental expenses.** Aside from the cost of the house itself, every home sale requires someone to pay for various incidentals such as escrow fees, a title search, city transfer tax, and the like. These items can range from a few hundred dollars to several thousand. By tradition, the seller usually picks up some of these costs, and the buyer picks up others (discussed in detail in Chapter 16). You could offer to pay for costs traditionally borne by the seller.
- **Write a cover letter.** It has become almost commonplace for prospective buyers to include a cover letter summarizing the main points of their offer and saying a bit about themselves—in particular, why they like the house and that they will take good care of it. You could also mention that you're ready to be flexible about the various terms of the offer. But don't put the seller in a position of having to discriminate in accepting or rejecting your offer, by emphasizing your family composition (which might suggest gender, sexual orientation, or marital status), religion, or ethnicity.
- **Show that you'll be easy to work with.** Chose an agent with a good reputation, or the seller's agent may advise, "Let's avoid this offer, or we'll spend all our time in hardball negotiations." Beyond this, try not to be too demanding in the initial offer. If the seller sees that you're insisting that he or she pay all the transaction fees, purchase a home warranty, and leave the curtains and basketball hoop behind as well, you might be shooting yourself in the foot.
- **Don't unreasonably limit the time by which the seller must accept.** Some buyers (usually egged on by aggressive agents) add a clause to their offer insisting that the seller accept (or reject) the offer "upon presentation" or within a few hours' time. Unfortunately, most sellers feel bullied. You can limit the time during which your offer remains open, but it's better to give the seller at least two or three days.

- **Don't waive the inspection contingencies.** Such a waiver would mean that you take the house without any inspections, or that, even if you conduct an inspection, you won't hold the seller responsible for any defects that are revealed. This is a risky proposition and most likely to be attractive to a seller who knows the home needs work. If you feel you must waive this contingency, ask to send in your own inspector *before* you make an offer.
- **Don't offer an open-ended amount.** Tired of being outbid, buyers have been known to resort to offers along the lines of, "We'll pay $5,000 more than your highest bidder." This is just plain foolhardy. If you are desperate enough to do this, at least put a cap on how high you'll go. Also add a provision giving you the right to review the other offer and preapproval letter to make sure it's legitimate. (However, viewing another buyer's offer materials raises confidentiality issues, and you may have to settle for seeing documents with portions blacked out.)

In Chapters 16 and 17 we delve further into the nitty-gritty of presenting your offer and dealing with counteroffers from the seller.

CHAPTER

16

Putting Your Offer in Writing

This chapter explains what should go into your written purchase offer. The next chapter discusses how to present it to the seller, and suggests good negotiating techniques. Read both chapters carefully even if your real estate agent is preparing the paperwork for you. Many important decisions are being made here, and it's essential that you know how to protect your interests—before signing your offer form. If anything in the offer form isn't clear to you, ask your real estate agent or attorney to explain it.

Although we've provided a sample offer form at the end of this chapter, we're going to assume that you'll use a standard form provided by your real estate agent and probably prepared by the California Association of Realtors® or by a company such as Realty Publications, Inc. or Professional Publishing. For that reason, this chapter will focus on all the topics that a real estate offer form normally covers. You should be able to use our discussion to evaluate any form that your agent uses, bearing in mind that the clauses won't necessarily appear in the same order.

What Makes an Offer Legally Valid

An offer to buy a house is legally useless unless it's in writing, has been delivered to the seller or the seller's agent, and contains specific financial and other terms so that if the seller says "yes," the deal can go through. The seller's acceptance, too, must be in writing.

Real estate offers almost always contain contingencies—events that must happen or else the deal won't become final. For example, your offer may be contingent on your qualifying for financing or the house passing certain physical inspections.

Most offers give the seller a certain period of time within which to accept. During this time, you may revoke (take back) your offer in writing so long as the seller hasn't yet communicated an acceptance to you or your agent. (See Chapter 17, Presenting Your Offer and Negotiating, for more on revoking.)

How Offers and Counteroffers Are Made

Before you look at your offer form, here are a few words on offer terminology and procedures. The exact same form may be called by different names, each with a different legal meaning, depending on when and by whom (buyer or seller) it's used.

- Making an *offer* is when you fill out a purchase agreement form and give it to the seller.
- A *counteroffer* is used by a seller who accepts some of your terms but modifies others. The seller may respond, for example, with a higher price or a shorter time for you to arrange financing. A counteroffer is sometimes (but not always) made using exactly the same form as the buyer's purchase offer, with the title changed to reflect that it's a counteroffer.
- A *multiple counteroffer* is when the seller counters a number of offers simultaneously—though not always identically. The seller may submit a

variety of counteroffers, including different prices, terms, or conditions, to different buyers. The seller will then ask for each buyer's "highest and best" offer in response. As if the seller wasn't already getting a good deal, the seller is likely to draft the counteroffers so as not to become obligated to accept any of the buyers' return offers. You're most likely to encounter this practice in Southern California.

- A *counter counteroffer* is when you accept some of the seller's counteroffer terms but modify others. Again, you can do this using a slightly modified version of the original offer form. (The back-and-forth dance can go on for a while with counter-counter counteroffers, and so forth.)
- The offer becomes a legally binding *contract* when you and the seller agree on all the terms in the offer (or counteroffer, and so forth) and sign it. You can both sign an offer form, or a separate written document stating that all terms of the offer (or counteroffer) are accepted. Not only must you both sign the agreement, you must both also initial every page.

EXAMPLE 1: Mitch gives Patricia a written offer to purchase her house for $750,000, which includes seven days to accept. Two days later, Patricia accepts in writing. A contract has been formed.

EXAMPLE 2: Now assume the same offer from Mitch, but before Patricia says "yes," Mitch finds a house he likes better. He immediately calls Patricia's agent and withdraws his offer. While this revokes his offer, he puts his revocation in writing and drops it off at Patricia's agent's office so there can be no misunderstanding. Mitch's offer has now been withdrawn; Patricia can't call Mitch up and say, "I accept," because no contract can be formed between them unless one or the other makes a second offer and the other accepts it in writing.

What Your Purchase Agreement Should Cover

Below is a review of the clauses traditionally found in a California purchase agreement.

Opening section. Your offer form will start with the obvious stuff: your name and the property's address. If you're married but buying a house using only your separate property (property acquired before marriage, by gift or inheritance during marriage, or after permanent separation), enter only your name. Normally, however, some community property (property acquired by either spouse during marriage, except gifts or inheritances) is used toward the down payment or monthly payments, so your spouse's name should also appear on the offer. (For more on this subject, see Chapter 20, Legal Ownership: How to Take Title.)

The street number, city, county, and state are sufficient for the address—a legal description isn't required. If the property has no street address, do your best to describe it ("the ten-acre Norris Ranch on County Road 305, two miles south of Andersonville").

You'll also be asked early on to state the purchase price you're offering, both written out (such as "four hundred seventeen thousand") and numerically ($417,000).

Also specify how soon escrow will close after the seller accepts your offer (in other words, the date on which you'll finalize the deal and the house will become yours). Be sure to give yourself ample time to remove all contingencies, such as arranging financing and inspections. Chapter 18 contains details on opening and closing escrow and tips on choosing a closing date.

Financial terms. Time to talk money—not just what you're offering, but how you can get out of the deal if your intended financing doesn't come through. The agreement should cover:

- **Your deposit.** You'll normally accompany your offer with an "earnest money" deposit, the amount of which should be stated here. If the seller accepts your offer, he or she will bank the deposit and may be able to keep it as damages if you back out of the deal for a reason not allowed by the contract. The deposit is usually about 1%–3% of the purchase price or sometimes a flat $1,000–$2,000 for lower-priced houses. The seller may counteroffer and ask for more. We advise limiting your initial deposit to 1%–2% of the purchase price. Also indicate the form of the deposit (personal check is most common).
- **Any increase to your deposit.** Buyers commonly increase the amount of the deposit after the offer is accepted, typically after 17 days or after removing the inspection contingencies (covered elsewhere in the agreement). For example, you might make an initial deposit of 1% of the purchase price and increase it to 3% upon removal of inspection contingencies.
- **Terms of the loans you'll be seeking.** If you already have your financing lined up, this will be easy. If a paragraph doesn't apply, enter N/A (for not applicable) in the blank. If you're applying for a government loan, be ready to demonstrate to the seller that you're eligible.
- **Down payment.** Specify your proposed down payment balance—your total down payment less your deposit and deposit increase.
- **Total.** Your deposit, loans, and the down payment should total up to your offer price.
- **Financing time limits and contingencies.** For your and the seller's protection, you'll need to state the number of days within which you'll provide a copy of your loan approval (if you have to start from scratch, expect to spend several weeks getting this); provide verification that you can pay the down payment and closing costs; arrange your financing and remove the loan contingency; and get the property appraised and remove the appraisal contingency.

Occupancy. You'll need to indicate whether you intend to occupy the property as your primary residence. The seller is interested in this because if you plan to rent out the property, you may have a harder time getting a loan. The agreement may also cover situations where tenants already live in the property, in which case you may agree to allow them to continue living there or propose a time by which they must move out.

Note that you buy subject to the tenants' rights and existing rental agreements. Many tenants will move on their own when they find out the house is being sold. In rent control areas, however, a long-term tenant with low rent may resist. After escrow closes, you may have to bring an eviction action on the grounds that you intend to occupy the house yourself.

Rent Control in California

About 15 California cities (listed below) have rent control ordinances, which may restrict the rent the owner can charge a tenant, as well as control the owner's rights and responsibilities. While this is most relevant with multiunit buildings, it can decrease the value of houses likely to be rented in the future. Even if you're not planning to rent your home now, your life may change. Rent control cities currently include:

Berkeley	Hayward	San Francisco
Beverly Hills	Los Angeles	San Jose
Campbell*	Los Gatos	Santa Monica
East Palo Alto	Oakland	Thousand Oaks
Fremont*	Palm Springs	West Hollywood
Gardena*		

* Rent not actually controlled, but landlord must agree to mediate over any increases.

RESOURCE

Buying property subject to tenants' rights or rental property? See *The California Landlord's Law Book: Rights and Responsibilities*, by David Brown, Ralph Warner, and Janet Portman (Nolo).

Although you'll probably want to take possession of the property on the day escrow closes, be prepared to give this up during your negotiations. Many sellers who are buying another house insist on not moving out until 60–90 days after escrow closes, normally in exchange for paying you rent. Some sellers who are renting new places won't want to move out until the first of the month when their lease begins—they, too, will pay you rent.

If you end up agreeing that the seller can stay on more than just a few days after closing, we suggest you and the seller sign a written rental agreement specifying a daily rent or security deposit, authorizing a final inspection, and indicating the rental term (length). (See Chapter 14 for resources on rental agreements.) Make sure your homeowners' insurance covers their stay; if not, you may need to buy rental insurance. The agreement should also state that you expect a per-day charge of your prorated monthly carrying costs.

Who pays for what costs. Your offer should indicate those items you agree to pay for, those you want the seller to pay for, and those you propose to split. Don't feel compelled to pay for every item—a lot depends on the particular house and market.

Use the chart below, "Who Pays for What," as a guide to how expenses are commonly

Who Pays for What		
Item	**Who usually pays**	**Comments**
Escrow fees	Buyer customarily pays in northern California, seller in southern California	Not uncommon for fees to be divided
Title search	Buyer customarily pays in northern California, seller in southern California	Buyer benefits—not unreasonable for buyer to pay
Title insurance for buyer/owner	Buyer customarily pays in northern California, seller in southern California	Buyer benefits—not unreasonable for buyer to pay
Title insurance for lender	Buyer	Buyer benefits—buyer should pay
Deed preparation fee	Buyer	Buyer benefits—buyer should pay
Notary fee	Buyer usually pays for grant and trust deeds; seller usually pays for reconveyance deed on the property	Grant and trust deeds help buyer purchase and finance property; seller receives reconveyance deed when paying off existing mortgage
Recording fee	Buyer usually pays for grant and trust deeds; seller usually pays for reconveyance deed on the property	Grant and trust deeds help buyer purchase and finance property; seller receives reconveyance deed when paying off existing mortgage
Attorney's fee (if attorney hired to clarify title)	Whoever hired attorney	
Documentary transfer tax	Seller usually pays except in probate sales, where buyer is usually required to pay by the terms of the notice of sale	
City transfer tax	Buyer and seller usually share the cost	
Pest control inspection report	Buyer usually picks inspector and pays for inspection in northern California; seller often has property inspected before listing it for sale in southern California	In southern California, lenders usually won't process buyer's loan application without termite inspection because termites are a serious problem; if seller didn't do inspection, buyer should pay to assure that report meets buyer's standard
General contractor report	Buyer usually picks inspector and pays for inspection	Buyer should pay to assure that report meets buyer's standard
Roof inspection report	Buyer usually picks inspector and pays	Buyer should pay to assure that report for inspection meets buyer's standard

Who Pays for What (continued)		
Item	**Who usually pays**	**Comments**
Other inspections	Buyer usually picks inspector and pays for inspection	Buyer should pay to assure that report meets buyer's standard
One-year home warranty	Seller	Sometimes seller offers to purchase a policy when listing the property—if seller doesn't, buyer can purchase one if desired or negotiate this as part of the contract
Real estate tax, Fire insurance, Bond liens (unless able to be paid off)	Buyer and seller usually prorate as of the date the deed is recorded (see these expenses listed in Clause 5)	Both parties benefit; should be prorated

divided. It's quite all right for you and the seller to agree to a different arrangement from that shown on the chart.

Escrow. Escrow is a process in which a disinterested third party, usually a title or escrow company, transfers the funds and documents among the buyer, the seller, and their lenders, in accordance with instructions provided by the buyer and seller (or their agents). (Escrow is described more thoroughly in Chapter 18.)

The standard contract will give you a place to enter the name and address of the escrow holder you choose. It's wise to do some preliminary investigation beforehand, so that you'll have at least a tentative idea about which company you'll use. However, if the seller has already set up a "listing escrow" with a company (a preliminary step that some take to speed up the process by a week or so), the expectation is that you'll use that company. There's little reason to argue, unless you've heard something negative about the company the seller has chosen. But if you're buying and selling a house in the same area, you'll ideally want to use the same escrow holder for both properties, to coordinate the closings.

Disclosures. Some parts of the standard offer form don't need to be filled out—for example, clauses intended to alert you to the seller's obligation to give you various disclosure statements within a certain time. Some of these seller disclosure statements are generic (like a pamphlet on lead-paint hazards), while others are specific to the property (the "Real Estate Transfer Disclosure Statement").

If you're buying a condo or a house in a planned development, the seller should provide you with all the rules and regulations, financial documents, and other pertinent paperwork. Study them carefully—you'll have an opportunity to cancel the agreement if you're not happy with them.

What Sellers Must Tell You About Registered Sex Offenders (Megan's Law)

Home sales contracts entered into after July 1, 1999 must include a notice, in eight-point type (at least), regarding the availability of a database maintained by law enforcement authorities on the location of registered sex offenders. (Civil Code § 2079.10a.)

The seller or broker is not required to provide additional information about the proximity of registered sex offenders. The law states, however, that it does not change the existing responsibilities of sellers and real estate brokers to make disclosures of "material facts" that would affect the "value and desirability" of a property. This arguably means that a seller or broker who knew for a fact that a registered sex offender lived nearby would be responsible for disclosing this "material" fact to the buyer. Since the law isn't clear, you should, if concerned, check the database yourself.

The California Department of Justice provides detailed information on Megan's Law and how to obtain information on sex offenders in your neighborhood (www.meganslaw.ca.gov).

Condition of property. Your offer contract should require the seller to keep the property in its current condition until you take possession. You will also require the seller to clear out all personal belongings and debris.

Fixtures included in the sale. Fixtures are items permanently attached to real property, like built-in appliances or bookshelves, chandeliers, and drapery rods (though usually not the drapes). If removing the item would cause damage, chances are it's a fixture. On the other hand, if the item is easily removed—like a refrigerator that can be unplugged and wheeled away—it's not a fixture, no matter how much it looks like a natural part of the house. Fixtures come with the house unless you and the seller agree that the seller can remove them.

Personal property included in the sale. Personal property doesn't come with the house unless the seller agrees in writing to include it. If the seller promises to include items such as rugs, beds, aboveground swimming pools, or appliances that aren't built in, list them in the agreement.

Title. This standard clause assures you that title to the house will be "clear" when you take possession. Someone will need to order a preliminary title report, either you or the seller (this differs based on local custom). If any clouds on the title are revealed in the preliminary report, and the seller is unable to clear up these difficulties before the close of escrow or you can't obtain a title insurance policy, you have the right to get out of the contract. We discuss checking out the title in Chapter 18.

Sale contingent on selling your property. Contingencies are conditions that either the seller or buyer must meet (or the other party must waive) before the deal will close. Once both of you have agreed that the other party has met all contingencies (that is, you've "removed" the contingency or, if you're no longer interested, "waived" it), you're legally bound to go forward with the purchase. The sale of your current home is perhaps the most common noninspection contingency.

Inspection contingencies and their removal. Your agreement will specify what inspections on the house you want and must approve before you complete the purchase (close escrow). You'll also note how soon after the acceptance of the offer the inspections must be done. Normally, 20 working days is reasonable. Most buyers request only a general contractor and a pest control report, unless the buyer or the general inspector suspects problems requiring an inspection by a specialist. As a very rough rule, you want to require more inspections when a house is older and expensive or vulnerable to special problems, such as being near an earthquake fault or a slide zone, or potentially containing toxic substances (lead, mold, or asbestos). With new houses, you may want to schedule inspections during key phases of construction, plus a final inspection. (See Chapter 7 regarding inspecting new houses.)

Other contingencies and their removal. The agreement will contain sections or allow space for you to specify other contingencies that must be met before you will close, and the dates by which you must agree to their removal:

- A title contingency is needed for all houses to make sure title is good, that is, no one has a lien on the house allowing them to foreclose, or claims an easement that might impact your use of the property. (See Chapter 18, After the Contract Is Signed, for a discussion of these terms and preliminary title reports.) In most cases, the buyer orders the preliminary title report within three days of acceptance.

Time Allowed for Removing Contingencies

Most offers call for the removal of all contingencies within 30–60 days after the seller's acceptance. You and the seller should decide depending on your time constraints and how long it will realistically take to remove each. If the house is in great physical shape, ten to 15 days should be adequate to remove all contingencies relating to its physical condition. Just don't hamper your ability to thoroughly check out the house in your eagerness to keep negotiations with the seller going smoothly.

A contingency based on your selling an existing house or obtaining a loan you haven't yet applied for will normally need 30–90 days for removal. If any contingencies aren't met in the specified time, the deal is over unless you and the seller agree in writing to extend the contingency release time.

Chapter 18 gives more detail on how to remove contingencies.

- You may request that the seller provide you with a written warranty covering certain items in the house. If so, be sure to also check "Seller" under the list of costs associated with the sale.
- California home buyers are finding it increasingly difficult to purchase hazard insurance with appropriate coverage (especially for earthquakes)

at affordable rates. To protect yourself, you can make your purchase contingent upon your applying, and receiving a commitment in writing, for reasonably priced hazard insurance on the property as required by your lender. Ask for as much time as possible to remove this contingency, at least 30 days if possible, depending upon your particular situation.

Final walk-through. The agreement should let you have one last look at the property right before the close of escrow to make sure the seller (or tenant) didn't damage the place before moving out or leave an old stained sofa and other junk behind, and that all promised repairs have been done to your satisfaction.

Liquidated damages. If you refuse to go through with the sale because a contingency can't be fulfilled, the seller must return your deposit. But if you back out simply because you change your mind, or you don't try in good faith to fulfill a contingency (for example, you don't even apply for a loan), it's considered a default. Assuming you both agree to a liquidated damages provision, the seller need not return your deposit. Your deposit turns into "liquidated damages," which in legal terms means you and the seller have agreed in advance on the maximum amount of the damages if you default. By setting the maximum amount in the purchase contract, you and the seller can save both time and money by avoiding court or arbitration, and you are protected from the risk of a court or arbitrator awarding the seller a larger amount.

How Clean Will It Be?

The sellers of the house are required to leave the premises vacant and undamaged, but not sparkling. Even if they have the house professionally cleaned before they leave (which some may do as a courtesy—feel free to ask), it may not look clean enough to you. After all, years of accumulated dirt and scuffs look invisible when they're in your own house but disgusting when created by someone else. As you plan your moving day, you might allow a day or two after the house is yours to tackle any cleaning tasks before your possessions arrive.

California law generally prohibits sellers from keeping more than 3% of the agreed-upon sale price as liquidated damages. (Civil Code § 1675.) But the seller generally must prove that the damages somehow relate to that amount. In some situations, where the seller immediately gets another acceptable offer, the damage is zero—and the seller won't be entitled to anything.

If your contract includes a liquidated damages provision, it must be in at least ten-point boldface type and signed or initialed by you and the seller.

Mediation of disputes. This clause lets you first try to settle any disputes that arise under the contract by nonbinding mediation. Mediation is a process where you and the seller pick someone to help you reach a mutually agreeable decision. It is cheap, fast, and avoids the emotional drain and hostility of litigation.

Arbitration of disputes. You can choose to resolve your dispute by arbitration should your attempt to settle any dispute informally or by mediation not succeed. You give up your right to a court trial, but like mediation, it's cheaper, faster, and less hostile than litigation.

In arbitration, you submit your dispute to one or more arbitrators for a decision. In the standard provision, most agreements are governed by either the American Arbitration Association (AAA) or the Judicial Arbitration and Mediation Services, Inc. (JAMS), both of which provide that the parties may get a lawyer to represent them (but don't have to) and that the decision is final—neither party can appeal it to a court.

Property tax and insurance prorations; assessment bonds. This type of clause allocates payment of property taxes, insurance policies carried over from seller to buyer, rents, interests, and any homeowners' association (HOA) dues or regular assessments. Each owner pays only for the period of actual ownership during the year the house is sold.

This clause also provides that the buyer assumes certain bond liens to finance local improvements such as curbs, gutters, or street lights. The seller may not even know whether the house has any such bond liens, but they'll show up on the title report.

Often bonds must be paid off when a house is sold, but sometimes they can't be. In that case, the buyer assumes responsibility to pay the lien, but the cost of doing so is credited by the seller to the buyer in escrow.

Attorney's fees. In any standard real estate purchase contract, the losing party in arbitration or litigation (you could wind up in litigation if you choose arbitration and the seller doesn't agree, or vice versa) is responsible for his or her own—and the other side's—attorneys' fees and court costs.

Time is of the essence. The statement that time is of the essence is standard contract language emphasizing the importance of the dates to which you and the seller agree. It means that a missed deadline by either party is considered a substantial breach of the contract, which can result in the other party being given money damages or being allowed to cancel the contract.

TIP

Put away your stopwatch. Despite this provision, many courts reject cries of "he breached the 'time is of the essence' clause" for a delay of a few hours or days, unless you can show that you have suffered, or will suffer, damages as a result.

Entire agreement. A standard contract will state that it is the entire and final agreement between you and the seller, and that all modifications to the contract must be in writing—in other words, that any other written or oral agreements floating around in the world don't count.

Agency disclosure and confirmation. Your offer contract must let you and the seller confirm your relationships with your agents. Long before you fill out this offer form, if you are working with an agent, you will have completed a "Disclosure: Real Estate Agency Relationships" form, which should have told you whether the agent is representing you, the seller, or both. In the agreement, you acknowledge that you've received that form, and confirm some of the information in the form.

Broker compensation. The contract may also clarify who pays which broker, and how much. Your options are outlined in Chapter 5.

When offer expires. Your offer should give the seller a deadline to accept. If the seller doesn't accept by that time, your offer automatically expires unless you extend it in writing. (See Chapter 17 on how to extend an offer. Chapter 17 also covers revoking your offer before the seller accepts or the deadline expires.)

Buyer's signature. By signing and dating the purchase agreement form, you agree to make your offer a binding contract if it's accepted by the seller. All buyers must sign, including your spouse if you're using community property to make the purchase. If you have a broker, the broker (or agent) must sign too (sometimes your broker will be referred to as "Selling Firm").

Seller's acceptance of offer. If the seller signs, it means your offer has been accepted, and the seller promises that he or she owns the property and has the right to sell it to you. If the sellers are a married couple, they both must sign, even if one spouse claims the house is separate property. A title company won't want to get involved in the complexities of California community property law and will want to see both signatures.

Seller's rejection of offer. Your offer form may provide a place for the seller to formally reject your offer. It will definitely make your life easier to know whether and when your offer is no longer being considered by the seller. However, not all sellers will take the time to fill this in and return it to you.

Other advisories. Your offer form may also contain various clauses whose primary purpose is to advise you and the seller of your rights and responsibilities. Most of these are warnings that you, as the buyer, can't rely on every word that the seller or any broker says, and should be a cautious consumer and investigate matters on your own.

Addenda containing other terms and conditions. Standard contracts don't necessarily contain space for every term that you might want to include in your agreement. You can create supplementary documents that are part of the agreement, for example to cover such issues as:

- your acknowledgment that the property contains unremitted units
- details outlining a probate or foreclosure sale (get help from a real estate agent or attorney experienced in these matters), or
- specification of who will pay to pump and certify a septic system or connect a sewer.

Backup offer. If the seller has already accepted another offer and you'd like to make a backup offer, you will in most cases need to prepare an addendum explaining this. For example, the San Francisco Association of Realtors® provides a one-page form that simply references your original offer and gives the seller a space to sign upon deciding to elevate your offer to primary position. If the seller does this, you'll normally be given a certain amount of time to approve the deal in writing. This lets you make more than one backup offer without being obligated to purchase more than one house if your offers are simultaneously accepted.

Contract to Purchase Real Property

Property address, including county: ______________________________

____

Date: ______________________

(Buyer) ______________________________,

makes this offer to purchase the property described above, for the sum of ______________________ dollars ($______________). Buyer includes a deposit, in the amount of ______________________________ dollars ($______________),

evidenced by ☐ cash ☐ cashier's check ☐ personal check ☐ promissory note ☐ other.

1. Financial Terms

This offer is contingent upon Buyer securing financing as specified in Items D, E, F, and G below within ______________ days from acceptance of this offer.

$ __________ **A. DEPOSIT TO BE APPLIED TOWARD THE DOWN PAYMENT**, payable to ______________________ (Payee), to be held uncashed until the acceptance of this offer. If this offer is accepted, the deposit shall be delivered to Payee and applied toward the down payment.

$ __________ **B. DOWN PAYMENT INCREASE**, to be paid into escrow ☐ within ________ calendar days of acceptance, or ☐ on or before ______________.

$ __________ **C. DOWN PAYMENT BALANCE**, to be paid into escrow on or before the close of escrow.

$ __________ **D. FIRST LOAN—NEW LOAN.** Buyer shall obtain a new loan, amortized over not fewer than __________ years. Buyer's financing shall be:

☐ Conventional (name of lender, if known) ______________________

☐ Private (name of lender, if known) ______________________

☐ Government (specify): ☐ VA ☐ FHA ☐ Cal-Vet ☐ CHFA

☐ Other: ______________________

Buyer's mortgage shall be

☐ at a maximum fixed rate of __________%

☐ an adjustable rate loan with a maximum beginning rate of ________%, or

☐ (fill in any other requirements here) ______________________

____

$ ____________ E. **FIRST LOAN—EXISTING LOAN.** Buyer shall ☐ assume ☐ buy subject to an existing loan under the same terms and conditions that Seller has with ______________________________, the present lender. The approximate remaining balance is $ ____________, at the current rate of interest of ______% on a ☐ fixed ☐ adjustable rate loan, for a remaining term of approximately ____________ years, secured by a First Deed of Trust.

$ ____________ F. **SECOND LOAN—NEW LOAN.** Buyer shall obtain a new loan, amortized over not fewer than ____________ years. Buyer's financing shall be:

☐ Conventional (name of lender, if known) ______________________________

☐ Private (name of lender, if known) ______________________________

☐ Government (specify): ☐ VA ☐ FHA ☐ Cal-Vet ☐ CHFA

☐ Other: ______________________________

Buyer's mortgage shall be

☐ at a maximum fixed rate of ________%

☐ an adjustable rate loan with a maximum beginning rate of ________%, or

☐ (fill in any other requirements here) ______________________________

____

____

$____________ G. **SECOND LOAN—EXISTING LOAN.** Buyer shall ☐ assume ☐ buy subject to an existing loan under the same terms and conditions that Seller has with ______________________________, the present lender. The approximate remaining balance is $ ____________, at the current rate of interest of ________% on a ☐ fixed ☐ adjustable rate loan, for a remaining term of approximately ________ years, secured by a Second Deed of Trust.

$____________ H. **TOTAL PURCHASE PRICE, EXCLUDING EXPENSES OF SALE AND CLOSING COSTS.**

$____________ I. **OTHER. (See Paragraph ________ of this contract for additional terms and conditions.)**

LOAN APPLICATION. Buyer shall submit complete loan application and financial statement to lender(s) within five days after acceptance. If Buyer, after making a good-faith effort, does not secure financing by the time specified, this contract shall become void, and all deposits shall be returned to Buyer.

GOVERNMENT FINANCING. In the event of FHA or VA financing, Buyer shall not be obligated to complete the purchase, nor shall Buyer forfeit the deposit, if the offer price exceeds the property's FHA or VA appraised value. Buyer shall, however, have the option of proceeding with the purchase from any above-named lender or a different lender without regard to the appraised value.

EXISTING LOAN. If Buyer is assuming any loans or purchasing the property subject to any loans, Seller shall, within seven days after acceptance, deliver to Buyer copies of all applicable notes and deeds of trust, loan balances, and current interest rates. Buyer's obligation under this contract is conditioned upon Buyer's written approval of the documents within seven days after receipt. If Buyer does not accept the documents, either party may terminate this contract.

SELLER FINANCING. The following terms apply only to financing extended by Seller.

1. The rate specified as the maximum interest rate in D or F, above, shall be the actual fixed interest rate for seller financing.
2. The loan documents shall be prepared in the form customarily used by Escrow Agent, identified in Clause 3.
3. The promissory note and deed of trust shall include the following:
   a. Request for Notice of Default on senior loans.
   b. Seller's right to have Buyer execute and pay for a Request for Notice of Delinquency.
   c. Acceleration clause making the loan due, at Seller's option, upon the sale or transfer of the property.
   d. Title insurance coverage insuring Seller's deed of trust interest in the property.
   e. Late charge of 6% of the amount of any installment received more than 10 days after the date it is due.
   f. Obligation of Buyer to maintain fire and extended insurance with Seller named as loss payee at least to cover lesser of replacement of improvements or the liens on the property.
4. Seller shall obtain at Buyer's expense a tax service to notify Seller in the event of a property tax delinquency by Buyer.

5. If the property contains 1–4 dwelling units, Buyer and Seller shall execute a Seller Financing Disclosure Statement as provided by the arranger of credit as soon as is practicable prior to the statements reflecting Buyer's financial condition in such detail as is customarily required by institutional lenders. Seller shall keep these documents confidential and use them only to approve Buyer's creditworthiness. Seller shall notify Buyer in writing within seven days after receipt of Seller's approval or disapproval of Buyer's credit.
6. Buyer shall notify Seller in writing within seven days after receipt of the Seller Financing Disclosure Statement of Buyer's approval or disapproval of the financing terms offered by Seller.

2. Occupancy

Buyer ☐ does ☐ does not intend to occupy the property as Buyer's primary residence.

3. Escrow

Buyer and Seller shall deliver signed escrow instructions to ______________________________ ____, escrow agent located at ____ ____, within a reasonable time before the close of this sale. Escrow shall close within __________ days of acceptance of this offer.

4. Prepayment Penalty and Assumption Fee

Seller shall pay any prepayment penalty or other fees imposed by any existing lender who is paid off during escrow. Buyer shall pay any prepayment penalty, assumption fee, or other fee that becomes due after the close of escrow on any loans assumed from Seller.

5. Expenses of Sale

Expenses of sale, settlement costs, and closing costs shall be paid for as follows:

	Buyer	Seller	Shared Equally	
A.	☐	☐	☐	Escrow fees
B.	☐	☐	☐	Title search
C.	☐	☐	☐	Title insurance for buyer/owner
D.	☐	☐	☐	Title insurance for buyer's lender
E.	☐	☐	☐	Deed preparation fee

	Buyer	Seller	Shared Equally	
F.	☐	☐	☐	Notary fee
G.	☐	☐	☐	Recording fee
H.	☐	☐	☐	Attorney's fee (if attorney hired to clarify title)
I.	☐	☐	☐	Documentary transfer tax
J.	☐	☐	☐	City transfer tax
K.	☐	☐	☐	Pest control inspection report
L.	☐	☐	☐	General contractor report
M.	☐	☐	☐	Roof inspection report
N.				Other inspections (specify): ______________________
1.	☐	☐	☐	______________________
2.	☐	☐	☐	______________________
3.	☐	☐	☐	______________________
4.	☐	☐	☐	______________________
O.	☐	☐	☐	One-year home warranty (specify covered items): ______________________
P.				Other (specify): ______________________
1.	☐	☐	☐	______________________
2.	☐	☐	☐	______________________
3.	☐	☐	☐	______________________
4.	☐	☐	☐	______________________

6. Property Tax and Insurance Prorations; Assessment Bonds

Seller shall be responsible for payment of Seller's prorated share of real estate taxes and assessments accrued until the deed transferring title to Buyer is recorded. Buyer understands that the property shall be reassessed upon change of ownership and that Buyer shall be sent a supplemental tax bill which may reflect an increase in taxes based on property value.

Any premiums on insurance carried over from Seller to Buyer and any homeowners' association dues and regular assessments, interests, and rents shall be prorated, that is, Seller shall pay the portion of the premiums and fees while title is in Seller's name and Buyer shall pay the portion of the premiums and fees while title is in Buyer's name.

Homeowners' association special assessments shall be ☐ paid current by Seller (payments not yet due shall be assumed by Buyer without credit toward the purchase price) or ☐ ______________ ____.

Buyer agrees to assume those assessment bond liens that cannot be paid off by Seller as follows. ____.

7. Fixtures

All fixtures and fittings that are permanently attached to the property or for which special openings have been made are included, free of liens, in the purchase price, including built-in appliances; electrical, plumbing, light and heating fixtures; garage door openers/remote controls; attached carpets and other floor coverings; screens; awnings; shutters; window shades; blinds; television antennas/satellite dishes and related equipment; private integrated phone systems; air coolers/conditioners; pool/spa equipment; water softeners (if owned by Seller); security systems/alarms (if owned by Seller); attached fireplace equipment; mailbox; in-ground landscaping including trees/shrubs, EXCEPT: ____

____

____

____

8. Personal Property

The following items of personal property, free of liens and without warranty of condition (unless otherwise provided), are INCLUDED in the sale:

☐ Stove ☐ Oven ☐ Refrigerator ☐ Washer ☐ Dryer ☐ Freezer
☐ Trash Compactor ☐ Dishwasher

____

____

9. Inspection Contingencies

This offer is conditioned upon Buyer's written approval of the following inspection reports. All inspections shall be carried out within ________ days of acceptance of the offer. Buyer shall deliver written approval or disapproval to Seller within three days of receiving each report. If Buyer does not deliver a written disapproval within the time allowed, Buyer shall be deemed to approve of the report.

Seller is to provide reasonable access to the property to Buyer, his/her agent, all inspectors, and representatives of lending institutions to conduct appraisals.

☐ A. Pest control report, covering the main building and ☐ detached garage(s) or carport(s) ☐ the following other structures on the property: ______________________________

____.

Buyer may elect to pay for all, a portion, or none of the cost of the work recommended by the report.

☐ B. General contractor report as to the general physical condition of the property including, but not limited to, heating and plumbing, electrical systems, solar energy systems, roof, appliances, structural, soil, foundation, retaining walls, possible environmental hazards, location of property lines, size/square footage of the property, and water/utility restrictions.

☐ C. Plumbing contractor report.

☐ D. Soils engineer report.

☐ E. Energy conservation inspection report in accordance with local ordinances.

☐ F. Seismic safety report.

☐ G. Environmental hazards inspection reports including, but not limited to, asbestos, radon gas, lead-based paint, mold, underground storage tanks, and hazardous wastes.

☐ H. City or county inspection report.

☐ I. Roof inspection report.

☐ J. General contractor report at the following phases of construction (specify) __________

____

____.

☐ K. Other (specify) ____

____.

If Buyer and Seller, after making a good-faith effort, cannot remove in writing the above contingencies by the time specified, this contract shall become void, and all deposits shall be returned to Buyer.

10. Other Contingencies

This offer is contingent upon the following:

☐ A. Buyer receiving and approving preliminary title report within ______ days of acceptance of this offer.

☐ B. Seller furnishing declaration of restrictions, CC&Rs, bylaws, articles of incorporation, rules and regulations currently in force, other governing documents, one year's homeowners' association minutes, financial statements of the owners' association for the past three years, a statement of reserves, assignment of parking spaces, within ________ days of acceptance.

☐ C. Sale of Buyer's current residence, the address of which is ________________________________
____, by ________________________________.

☐ D. Seller furnishing rental agreements within _________________________ days of acceptance.

☐ E. Seller providing Buyer with a home warranty to cover the following: ____________________
____.

☐ F. Buyer applying for insurance acceptable to Buyer and Lender so as to indemnify both in the event of casualty loss upon Buyer's taking title to the property, and Buyer receiving written commitment of said insurance within _____ days of acceptance of this offer. Seller to furnish Buyer with written disclosure of existing insurance policy and any previous claims within three business days of acceptance of this offer.

☐ G. Other: ____
____
____
____
____
____.

Buyer shall deliver written approval or disapproval to Seller within three days of receiving each report, statement, or warranty. If Buyer does not deliver a written disapproval within the time allowed, Buyer shall be deemed to approve of the report, statement, or warranty. If Buyer and Seller, after making a good-faith effort, cannot remove in writing the above contingencies, this offer shall become void, and all deposits shall be returned to Buyer.

11. Condition of Property

Seller represents that the roof, heating, plumbing, air conditioning, electrical, septic, drainage, sewers, gutters and downspouts, and sprinklers, as well as built-in appliances and other equipment and fixtures, are in working order. Seller agrees to maintain them in that condition, and to maintain all landscaping, grounds, and pools, until possession of the property is delivered to Buyer. Seller shall, by the date of possession, replace any cracked or broken glass.

12. Foreign Investors

If Seller is a foreign person as defined in the Foreign Investment in Real Property Tax Act, Buyer shall, absent a specific exemption, have withheld in escrow ten percent (10%) of the gross sale price of the property. Buyer and Seller shall provide the escrow holder specified in Clause 3 above with all signed documentation required by the Act.

If Seller has a last known address outside of California or if Seller's proceeds will be paid to a financial intermediary of Seller, under California Revenue and Tax Code, Buyer, unless an exemption applies, must deduct and withhold 3⅓% of the gross sales price from Seller's proceeds and send it to the Franchise Tax Board.

13. Rent Control

The property ☐ is ☐ is not located in a city or county subject to local rent control. A rent control ordinance may restrict the rent that can be charged for this property, limit the right of the owner to evict the occupant for other than "just cause," and control the owner's rights and responsibilities.

14. Title

At close of escrow, title to the property is to be clear of all liens and encumbrances of record except those listed in the preliminary title report and agreed to be assumed by Buyer. Any such liens or encumbrances assumed by Buyer shall be credited toward the purchase price. If Seller cannot remove liens or encumbrances not assumed by Buyer, Buyer shall have the right to cancel this contract and be refunded his/her deposit and costs of inspection reports.

15. Possession

Buyer reserves the right to inspect the property three days before the close of escrow. Seller shall deliver physical possession of property, along with alarms, alarm codes, keys, garage door openers, and all other means to operate all property locks, to Buyer: ☐ at close of escrow ☐ no later than ______________ days after the close of escrow.

If Buyer agrees to let Seller continue to occupy the property after close of escrow, Seller shall deposit into escrow for Buyer a prorated share of Buyer's monthly carrying costs (principal, interest, property taxes, and insurance) for each such day, subject to the terms of a written agreement, specifying rent or security deposit, authorizing a final inspection before Seller vacates, and indicating the length of tenancy, signed by both parties.

16. Agency Confirmation and Commission to Brokers

The following agency relationship(s) are confirmed for this transaction:

Listing agent: ____ is the agent of:

☐ a Seller exclusively ☐ Buyer and Seller

Selling agent: ____ is the agent of:

☐ Buyer exclusively ☐ Seller exclusively ☐ Buyer and Seller

Notice: The amount or rate of real estate commissions is not fixed by law. They are set by each Broker individually and may be negotiable between the Seller and Broker.

Buyer and Seller shall each pay only those broker's commissions for which Buyer and Seller have separately contracted in writing with a broker licensed by the California Commissioner of Real Estate.

$____________ or __________% of selling price to be paid to ________________________

____ by ☐ Seller ☐ Buyer.

$____________ or __________% of selling price to be paid to ________________________

____ by ☐ Seller ☐ Buyer.

17. Advice

If Buyer or Seller wishes advice concerning the legal or tax aspects of this transaction, Buyer or Seller shall separately contract and pay for it.

18. Backup Offer

☐ This offer is being made as a backup offer. Should Seller accept this offer as a backup offer, the following terms and conditions apply:

If Seller accepts this offer as a primary offer, he/she must do so in writing. Until that time, Buyer's deposit check shall be held uncashed.

Buyer has 24 hours from receipt of Seller's written acceptance to ratify it in writing. If Buyer fails to do so, Buyer's offer shall be deemed withdrawn and any contractual relationship between Buyer and Seller terminated.

19. Duration of Offer

This offer is submitted to Seller by Buyer on ____________________, at ________ ☐ a.m. ☐ p.m. Pacific Time, and will be considered revoked unless a copy of this contract with Seller's signature accepting it is delivered in person, by mail, or by fax and personally received by Buyer or Buyer's real estate agent not later than ______ ☐ a.m. ☐ p.m. on ____________________, or, if prior to Seller's acceptance of this offer, Buyer revokes this offer in writing.

20. Other Terms and Conditions

____

____

____

____

____

21. Risk of Damage to Property

All risk of loss to the property that occurs after this offer is accepted shall be borne by Seller until title has been conveyed to Buyer. Any damage totaling ____________% or less of the purchase price shall be repaired by Seller prior to the transfer of title. If the land or improvements are destroyed or material damaged in an amount exceeding ____________% of the purchase price, Buyer shall have the option of either terminating this agreement and recovering all deposits made or purchasing the property in its then condition.

22. Liquidated Damages

If Seller accepts this offer, and Buyer later defaults on the contract, Seller shall be released from Seller's obligations under this contract. By signing their initials here, Buyer (____________) and Seller (________) agree that if Buyer defaults, Seller shall keep no more than three percent (3%) of the purchase price stated above if the property is a dwelling with no more than four units, one of which Buyer intends to occupy as Buyer's residence.

Seller shall retain the right to proceed against Buyer for any other claim or remedy Seller may have, other than for breach of contract. In the event of a dispute, funds deposited into escrow are not released automatically and require mutual, signed release instructions from Buyer and Seller, a judicial decision, or an arbitration award.

23. Mediation of Disputes

If a dispute arises out of, or relates to, this agreement, Buyer and Seller ☐ agree ☐ do not agree to first try in good faith to settle the dispute by nonbinding mediation before resorting to court action or binding arbitration. Mediation is a process in which parties attempt to resolve a dispute by submitting it to an impartial, neutral mediator who is authorized to facilitate the resolution of the dispute but who is not empowered to impose a settlement on the Buyer and Seller.

To invoke mediation, one party shall notify the other of his/her intention to proceed with mediation and shall provide the name of a chosen mediator. The other party shall have seven days to respond. If he/she disagrees with the first person's chosen mediator, the parties shall ask the escrow holder to choose the mediator or to recommend someone to choose the mediator. The mediator shall conduct the mediation session or sessions within the next three weeks. Before the mediation begins, Buyer and Seller agree to sign a document limiting the admissibility in arbitration or a lawsuit of anything said or admitted, or any documents prepared, in the course of the mediation.

Costs of mediation shall be divided equally between Buyer and Seller.

______________________________ Buyer ______________________________ Seller

______________________________ Buyer ______________________________ Seller

24. Arbitration of Disputes

Any dispute or claim in law or equity between Buyer and Seller arising out of this contract or any resulting transaction which is not settled by mediation shall be decided by neutral, binding arbitration and not by court action except as provided by California law for judicial review of arbitration proceedings.

The arbitration shall be conducted in accordance with the rules of either the American Arbitration Association (AAA) or Judicial Arbitration and Mediation Services, Inc. (JAMS). The selection between AAA and JAMS rules shall be made by the claimant first filing for the arbitration. The parties to an arbitration may agree in writing to use different rules and/or arbitrator(s). In all other respects, the arbitration shall be conducted in accordance with Part III, Title 9, of the California Code of Civil Procedure.

Judgment upon the award rendered by the arbitrator(s) may be entered in any court having jurisdiction thereof. The parties shall have the right to discovery in accordance with Code of Civil Procedure § 1283.05. The following matters are excluded from arbitration hereunder: (a) a judicial or nonjudicial foreclosure or other action or proceeding to enforce a deed of trust, mortgage, or installment land sales contract as defined in Civil Code § 2985; (b) an unlawful detainer action; (c) the filing or enforcement of a mechanic's lien; (d) any matter which is within the jurisdiction of a probate or small claims court; and (e) an action for bodily injury or wrongful death, or for latent or patent defects, to which Code of Civil Procedure § 337.1 or § 337.15 applies. The filing of a judicial action to enable the recording of a notice of pending action, for order of attachment, receivership, injunction, or other provisional remedies, shall not constitute a waiver of the right to arbitrate under this provision.

Any dispute or claim by or against broker(s) and/or associate licensee(s) participating in this transaction shall be submitted to arbitration consistent with the provision above only if the broker(s) and/or associate licensee(s) making the claim or against whom the claim is made shall have agreed to submit it to arbitration consistent with this provision.

"NOTICE: BY INITIALING IN THE SPACE BELOW YOU ARE AGREEING TO HAVE ANY DISPUTE ARISING OUT OF THE MATTERS INCLUDED IN THE 'ARBITRATION OF DISPUTES' PROVISION DECIDED BY NEUTRAL ARBITRATION AS PROVIDED BY CALIFORNIA LAW, AND YOU ARE GIVING UP ANY RIGHTS YOU MIGHT POSSESS TO HAVE THE DISPUTE LITIGATED IN A COURT OR JURY TRIAL. BY INITIALING IN THE SPACE BELOW YOU ARE GIVING UP YOUR JUDICIAL RIGHTS TO DISCOVERY AND APPEAL, UNLESS THOSE RIGHTS ARE SPECIFICALLY INCLUDED IN THE 'ARBITRATION OF DISPUTES' PROVISION. IF YOU REFUSE TO SUBMIT TO ARBITRATION AFTER AGREEING TO THIS PROVISION, YOU MAY BE COMPELLED TO ARBITRATE UNDER THE

AUTHORITY OF THE CALIFORNIA CODE OF CIVIL PROCEDURE. YOUR AGREEMENT TO THIS ARBITRATION PROVISION IS VOLUNTARY."

"WE HAVE READ AND UNDERSTAND THE FOREGOING AND AGREE TO SUBMIT DISPUTES ARISING OUT OF THE MATTERS INCLUDED IN THE 'ARBITRATION OF DISPUTES' PROVISION TO NEUTRAL ARBITRATION."

Buyer's(s') Initials ____________/____________ Seller's(s') Initials ____________/____________

25. Attorneys' Fees

If litigation or arbitration arises from this contract, the prevailing party shall be reimbursed by the other party for reasonable attorneys' fees and court or arbitration costs.

26. Entire Agreement

This document represents the entire agreement between Buyer and Seller. Any modifications or amendments to this contract shall be made in writing, signed and dated by both parties.

27. Time Is of the Essence

Time is of the essence in this transaction.

28. Disclosures

_______ By initialing here, Buyer requests a copy of the Real Estate Transfer Disclosure Statement.

_______ By initialing here, Buyer requests copies of the Natural Hazards Disclosure Statement.

_______ By initialing here, Buyer requests a copy of *The Homeowner's Guide to Earthquake Safety.*

_______ By initialing here, Buyer requests a copy of *Environmental Hazards: A Guide for Homeowners and Buyers.*

_______ By initialing here, Buyer requests a lead-based paint hazards disclosure.

_______ By initialing here, Buyer requests a copy of the following disclosures: (specify) ___________
____

29. Buyer's Signature

This constitutes an offer to purchase the above listed property.

Selling Broker ______________________ Buyer ______________________

By Selling Agent ______________________ Buyer ______________________

Broker's Address ______________________ Broker's Telephone ______________________

______________________ Broker's Fax ______________________

______________________ Broker's Email ______________________

Date ______________________

30. Seller's Acceptance

The undersigned Seller ☐ accepts ☐ accepts subject to the attached counteroffer the foregoing offer, and agrees to sell the property on the terms and conditions stated above.

Seller agrees to pay compensation for services as follows:

☐ ____% of the sales price or ☐ $________ to (Listing Broker) ______________________

____

☐ ____% of the sales price or ☐ $________ to (Selling Broker) ______________________

____

payable on recordation of the deed or other evidence of title. If the sale is prevented due to the default of Seller, the commission shall be paid at default. If the sale is prevented due to the default of Buyer, the commission shall be paid only if and when Seller collects damages from Buyer.

Listing Broker ______________________ Seller ______________________

By Listing Agent ______________________ Seller ______________________

Broker's Address ______________________ Broker's Telephone ______________________

______________________ Broker's Fax ______________________

______________________ Broker's Email ______________________

Date ______________________

CHAPTER

17

Presenting Your Offer and Negotiating

This chapter discusses presenting your offer to the seller and, if necessary, negotiating the price and other terms. If you haven't done so already, read Chapter 16, Putting Your Offer in Writing.

GO BACK

If you're looking to buy a new house. This chapter focuses on negotiating to purchase an existing house. We discuss negotiating with the developer to purchase a new house in Chapter 7.

Notify the Seller of Your Offer

Once you notify your agent that you are ready to make an offer and draw it up, your agent will contact the seller's agent (or the seller directly, if the house is for sale by owner). The seller or agent may respond by either:

- setting up an appointment to receive your offer (common in cold markets)
- telling you a date and time when offers will be accepted (common in hot markets, when sellers expect multiple offers), or
- stringing you along or coming up with a delaying strategy, if the seller thinks he or she may get a better deal by waiting.

No matter which strategy the seller employs, unless your offer is rejected outright, you should eventually be able to coordinate a meeting so your offer can be presented.

Don't Reveal Your Offer Too Early

If the seller asks questions about the terms of your offer, it's usually best to politely decline to answer until you can make a formal presentation. This is especially true if your offer is on the low side or contains a number of contingencies. Once you're in the same room, it's harder for the seller to dismiss your offer out of hand, and you can build rapport and ask for a counteroffer. On the other hand, an offer revealed prior to the formal presentation may be used by the seller or her agent to try to get you, and others, to bid higher.

Strategies in a Competitive Market

In real estate markets where demand is high, homes sell quickly—often above the asking price—as bidding wars erupt. If you're buying in a competitive market, it's crucial to develop a bidding strategy. For example, you might bid on several houses at once as discussed under "Bid on Two or More Houses," below. Another option is to prepare several bids at different prices. Present the lowest bid if you're the only one making an offer, the next highest if there are only one or two other people making offers, and your highest price if there are three or more bidders.

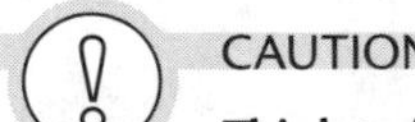

CAUTION

Think twice before you get caught up in a bidding war. When a number of people bid on a house, competitive juices begin to flow, and a

kind of "auction mentality" prevails. Be careful not to exceed your budget.

Remember, price alone is not the only consideration for sellers. Your ability to close the deal quickly—for example, by getting loan preapproval—is crucial in hot markets. Finally, your flexibility and sensitivity to the seller's needs—whether it's extending the closing date for a seller who can't move for a few months or paying for repairs—may make or break your offer.

Strategies in a Cold Market

When prices are dropping, you can bid less than the sellers' asking price. Assuming the sellers are anxious to close the deal, they will probably counter with a price somewhere between their most recent offering price and the amount you proposed. For example, let's say you bid $750,000 on a house offered at $825,000. The sellers counter by lowering their price to $795,000.

Your next step is to decide whether you want to raise your offer. Hide your eagerness to buy the house. Here are some ways to do this:

- Don't respond immediately. Instead, either wait until the sellers' deadline for a response or ask for a little more time.
- Make it clear, either directly or through your agent, that you are still looking at other properties.
- If you are willing to risk losing the property, consider breaking off negotiations for a week or two.

When you make a counteroffer, make it on the low side to get the best deal you can. You can raise your offer later if the seller says no.

Present Your Offer

Buyers don't usually accompany the agent to the offer presentation or subsequent negotiations. Most real estate people believe it's unwise for buyers to be there, fearing that you'll muck up the process or say something that the seller or agent could use against you. But it's your purchase, not the agent's, and you can call the shots if you want to.

What to Bring to the Offer Conference

Prepare the following materials for the offer conference:

1. A completed offer.
2. Proof that you can afford the purchase, such as, in order of effectiveness:
   - a preapproval letter
   - a credit report, or
   - a family financial statement (see Chapter 2).
3. A brief letter about you and why you love the house and will take great care of it yourself. Consider including a photo of you or your family.

If you are attending the conference, or representing yourself, you have two goals, in addition to presenting your offer:

- to fully understand the seller's needs so you can adjust your offer to meet

them, without compromising your own objectives
- to convince the seller that you can afford to buy the house and are a reasonable person to work with.

Starting Off on the Right Foot

Don't overlook the basics when meeting with a seller to negotiate:

- Show up on time.
- Dress reasonably, but conservatively.
- If you don't own a decent car, borrow one (or ride with your agent).
- Leave your kids at home.

You want to convey to the seller that you are reasonably knowledgeable about the real estate market—though you don't want to come off like a know-it-all.

Approach the seller in a straightforward, friendly manner. As an opener, say something nice about an aspect of the house that reflects the owner's personal taste, such as the garden or artwork. But don't gush—you'll only drive up the price. On the other hand, don't criticize anything that reflects the seller's taste.

Bring a preapproval letter for an amount that shows you can afford the home. Another way to establish your economic bona fides is to casually mention your job, or jobs, such as, "One reason we like this house is that it's a convenient commute to both of our jobs—Sidney is a law librarian and works at the county courthouse, and I'm a nurse at the hospital, which is only about 20 minutes away."

Even though you have decided on the terms you need, it's not too late to glean some useful information from the seller. Encourage the seller to talk. If the seller needs to move quickly to close on another house, relocate before school starts, or cope with a divorce, you may be able to get a better price if you can close quickly.

TIP

Need to regroup? If you get information from the seller that surprises you and you want to modify your offer, ask to speak privately with your agent. This may mean no more than walking around the block or it could mean recessing for hours or even days to get legal, tax, or other specialized advice.

Bid on Two or More Houses

If you are in a hot market where you may bid on multiple houses before an offer is accepted, or if you are in a cold market and want to aggressively pursue several options and give each the pressure of competing with others, you can bid on more than one house at a time without encountering any legal problems. Here's how:

- Make each formal written offer open to acceptance for a very short period of time, such as 24 or 48 hours. You can extend the time in writing if you want to.
- If you make a subsequent offer while your first offer is still outstanding,

be sure at least one of the offers has enough contingencies so that you can avoid the multiple-acceptance trap—should both sellers accept your offers simultaneously. For example, if you're bidding on an older house that obviously has some problems, include a contingency that you approve, in writing, a structural pest control report and any other inspections and reports that you'd like to obtain.

- Make your offer contingent on your written ratification of the seller's acceptance of your offer. This is commonly done with backup offers, but can just as easily be done in your original offer. Wouldn't a seller be less likely to accept this type of offer? Yes, but if you make your ratification time short (for example, six hours from the written notification), and yours is otherwise the best offer in terms of price and other conditions, a seller will probably give you a chance to say yes. And, of course, while you are doing so, be sure to formally revoke any outstanding offers.

The Seller's Response to Your Offer

The seller and his or her agent will read your offer and any others that are submitted. Sellers normally focus on price, financing, and contingencies:

- **Price.** If it's in the ballpark of what the seller expected, the negotiation process will likely begin. If your bid is way out of line, the seller may reject it or not bother to respond at all. If there are several bidders, the seller will normally look at which is highest and then will focus on the quality of the offers—seeking, for example, a buyer who is preapproved by a mortgage lender, will make a substantial down payment, has few contingencies in the offer, and can close within a short period of time.

True Story

Li and Sam: How to Pursue Several Houses at Once

When they needed to move, Li and Sam discovered there was fierce competition for houses in their community and price range. After bidding on several houses and losing all of them, they tried something new.

In a weekend marathon of house hunting, the couple saw four houses they liked—and bid on all of them. Li and Sam's offer included a clause stating that the seller had to accept or reject the offer within two days. Also, if the seller accepted their offer, then the couple would be allowed six hours to ratify it or back out. On Wednesday morning, two of their offers were accepted almost simultaneously. They accepted the better one, and even though not legally bound to do so, immediately withdrew the other three offers in writing.

- **Financing.** The seller will look at your financing information and is likely to reject your offer on the spot if it seems unrealistic. If multiple offers come in at similar prices, a seller who needs to close quickly will probably prefer the buyer with the strongest financial profile.
- **Contingencies.** If the seller wants to sell fast, he or she will be particularly concerned with any difficult or time-consuming contingency, such as your need to sell an existing house.

The Seller Accepts on the Spot

If the seller says "yes" to your entire offer, make sure he or she immediately follows up by putting it in writing. An oral acceptance is not legally enforceable.

The seller will ordinarily accept by completing the acceptance blank at the bottom of your Contract to Purchase Real Property form. If the seller accepts all but even one term, it technically isn't an acceptance, but a counteroffer, which you, in turn, can accept or reject. In fact, it is rare for a seller to say yes to all of the terms of an offer on the spot.

The Seller Rejects on the Spot

If the seller rejects your offer, try to get it in writing. An oral rejection can cause problems if your original offer gives the seller additional time to accept. In theory, the seller could

True Story

Chuck and Ming: Buying a Good House in a Bad Way

Chuck and Ming spot a house they like. Frederick, their agent, arranges with the sellers' agent, Shirley, to present the offer to the sellers, Mike and Gail, at 11:00 a.m. the next day. Frederick is 20 minutes late.

When he arrives he bursts in and slaps the offer on the table, barely saying hello. The offer is $15,000 less than the list price, but Chuck and Ming love the house and will meet the asking price, if necessary.

Shirley asks Chuck how they like the house. Ming interrupts, saying they really love it and adds that they're exhausted from looking at dozens of others.

Shirley, Mike and Gail excuse themselves. They're hardly out of the room when Chuck and Ming criticize Frederick for being late; he, in turn, expresses anger at Ming for not letting a more knowledgeable person do the negotiating.

In the meantime, Shirley, Mike, and Gail are pleased; Ming and Chuck have offered a good price, they can obviously afford the purchase, and the only contingency is a routine inspection. The offer is so solid, Mike and Gail probably would have accepted it as is, but based on Ming's revelations about how they love the house, they counteroffer $13,000 higher than Chuck and Ming's offer. After some negotiating a deal is finally struck for $9,000 above the first offer. Ming and Chuck overpaid because they weren't prepared to negotiate properly.

change his or her mind and accept your offer in writing two days later, when you may no longer want the house. If the seller refuses to go to the trouble of putting a rejection in writing, simply withdraw your offer using a written Revocation of Offer to Purchase Real Property form. (See "Revoking an Offer or Counteroffer," below.)

Normally, if the seller thinks a deal can be made, the seller will counter your offer, not reject it outright. Most outright rejections happen when the seller already has a better offer or thinks the buyer's offer is ridiculously low or otherwise weak. If you think you can make your offer more attractive—for example, by upping the price or getting rid of a contingency that you sell your current home—and you're willing to follow through, you can write another offer.

Concerned About Discrimination?

What are your rights if the seller refuses your offer and then promptly sells to another buyer at the same or a lower price, or on less favorable terms? If you think the seller's decision not to sell to you was based on your race, ethnic background, religion, sex, sexual orientation, marital status, age, family status, or disability, the seller may be violating laws prohibiting discrimination. Contact the California Department of Fair Employment and Housing at 800-233-3212, www.dfeh.ca.gov.

The Seller Asks for More Time

It's reasonable (although not required) to give the seller one to three days to decide whether to accept, reject, or counter your offer. If the seller wants more time than you have specified in your offer, and you are so anxious to get the house you decide to oblige, prepare an Extension of Offer to Purchase Real Property form. A sample is shown below.

If you make a take-it-or-leave-it offer to force a quick decision, you won't want to give the seller extra time. This preemptive bid strategy is a good one in a hot market, if you bid aggressively on a new listing (maybe even overbid the asking price) in an effort to grab the house fast. In addition, the strategy may be necessary if you're interested in more than one house and want to force a quick decision on one so you can bid on another if the first seller says no.

The Seller Is Waiting for Other Bids

If a seller is expecting other offers, he or she is unlikely to make a decision until all offers are in (unless the seller receives one too good to resist saying "yes" to). If you want the house, there's nothing you can do but wait, unless you want to force the matter by making an attractive offer that requires an immediate decision.

Extension of Offer to Purchase Real Property

(Buyer) ____

extends the offer made to purchase the real property at (address) ______________________

____

____

made on (date) ______________________, until (time) ____________ ☐ a.m. ☐ p.m.

on (date) ______________________.

______________________________ ______________________

Offerer/Buyer Date

______________________________ ______________________

Offerer/Buyer Date

The Seller Has Received a Higher Bid

A seller may say that he or she has already received a higher offer and that you'll need to raise yours to be seriously considered. Ask to see the higher written offer, so you know what you're bidding against, and then ask the seller to give you a written counteroffer.

The seller is unlikely to show you the competing offer; even so, it doesn't hurt to ask.

If you're shown another offer contract, don't stop reading when you find out the amount offered. Check whether the financing is solid and whether there are any contingencies that make the offer chancy. If the offer has problems, the seller may accept your more solid, lower offer, or you may get another chance if the first deal falls through.

If the higher offer has real potential, and the seller counters your offer at, or above, the amount of the other offer, consider how much you can afford, how much you believe the house is worth, and your overall house purchase strategy.

Don't get so caught up in negotiating that you make a decision you'll regret later. If you do bid higher, take time away from the negotiating table to carefully consider each increase. A house you concluded was worth $600,000 on Sunday is unlikely to be worth $700,000 on Tuesday, just because another buyer wants it.

Your other option if you appear to be second in line is to accept a backup offer position, as discussed later in this chapter.

The Seller Responds With a Counteroffer

Typically, the seller responds with a written counteroffer accepting most of the offer terms but proposes certain changes. If the seller orally states a counteroffer, insist that it be put in writing before you consider or discuss it.

Major Provisions of a Typical Counteroffer

Most counteroffers correspond to these provisions of an offer:

- **Price.** Unless your offer meets or exceeds the asking price, the seller may ask for more money. If you decide to increase your initial bid (in a counter counter-offer or by accepting the counteroffer):
  - Make the increases small.
  - Try to get something in return for each increase. For example, ask the seller to pay for certain repairs.
  - Walk away if the price and the terms aren't right and you can't reasonably expect to come to agreement—for instance, if you want the seller to pay for expensive mold remediation, and he or she refuses.
- **Financing.** If the seller believes your financing is impractical, he or she will likely propose a change. Similarly, if you offer to put 10% down with the seller taking back a second mortgage, and the seller wants all of his or her equity in cash, he or she will counter-offer.
- **Occupancy.** The seller may want additional time to move out.
- **Your selling a current house.** If your offer is contingent on selling a current home, the seller may reject this in a counteroffer if the market is hot and the seller believes he or she can easily find another buyer. Or the seller may counteroffer with a wipe-out clause (see Chapter 18).
- **Inspections.** A seller's counteroffer for dealing with inspections may suggest a shorter period of time, eliminate one or more of your proposed inspections, or offer the house for sale "as is," meaning the seller won't pay for any defects the inspections turn up. Another increasingly common scenario is for the seller to propose that the buyer be responsible for the first "X" dollars of any needed repairs. While it's reasonable for you to complete inspections in a timely manner, it's completely unreasonable (and a possible red flag indicating physical problems) for the seller to limit the type of inspections you can conduct or insist that you purchase "as is."

Sample Counteroffer

The sample counteroffer shown in this chapter may be used by either the seller or buyer when only limited changes are proposed in the counteroffer (or counter counteroffer). A seller can also counteroffer using a detailed offer form. Study any new form carefully—no two are the same. An experienced broker or real estate lawyer should review the paperwork. If one provision of the counteroffer is unacceptable and you no longer want the house, do nothing. A counteroffer not accepted by the deadline simply expires.

> **EXAMPLE:** Leili offers to buy Tony and Jackie's house for $480,000, leaving the offer open for 48 hours. They counter-offer for $510,000 and permission to remove some built-in bookshelves. In addition, they require Leili to drop her contingency to sell her existing house first. Tony and Jackie give Leili 12 hours to accept the counteroffer. Leili, who has found a house she likes better, does nothing, and the counteroffer simply expires.

Negotiate by Counteroffers

For many sales, the written offer acceptance process is completed relatively quickly: The buyer makes an offer, the seller suggests a few changes, the buyer agrees. Sometimes, however, the process drags on, with counter-offers, counter counteroffers, and counter counter counteroffers flying back and forth for days, or even weeks. This can work well, if you and the seller narrow your differences with each counteroffer. But don't get so caught up in negotiating that you pay more than the house is worth, or otherwise make a bad deal.

If you participate in a counteroffer dance, make sure:

- All counteroffers are in writing.
- You and the seller meet all deadlines.
- All counteroffers contain a time limit by which responses must be accepted.
- You and the seller keep clear on what's being offered and what's being accepted. At some point, using short counteroffer forms that don't restate the entire offer will become confusing. Before that happens, use a new purchase agreement form. Retitle it "Counteroffer" (or "Counter Counteroffer" or whatever), state the terms you and the seller have agreed on, and make appropriate changes.

Multiple Counteroffer

Occasionally, the seller will counter several buyers' offers with a "multiple counteroffer." The terms of each offer need not be the same. Buyers who remain interested (some will drop out) must accept or counter the terms of the counteroffer. If you're really eager to get this house, you'll need to act strategically to set your offer apart from the competition. Consider bumping up your offer price a little or improving the offer's other terms. Multiple counteroffers are common in southern California, less so in northern California.

Counteroffer [Counter Counteroffer]

Date: ______________________________ Time: ________ ☐ a.m. ☐ p.m.

In response to the offer [counteroffer] to purchase real property at (address) ____________
____,
dated ______________, ____
______________, Buyer [Seller] submits the following counteroffer [counter counteroffer]:
____
____.

All other terms of the offer [counteroffer] remain the same. This counteroffer [counter counteroffer] expires on __________ at (time) ______ ☐ a.m. ☐ p.m. unless Buyer [Seller] delivers a written acceptance to Seller [Buyer] or his/her agent before then.

____ ____________________
Signature Date

____ ____________________
Signature Date

Acceptance

The undersigned Buyer [Seller] ☐ accepts ☐ accepts subject to the attached counteroffer the foregoing offer and agrees to sell the property on the terms and conditions stated above.

Seller agrees to pay compensation for services as follows:

☐ ____% of the sales price or ☐ $ ________ to (Listing Broker) ________________________

☐ ____% of the sales price or ☐ $ ________ to (Selling Broker) ________________________

payable on recordation of the deed or other evidence of title. If the sale is prevented due to the default of Seller, the commission shall be paid at default. If the sale is prevented due to the default of Buyer, the commission shall be paid only if and when Seller collects damages from Buyer.

Buying [Listing] Broker ____

By Buying [Listing] Agent ____

Buyer [Seller] ____

Buyer [Seller] ____

Broker's Address ____

Broker's Telephone ____________________ Broker's Fax ____________________

Date: ______________________________ Broker's Email ____________________

True Story

Christina: I'm Glad Our First Few Offers Fell Through

After eight years of renting a small apartment my husband and I decided we wanted a larger place with more grass and trees—someplace good to raise the kids we planned to have in a few years.

Our first weekend house hunting, we fell in love with a beautiful house in a nearby suburb, but it was $30,000 above our maximum price and needed some major structural work. The sellers were anxious to sell quickly for full price and "as is," because they had already bought a second house.

We made the classic mistake of thinking this house was the only one in the world; we counteroffered for days. Our real estate agent, who was anxious for a quick sale, fanned the flames. When this deal fell through, we repeated the same mistake with the next house. A few weeks later, we finally came to our senses and realized there were lots of houses out there. We got a new agent, slowed down our house search, and became more realistic—after, all, we were in no real hurry to move. Once we relaxed, we found a lovely place—much nicer than the first one—for $15,000 less than we expected to pay. Now our advice to others is get out of the fast lane and enjoy the process.

An Offer Is Accepted—A Contract Is Formed

A contract is formed when either the buyer or the seller accepts all of the terms of the other's offer or counteroffer in writing within the time allowed. After this happens:

- Make copies of the contract; keep one and make sure the seller has or gets one. If short-form counteroffers were used to change a long offer, all contract terms won't be stated in one document. It's best to retype all the accepted terms onto one form.
- Give the seller's agent a deposit check made out to an escrow or title company in the amount called for in the contract.
- Give copies of documents to any real estate agent, attorney, or tax adviser who's assisting you.
- Take steps to begin removing the contingencies—you usually have only a few days to act. At the least, you'll need to arrange inspections and apply for financing if you haven't already done so.

Revoking an Offer or Counteroffer

You may revoke (take back) your offer in writing any time before the seller accepts in writing. You needn't state a reason. If you want to revoke an offer (or counter counteroffer), do so immediately. Call the seller or her agent and say that you're revoking your offer; immediately follow up in writing. The best ways to do this are by email or fax (follow up by sending a signed original to the seller or agent), hand delivery, or overnight mail.

A sample Revocation of Offer to Purchase Real Property form is shown below.

Making a Backup Offer

If you locate a house you love, but end up losing out to another bidder, consider making a backup offer.

One way to do this by submitting a short addendum to your original purchase offer. Your addenda should give you the right to say yes or no in writing within a certain number of hours should the seller inform you in writing that the primary offer has fallen through and the seller now wants to accept yours. You will, however, typically need to remove certain contingencies within those hours, including the financing and inspection contingencies.

Many cautious sellers are delighted to receive backup offers and accept desirable ones. If a seller accepts more than one, priority is set by the date and time of acceptance.

Revocation of Offer to Purchase Real Property

(Buyer) ______________________________

hereby revokes the offer made to purchase the real property at (address) ______________

______________________________,

made on (date) ______________.

______________________________ ______________
Offerer/Buyer Date

______________________________ ______________
Offerer/Buyer Date

CHAPTER

18

After the Contract Is Signed: Escrow, Contingencies, and Insurance

Congratulations! Your offer to purchase a house has been accepted. But it's not yet time to buy a new doormat. Many tasks remain before the house is yours—opening an escrow account, removing contingencies, obtaining title insurance, and closing escrow—and all are discussed in this chapter.

The time it takes between the contract signing and the close of escrow (when you become the owner) depends on what deadline you and the seller agreed to, probably based on what remains to be done following the signing. If you have your financing lined up in advance and the house is in excellent condition, you shouldn't have any trouble meeting the standard 30- to 60-day closing date. If, however, your offer is contingent upon your selling an existing house, the inspections turn up lots of physical problems, or you need to arrange a complicated financing package, it could take several months or more. If your deadline is too soon, you and the seller can agree to extend it.

CAUTION

Understand escrow before you begin the process. Opening and successfully closing escrow involves detailed, picky, and often overlapping steps. Read through your purchase contract and draw up a list, calendar, or flowchart that shows you who needs to perform what tasks, and when.

Open Escrow

In finalizing the purchase of your house, you and the seller need a neutral third party to hold onto, and then exchange, deeds and money, pay off existing loans, record deeds, prorate the property tax payments, and help with other transfer details.

To begin this process, you and the seller "open an escrow account" with a person or organization legally empowered to act as an escrow agent. Lawyers need not be involved with escrow in California, and usually aren't, unless an unusual problem arises (for example, the seller's title isn't clear)—in which case either buyer or seller may wish to consult an attorney.

By custom, escrow is done differently in northern and southern California. The common "dividing line" between northern and southern California escrow approaches is somewhere near the Tehachapi Mountains. Nevertheless, both escrow styles routinely appear in the middle of the state, and some northern California escrow agents are beginning to adopt southern California practices.

Northern California. An escrow account is normally opened with a title insurance company (often just called a title company) immediately after the purchase contract is signed. Title companies not only provide the necessary title insurance, but also handle financing arrangements such as collecting your down payment and funds for your lender, paying off the seller's lender, and preparing and recording a deed from the seller to you and a deed of trust for your lender.

Southern California. An escrow account is usually opened by the buyer and seller with an escrow company, which prepares the necessary papers and exchanges the seller's ownership interest for your money after

Escrow Terminology

Here are common real estate terms used during escrow.

Close of escrow or Closing. The final transfer of ownership of the house to the buyer. It occurs after both the buyer and seller have met all terms of the contract and the deed is recorded. "Closing" also refers to the time when the transfer will occur, such as, "The closing on my house will happen on January 27 at 10:00 a.m."

Closing costs. The expenses involved in the closing process, including broker commissions, title insurance, loan fees, lender's appraisal, inspection fees, private mortgage insurance, deed recording, and incidental fees charged by the escrow agent and lender.

Closing statement. A document prepared by the escrow holder containing a complete accounting of all funds, credits, and debts involved in the escrow process. Basically this amounts to a statement of the amount of cash the buyer and the buyer's lender have put into escrow, how much the seller has received, and how much money was used for other expenses.

Demand or Request for beneficiary statement. A letter from the seller's lender to the escrow holder telling how much the escrow holder must send the lender to pay the seller's existing mortgage in full. The lender sends it after being notified by the escrow holder that the seller is selling the house and expects to close escrow by a certain date. If the time between opening and closing escrow is reasonably short, the seller wants to receive the demand fast to include the calculations in the closing. If the time between opening and closing will take some time, however, the seller won't rush the demand. A demand is typically good for only 30 days; if it comes too soon, it will expire before escrow closes and the seller will have to request a second one.

Final title report or Final. Just before the close of escrow, the title company rechecks the condition of the title established in the preliminary title report. If it's the same (it usually is), the preliminary title report becomes the final report, and title insurance policies are issued.

Funding the loan. California law requires that checks and drafts be collected prior to disbursement. This means that to close escrow, funds must be deposited with the escrow holder one or more days prior to the close of escrow, except for cash and funds deposited by electronic transfer.

Good-faith estimate or Reg. Z Disclosure. Federal law requires the lender to disclose to you all the material terms of the loan (such as negative amortization, the annual percentage rate, and caps) you are applying for, on this form.

Legal description or Legal. The description of the parcel of land being sold that appears on the deed to the property. It has nothing to do with the buildings, but rather the land itself. The legal may specify Lot and Block numbers or metes and bounds (a complicated exercise in map reading), none of which should concern you. (If you want to know more about legally describing California real

Escrow Terminology (continued)

property, see *Deeds for California Real Estate*, by Mary Randolph (Nolo).)

Loan commitment. A written statement from a lender promising to lend you a certain sum of money on certain terms.

Opening escrow. Escrow is opened when you and the seller select an escrow agent to hold onto and transfer documents and money during the house purchase process.

Preliminary, Prelim, or Pre. The preliminary title report issued by a title company soon after escrow opens. It shows current ownership information on the property (including any liens or encumbrances). If any problems are found, the seller can take steps to resolve them before escrow closes. The title insurance policy issued at the close of escrow is usually based on this report.

Taking title. Describes the transfer of ownership from seller to buyer. For example, "The buyer takes title [gets his or her name on the deed] next Tuesday."

deducting the amount needed to pay off the seller's existing mortgage, past taxes, and other liens. Title insurance is obtained from a title insurance company, which isn't usually otherwise involved in the escrow process.

Other escrow holders. Although it's unusual, escrow can be legally handled by someone other than a title or escrow company. The buyer or seller's attorney, a real estate broker who has a trust account for supervising escrows, or the escrow department of a bank are all legally empowered to do the job.

How to Open Escrow

When the seller accepts your offer, you'll normally give your agent a deposit check made out to the escrow holder. The deposit is taken to the title or escrow company, and an escrow account is opened. The deposit will be applied to the purchase price, or it will be returned to you if you back out of the deal for a valid reason allowed by the contract—for example, a contingency can't be met.

TIP

Consider getting a power of attorney. If you or a cobuyer will be traveling, consider filling out a power of attorney so the nontraveling buyer can sign the final papers. Ask your escrow company to draft the power of attorney.

How to Find an Escrow Holder

In your offer contract, you'll enter the name and address of the escrow holder you choose. In some situations, the seller may disagree and list his or her choice in the counteroffer. As the basic task to be accomplished and prices charged are similar, this should not be an issue to hold up the acceptance of an offer. Unless you feel very strongly about using "your" escrow agent or not using the seller's, give in.

How do you know which title company or escrow company to enter on the offer form? As with finding any service provider, it's best to get a recommendation from someone you trust, such as your agent. But be sure to confirm that your escrow officer won't be taking any long leaves or vacations during your escrow period.

If you are considering several recommended firms, you may be inclined to call around and compare prices. You may save a few dollars, but prices tend to be pretty similar. Because of the small potential savings involved, it normally makes more sense to concentrate on finding a company that offers superior service.

How to Work With the Escrow Holder

What happens after escrow opens depends to a considerable extent on your escrow agent, whether you're in northern or southern California, and your contract with the seller. If the contract contains contingencies, the escrow holder may do very little until you and the seller remove them, although many escrow holders in southern California routinely confer with agents, or with sellers and buyers without agents, to make sure steps are being taken to remove contingencies. Southern California escrow holders also frequently try to help resolve any title disputes. Even if your escrow holder is less involved, be sure the escrow holder gives you a list of what you need to provide and the dates when you need to provide each item.

Your agent should help the escrow process go smoothly. If neither you nor the seller is working with an agent, however, you'll need to handle the details yourselves. Fortunately, it's not difficult. Make an initial appointment with the escrow agent. Bring the timeline from Chapter 13, Obtaining a Mortgage, and use it as your guide to ask questions. Check in regularly—about once a week—to be sure you're doing what's expected and that everything is on track.

If a dispute arises between you and the seller during escrow, don't look to the escrow holder to resolve it—or to transfer the money and deed. The escrow holder is a neutral party. You'll have to solve the problem (see Chapter 21, If Something Goes Wrong During Escrow); until you do, the escrow holder sits still. If the dispute drags on long enough, the escrow holder may get tired of being stuck in the middle and may initiate a lawsuit (called an "interpleader") to have the court resolve the dispute and direct the distribution of the deposited money.

Ordering Title Insurance

Ordering title insurance from a title insurance company (usually the same company handling the escrow in northern California) is the buyer's responsibility. The title company issues a preliminary title report and then, just before closing, a final title report and two title insurance policies. If you're represented by a real estate professional, he or she will be able to help you with this.

The Cost of Escrow

Closing costs are typically about 2%–5% of the purchase price, with the lion's share made up of loan points and fees. Escrow costs, which are considered part of closing costs, tend to be under 1% of the purchase price. (In southern California, the costs are divided between the escrow company and a title insurance company.) Included in the escrow costs are fees for the preliminary and final title reports, recording of the deed, notarization, the title company, the escrow company (if necessary), and two title insurance policies. One policy is for the buyer (CLTA policy), and one is for the lender (ALTA policy). (See "Obtain Title Report and Title Insurance," below, for more.)

No law specifies who pays escrow costs; you and the seller negotiate this as part of the forming of the contract. For our discussion on who *customarily* pays which fee, see Chapter 16.

Complying With IRS Foreign Investor Rules

The seller must complete a form, available from the escrow or title company or the IRS, stating whether he or she is a foreign investor as defined by law. (This is required by a federal law called FIRPTA, the Foreign Investment in Real Property Tax Act, Internal Revenue Code § 1445.) If the seller is a foreign investor, you must withhold in escrow 10% of the sale price of the house and fill out and file some papers with the IRS. The escrow agent can help you.

If the seller is located outside of California or the proceeds of the sale will be paid to an intermediary of the seller, you must withhold and send some money to the Franchise Tax Board (California's taxing authority). Again, the escrow agent can help you.

Remove Contingencies

If your contract contains contingencies, you must remove them in writing and let the escrow holder know they've been removed before the purchase becomes final. Removing the most common contingencies, and extending the time for doing so, is discussed below.

Inspection Contingencies

Most house purchase contracts give the buyer the right to have the house inspected by specified inspectors, and approve the results of their reports, before going through with the sale. This is an important part of the process, in which you'll learn a lot about your new house's foundation, structure, internal systems such as heating and electrical, and pest activity. You will normally hire one or more professional inspectors, including at a minimum a general contractor and a pest inspector.

Give each inspector a copy of the seller's Real Estate Transfer Disclosure Statement, Natural Hazard Disclosure Statement, and any other inspection reports and disclosures the seller provides you. The seller must let the inspectors have access to the house, although you may need authorization from a homeowners' association for the contractor to inspect common areas of a condominium. We suggest that you accompany the inspectors on their rounds. Chapter 19 discusses the seller's legally required disclosures and the house inspection system in detail.

Inspections often find problems. For example, the house may have termite damage, need new wiring, or require roof repairs. You have various options to deal with such problems:

- If your offer is contingent on approving inspection reports, you can ask the seller to fix the problem before you go through with the purchase.
- If your offer is contingent upon your approving inspection reports, and a report indicates serious problems, you can back out of the deal.
- If the problem was disclosed before you made your offer, and you nevertheless offered to purchase the house "as is," you can't legally claim that it must be repaired at the seller's expense before you'll buy.

Assuming the house needs repairs and your offer wasn't "as is," your first question is, do you still want the house if it's repaired? If the problem is extremely serious (the house is in a hazardous slide zone or near an earthquake fault), you may say, "No." But if you still want the house, you and the seller must negotiate over who pays for what.

Negotiating the Cost of Repairs

By the time an offer has been accepted and inspections have been done, neither you nor the seller wants to spend more money. At the same time, both of you have already invested considerable time and energy in the transaction and don't want to walk away and start over. If either of you needs the sale to go through to meet other commitments, time pressure (and, often, the other's leverage) can cause great stress and short tempers.

Who pays what usually comes down to who is perceived to have more negotiating clout. If the seller thinks he or she has agreed to sell at too low a price or can easily find another buyer, the seller will probably refuse to pay for all or most repairs. If you think the seller is right, you'd be smart to share modest repair costs. If, however, you believe you've offered top dollar for the house and don't think it's worth a penny more, you'll want to insist that the seller pay most or all of the repairs and refuse to finalize the deal otherwise.

Paying for Repairs

A seller willing to reduce the purchase price to allow for the cost of repairs normally does so through an "escrow credit." This means the seller agrees to leave money in escrow from the sale proceeds to cover the amount of the repairs. The exact amount the repairs will cost is normally agreed to by all parties based on contractors' bids. You want to be sure that the cost reflects all needed work using quality labor and materials.

If expensive repairs are needed, the lender often requires that work be done before escrow closes. Assuming the seller has agreed to cover the cost, a portion of the money placed in escrow can be paid to a contractor before the close of escrow, or held by the escrow holder after the sale closes, pending the contractor completing the work.

But if you've agreed to pay for a portion of the repairs, you must come up with the money. If this is difficult to do, explore having the seller mark up the price of the house by the amount of the repairs. This still results in your paying for the repairs through the higher price, but if the mortgage lender will go along, and if the appraisal value of the house justifies the higher price, it will help cover the extra expense. The seller who gets the artificially high price uses the extra money to pay for the repairs.

In some situations, especially where repairs aren't major, a lender will let escrow close without requiring the repairs to be made. In this situation, if the seller has agreed to pay a credit into escrow for the work, the buyer is free to use this money for other purposes, such as contributing to the down payment.

EXAMPLE: Mary agrees to sell her house to Albin for $581,000. Albin's offer is contingent upon his approval of a pest control and general contractor's inspection. The inspections turn up $30,000 worth of beetle damage and drainage problems. Albin refuses to go through with the sale unless Mary credits him $30,000 in escrow for the repairs. They negotiate and agree to share the costs, with Mary paying $24,000 and Albin $6,000. The compromise reflects the fact that Albin was ready to walk away from the deal if Mary didn't pay most of the cost. Mary, on the other hand, needed to move and didn't have time to find another buyer in a slow sales market.

A problem remains, however. Albin doesn't have $6,000 to pay his share. This problem is solved when his lender agrees to let the price of the house be raised to $587,000, with Mary now

True Story

Mitchell: How I Used an Escrow Credit to Reduce My Down Payment

I was going to offer $362,000 for a house I liked but changed my mind after reading an inspection report commissioned by another buyer. It identified leaks in an old roof and pest problems in the foundation. I offered $359,000 and asked for a $5,000 credit for roof work and a $12,000 credit for pest work. The seller agreed to install a new roof and give me $3,000 toward closing costs and $6,000 for pest work.

The pest problem was old and not getting worse, however, so the repair work wasn't immediately necessary, and I decided to hold off. I got to use $9,000 to reduce my out-of-pocket costs for closing and the down payment.

paying for all repairs. The lender is willing to do this based on its appraisal, which concludes that once the $30,000 of repairs are made, $590,000 reflects a fair market value.

If the lender doesn't require that work be done, and you have enough cash to pay for the repairs yourself, consider asking the seller to reduce the asking price instead of giving you a credit in escrow. This saves you money because escrow and title fees, as well as annual property taxes, are based on the purchase price. The seller is often pleased, because the commission the sellers pay is based on the sale price. However, since the real estate commissions are reduced, the agents might not be excited about this arrangement.

Removing Inspection Contingencies

As you satisfy or waive an inspection contingency, you must remove it in writing. The section titled "Releasing Contingencies," below, shows how.

Financing Contingencies

In any standard purchase contract, the buyer makes the offer to buy contingent on arranging satisfactory financing. To remove (release) this contingency you should provide the seller written evidence that you have obtained financing sufficient to purchase the house, along with a contingency release form. Evidence of financing is usually a loan commitment letter from a lender or a bank confirmation if you arrange private financing. If you're assuming the seller's mortgage, order the assumption documents from the lender to start the process of taking over the loan.

Extending Time to Meet a Contingency

Buyers frequently need extra time to satisfy a contract contingency. Without the extra time, the contract ends (that is, the deal falls through) unless you and the seller agree to extend it. If the seller wants out, he or she won't extend the time. More commonly, however, the seller wants the deal to go through but needs reassurance that you're still serious about buying the house. The seller may demand that you increase your deposit in exchange. The amounts vary, but to extend a $300,000 offer for a few weeks, $1,000 or so is reasonable.

Any agreement to extend the time to meet a contingency (or to change any other term of the contract) must be in writing and signed. A sample is below.

> **EXAMPLE:** Julie agrees to buy Shawn's house for $700,000, contingent upon securing an adjustable rate mortgage at 6% or lower for 80% of the purchase price and selling her own house within 90 days. Julie arranges the financing easily but has trouble selling her house. She offers Shawn $3,000 cash to extend her time to purchase (to let her sell her existing house) for another 60 days. Shawn agrees.

Extending Time to Meet Contingencies

The material set out below is hereby made a part of the contract dated ____________________
between (Buyer) ____________________
and (Seller) ____________________
to purchase real property located at ____________________
____________________.

The final date for Buyer's removal of all contingencies set out in Clause ____ of the contract, is hereby extended until (month, day, year) ____________ at (time) ________ ☐ a.m. ☐ p.m.

____________________ ____________________
Signature of Buyer Date

____________________ ____________________
Signature of Buyer Date

____________________ ____________________
Signature of Seller Date

____________________ ____________________
Signature of Seller Date

Releasing Contingencies

As you satisfy or abandon (waive) a contingency, you must remove (or release) it in writing. Don't wait until all contingencies are met to do this. Remove each one as it is satisfied or abandoned. You remove a contingency by executing a contingency release form such as the one below. Give the original to the seller and keep a copy for yourself.

If the seller has agreed to credit you for the cost of any repairs, add the following to the release, after the word "report":

"providing that by ____ ___.m. on ____________, Seller agrees in writing to extend to Buyer an escrow credit in the amount of $____________ against the purchase price to cover the cost of needed repair and rehabilitation work to be paid by Buyer."

Release Clauses (Wipe-Outs)

Some contracts let the seller demand in writing that you remove all contingencies within a certain time (usually between 24

Contingency Release

(Buyer) ______________________________
of the property at (address) ______________________________,
hereby removes the following contingency(ies) from the purchase contract dated __________:
____
____
____
____

If this release is based on accepting any inspection report, a copy of the report, signed by Buyer, is attached, and Buyer releases Seller from liability for any physical defects disclosed by the attached report.

Signature of Buyer	Date
Signature of Buyer	Date
Signature of Seller	Date
Signature of Seller	Date

and 72 hours). This is sometimes called a "notice to perform" or a "72-hour release clause," and we call it a "Seller's Demand for Removal of Contingencies" in the sample below.

If you can't, the seller can give you written notice ending your contract (wiping it out) and go ahead with a backup offer. The seller can do this to you only if a wipe-out clause was included in the original contract. Wipe-out clauses are most common when an offer is contingent upon your selling an existing house or arranging financing that the seller believes may not come through.

When You Can't Fulfill a Contingency

If, after trying in good faith, you or the seller can't meet a contingency, the deal is over. The most common reasons sales fall through are:

- An inspection turns up expensive physical problems and you decide you no longer want the house, or you and the seller can't agree who will pay.
- You're unable to sell your existing house within the time provided.
- You can't secure adequate financing within the time provided.

Seller's Demand for Removal of Contingencies

Under the terms of the contract dated ________________, between (Buyer) ________________ and (Seller) ________________ for the purchase of the real property at (address) ________________, Seller hereby demands that Buyer remove the following contingency specified in Clause ______ of the contract:

____

____

____

within ☐ ninety-six (96) hours from receipt of this demand if personally delivered.
☐ five (5) days from mailing this demand if mailed by certified mail.

If Buyer does not remove this contingency within the time specified, the contract shall become void. Seller shall promptly return Buyer's deposit upon Buyer's execution of a release, releasing Buyer and Seller from all obligations under the contract.

Signature of Seller ________________ Date ________

Signature of Seller ________________ Date ________

Personally delivered on: ________ Mailed by certified mail on: ________

You and the seller should sign a release canceling the contract and authorizing the return of your deposit. The seller has no right to keep your deposit if the deal falls through for failure to meet a contingency spelled out in the contract. If the seller refuses, or you refuse, to sign the release within 30 days following a written demand, the person who refuses to sign may be liable to the other for attorneys' fees and damages of three times the amount deposited in escrow, no more than $1,000 and no less than $100. (Civil Code § 1057.3.)

If an inspection turns up negligible problems and you refuse to go ahead with the purchase (or you refuse to proceed for another nonlegitimate reason), the seller can keep your deposit. A seller rarely keeps an entire deposit, however, because the seller will have trouble completing a subsequent sale until the escrow with you terminates; and termination of escrow normally can't happen until your deposit is released. Also, state law generally limits the amount sellers can keep if you default. (See Chapter 16 for our discussion of liquidated damages.)

Even if a buyer withdraws for a non-legitimate reason, it's common for the buyer and seller to compromise, with the seller keeping part of the deposit and some of it being returned to the buyer.

A sample release form is shown below.

Obtain Hazard Insurance

Before finalizing your loan, your lender will require that you purchase hazard coverage to pay the lender in the event your house is damaged or destroyed by fire, smoke, wind, hail, riot, vandalism, or another similar act. Don't balk at the insurance. You're going to want what's required, and probably more. And don't wait until right before escrow closes to start shopping for insurance—it's

Release of Real Estate Purchase Contract

(Buyer) ______________________________

and (Seller) ______________________________.

hereby mutually release each other from any and all claims with respect to the real estate purchase

contract dated ______________ for the property located at: ______________

______________________________.

It is the intent of this release to declare all rights and obligations arising out of the real estate purchase contract null and void.

☐ Buyer has received his/her deposit.

☐ Seller has directed the escrow holder to return Buyer's deposit.

Signature of Buyer	Date
Signature of Buyer	Date
Signature of Seller	Date
Signature of Seller	Date

getting harder and harder to find a good policy at a reasonable price, due to recent losses and clampdowns in the insurance industry.

Typical Coverage

Virtually all homeowners buy comprehensive homeowners' insurance, not just the minimum hazard insurance required by the lender. In addition to covering your house, homeowners' insurance protects other structures on the property (such as a pool or in-law unit) and your personal property, usually for 50% of the liability limit on your house, unless you pay extra.

A few valuable items, such as art, computer equipment, and antiques, are covered to a specific (low) amount; if you own more, you'll have to itemize them and pay extra. But this may not be the time to skimp—if everything you own is destroyed, say in a fire, being able to rebuild the bare house will be small comfort.

A comprehensive policy will also cover you for some types of personal liability—if the letter carrier trips over your kid's skateboard, your policy will pay for his or her medical expenses and other losses. In addition, if you injure someone off your property, you will likely be covered if the injury doesn't involve a motor vehicle or your business.

CAUTION

Beware of dogs raising your premiums. Most insurance companies are attaching canine exclusions for dog breeds that are particularly large or have bad reputations. While the various insurance companies are not consistent about which pooches they prohibit, owning an "ineligible" breed could impair your chances of purchasing a policy or result in your paying a policy surcharge.

How much insurance do you need? You should cover the full replacement value of your real property (not including the land) and your personal property. (At least 40%, and often more, of the value is the land itself, which will likely still be there even if your house is destroyed.) The coverage most people select is "extended replacement cost." This pays for replacement of your house up to a certain percentage (often 125%) of what the policy states is the house's value. Such coverage helps protect you if your house's stated value turns out to be less than what it would cost to replace it.

For added protection, you can also buy what's called an "inflation guard." This automatically amends your policy to raise the stated value of your house by a fixed percentage every year. You choose the percentage when you buy the inflation guard.

Fewer and fewer insurance companies write policies for "100% guaranteed replacement." This is because such a policy replaces your house at full value even if construction and labor costs have skyrocketed past the house's value as stated in the policy.

Special Insurance Concerns for Home-Based Businesses

If you run a home-based business, don't rely on the standard homeowners' policy to cover business-related losses. For example, many homeowners' policies don't cover damage to detached garages and storage sheds you were using to run a business out of (though storage of business goods is usually okay). If that's where your business will be located, you'll need to purchase extra coverage. If you'll have business-related visitors, you should also consider buying liability coverage in case they're injured. And even if your home is not your business's central location, inventory or equipment that you keep at home, particularly if it's worth more than $2,000, will not be covered by the standard homeowners' policy. Ask your insurance broker for more information.

Earthquakes and Floods

Two of the greatest risks facing California homeowners are not even covered in the standard homeowners' insurance policy: earthquakes and floods.

Because of the huge losses earthquakes have caused Californians in the past, the state of California now mandates that your insurance company offer you state-sponsored earthquake insurance, both when you first buy the policy and at every alternate renewal. You actually have to sign something if you decide to decline this coverage.

Finding Earthquake Insurance Can Be Risky

Whenever an insurance company issues a homeowners' insurance policy in California, it must offer earthquake insurance. The offered policy must cover loss or damage to the dwelling and its contents and living expenses for the occupants if the house is temporarily uninhabitable. (Insurance Code §§ 10081, 10089.) As a result of several earthquakes in California, insurance companies have been seeking ways to circumvent their legal requirement to offer earthquake insurance.

Many homebuyers have been unable to close escrow because they could not purchase property insurance—because the carrier writing the property insurance would then have to offer earthquake insurance. The Insurance Code enables insurers to offer applicants a "mini" earthquake policy on the dwelling structure and personal property. These mini-earthquake policies are generally very expensive, have limited coverage, and contain large deductibles. In many cases, even the mini-policies are difficult to find.

The end result is the extraordinary unavailability of earthquake insurance. To protect yourself when buying a house, we recommend you include a contingency in your offer dependent upon your securing adequate hazard insurance. That way if getting earthquake insurance is important to you and you're not able to, you can back out of the agreement.

Unfortunately, the state-sponsored coverage is not highly regarded, so you're better off looking for a private earthquake insurer. Whether you can find private coverage at a price you can afford will depend on where you live and when the last earthquake occurred (immediately after an earthquake, insurance companies stop selling earthquake coverage for a while).

Buying earthquake coverage typically costs a few hundred dollars or more per year. Houses near active faults or made of brick may be more expensive to insure. The problem with earthquake insurance is the high deductible—typically 10% to 15% of the policy amount. That means if you have a $200,000 policy, you won't get any benefits unless the damage is more than $20,000 (with a 10% deductible) or $30,000 (with a 15% deductible).

Another endorsement to consider, if you're one of the thousands of California residents buying a home in a flood zone, is flood coverage. Unfortunately, the extra coverage can be expensive and contain high deductibles. However, lenders require flood insurance for property in designated flood hazard areas. This is an irritant to property owners who live in designated flood areas but who haven't seen a real flood in years. If you're buying a house in such an area, you may be able to avoid buying flood insurance by having your property surveyed to show that it lies above the flood plain. (And, though it's many years away, once your house is paid off, the lender will have no say in whether you buy flood insurance!)

See Chapter 19 for a discussion of seller disclosures regarding flood, fire, and seismic hazards. Also, see Appendix A for information on the areas of California susceptible to earthquakes, fires, and floods.

Condominiums

If you are buying a condominium, a town house, or some other planned unit development property, consult the CC&Rs to determine what type of insurance protection you should or must buy. Often the homeowners' association buys insurance for all the buildings and the common areas. That leaves you responsible for buying coverage for your personal property (the contents of your unit) and personal liability (that is, claims made against you).

If you have any thoughts of replacing or improving the features of your unit, you should also invest in what's called "alterations and additions" coverage. For example, if you were to replace the unit's existing cheap painted cabinetry with polished teak, and your unit burnt, the association's homeowners' insurance would only cover the value of the cheap cabinets.

CAUTION

Be ready for CC&Rs that make you responsible for holes in the homeowners' association's insurance coverage. For example, if the club house burns down and the association insurance won't cover the entire loss, a typical set of CC&Rs would allow the association to collect the shortfall from the unit owners. Insurance for this type of unhappy event, called "loss assessment" coverage, can be very cheaply included in your policy.

Shop Around for Insurance

Homeowners' insurance rates can vary up to 30% from company to company, so try to compare rates of several companies. Another way to save money is to opt for a larger-than-usual deductible. By increasing your deductible to $1,000 (or more), you may save 10% or more on your premiums. Also, ask your insurance agent what discounts are available for new or remodeled houses, or houses with a security system or near a fire hydrant. Some companies also offer discounts if you buy more than one policy from them, for example, an auto as well as a home policy. And, if you're a retiree age 55 or over, you may qualify for a discount of up to 10% at some companies.

Price isn't the only factor to consider when choosing insurance. Some companies are better at processing claims fairly and quickly. If you live near an area where there was a severe fire, earthquake, or flood, ask community organizations which insurers were particularly responsive to consumers (and which ones to avoid).

And then there's the matter of convincing the insurance company that you qualify for insurance. Because the insurance industry in California has taken some economic hits recently, it has gotten skittish about doing the very thing it's supposed to do: sell insurance. You may be refused affordable coverage, or any coverage, based on your home's location, your credit score, your history of filing claims due to mold or water damage, or your history of filing other homeowners' insurance claims.

Your Home's Location

The insurance industry is not allowed to use outright discrimination (known as red-lining) when deciding which localities it will offer policies within. However, insurance underwriters come close to the wire, by following their home offices' guidelines stating that no insurance can be offered in certain "capacity exposure areas." When you apply for homeowners' insurance, the first thing the underwriter will do is to "map" the property. If you reside in a brush area, for example, the underwriter may turn down your application for insurance. If you promise to clear the brush away from your home, you may get a second chance, but woe unto you (and your coverage) if you fail to clear the brush or you allow it to grow back.

Soil instability in the area where your new home is located could also make the home difficult to insure. This seems especially odd given that most homeowner's policies do not even pay claims for earth movement, earthquakes, or soil slippage. However, some underwriters fear that our courts will be overly generous to a homeowner whose house has just been shaken into the mud, and they refuse to issue insurance policies in unstable soil areas.

Your Credit Score

Most insurance companies and their underwriters now order a copy of your credit report before they decide whether to sell you coverage. (That's why they'll ask you for your Social Security number.) Their theory is

How to Make Sure Your Policy Gets Renewed

After making the important decision of which home insurance policy to buy, it's worth taking steps to hang onto it for more than a year. Try to:

- **Pay your premiums when they are due.** Don't allow your insurance policy to lapse or be cancelled due to late payments. Once you've had a policy cancelled for any reason, finding a replacement policy will be an uphill battle.
- **Think twice about turning in claims.** Unless your house has gone through major damage, any money that you realize by filing a claim may be wiped out by a resulting increase in your premium, or the cancellation of your insurance when it's time for renewal. With this in mind, ask your agent to increase your policy deductible—up to $2,500 to $5,000 is a safe amount, if your lender will allow it—and take advantage of the premium credit that will result. (Why have a low deductible if you won't be filing claims for these relatively low amounts, anyway?) Then fix those minor problems yourself, without even contacting your insurance company.
- **Cooperate with your insurance company.** If your insurance underwriter asks numerous questions during the application process, or sends you a questionnaire about you and your home at renewal time, call your agent. Find out what's going on and get back to the underwriter as soon as you can. Don't give the company an excuse to cancel your policy based on noncooperation.
- **Keep up with basic home maintenance.** Don't ignore little problems that could turn into big ones, such as leaking roofs and plumbing problems. If you aren't attuned to home repair issues, bring in a professional to assess your home's condition.
- **If you need additional help, get in touch with an experienced insurance broker.**

By the way, if you've got a decent insurance policy, hang onto it. Jumping from one insurance company to another in an effort to save a few dollars is not worth your time. Just when you get another policy, your new company is likely to institute a rate increase to catch up with the competition.

that if you have bad credit, you might turn in maintenance claims to the insurance company instead of taking care of the property yourself. They call this the "moral hazard."

Past Claims for Water Damage and Mold

The prospect of mushrooming mold claims makes the insurance industry very nervous—especially given the lack of medical information about which molds are dangerously toxic. If you have ever submitted a claim for water damage (in a past home), or if the home you are buying has had any history of water damage, expect difficulty in getting the underwriters to insure your property. Or, if they do agree to insure you, count on a complete mold exclusion or, at best, a pitifully low amount of coverage for any future mold claims, plus a large deductible for claims based on mold or water damage.

Other Past Claims

You might have thought that the purpose of insurance was to collect on it when you need to—but think again. To keep its risks low, insurance companies have recently been trying to insure only those homeowners who won't actually use the insurance! Your history of filing claims on the home you are leaving, as well as the seller's history of filing claims on the home you are buying, will all be taken into account. Yes, you heard right, even claims on your former home and claims that someone else made will be counted against you in the underwriting process. (Of course, if you are purchasing a brand new home or one in which you are the first owner, you'll have only your own past claims to contend with.)

How Insurance Relates to the Closing

Once you arrange your insurance, have your insurance agent deliver your policy to the escrow holder before closing. Your lender will not approve your loan until your insurance takes effect. Many lenders will want you to prepay the first year of hazard insurance by the closing; ask if you can pay semiannually, quarterly, or monthly, if your budget is tight.

Do You Need Life Insurance?

Some insurance companies will try to sell you life insurance or credit insurance so your heirs can pay off the mortgage if you die. Unless your survivors could not afford the monthly payments without you, don't bother. Even then, look for a policy that lets your survivors use the money as they wish, not just to pay off the mortgage. For this purpose, a term policy covering the period for which survivors (often small children) are vulnerable to losing the house if you die is far cheaper than a whole life policy, and just as good.

RESOURCE

Insurance information. For general information on homeowner's insurance, including premium comparisons among some of the state's larger companies, or to file a complaint about an insurance company, contact the Department of Insurance Consumer Hotline, 300 South Spring Street, South Tower, Los Angeles, CA 90013, 800-927-4357; www.insurance.ca.gov. Insurance News Network, www.insure.com, has a wide variety of useful information on homeowner's insurance. You can also check the websites of individual companies such as State Farm or Allstate.

CAUTION

After you find earthquake insurance, make sure your mortgage lender won't claim first dibs on the proceeds. Some mortgage agreements (deeds of trust) require that the lender be the primary payee of any earthquake insurance proceeds. The lender then collects amounts owing on the mortgage and dictates how whatever is left will be used for repairs. Worse yet, a California court has upheld this practice. (*Martin v. World Savings*, 92 Cal.App.4th 803 (2001).) Read your loan paperwork carefully.

Obtain Title Report and Title Insurance

Title insurance protects both you and your lender against unknown clouds on the legal title to the property. The title insurance company insures against the possibility of undisclosed legal challenges or liens against the property, such as an unrecorded deed, a forged deed, or an unrecorded easement—the right of someone else to use your property for a specific purpose (for example, the right the previous owner granted your neighbor to share your extra-wide driveway). If you think you might sell the house within the next two years, ask your title insurer about a "binder" policy that will give you a refund when you resell.

What Are Liens?

A lien is a claim for money, with property as security (collateral) for payment. Other common liens are for unpaid taxes and debts owed to contractors who worked on the property but were never paid (called a mechanic's lien).

Financial institutions require title insurance whenever they finance a house sale. As soon as you and the seller sign the house purchase contract, you should order a preliminary title report (also called a prelim or pre) on the property. Your offer should make your approval of a preliminary title report a contingency. (In northern California, the escrow holder—a title insurance company—will often order the policy itself.) This report is a statement summarizing the current condition of the title to the property, including liens; encumbrances; covenants, conditions, and restrictions (CC&Rs); and easements. You want the prelim early in escrow so that you, the seller, and the lender have time to address any problems that turn up.

The most common problems require the seller to pay off liens from the sale proceeds. These problems threaten your deal with the seller only if the seller disputes the lien and refuses to instruct the escrow holder to pay the lienholder. Other problems include a newly discovered easement, lawsuits disputing the boundary line or filed against the seller, an unknown heir (if the previous owner recently died), or an unexpected owner (such as a previous spouse). If any of these situations come up, the seller will likely need the help of a lawyer.

If problems arise with the title that the seller cannot quickly resolve, you can refuse to go through with the sale, give the seller an extension of time (if you think the extra time will help), or buy the house with less-than-perfect title. Deciding to do this is beyond the scope of this book; consult an experienced real estate lawyer.

If you pay all cash or borrow from Uncle Stanley, or if the seller takes back a second, you (or you and Uncle Stanley or you and the seller) must decide whether to buy title insurance. We recommend it, even if you search the title yourself at the county recorder's office and believe title is clear. In the future, you don't want any unpleasant surprises.

Financial institutions require a California Land Title Association (CLTA) policy and an American Land Title Association (ALTA) policy. The CLTA policy covers items in the public record, such as mortgage liens, trust deed liens, or judgment liens. The ALTA policy is more extensive, insuring against claims found both in the public record and by physically inspecting the house, such as unrecorded easements, boundary disputes, and physical encroachments.

The policies also differ regarding how much they cover and whom they benefit. The CLTA policy insures to the amount of the purchase price and benefits you. The ALTA policy insures to the amount of the loan and benefits the lender. If you'll occupy the house, the CLTA policy you receive will include the same extended coverage the lender gets on the ALTA policy. If you won't be occupying the house, you can buy the extended coverage for about 30% above the policy cost.

RESOURCE

CLTA and ALTA policies. For more information on CLTA policies, phone 916-444-2647 or check the CLTA website at www.clta.org.

For information on ALTA polices, phone 800-787-ALTA or check the ALTA website at www.alta.org.

Before closing, the title insurance company will check the public records for any changes since the prelim was issued. If all is the same (as is the usual case), the prelim becomes the final title report. If there are any changes, they'll be reported in a supplemental title report. You and your lender must decide whether to close or call the deal off.

Conduct Final Physical Inspection of Property

A few days before escrow closes, reinspect the property to make sure everything is in order. Your contract should give you the right to do so. You'll want to make sure:

- No damage has occurred to the house since you agreed to buy it.

- The fixtures and personal property the seller agreed to sell you are still in the house.
- Smoke detectors are installed in all sleeping rooms as required by state law. (Health and Safety Code §§ 13113.7 and 13113.8.)
- All agreed-upon work has been done to your satisfaction (this is especially important with new houses).
- The house is empty—that is, the seller (or tenant) has moved (unless your agreement lets him or her stay longer) and hasn't left piles of unwanted possessions behind.

If you discover a problem during this final inspection, you can:

- Insist that the closing be delayed until the seller fixes the problem.
- Insist that the seller credit you in escrow with a sum of money sufficient for you to remedy the problem—this means you pay that much less for the house.
- Conclude that the problem isn't significant and close anyway.

If you're at a real deadlock, consider mediation, as many standard real estate contracts require.

If you're buying a new house, be sure to reread Chapter 7 on dealing with final inspections, construction delays, and other problems.

TIP

Ask the sellers to accompany you during the final inspection or to give you a post-inspection "tour." Every house has its quirks and mysteries—how to light the old gas oven, the identity of garden plants, and more. If negotiations have remained friendly, going through the house with the sellers can yield a wealth of information. Prepare questions in advance. If you're happy with how the house has been maintained, ask for the names of the sellers' gardener, painter, and other servicepeople.

Closing Escrow

Until all contingencies in your offer are removed, no firm closing date can be set. Thus, during the early and middle stages of an escrow, the closing date is projected, not firm.

The paperwork necessary for closing escrow should be completed a minimum of four working days before the expected closing date. This allows for delays in the transmittal of the loan documents between the lender(s) and the escrow holder. The buyers and sellers usually sign closing documents at different times, making separate visits to the escrow holder's office.

Once the escrow officer has the necessary documents from both seller and you, along with your down payment and the loan proceeds, the officer will prepare a new deed, naming you as the owner. The escrow officer will send the new deed to the county recorder's office, which will record the deed the next day. The seller will receive his or her check late in the day that escrow closes. Others may also be paid out of the sale proceeds, for example, the seller's lender and any lienholders. (These procedures are very different from those in many other states, where the buyer, seller, and agents sit around the closing table, swap deeds and cashier's checks, and complete the sale the same day.)

The forms you'll be required to sign may include:

- Final escrow instructions. In northern California, the escrow holder prepares two slightly different sets of instructions—one for the seller and one for the buyer—so read them carefully to be sure that you and the seller are in agreement; in southern California, the buyer and seller sign identical escrow instructions.
- Copy of the preliminary title report.
- Deed of trust (and other forms) from the lender.
- Copies of structural pest control and other inspection reports.
- FIRPTA (Foreign Investment in Real Property Tax Act) statement.
- Fund disbursement (or loan assumption) documents provided by the lender.
- Any rental agreement between you and the seller if the seller will live in the house for a while after the close.
- Settlement statement listing all costs, prepared by the escrow holder.
- Statements authorizing an impound account.
- A perjury statement where you attest to the truth of the information you provided.
- Statement showing your hazard insurance coverage.

If rehabilitation work must be done to repair damage or substandard conditions discovered in an inspection report, money

County Property Taxes and Exemptions

When real estate is sold in California, the county assesses the value of the property and imposes property taxes accordingly. This will be done shortly after you close on the sale.

Take a careful look at the assessment statement. If you will live in the house, most counties allow you to a yearly homeowner's property tax exemption of up to $7,000 on the assessed value of the property. If you move in after March 1, you are entitled to 80% of the full amount for the first year. If the assessment statement does not include the exemption, call your county tax assessor's office and find out how to file for it.

When a house sells for more than the previous assessed value, the county will issue a supplemental tax bill that accounts for the difference in price. The county issues this bill during the first year after you buy your home. If, for example, the house was previously assessed at $180,000, and you paid $540,000, you'll receive a supplementary tax bill representing the $360,000 difference—or, depending on the timing of your purchase, a portion of the difference. The bill will be prorated according to how far into the tax year you bought the house. Tax years run from July 1st to June 30th of the following year. So if you purchase your home on September 30, 2009, your tax bill will cover only the period from October 1, 2009 through June 30, 2010.

may be held by the escrow holder after the sale closes to pay the contractor.

After you've completed all your inspections and both you and the seller have signed all the closing papers, you can either bring in your cashier's check or have money wired from your bank for the down payment and closing costs.

TIP

Don't be in a hurry to deposit your check or wire your money. Once your money is in escrow, you're no longer earning interest on it. More important, if something goes wrong, it will be hard to get your money back.

If you deposit your money by check, it must actually be available by the closing date. Especially if you will use a nonlocal check, ask the escrow holder to tell you how many days in advance of closing your check must be submitted. Using a cashier's check will be cheaper than arranging for a wire transfer from your bank to the escrow holder's bank.

Chapter 21 covers what happens if there are delays or problems during escrow.

RESOURCE

Where to complain about an escrow or title insurance company. If you have any problem with your escrow company, contact the Department of Corporations at 800-275-2677, or check www.corp.ca.gov ("Consumer Complaints" area); this state agency regulates independent escrow companies. The Department of Insurance oversees title insurance companies and can be reached at 800-927-4357 or www.insurance.ca.gov.

Tips on Choosing a Closing Date

Your contract should specify the date for closing escrow. But sometimes the closing date will later need to be postponed to allow for all contingencies to be removed. You'll need to negotiate the date with the seller depending on your individual needs—for example, if you want the closing date to coincide with the end of your lease. If you have a choice, here's some money-saving advice on choosing a closing date:

- The later in the month your closing date, the less prorated interest you'll owe in closing costs. If you close on the second of June, you'll need to prepay interest from June 2 through the end of the month. If you close on June 28, you'll need to prepay interest for only a few days.
- Don't close escrow on a Monday (or a Tuesday following a three-day weekend), because you may end up paying extra interest. Lenders must fund a loan, and start charging the buyer interest, the day before escrow closes. Closing on a Monday requires the lender to fund the loan on the previous Friday; this means you end up paying interest over the weekend, before you even own the property.

Closing Costs and Loan Fees

Closing costs and loan fees usually add up to 2%–5% of your purchase price. Some fees are paid when you take out the loan, or at the same time you arrange inspection reports, but most are paid the day you close escrow. Not all lenders and escrow holders require all the fees (some are waived as part of special offers). When escrow closes, you'll receive a statement with an itemized list of the closing costs.

Here are typical closing costs and loan fees.

Appraisal fees. Charged by an appraiser hired by the lender to be sure the property is worth what you've agreed to pay. Fees usually run between $325 and $450 for a regular-sized single-family home, and somewhat more for a very large or multiple-unit building. (See Chapter 13 for more on appraisals.)

Lender fee. Loan application fees (typically $1,000) cover the lender's cost of processing your loan.

Assumption fee. Typically 1% of the loan balance to assume the seller's existing ARM; to assume an FHA or VA loan, the fee will range from $50 to $100.

Attorneys' fees. If problems develop, such as the need to evaluate or clear title, you may need to hire an attorney.

Credit report. Should cost around $20 to check your credit. While standard credit checks cost less, for home loans the lender checks at least two credit reporting agencies and the county records for judgment and tax liens.

Escrow company fees. An escrow company that is not a title insurance company may charge a nominal fee for doing the escrow work.

Junk fees. Real estate business slang for a number of small and unexpected fees, including administrative, courier, and filing fees, which typically run from $150 to $250. You can negotiate to have the more ridiculous ones removed.

Loan fees. This includes points (one point is 1% of the loan principal) and an additional fee, usually between $100 and $450.

Physical inspection reports. May add several hundred dollars or more, depending on how many are requested. If you pay these at the time of the inspection directly to the inspectors, you can save a few dollars. Escrow companies will charge $25–$50 if they pay off your inspectors in escrow.

Prepaid homeowners' insurance. Amount as required by lenders, typically one year; depends on the house's value, level of coverage, and location.

Prepaid interest on the loan. You'll be asked to pay per diem interest in advance, from the date your loan is funded to the end of that month. The maximum you'll be charged is 30 days of interest.

Prepaid property taxes. Depends on tax assessment; covers the time period between closing and your first monthly mortgage payment. Some lenders have you prepay one or two months in addition.

Private mortgage insurance. As discussed in Chapter 4, if you make a down payment of less than 20%, most lenders will require private mortgage insurance, or PMI. You will probably need to pay a few months' worth

Closing Costs and Loan Fees (continued)

of PMI premiums at the close of escrow. It's usually calculated at 0.52 of the loan amount, divided by 12. On a $300,000 loan, that's $130 per month.

Recording and filing fees. The escrow holder will charge about $100 for drawing up, reviewing, and recording the deed of trust and other legal documents. The total escrow and title fees can amount to 0.5% of the loan.

Survey fee. May be needed to show plot measurements if house has easements; will run about $300.

Tax service fee. Issued to notify the lender if you default on your property taxes; usually costs about $75 to $80.

Title search and title insurance. Only in northern California does the buyer pay the title costs. Most lenders require title insurance for the face amount of their mortgage or for the value of their loan. Title insurance is a one-time premium that averages about $900.

Transfer tax. Tax assessed by the county when the property changes hands. Usually split with seller, in which case it costs about $1.10 per $1,000. Many cities also charge transfer tax; it varies city to city, but usually is not more than 1.5% of the purchase price.

CHAPTER

19

Check Out a House's Condition

Before you finalize your house purchase, you'll want to check out its condition. If the house is in good shape, you can proceed knowing that you're getting what you paid for. But the few hundred dollars you spend may save you thousands later. If inspections discover problems, you can negotiate with the seller to pay for necessary repairs or back out of the deal, assuming your contract is written to allow that.

CAUTION

Don't rely solely on inspection reports from the seller. Sellers often commission a full set of inspections and provide buyers with a comprehensive "Disclosure Package" that can be over 100 pages long. Read these carefully, but don't rely on them solely. The seller's report may be from the most optimistic inspector they could find. Even if the inspector spots a problem, his or her analysis of what's needed to correct it may tend toward the low-cost solutions. What's more, the California Department of Real Estate reports that it is "not uncommon" for sellers who don't like the results of one report to commission a second one, and then present the more favorable-looking one to buyers.

Short History of California House Inspections

Until the mid-1980s, California houses, like houses in most states, were sold with a caveat emptor (buyer beware) approach. As long as the seller didn't fraudulently conceal defects, the buyer was responsible for discovering the physical problems. Not surprisingly, with this system, buyers and their lenders were very concerned not to miss major defects in the house. Unfortunately, this usually only involved hiring a pest inspector—and pest inspectors rarely know about or checked the complex systems in the house (like electricity or plumbing) or structural defects unrelated to pests.

Sometimes, it later became obvious that the seller (and sometimes his agent) knew about a particular undiscovered defect but never said a word. California courts began to question this "find-it-if-you-can" system and started holding sellers and their agents financially liable for not disclosing known problems. Several state and local laws now require sellers to provide specific information on the condition of the house as well as disclose potential hazards like floods, earthquakes, and environmental hazards

The new statutes aren't the end of the story—California courts still require sellers to disclose any negative fact that could reasonably be expected to lower the value of the property. (See *Reed v. King*, 145 Cal. App.3d 261 (1983).) The sellers must even disclose any "psychological defects," or that the house is of "ill repute"—or else face liability. For example, in the *Reed* case, the sellers sold their house without revealing that it had been the site of a multiple murder ten years before—a fact that appraisers said brought the property's value down significantly. Courts in have looked to the *Reed* case to decide that sellers should have disclosed a previous suicide, neighborhood noise, groundwater contamination, and more.

Real Estate Transfer Disclosure Statement

State law requires sellers to tell you considerable information about the condition of the house on a Real Estate Transfer Disclosure Statement form ("TDS" in real estate shorthand). (Civil Code § 1102.) The TDS includes three types of disclosures:

- items included in the property, such as a burglar alarm or trash compactor
- information on defects or malfunctions in the building's structure, such as the roof or windows
- a variety of special issues, such as the existence of a homeowners' association (and any covenants, conditions, and restrictions, or CC&Rs), environmental hazards like asbestos and lead-based paint, whether remodeling was done with permits and met local building codes, and neighborhood noise problems or nuisances.

We include a sample Real Estate Transfer Disclosure Statement (TDS) here. The TDS you'll be handed as part of your purchase should contain the identical language, as the disclosures are specified by state law. (Civil Code § 1102.6.)

CAUTION

Exemptions from transfer disclosure statement. Certain properties, including foreclosures and probate sales and buildings with more than four units, are exempt from state disclosure laws. In these cases, be sure to get a professional home inspection before closing the deal.

Examining the Seller's Disclosure Statement

Sellers must provide you a copy of the Transfer Disclosure Statement "as soon as practicable before transfer of title." (Civil Code § 1102.3.) It's to your advantage to get a copy of the TDS as soon as possible; you don't want to invest the time and money in the house-buying process only to discover problems just before you close escrow.

Often, seller's disclosure forms are only cursorily filled out, and you'll need to ask questions for additional information. If the form you receive is sparse, you're confused about any of the seller's disclosures, or you simply want more details, make a written request for more information; send a copy to the seller's agent and keep a copy for yourself. Insist on a written response from the seller.

In your request, ask not only for elaboration on the Real Estate Transfer Disclosure Statement, but also for any other recent inspection reports the seller may have authorized, such as a pest inspection (especially if you're in southern California). In addition, ask for copies of any home insurance claims reports. The key here is not merely to discover previous damage, but to see how much insurance claim activity took place. As discussed in Chapter 18, a history of "too many" claims can lead to high premiums on your policy, or even to an uninsurable house. Be particularly concerned if you see any past claims for water damage, which make insurance companies skittish.

Real Estate Transfer Disclosure Statement

(California Civil Code § 1102.6)

THIS DISCLOSURE STATEMENT CONCERNS THE REAL PROPERTY SITUATED IN THE CITY OF ______________________, COUNTY OF ______________________, STATE OF CALIFORNIA, DESCRIBED AS ______________________ ______________________. THIS STATEMENT IS A DISCLOSURE OF THE CONDITION OF THE ABOVE-DESCRIBED PROPERTY IN COMPLIANCE WITH SECTION 1102 OF THE CIVIL CODE AS OF ______________________, 20________. IT IS NOT A WARRANTY OF ANY KIND BY THE SELLER(S) OR ANY AGENT(S) REPRESENTING ANY PRINCIPAL(S) IN THIS TRANSACTION, AND IT IS NOT A SUBSTITUTE FOR ANY INSPECTIONS OR WARRANTIES THE PRINCIPAL(S) MAY WISH TO OBTAIN.

I
Coordination With Other Disclosure Forms

This Real Estate Transfer Disclosure Statement is made pursuant to Section 1102 of the Civil Code. Other statutes require disclosures, depending upon the details of the particular real estate transaction (for example: special study zone and purchase-money liens on residential property).

Substituted Disclosures: The following disclosures and other disclosures required by law, including the Natural Hazard Disclosure Report/Statement that may include airport annoyances, earthquake, fire, flood, or special assessment information, have been or will be made in connection with this real estate transfer, and are intended to satisfy the disclosure obligations on this form, where the subject matter is the same:

☐ Inspection reports completed pursuant to the contract of sale or receipt for deposit.

☐ Additional inspection reports or disclosures: ______________________
____
____

II
Seller's Information

The Seller discloses the following information with the knowledge that even though this is not a warranty, prospective Buyers may rely on this information in deciding whether and on what terms to purchase the subject property. Seller hereby authorizes any agent(s) representing any principal(s) in this transaction to provide a copy of this statement to any person or entity in connection with any actual or anticipated sale of the property.

THE FOLLOWING ARE REPRESENTATIONS MADE BY THE SELLER(S) AND ARE NOT THE REPRESENTATIONS OF THE AGENT(S), IF ANY. THIS INFORMATION IS A DISCLOSURE AND IT IS NOT INTENDED TO BE PART OF ANY CONTRACT BETWEEN THE BUYER AND SELLER.

Seller ☐ is ☐ is not occupying the property.

A. The subject property has the items checked below (read across):

☐ Range	☐ Oven	☐ Microwave
☐ Dishwasher	☐ Trash Compactor	☐ Garbage Disposal
☐ Washer/Dryer Hookups		☐ Rain Gutters
☐ Burglar Alarms	☐ Smoke Detector(s)	☐ Fire Alarm
☐ TV Antenna	☐ Satellite Dish	☐ Intercom
☐ Central Heating	☐ Central Air Conditioning	☐ Evaporator Cooler(s)
☐ Wall/Window Air Conditioning	☐ Sprinklers	☐ Public Sewer System
☐ Septic Tank	☐ Sump Pump	☐ Water Softener
☐ Patio/Decking	☐ Built-in Barbecue	☐ Gazebo
☐ Sauna	☐ Hot Tub ☐ Locking Safety Cover*	
☐ Pool ☐ Child-Resistant Barrier*	☐ Spa ☐ Locking Safety Cover*	
☐ Security Gate(s)	☐ Automatic Garage Door Opener(s)*	☐ Number of Remote Controls
☐ Garage: ☐ Attached	☐ Not Attached	☐ Carport
☐ Pool/Spa Heater: ☐ Gas	☐ Solar	☐ Electric
☐ Water Heater: ☐ Gas	☐ Water Heater Anchored, Braced, or Strapped*	
☐ Water Supply: ☐ City	☐ Well	☐ Private Utility or
☐ Gas Supply: ☐ Utility	☐ Bottled	☐ Other ____________
☐ Window Screens	☐ Window Security Bars ☐ Quick Release Mechanism on Bedroom Windows*	
☐ Exhaust Fan(s) in	☐ 220 Volt Wiring in	☐ Fireplace(s) in
☐ Gas Starter ____________	Roof(s): Type: ____________	Age: (approx.) ____________

Other: ____

Are there, to the best of your (Seller's) knowledge, any of the above that are not in operating condition? ☐ Yes ☐ No. If yes, then describe. (Attach additional sheets if necessary):

____

*This garage door opener or child-resistant pool barrier may not be in compliance with the safety standards relating to automatic reversing devices as set forth in Chapter 12.5 (commencing with Section 19890) of Part 3 of Division 13 of, or with the pool safety standards of Article 2.5 (commencing with Section 115920) Chapter 5 of Part 10 of Division 104 of, the Health and Safety Code. The water heater may not be anchored, braced, or strapped in accordance with Section 19211 of the Health and Safety Code. Window security bars may not have quick-release mechanisms in compliance with the 1995 Edition of the California Building Standards Code.

B. Are you (Seller) aware of any significant defects/malfunctions in any of the following?

☐ Yes ☐ No. If yes, check appropriate space(s) below.

☐ Interior Walls ☐ Ceilings ☐ Floors ☐ Exterior Walls ☐ Insulation
☐ Roof(s) ☐ Windows ☐ Doors ☐ Foundation ☐ Slab(s)
☐ Driveways ☐ Sidewalks ☐ Walls/Fences ☐ Electrical Systems ☐ Plumbing/Sewers/Septics

☐ Other Structural Components (describe): ______________________________

If any of the above is checked, explain. (Attach additional sheets if necessary): ______________________________

____

____

C. Are you (Seller) aware of any of the following?

☐ Yes ☐ No 1. Substances, materials, or products which may be an environmental hazard such as, but not limited to, asbestos, formaldehyde, radon gas, lead-based paint, mold, fuel or chemical storage tanks, and contaminated soil or water on the subject property.

☐ Yes ☐ No 2. Features of the property shared in common with adjoining landowners, such as walls, fences, and driveways, whose use or responsibility for maintenance may have an effect on the subject property.

☐ Yes ☐ No 3. Any encroachments, easements, or similar matters that may affect your interest in the subject property.

☐ Yes ☐ No 4. Room additions, structural modifications, or other alterations or repairs made without necessary permits.

☐ Yes ☐ No 5. Room additions, structural modifications, or other alterations or repairs not in compliance with building codes.

☐ Yes ☐ No 6. Fill (compacted or otherwise) on the property or any portion thereof.

☐ Yes ☐ No 7. Any settling from any cause, or slippage, sliding, or other soil problems.

☐ Yes ☐ No 8. Flooding, drainage, or grading problems.

☐ Yes ☐ No 9. Major damage to the property or any other structures from fire, earthquake, floods, or landslides.

☐ Yes ☐ No 10. Any zoning violations, nonconforming uses, or violations of "setback" requirements.

☐ Yes ☐ No 11. Neighborhood noise problems or other nuisances.

☐ Yes ☐ No 12. CC&Rs or other deed restrictions or obligations.

☐ Yes ☐ No 13. Homeowners' Association which has any authority over the subject property.

☐ Yes ☐ No 14. Any "common area" (facilities such as pools, tennis courts, walkways, or other areas co-owned in undivided interest with others).

☐ Yes ☐ No 15. Any notices of abatement or citations against the property.

☐ Yes ☐ No 16. Any lawsuits by or against the Seller threatening to or affecting this real property, including any lawsuits alleging a defect or deficiency in this real property or "common areas" (facilities such as pools, tennis courts, walkways, or other areas co-owned in undivided interest with others).

If the answer to any of these is yes, explain (attach additional sheets if necessary):__________

____

____

____

Seller certifies that the information herein is true and correct to the best of the Seller's knowledge as of the date signed by the Seller.

Seller ____________________ Date __________

Seller ____________________ Date __________

III
Agent's Inspection Disclosure (Listing Agent)

(To be completed only if the Seller is represented by an agent in this transaction.)

THE UNDERSIGNED, BASED ON THE ABOVE INQUIRY OF THE SELLER(S) AS TO THE CONDITION OF THE PROPERTY AND BASED ON REASONABLY COMPETENT AND DILIGENT VISUAL INSPECTION OF THE ACCESSIBLE AREAS OF THE PROPERTY IN CONJUNCTION WITH THAT INQUIRY, STATES THE FOLLOWING:

☐ Agent notes no items for disclosure.

☐ Agent notes the following items:____________________

____

____

____

____

Agent (Print Name of Broker Representing Seller) ____________________

By (Associate Licensee or Broker's Signature) ____________________

Date ____________________

IV
Agent's Inspection Disclosure

(To be completed only if the agent who has obtained the offer is other than the agent above.)

THE UNDERSIGNED, BASED ON A REASONABLY COMPETENT AND DILIGENT VISUAL INSPECTION OF THE ACCESSIBLE AREAS OF THE PROPERTY, STATES THE FOLLOWING:

☐ Agent notes no items for disclosure.

☐ Agent notes the following items: ____________________

Agent (Print Name of Broker Obtaining Offer) ____________________

By (Associate Licensee or Broker's Signature) ____________________

Date ____________________

V

BUYER(S) AND SELLER(S) MAY WISH TO OBTAIN PROFESSIONAL ADVICE AND/OR INSPECTIONS OF THE PROPERTY AND TO PROVIDE FOR APPROPRIATE PROVISIONS IN A CONTRACT BETWEEN BUYER(S) AND SELLER(S) WITH RESPECT TO ANY ADVICE/INSPECTION/DEFECTS.

I/We acknowledge receipt of a copy of this statement.

Seller ____________________ Date ____________________

Seller ____________________ Date ____________________

Buyer ____________________ Date ____________________

Buyer ____________________ Date ____________________

Agent (Print Name of Broker Representing Seller) ____________________

By (Associate Licensee or Broker's Signature) ____________________

Date ____________________

Agent (Print Name of Broker Obtaining the Offer) ____________________

By (Associate Licensee or Broker's Signature) ____________________

Date ____________________

SECTION 1102.3 OF THE CIVIL CODE PROVIDES A BUYER WITH THE RIGHT TO RESCIND A PURCHASE CONTRACT FOR AT LEAST THREE DAYS AFTER THE DELIVERY OF THIS DISCLOSURE, IF DELIVERY OCCURS AFTER THE SIGNING OF AN OFFER TO PURCHASE. IF YOU WISH TO RESCIND THE CONTRACT, YOU MUST ACT WITHIN THE PRESCRIBED PERIOD.

A REAL ESTATE BROKER IS QUALIFIED TO ADVISE ON REAL ESTATE. IF YOU DESIRE LEGAL ADVICE, CONSULT YOUR ATTORNEY.

Sample Letter Requesting Further Seller's Disclosure

February 22, 20xx

Dear ________________:

I have received your Real Estate Transfer Disclosure Statement, dated ____________. In item ____, you indicate that ______________ ____________________________________.

Please explain this condition more fully. Specifically, I would appreciate your letting me know in writing answers to the following questions:

1. ______________________________

2. ______________________________

3. ______________________________

Also, please send me copies of any inspectors' reports that deal with any aspect of the physical condition of the property, and copies of all home insurance claim reports. Thank you for your cooperation.

Sincerely,

Also, be sure to carefully read the visual disclosures made by your agent and the seller's agent. The seller may not notice obvious defects he or she has lived with every day (such as cuts in linoleum or spots of mold on the walls). Therefore, the agent might be the only one to mention these issues.

When to Go Beyond the Real Estate Transfer Disclosure Statement

In addition to considering at face value the information disclosed, examine the disclosure statement for clues to other problems, and follow up with a professional inspection.

For example, if the seller says that several windows won't open, they may simply be painted shut. But it's also possible that the house has settled and the window frames are no longer properly aligned. Similarly, cracks in the dining room ceiling may mean no more than that the plaster is old, or they may be a clue to significant earth movement or to an otherwise unstable foundation. In either case, have the foundation checked extra carefully.

Real Estate Agents' Disclosures

California law requires licensed real estate agents (brokers and salespeople) to conduct a "reasonably competent and diligent" visual inspection of property and to disclose to you anything that would affect the "value or desirability" of the property—that is, anything that would be likely to affect your decision to buy. (Civil Code §§ 2079, 2079.3.)

This obligation is on both your agent and the agent representing the seller. Agents do not have to inspect inaccessible areas (such as the sealed-off underside of the porch) or review public documents affecting title to or use of the property. Similarly, agents are not required to explain the legal ramifications of their disclosures.

Handling Problems With the Transfer Disclosure Statement

The law specifically allows buyers, in deciding whether and on what terms to buy the house, to rely on a seller's disclosure statement. Even if your offer was not contingent upon your approving inspection reports, state law allows a person to terminate his or her offer to purchase real property three days after personal delivery of a Real Estate Transfer Disclosure Statement (five days from mailing). (Civil Code § 1102.3.) A buyer may alternatively decide to proceed with the sale and negotiate the cost of making repairs with the seller.

Although sellers and agents need disclose only defects within their personal knowledge, some sellers worry about being sued. They're afraid they won't be able to prove that they didn't know about a certain problem. In short, they now have a good reason to discover and disclose defects, just as do buyers.

A wise seller will disclose all possible (and sometimes even imagined) defects to protect against possible future lawsuits, often in a supplement to the TDS. On a supplementary form recommended by some San Francisco real estate agents, for instance, sellers are asked to answer if they are aware of any problems, such as damages caused by animals, neighborhood animal problems, criminal activities on the property, or diseased trees on the property.

Not all sellers and agents are savvy enough to provide detailed disclosures. Some still try to cover up serious problems, hoping that you and your inspector won't find them. The seller may be sued later, but some sellers don't think this far ahead. (For handling these types of legal problems, see Chapter 21.)

Disclosures Required With FHA Loans

The Department of Housing and Urban Development (HUD) requires disclosures regarding home inspections for borrowers seeking Federal Housing Administration (FHA) financing. All FHA borrowers must be given a new form, "The Importance of a Home Inspection." This form must be signed and dated by the borrower before the execution of the sales contract. For more information on FHA loans, see Chapter 11.

Natural Hazard Disclosure Statement

The Transfer Disclosure Statement discussed in the previous section includes information on many hazards affecting the house, some of which require additional disclosures. Many of these are made on the Natural Hazard Disclosure Statement, which indicates whether the property is in one of the following hazard zones (Civil Code § 1103.2):

- a flood hazard zone designated by the Federal Emergency Management Agency (FEMA)

- an area of potential flooding due to failure of a dam as identified by the Office of Emergency Services on an "inundation map" (Government Code § 8589.5)
- a very high fire hazard severity zone designated by a local agency (Government Code §§ 51178, 51179)
- a state-designated wildland fire area zone (Public Resources Code § 4125)
- a delineated earthquake fault zone as identified by the California State Geologist (Public Resources Code § 2622)
- a seismic hazards zone (area where landslides and liquefaction are most likely to occur) as defined under Public Resources Code § 2696, or
- an airport annoyance area or one subject to special tax assessments (Civil Code § 1103.4).

These designations are often puzzling, at least to a layperson. For example, San Francisco is not within an earthquake fault zone. That's because the fault line isn't in San Francisco—although San Francisco has certainly experienced the ravages of earthquakes.

Also, sometimes the available maps and information are not of sufficient accuracy or scale for a seller to determine whether the property falls inside a designated hazard zone, such as a high fire hazard severity zone. In this case, the law requires the seller to mark "Yes" on the Natural Hazard Disclosure Statement—unless the seller has evidence, such as a report from a licensed engineer, that the property is not in the particular zone. (Civil Code § 1102.4.) More and more sellers, however, don't even fill this form out on their own, but instead pay a few hundred dollars to a company that generates a report based on the lot and block number of the home in question (or using the street address, to make it even easier). The reports carry explanatory language about how the various zones are set up legally and what their designations mean.

We include a sample Natural Hazard Disclosure Statement (NHDS) here so that you can familiarize yourself with this form. The NHDS you receive should contain identical language, as the disclosures are specified by state law (but it may contain extra language if prepared by an outside company). Examine the Natural Hazard Disclosure Statement and follow up on any questions or problems. Also, check with the local planning department for more information on earthquake hazards in the area. And see Appendix A, Welcome to California, which discusses areas of the state susceptible to various natural disasters and includes resources for more information on fires, floods, and earthquakes.

TIP

Alternative disclosure form. A seller may provide these disclosures on a Local Option Real Estate Disclosure Statement, described under "Local Disclosures," below.

Natural Hazard Disclosure Statement

This statement applies to the following property: ______________________________.

The transferor and his or her agent(s) or a third-party consultant disclose the following information with the knowledge that even though this is not a warranty, prospective transferees may rely on this information in deciding whether and on what terms to purchase the subject property. Transferor hereby authorizes any agent(s) representing any principal(s) in this action to provide a copy of this statement to any person or entity in connection with any actual or anticipated sale of the property.

The following are representations made by the transferor and his or her agent(s) based on their knowledge and maps drawn by the state and federal governments. This information is a disclosure and is not intended to be part of any contract between the transferee and the transferor.

THIS REAL PROPERTY LIES WITHIN THE FOLLOWING HAZARDOUS AREA(S):

A SPECIAL FLOOD HAZARD AREA (any type Zone "A" or "V") designated by the Federal Emergency Management Agency.

☐ Yes ☐ No ☐ Do not know and information not available from local jurisdiction

AN AREA OF POTENTIAL FLOODING shown on a dam failure inundation map pursuant to Section 8589.5 of the Government Code.

☐ Yes ☐ No ☐ Do not know and information not available from local jurisdiction

A VERY HIGH FIRE HAZARD SEVERITY ZONE pursuant to Section 51178 or 51179 of the Government Code. The owner of this property is subject to the maintenance requirements of Section 51182 of the Government Code.

☐ Yes ☐ No

A WILDLAND AREA THAT MAY CONTAIN SUBSTANTIAL FOREST FIRE RISKS AND HAZARDS pursuant to Section 4125 of the Public Resources Code. The owner of this property is subject to the maintenance requirements of Section 4291 of the Public Resources Code. Additionally, it is not the state's responsibility to provide fire protection services to any building or structure located within the wildlands unless the Department of Forestry and Fire Protection has entered into a cooperative agreement with a local agency for those purposes pursuant to Section 4142 of the Public Resources Code.

☐ Yes ☐ No

AN EARTHQUAKE FAULT ZONE pursuant to Section 2622 of the Public Resources Code.

☐ Yes ☐ No

A SEISMIC HAZARD ZONE pursuant to Section 2696 of the Public Resources Code.
☐ Yes (Landslide Zone) ☐ Yes (Liquefaction Zone) ☐ No ☐ Map not yet released by state

THESE HAZARDS MAY LIMIT YOUR ABILITY TO DEVELOP THE REAL PROPERTY, TO OBTAIN INSURANCE, OR TO RECEIVE ASSISTANCE AFTER A DISASTER.

THE MAPS ON WHICH THESE DISCLOSURES ARE BASED ESTIMATE WHERE NATURAL HAZARDS EXIST. THEY ARE NOT DEFINITIVE INDICATORS OF WHETHER OR NOT A PROPERTY WILL BE AFFECTED BY A NATURAL DISASTER. TRANSFEREE(S) AND TRANSFEROR(S) MAY WISH TO OBTAIN PROFESSIONAL ADVICE REGARDING THOSE HAZARDS AND OTHER HAZARDS THAT MAY AFFECT THE PROPERTY.

Signature of Transferor(s) ______________________ Date ____________

Signature of Transferor(s) ______________________ Date ____________

Agent(s) ______________________ Date ____________

Agent(s) ______________________ Date ____________

Check only one of the following:

☐ Transferor(s) and their agent(s) represent that the information herein is true and correct to the best of their knowledge as of the date signed by the transferor(s) and agent(s).

☐ Transferor(s) and their agent(s) acknowledge that they have exercised good faith in the selection of a third-party report provider as required in Civil Code Section 1103.7, and that the representations made in this Natural Hazard Disclosure Statement are based upon information provided by the independent third-party disclosure provider as a substituted disclosure pursuant to Civil Code Section 1103.4. Neither transferor(s) nor their agent(s) (1) has independently verified the information contained in this statement and report or (2) is personally aware of any errors or inaccuracies in the information contained on the statement. This statement was prepared by the provider below:

Third-Party Disclosure Provider(s) ______________________ Date ____________

Transferee represents that he or she has read and understands this document. Pursuant to Civil Code Section 1103.8, the representations made in this Natural Hazard Disclosure Statement do not constitute all of the transferor's or agent's disclosure obligations in this transaction.

Signature of Transferee(s) ______________________ Date ____________

Signature of Transferee(s) ______________________ Date ____________

Earthquake and Seismic Disclosures

To help buyers make earthquake-informed decisions, the seller must indicate on the Natural Hazard Disclosure Statement whether the property is in an earthquake fault zone or a seismic hazard zone. In addition, state law requires sellers to provide information on the safety of the house itself and its ability to resist earthquakes.

Residential Earthquake Hazards Report

The seller must tell you whether the property has any known seismic deficiencies, such as whether or not the house is bolted or anchored to the foundation and whether cripple walls, if any, are braced. (Government Code § 8897.) The seller is not required to hire anyone to help evaluate the house or to strengthen any weaknesses that exist. If the house was built in 1960 or later, oral disclosure is enough.

If the house was built before 1960, the seller must disclose in writing and sign the disclosure form, Residential Earthquake Hazards Report, included in a booklet called the *Homeowner's Guide to Earthquake Safety.* The seller must give the buyer a copy of this booklet and disclosure "as soon as practicable before the transfer." (Government Code § 8897.1.)

RESOURCE

The *Homeowner's Guide to Earthquake Safety* is available from the California Seismic Safety Commission (CSSC) at 916-263-5506, or www.seismic.ca.gov. This booklet provides valuable information, including how to find and fix earthquake weaknesses and a detailed list of earthquake resources.

Water Heater Bracing

If the property you are buying has had a new or replacement water heater installed since January 1, 1991, it must be braced, anchored, or strapped to resist falling or displacement during an earthquake. (Health and Safety Code § 19211.) Anyone selling property with such a water heater must certify in writing that the heater complies with the law.

Environmental Hazards

Item C.1 on the Transfer Disclosure Statement asks the seller to identify environmental hazards on the property such as radon gas and contaminated soil. Mold was added to the hazard list in 2001. In addition, sellers should provide prospective home buyers a copy of *Residential Environmental Hazards: A Guide for Homeowners, Homebuyers, Landlords and Tenants*, which provides information on different environmental hazards that may be on or near the property, such as asbestos, formaldehyde, lead, and hazardous wastes.

Lead

HUD rules require that applicants for FHA mortgages be given a lead-based paint notice disclosure form before signing the final sales contract. Lead paint in homes financed by the FHA must be removed or repainted.

California law requires that a seller disclose lead-based paint hazards to prospective buyers on the Transfer Disclosure Statement. (Civil Code § 1102.6.) Furthermore, sellers of houses built before 1978 must comply with the Residential Lead-Based Paint Hazard Reduction Act of 1992 (42 U.S. Code § 4852d), also known as Title X [Ten]. Sellers must:

- disclose all known lead-based paint and paint hazards in the house
- give buyers a pamphlet prepared by the U.S. Environmental Protection Agency (EPA) called *Protect Your Family From Lead in Your Home.*
- include certain warning language in the contract, as well as signed statements from all parties verifying that all requirements were completed
- keep signed acknowledgments for three years as proof of compliance, and
- give buyers a ten-day opportunity to test the housing for lead.

If a seller fails to comply with Title X requirements, you can sue the seller for triple the amount of your resulting damages.

RESOURCE

Lead. The National Lead Information Center has extensive information on lead hazards, prevention, and disclosures. For more information, call the Center at 800-424-LEAD or check www.epa.gov/lead.

Disclosure of Deaths and/or AIDS

State law implies that the seller should disclose any death within the last three years that he or she knows occurred on the property. (Civil Code § 1710.2.) If a death occurred more than three years before, the seller need disclose it only if asked by the buyer—unless the circumstances of the death (for example, a multiple murder) would significantly lower the house's value. (*Reed v. King*, 145 Cal.App.3d 261 (1983).)

Disclosing Ghosts and Haunting

Do the sellers need to tell you if they think their house is haunted? Based on California's broad disclosure rules, most experts would say yes. You're not likely to see a seller boldly declare on the TDS form that the house is haunted—but if you see statements such as "dining room furniture tends to move around at night," "cats won't go near the attic stairs," or "unexplained vapors," you might want to ask further questions.

Despite *Reed*, a seller need not disclose that an owner had, or died from, AIDS, but the property owner or his agent should answer honestly any direct questions on this subject. (Civil Code § 1710.2.) The legislature didn't address any diseases other than AIDS—its concern was that the widespread fear and stigma around this disease would lead to sellers having to disclose their private health information.

Disclosure of Military Ordnance

Sellers who know of any former federal or state ordnance locations (once used for military training purposes and potentially containing explosive munitions) within one mile of the property must provide written disclosure to the buyer as soon as practicable before transfer of title. (Civil Code § 1102.15.)

Local Disclosures

Many cities and counties have local disclosure requirements. To make sure the seller complies, check with the local city or county planning or building department for any local requirements. For example:

- Many municipalities require sellers to upgrade insulation before selling and take specific energy-efficiency measures.
- Many coastal areas restrict owners from making structural modifications to their property without a permit.
- Some communities adjacent to agricultural or timber production zones require sellers to disclose agricultural nuisances such as noise, odors, and dust.
- Sellers of property in designated "community facilities" districts must disclose information on special taxes for police or fire departments, libraries, parks, and schools. (Civil Code § 1102.6b.)

Sellers in communities with local disclosure requirements passed after July 1990 may use a special form, the Local Option Real Estate Disclosure Statement. (Civil Code § 1102.6a.)

Inspecting the Property Yourself

At some point, you'll want to arrange professional inspections. Before you get this far, you should first conduct your own inspection—ideally, before you make a formal written offer so that you can save yourself the trouble should you find serious problems.

Various books can help you prepare for your preliminary home inspection, including *The Complete Book of Home Inspection,* or *Home Inspection Checklists*, both by Norman Becker (McGraw-Hill), as well as two good ones by Robert Irwin, *The Home Inspection Troubleshooter* (Dearborn Publishing) and *Home Buyer's Checklist* (McGraw-Hill). Books written for professional inspectors can also be excellent guides, such as *Inspecting a House,* by Rex Cauldwell (Taunton Press).

Make a list of areas you can check out without needing expertise or having to climb around in dangerous places. Focus on items of particular importance to you and your family. Bring along a note pad, tape measure, camera, and flashlight and a copy of the Ideal House Profile you prepared in Chapter 1. If you're buying a condo, be sure to visit the unit in the evening when neighbors are more likely to be home, to hear any loud noises.

CAUTION

Look hard at "do-it-yourself" home repair jobs. If you see signs that the previous owners took on major repairs or remodeling work without professional help, ask the inspector to take an especially hard look. Amateur home repair projects are notorious for violating codes and containing hidden—or not-so-hidden—defects. Be sure the work was done with permits, and that all the permits have been "finaled."

Arranging Professional Inspections

In addition to inspecting the house yourself and examining the seller's disclosure and inspection reports, you'll want to hire a general contractor to inspect the property and a licensed structural pest control inspector to check for pest damage. (A few inspectors are qualified to do both.) This should be done after your written purchase offer has been accepted by the seller (which should be contingent upon your approving the results of one or more inspections). Make sure you have the seller's Transfer Disclosure Statement and Natural Hazard Disclosure Statement so that the inspectors can follow up on any problems identified therein. You may also want to arrange more specialized inspections after reviewing disclosure reports.

Even if you are an expert, such as an architect or investor, don't forgo the professional home inspection. The inspector may find defects that you missed—and his or her report of the cost of repairs will be given more weight than your own estimate. That means the cost of the inspection can be readily offset by negotiating price concessions or repairs by the seller.

If, on the other hand, the seller is not willing to negotiate on price, the inspection contingency gives you a ready opportunity to back out of the sale.

TIP

In a hot market, consider a professional inspection before you make an offer. In a hot market, it allows you to close the deal quickly, giving you an edge over the competition. Obviously, you'll need the seller's permission first to do a preoffer inspection.

Request Copies of Utility and Water Bills

While sellers are not required to tell you how much they pay the gas and electric company every month, ask to see past bills, especially for the winter months. Gas and electric bills can vary a lot, depending on a house's location, size, and insulation, and the type and age of the furnace and hot water heater.

If utility bills are high, ask the local gas and electric company to conduct an energy check or audit. Many do it at no charge, identifying the problems, recommended solutions, and costs. If your utility company won't help or will take too long, ask for the names of private companies who conduct energy audits.

With water bills, look for any sudden increase in water usage. In older houses especially, this may be a tip-off that main pipes are leaking.

Structural Pest Control Inspection

An inspection by a licensed structural pest control inspector, covering infestation by termites and flying beetles, dry rot, and other fungal conditions, is almost always required by the lender. If you don't make it a condition of the contract, your lender may, particularly if you put down less than 20% of the purchase price.

If the seller has a pest report done before putting the house up for sale, you should still get your own done. Some inspectors are less picky than others, and the seller has a motive (wanting the deal to go through) to pick someone who won't be too fussy. Pest control reports are not costly, beginning at about $150 for a typical single-family dwelling. In a condo, you may need an authorization from the homeowners' association for the pest control inspector to look at common areas.

RESOURCE

More information on pest control inspection. The Structural Pest Control Board keeps files of all pest control reports commissioned within the past two years and provides useful consumer information on pest control inspections and reports. The Board can provide complaint information on individual pest control companies and help mediate disputes. For more information, call 800-737-8188 or 916-561-8708, or go to www.pestboard.ca.gov.

General Inspection

A licensed inspector (usually with a background as a general contractor) inspects all major house systems, from top to bottom. The inspector will examine the general conditions of the site, such as drainage, retaining walls, fences (some skip the fences—remind them to look), and driveways; the integrity of the structure and the foundation; and the condition of the roof, exterior and interior paint, doors and windows, and plumbing, electrical, and heating systems. A growing number of inspectors test for lead in water or radiation exposure around a built-in microwave. You might also want to arrange specialized inspections, such as for seismic safety or asbestos hazards (described below). If you're concerned about toxic mold, make sure the inspector has expertise in finding and assessing it.

How to Find a Good Inspector

A reliable personal recommendation is the best way to find a house inspector and structural pest control inspector. Remember, you want someone who will be thorough and tough. Ask your real estate agent for a referral to an inspector, but be sure to double-check any leads from your agent. Some agents are anxious that the deal go through and therefore may recommend an inspector not overly persnickety about identifying problems. The better agents, however, realize that referrals to tough inspectors work in everyone's interests—after all, most real estate lawsuits are filed by buyers against sellers as well as real estate agents, claiming that problems with the home weren't disclosed to them.

You can also get local referrals from two professional associations: the American Society of Housing Inspectors (ASHI) or the California Real Estate Inspection Association (CREIA) (contact information below).

Get at least two or three specific proposals from recommended home inspectors and check the status of each individual's license and any outstanding complaints with the Contractor's State License Board or the Structural Pest Control Board (contact information below). Ask for references from customers who have owned their homes for a few years, so that any problems the inspector didn't discover have had a chance to pop up. Ask the inspector about his or her liability insurance coverage, including "errors and omissions" (E&O) or malpractice insurance to cover negligence.

Recognizing that there is an inherent conflict of interest in inspecting and bidding on the same job, state law prohibits this practice. Home inspectors may not perform any repairs to a house on which the inspector, or the inspector's company, has prepared a home inspection report in the past 12 months. (Business and Professions Code §§ 7195, 7197.) Note, however, that this law only covers home inspectors. There's nothing to stop you from asking a general contractor to examine your roof or foundation and then prepare a bid to do any necessary work.

RESOURCE

Finding a good general inspector. A useful brochure, *What You Should Know Before You Hire a Contractor,* is available free from the Contractors State License Board by calling 800-321-CSLB or checking their website at www.cslb.ca.gov. There, you can also check a contractor's license and complaints. Or for referrals to local inspectors and information on buying a home in good shape, contact the American Society of Housing Inspectors (ASHI), 800-743-2744, www.ashi.com, or the California Real Estate Inspection Association (CREIA), 800-848-7342, www.creia.com.

Inspections and Reports

The general inspection should take at least two to three hours, while the pest control inspection should take about an hour. Accompany the inspector during the examination. You will learn a lot and better understand the report the inspector will later write. You can also find out about the maintenance and preservation of the house and ask questions.

If a friend or relative has experience in any aspect of construction, bring him or her along. Another set of eyes that know what to look for is always a help. It's also a good idea to bring along a video camera to record the inspection—you may want to view it years later to remind yourself about maintenance issues.

Expect to receive the general inspector's report after a short time (a few days or up to a week), and the pest control report within about five days. Both reports should detail the condition of all major components of the house inspected or checked for infestation and estimated repair costs. The inspector should point out any problems and indicate which are truly important and which are minor, and give a rough estimate of the costs involved for repairs. The inspector may also recommend additional specialized inspections such as those listed below.

House inspection contractors often worry about their liability should they fail to discover a serious defect. While this encourages thoroughness, it can also result in overly defensive inspecting. Here's how to filter out inspector paranoia while reading an inspection report:

- Don't focus on the long-winded disclaimers written by lawyers. While this boilerplate language may sound scary, it's usually not a tip-off that all sorts of problems are lurking just out of sight.
- Pay attention to statements describing the tests the inspector didn't conduct or areas not inspected. If you have educated yourself by reading good house-inspection books, you'll be in a fairly decent position to determine whether any areas or systems were left out that shouldn't have been. (Sometimes, the seller will block off certain areas, in which case you should insist that they be opened for reinspection.) Next, focus on what the inspector did discover. You'll have to decide whether the identified problems merit a specialized inspection (for example, by a structural engineer) and whether you still want to go through with the transaction, based on what the inspection revealed.
- Get a second opinion if a general contractor or pest control inspector discovers a potentially serious problem or doesn't inspect important areas. Arrange for the follow-up inspection to be conducted by a specialist.

Specialized Inspections Common in California

Here are some specialized inspections that may be necessary:

Asbestos. Exposure to asbestos has been linked to an increased risk of cancer. Normally, a separate asbestos inspection is not necessary unless you suspect problems (generally not the case with homes built since the mid 1970s). A general contractor should tell you if the house contains asbestos insulation around heating systems, in ceilings, or in other areas.

RESOURCE

Information on asbestos inspections. Contact the Contractors State License Board, 800-321-2752, www.cslb.ca.gov, or the American Lung Association, 800-LUNG-USA, 586-4872, www.lungusa.org.

To check the license of an asbestos inspector, contact the California Department of Industrial Relations, Division of Occupational Safety and Health (Cal/OSHA), 916-574-2993, www.dir.ca.gov (search for "asbestos").

Electrical. If you or a general contractor suspects problems (more likely if the house was built 25 years ago or more), have an electrician or an electrical engineer do a specialized electrical report. Many general contractors don't have enough knowledge of electrical codes to do an adequate job on a large older house.

Electromagnetic radiation. If you're considering a home near high-voltage electrical power lines, you may be worried about possible health hazards. Although links between electromagnetic radiation and diseases such as cancer have not been proven, you may still want to call the local utility company for a test and evaluation of the electromagnetic radiation levels. Some general contractors can test for this as well.

Foundation and structure. A general contractor can report on these; if the contractor suspects a problem, or you're concerned based upon the seller's disclosures, you'll want an expert to inspect the foundation and structure.

Lead. Exposure to lead-based paint and lead water pipes may lead to serious health problems, especially for children. For information on home testing for lead hazards and a list of state-certified lead inspectors and testing laboratories, contact the California Department of Health Services, 800-597-5323, www.dhs.ca.gov/childlead. For information on lead in drinking water, contact the EPA Safe Drinking Water Hotline at 800-426-4791, www.epa.gov/safewater. See the discussion, above, of state and federal disclosures regarding lead, including how to contact the National Lead Information Center.

Mold. Recent concerns about mold's effect on human health have brought it into the public spotlight. The concern is not with the relatively benign mold that appears on shower tiles—it's with the layers of mold that develop around leaky pipes or other major moisture problems. These villains are reputed to cause everything from allergic coughs to brain damage and death. Some people have major reactions to mold, while others have none at all.

Regardless of your sensitivity level, if the house you're hoping to buy has a mold problem, you'll want to know about it. Your first step is to look closely when you visit the house yourself. Look not only for visible signs, but also for unpleasant smells or areas of obvious moisture or water damage. Unfortunately, not all molds have a smell, and mold may hide in air ducts, crawl spaces or ceilings, and attics. For this reason, you should choose a home inspector who has experience in identifying mold problems. Many of them have been attending special trainings of late. For more information, see the website of the California Real Estate Inspection Association, www.creia.com, or call them at 800-848-7342.

To further protect home buyers, the California Legislature passed the Toxic Mold Protection Act of 2001. (Health & Safety Code §§ 26100 and following.) This requires sellers to disclose any significant known or suspected mold problems. However, sellers are not required to test for mold (reliable tests haven't yet been developed)—and it's entirely possible the sellers won't notice any mold on their own.

RESOURCE

Mold. For information on the detection, removal, and prevention of mold, see the EPA website at www.epa.gov/iaq. By clicking "Mold," you'll find their document "A Brief Guide to Mold, Moisture, and Your Home." Additional publications are available from the California Department of Health Services at www.cal-iaq.org. This site includes many helpful links to other states' health departments and to academic and scientific studies on the subject of mold.

Plumbing. If the general inspector's report indicates plumbing problems, get an in-depth report from a plumber. Your local water department may provide some useful information regarding water pressure and hardness or softness of water. If a house is more than 50 years old, the main sewer line to the street may need replacing before long. General contractors typically do not inspect wells and septic tanks; you'll need to hire a specialist if you want these checked out.

Radon. Radon is a naturally occurring radioactive gas associated with lung cancer that enters and can contaminate a house built on soil and rock with uranium deposits or through water from some private wells. Radon concentrations tend to be highest in newer buildings, whose tight sealing doesn't allow the gas to escape. It is not a problem in most of California, but if you're concerned, contact the National Safety Council (NSC) Radon Hotline at 800-767-7236 or visit www.nsc.org. The California Department of Health Services Radon Information Line can also provide information at 800-745-7236, or check the Department's website at www.cdhs.ca.gov (search for "radon").

Subsoil. If earth movement, especially subsidence or slippage, is a problem or possibility (or if the house is on fill), contact your local building or planning department for any soil reports on file. For information sources on earthquake study zones and hazardous landslide and flood areas in California, see Appendix A, Welcome to California. In addition, you may want to consult a soils expert, who may recommend soil borings.

Which Inspections Do You Really Need?

Some very cautious buyers have different specialists check all major areas of the house, such as heating, plumbing, roof, and foundation. Involving specialists makes excellent sense if the house is old, large, expensive, or in obvious poor condition. But weigh the benefit against the cost. If you're buying a five-year-old house in apparently great shape, you have read up on inspections, and an experienced general inspector and pest control inspector have discovered no problems, spending any money on additional inspections is probably overkill. These guidelines should help you decide how many inspections you need:

- **Let your eyes be your first guide.** The poorer-looking the condition, the more you should use a fine-tooth comb.
- **Age is a factor.** Houses deteriorate over time, and construction techniques (especially for foundations) weren't always the best years ago. So the older the house, the more it makes sense to examine it closely.
- **Mansions deserve a third look.** The more expensive the house, the more you want to be sure you're getting your money's worth.
- **In areas where the earth moves often, check the foundation and the subsoil carefully.** This is especially true for houses in landslide- or earthquake-vulnerable areas and houses built on landfill.

- **Look for evidence of seasonal problems.** If you buy a house in the middle of August, the roof won't be leaking or the basement flooding—but they may in December. So look carefully at ceilings, attic spaces, and basements for stains or water marks. If ceilings have recently been repainted, ask why. If you aren't satisfied with the answer, ask your inspector to check these areas extra carefully and the seller to state in writing that no problems have been covered up.
- **Question new construction.** If you have any questions about a room addition or any remodeling done on the house, check permits on file at the local planning department. Make sure that all the work was done with permits and that the final permits were issued.

EXAMPLE: Amy is making an offer on an older, two-story stucco house in the Berkeley hills. She read that pest control inspectors often fail to probe corners of buildings under inset gutters for hidden rot caused by overflowing and don't usually get behind the stucco. She also learned that in earthquake zone areas, like Berkeley, this is dangerous, because rotten wood at the corners can make buildings structurally unsafe. Sure enough, when she read the pest control report, no behind-the-stucco probing had been done. She hires another inspector who has a solid reputation. He probes the corners and discovers serious damage, which costs $22,000 to repair. Fortunately, Amy gets the seller to credit the full amount in escrow.

Why Some Inspectors Are Paranoid

In recent years, many buyers, discovering defects after the purchase, have sued the property inspector, claiming that the defects should have been discovered and disclosed. The possibility of being sued has made some inspectors ultracareful when it comes to emphasizing what's wrong with a house.

Who Pays for Inspections?

A general inspection typically costs about $500–$800 for a single-family home, and more for a multiple-unit dwelling. Structural pest control inspections cost about $150 for an average single-family house. Normally, the buyer pays for inspections required as part of the offer to purchase. This is custom, however, not law, and it's possible to negotiate an arrangement where the seller pays or shares in the cost of inspections. Just make sure that even if the seller pays, you choose the inspector.

Are the Repairs Really Needed?

If the inspection reports identify expensive repair needs, here are some questions to ask:

- **Did you get a second opinion?** Especially if the problem is serious or requires specialized knowledge, you might want one.

- **Has one inspector called for very different types of repairs from another?** If so, some work probably needs to be done, but you still need to figure out exactly what.
- **Is the problem real or potential?** Can the situation be monitored? Will less-expensive work solve the problem? Pest control inspectors must notify the person requesting the report that the information can be divided into two sections: corrective measures for damage from evident infestations and corrective measures for conditions deemed likely to lead to infestation and future problems. For potential problems, ask whether the expensive work needs to be done now.
- **Is the problem getting worse?** If so, it's an indicator that you'll probably have to take immediate steps to either repair it or at least prevent it from spreading.

Don't simply accept as gospel what the expert tells you. If the costs seem too high, get a second opinion from someone committed to helping you arrive at a less-expensive solution.

Who Pays for Defects?

If inspections turn up a laundry list of expensive defects, you and the seller will have to negotiate who pays what. If your offer is contingent upon your approving inspection reports, you have no obligation to proceed with the purchase until you approve of the plan to remedy the defects.

Earthquake Reinforcements

Earthquakes in the late 1980s and 1990s have cast much new light on making houses earthquake safe. The time-tested advice to bolt a house to its foundation and install stiff plywood cripple walls in the basement proved to be helpful. These reinforcements typically cost only a few thousand dollars, won't trigger a reappraisal of your home for property tax purposes (Revenue and Tax Code § 74.5), and are frequently a condition of getting earthquake insurance.

Recent earthquakes have also focused attention on the possibility that vertical earth movements can make houses vulnerable to literally jumping off their foundations. To cope with this danger, it's best to secure the house to the foundation using steel ties, straps, and, in some cases, cables. You might also want the cripple walls strengthened with heavy-gauge metal fasteners and cross bracing. A thorough retrofit of this type typically costs $2,000–$8,000 or more, depending on the size and age of the house, but should be done only after an earthquake expert is consulted.

In addition, it's important to repair termite and other structural damage, or else earthquake retrofit work can actually make a house more susceptible to earthquake damage. Earthquake retrofit services are advertised heavily; many people sound convincing but actually know so little that they are apt to make the problem worse. For more information on earthquake-proofing your house, see the *Homeowner's Guide to Earthquake Safety*, discussed above.

Ask for a Home Warranty

Several companies sell home repair warranty contracts. Typically, these policies cover the heating, air conditioning, plumbing, and electrical systems, as well as the water heater and built-in kitchen and laundry appliances. For an extra charge, the policy can also cover pools, spas, and even roofs. Under standard home warranties, if one of these systems fails during the coverage period (usually one year), you call the warranty company, which sends out a repair person. You'll have to pay a fee of $35 to $50 per visit, depending upon the particular policy. In addition, there may be a modest deductible.

CAUTION

You shouldn't have to buy a home warranty policy for a new home. Most home warranty policies are geared toward existing homes. If you're buying a newly built home, it will normally come with a warranty between you and the builder.

A growing number of sellers voluntarily include a year's service contract as part of the price of the house, particularly with new houses. If the seller doesn't offer you one, it doesn't hurt to ask. Depending on the size and age of the house, a service contract might cost $300–$900. A seller may see this as a bargain if it clinches the sale. Sometimes a buyer's real estate agent will provide a buyer with a home warranty—again, as incentive for the deal to close. Around 90% of the houses sold in California now come with a home warranty.

If no one offers you a policy, you can buy one yourself (but must do so now, as part of your purchase transaction). Although these policies can be renewed indefinitely, having the coverage makes the most sense during the first year of ownership, when systems and appliances likely to give you trouble will probably do so. Coverage usually begins at the close of escrow.

Several companies offer home warranties. Here are some keys to finding good coverage:

- Be sure the contract covers preexisting conditions that were not known to the seller or discovered in an inspection.
- Be sure you're aware of all restrictions and dollar limits of coverage. For example, while a home warranty might cover the cost of repairing a burst pipe, secondary damage to furniture or carpeting typically won't be covered.
- Find out how disputes are handled and whether the warranty requires mediation or arbitration.
- If an appliance or system is still covered by its own warranty, don't bother including it in the home warranty unless the warranty that came with the appliance or system will expire shortly. Instead, ask for a fee reduction.

TIP

Don't worry—filing home warranty claims won't raise the price or availability of your homeowners' insurance coverage. Home warranty contracts are a different animal from regular homeowner's insurance. The offering companies don't even communicate with one another. And since home warranty claims don't tend to run into high dollar figures, the industry isn't paranoid about the number of claims you file per year—the current average per customer is two.

RESOURCE

Home warranties. For more information on home warranties, contact the Home Warranty Association of California at www.warrantyassn.com or 805-653-1648. Ask for a copy of their free brochure.

The California Department of Insurance licenses home warranty firms and can provide information on the current status of a particular company's license. Call them at 800-927-4357, or check their website at www.insurance.ca.gov.

For a discussion of developer's warranties on new homes, see Chapter 7.

CHAPTER

20

Legal Ownership: How to Take Title

Before escrow closes on your new house, you'll need to choose how to take "title" (documented legal ownership). Title is evidenced by a deed recorded at the county recorder's office. The deed contains a description of the property and includes the name(s) of the seller(s) and buyer(s).

SKIP AHEAD

If you've owned a house before, you may be familiar with your options and already know how you want to take title. If so, you can skip this chapter. If you're a first-time homeowner or new to California and its community property ownership system, however, read on carefully.

One Unmarried Person

If you're in this category, you simply take title in your own name. Many title companies may add "an unmarried man" or "an unmarried woman" to the deed. This isn't legally required, but it helps dispel any later questions about whether there's a spouse of yours out there with a community property interest in the house.

The name to put on the deed is the one that appears on your checks, driver's license, passport, and other similar documents. This need not be your birth name. If you use more than one name, list the name you most commonly use for business purposes first, followed by A.K.A. ("also known as") and the other name.

Two or More Unmarried People

Unmarried people who purchase a house together may take title in one of four ways:

- joint tenancy
- tenancy in common
- partnership, or
- if you've registered as domestic partners, as community property.

The overwhelming majority of unmarried couples or groups own property in joint tenancy or tenancy in common. Partnership is typically appropriate only if you already own a business together and purchase the house as a business asset, or if you buy the house as a business investment to fix up for resale.

Joint Tenancy

If you take title to real property as joint tenants, all buyers will share property ownership equally and have the right to use the entire property. The key feature of joint tenancy is "the right of survivorship." When one joint tenant dies, his or her share automatically goes to the survivor(s), even if the deceased attempted to leave a portion of the house to someone else by will or living trust.

The right of survivorship lets the survivor take the property right after the other's death, without the expense and trouble of probate. Property left in a will must go through formal probate court before being transferred to the new owner (although there is a simplified procedure for property left to a spouse). If, however, you're the property's primary owner and just adding someone's name to the title to avoid probate, consider

Forms of Real Property Co-Ownership

	Tenancy in Common	Joint Tenancy	Partnership	Community Property	Community Property With Right of Survivorship
Creation	Deed must transfer property to two or more persons "as tenants in common" or without specifying how title is to be held.	Deed must transfer property to two or more persons "as joint tenants" or "with right of survivorship."	Deed must transfer property to the name of the partnership, or partnership funds must be used to buy it.	Deed must transfer property to a married couple or to registered domestic partners "as community property."	Deed must transfer property to married couple as "community property with right of survivorship."
Shares of co-owners	May be unequal. (This is specified on the deed.)	All joint tenants must own equal shares.	Determined by partnership agreement or Uniform Partnership Act.	Each spouse owns half.	Each spouse owns half.
Survivorship	On co-owner's death, interest passes to heirs under intestate succession law or beneficiaries under will or living trust.	Deceased joint tenant's share automatically goes to surviving joint tenants.	Interests usually go to partner's heir or beneficiaries, but partnership agreement may limit this.	Spouse can leave his or her half to anyone; if nothing to the contrary, goes to surviving spouse.	When one spouse dies, survivor automatically owns entire property.
Probate	Interest left by will is subject to probate. Simplified procedure available if left to spouse.	No probate necessary to transfer title to surviving joint tenants.	Interest left by will is subject to probate.	Simplified probate procedure available to transfer title to surviving spouse.	No probate necessary to transfer title to surviving spouse.
Termination	Any co-owner may transfer his or her interest or get partition order from court. Co-owners can change the form of ownership by signing a new deed.	Joint tenant may transfer interest to him- or herself or another as tenants in common, or may get partition order from court.	Governed by partnership agreement or Uniform Partnership Act.	Both spouses must agree to transfers.	Both spouses must agree.

Source: *Deeds for California Real Estate*, by Mary Randolph (Nolo).

using a living trust instead; it allows you to change your mind later. See *Make Your Own Living Trust*, by Denis Clifford (Nolo).

While the joint tenants are alive, any owner can end the joint tenancy by selling his or her share of the property, or by deeding it from him- or herself in joint tenancy to him- or herself in tenancy in common. (Civil Code § 683.2.) This ends the joint tenancy and, with it, the automatic right of survivorship.

Joint tenancy isn't a good choice for all unmarried couples or groups. First, it necessitates equal ownership shares, so if people want to own the house in unequal shares, joint tenancy won't work. Second, contrary to popular belief, joint tenancy won't necessarily protect a surviving owner from state tax authorities coming to reappraise the house's value after one owner dies. Although married couples and registered domestic partners are exempt from this reappraisal, unmarried couples are not. It's most appropriate for people in intimate, long-term relationships who wish to provide for each other after one dies.

Joint Tenants: What Your Deed Should Say

If you want to take title as joint tenants, the deed should specify that you hold title as joint tenants with right of survivorship. You need not use a form with "Joint Tenancy Deed" printed on it, though it's fine if you do. A "Grant Deed" or a "Quitclaim Deed" will also form a legal joint tenancy as long as the proper legal language is used.

Tenancy in Common

Tenancy in common ("TIC") is the appropriate way for many unmarried co-owners to take title to property, because co-owners need not own equal shares. For example, one person could own 70% of the property and the other person own 30%. If ownership is to be unequal, it's best to write a separate contract specifying each person's ownership percentage and what happens if one person wants to sell or dies. Two Nolo books—*Living Together: A Legal Guide for Unmarried Couples*, by Ralph Warner, Toni Ihara, and Frederick Hertz, and *A Legal Guide for Lesbian & Gay Couples*, by Denis Clifford, Frederick Hertz, and Emily Doskow—contain tenancy in common (and joint tenancy) contracts as well as lots of other useful information for unmarried couples buying together. Regardless of the percentages, however, each person owns an undivided portion of the entire house, not a particular part of it.

Tenancy in common has no right of survivorship—when a tenant in common dies, his or her share passes to the person named in a will or living trust, or by intestate succession (the laws that govern who gets your property if you fail to specify whom you want to receive it). If you're doing an equity share (described in Chapter 3), you must, unless there is some compelling reason against it, hold title as tenants in common.

If you wish to provide for the survivor without going through probate when the first partner dies, you can hold property as tenants in common and each put your share into a revocable living trust. Simply name each other as beneficiary to receive the owner's share on the owner's death. If you change your mind and decide not to leave your co-owner your share, simply change the trust beneficiary of the living trust.

Tenants in Common: What Your Deed Should Say

In California, a transfer of real property to two or more persons automatically creates a tenancy in common unless the deed says otherwise. No special words are necessary.

Couple or Domestic Partners Owning Together

Married persons and registered domestic partners ("RDPs") who wish to co-own may take title as joint tenants, tenants in common, or as community property with right of survivorship. The last one is the choice we recommend for most married couples and RDPs.

CAUTION

Get more details if you're in a registered domestic partnership or married to a person of the same sex. Because federal laws treat these statuses differently than state laws do, tax issues are considerably more complex. You'll want to consult an estate planning attorney before buying a house. For further information about related issues, contact Equality California (www.eqca.org, 415-581-0005) or the National Center for Lesbian Rights (NCLR) (www.nclrights.org, 415-392-6257).

Community Property With Right of Survivorship

CAUTION

If you don't want to leave the property to your spouse or registered domestic partner, hold title a different way. If you and your spouse or partner own the property as "community property with right of survivorship," at your death your spouse or partner will inherit your half—even if your will contains instructions to the contrary. If you want the other advantages of community property without the automatic right of survivorship, you can hold title as plain "community property." Simply leave the words "with right of survivorship" off the deed. The deceased person's half of the property will then go to whoever is named in the will.

Taking title as community property with right of survivorship offers two advantages:

- avoiding formal probate when a spouse or partner dies, and
- easy qualification for a federal income tax break (for married couples only, not RDPs).

Probate Avoidance

When one spouse or partner dies, property held as community property with right of survivorship goes directly to the surviving person without formal probate. A surviving spouse or partner who inherits needs only to record a simple document with the county recorder. This can be done without a lawyer; the survivor avoids not only lengthy delays in transferring the property (and title), but also costly probate fees.

RESOURCE

The petition and instructions for completing and filing an affidavit with the probate court are included in *How to Probate an Estate in California,* by Julia Nissley (Nolo).

Tax Planning

Normally, if someone sells a house, taxable profits are determined by adding the price originally paid for the house to the cost of capital improvements, and then subtracting this total from the amount the house sells for less the costs of sale.

When title is held by a married, heterosexual couple as community property with right of survivorship, a surviving spouse who inherits the property automatically qualifies for a significant tax advantage. (One that's more difficult to achieve if the same property is held in tenancy in common or joint tenancy.) The cost basis of the entire property—the cost of the house and improvements—increases ("steps up") to the property's value at the deceased person's death. Because the higher the cost basis is, the lower the taxable profit will be, a stepped up basis can significantly reduce your overall tax liability if one spouse dies. If the property isn't community property, the basis of the survivor's share stays the same. Only the half inherited from the deceased spouse gets a stepped-up basis.

CAUTION

Domestic partners and couples in same sex marriages take note. Legal experts are doubtful about whether the IRS will permit registered domestic partners or couples in same sex marriages the same tax advantage. The issue is whether the step up in basis is available to anyone who can claim community property ownership, or whether the owners must also be a married, opposite-sex couple. The news is better when it comes to property reappraisal upon one owner's death: like opposite sex married couples, the surviving registered domestic partner or same sex spouse will be exempt from reappraisal by the California tax authorities.

Community Property With Right of Survivorship: What Your Deed Should Say

For a married couple and registered domestic partners, the deed need simply say, "Fred Parks hereby grants to Mabel Rivera and Albert Riviera, [either "spouses" or "registered domestic partners"] as community property with right of survivorship, [the legal description of the property]."

EXAMPLE: Carmen and Al brought a house in 1976. In tax lingo, what Carmen and Al originally paid for the house ($60,000), plus the cost of improvements ($40,000), is their "adjusted cost basis" in the property ($100,000). If they sell for $850,000, their taxable profit would be

$750,000: the selling price less the cost basis.

If instead Carmen dies, leaving everything to Al, and they owned their house as tenants in common, the cost basis on Carmen's half of the property would increase from $50,000 (half of the $100,000 adjusted cost basis) to $425,000 (half of the $850,000 value at the time of her death). The basis on Al's half remains $50,000; as owner of the entire property, his total cost basis becomes $475,000. If Al later sells the house for $975,000, his taxable profit will be $500,000.

But if Carmen and Al had taken title to the house as community property, Al would qualify for a 100% stepped-up federal cost basis, not just on the half of the house belonging to Carmen. Now, if Al sold the property for $975,000, he'd have no taxable profit from the sale, because his gain is less than $250,000.

It's possible to argue, even if you didn't hold title as community property, that the property was in fact community property, held in joint tenancy or tenancy in common "for convenience." But there are no draw-backs to holding title as community property, and you can save yourselves an argument with the IRS.

Joint Tenancy

What about holding co-owned property in joint tenancy? Some spouses need to do this, for example, because their bank or savings and loan insisted on it, for separate reasons. Other than this type of situation, however, there is very little reason for a married couple to choose a joint tenancy. Community property with right of survivorship offers the same advantages and more.

What about qualifying for a stepped-up tax basis? Do you lose this big advantage if you hold title in joint tenancy? Not necessarily. If you want to put your co-owned property in joint tenancy and qualify for a stepped-up cost basis, too, you simply need to be able to convincingly document to the IRS that the property is community property. Some experts recommend that you place the words "community property held in joint tenancy" on the deed. Before taking property in joint tenancy, read the section above on joint tenancy for unmarried people.

Separate Versus Community Property

Separate property is property acquired by one spouse or registered domestic partner prior to marriage or registration, after permanent separation, or during marriage or registered partnership by gift or inheritance. If separate property is sold, and other property is bought with the proceeds, it, too, is separate property.

Community property is all money earned or otherwise acquired by either spouse or partner during the marriage or registered partnership (except for rents, dividends, interest, and the like earned on separate property). A spouse or partner can turn his or her separate property into community property by stating that intention in writing.

Tenants in Common

While married couples rarely hold property as tenants in common, it is occasionally done. If, for example, the house was bought with the separate property of the husband and the separate property of the wife, and they want to keep it in separate shares, tenancy in common makes sense.

Tenancy in common lets spouses own the property in unequal shares. The specific shares, however, must be identified in writing, and the document should be recorded with the county recorder. Otherwise, property held in tenancy in common is presumed to be community property if you die or divorce. Marital Property Agreement #1, below, is a sample agreement for spouses who hold unequal shares of their house as tenants in common. This is a tricky area of law; have a real estate lawyer look at any agreement you draft.

Married Person Owning Alone

If a married person wants to own a house separately, title should be in that person's name alone, and the couple should sign and record (with the deed) an agreement declaring their intention that one spouse owns the house as separate property. Otherwise, if the couple divorces and disagrees about ownership, a court will characterize the house as community or separate property depending on what funds (community or separate) paid for it, not whose name is on the deed. Because most couples mix and spend separate and community funds without regard to type, what property was used to pay the mortgage, insurance, improvements, and taxes won't always be clear.

CAUTION

A house that starts out as separate property may easily become a mix of separate and community. For example, if Jeff and Maida, a married couple, buy a house using Jeff's premarital earnings for the down payment and then use income earned during marriage for the insurance, taxes, mortgage payments, and improvements, everything but the down payment is community property, no matter what the deed says. Jeff and Maida can change this only by signing a written agreement. However, if Jeff had spent his separate property on a house that Maida owned before their marriage, not only would it not become community property, but he couldn't expect reimbursement in the event of their divorce. (See *In Re Marriage of Cross*, 94 Cal.App.4th 1143; 114 Cal. Rptr.2d 839 (2001).)

To put your understanding in writing, use an agreement like Marital Property Agreement #2, below.

CAUTION

Be careful if one spouse gives up property rights. If you or your spouse or partner gives up valuable property rights in the agreement, a court might later conclude that that person was unduly influenced by the other. The court could throw out the whole agreement. To be safe, consult a lawyer—who may recommend that you each see separate lawyers.

Marital Property Agreement #1

Diane Holst and James Kelvin, husband and wife, agree as follows:

1. We purchased the house at 9347 24th Street, Laguna Niguel, California, using as a down payment Diane's separate property plus a small amount of community property.
2. We hold title to the house as tenants in common.
3. Diane agrees to pay mortgage payments and taxes from her separate property, with only a small amount of community property being used for improvements.
4. As a result, Diane owns 80% of the equity in the house, and James owns 20%.
5. We intend this document to rebut the presumption of Civil Code § 4800.2 that, at dissolution, property held in joint title is community property. We do not wish the property to be treated as community property if we dissolve our marriage.

Diane Holst — *9/30/08*
Diane Holst — Date

James Kelvin — *9/30/08*
James Kelvin — Date

State of California
County of *Orange*

On *September 30*, 20*08* before me, *Nora Public, Notary Public*, personally appeared *Diane Holst* and *James Kelvin*, personally known to me (or proved to me on the basis of satisfactory evidence) to be the persons whose names are subscribed to the within instrument and acknowledged to me that they executed the same in their authorized capacities, and that by their signatures on the instrument the persons, or the entity upon behalf of which the persons acted, executed the instrument.

WITNESS my hand and official seal.

Signature *Nora Public*

[SEAL]

Marital Property Agreement #2

We, Brian Morgan and Laura Stein, husband and wife, hereby agree that:

1. Brian Morgan holds title to a vacation cabin near Lake Tahoe, the address of which is 43566 Lake Tahoe Drive, Lake Tahoe, California, which he owned prior to our marriage as separate property.
2. Although the mortgage, maintenance, and improvements on the cabin have been, and will be, paid during our marriage with savings that are partially community property, we intend that Brian Morgan own the cabin as his separate property.
3. We make this agreement in light of the fact that Brian's earnings constitute a greater portion of our community savings, and that upon Brian's death, we both want the cabin to be inherited by Scott Morgan, Brian's son.

Brian Morgan — *9/30/08*
Brian Morgan — Date

Laura Stein — *9/30/08*
Laura Stein — Date

State of California
County of *Alameda*

On *September 30*, 20*08* before me, *Jon Dough, Notary Public*, personally appeared *Brian Morgan* and *Laura Stein*, personally known to me (or proved to me on the basis of satisfactory evidence) to be the persons whose names are subscribed to the within instrument and acknowledged to me that they executed the same in their authorized capacities, and that by their signatures on the instrument the persons, or the entity upon behalf of which the persons acted, executed the instrument.

WITNESS my hand and official seal.

Signature *Jon Dough*

[SEAL]

Partnership

Partnership may be appropriate for people already in a business together who purchase a house as a business asset, or people buying a house purely as an investment to fix up and resell.

Property acquired with partnership funds is presumed to belong to the partnership, absent an agreement to the contrary. What the partners can do with the property once it's transferred to the partnership is governed either by their partnership agreement or, if they have no agreement, the Uniform Partnership Act. (Corp. Code §§ 16100 and following.)

RESOURCE

Partnership law. Home buyers don't usually form a partnership to purchase a house, so we do not discuss partnership rules in detail here. For more information on partnership law and written partnership agreements, see *Form a Partnership: The Complete Legal Guide,* by Denis Clifford and Ralph Warner (Nolo), and Nolo's *Quicken Legal Business Pro* (software), to create a partnership agreement.

Partnership: What Your Deed Should Say

When a partnership buys a house, the deed states the business name used by the partnership, or the partners' names themselves, such as, "Fred Parks hereby grants to the Stobert Partners, [the legal description of the property]."

Placing the Property in a Living Trust

Now is a good time to think about keeping the house from going through probate at your death. Probate is a long and expensive court process where assets are distributed by the terms of a will or, if there is no will, by the laws of the state.

TIP

Already taking title as joint tenants or as community property with right of survivorship? If so, the house will pass to the surviving spouse without probate anyway. Realize, however, that this doesn't cover you against all eventualities. You might, for example, want to think about avoiding probate in case both spouses die at once, or if you're both at a stage in life where you're planning who will inherit the house when you're gone.

Fortunately, avoiding probate is relatively easy. You set up a revocable living trust, name yourself as the trustee (which means you keep control over the property), and name a beneficiary to receive the property when you die. The beneficiary can be anyone: a spouse, lover, child, charity, or whoever. You prepare, sign, and record a deed transferring ownership from yourself to yourself as trustee of the living trust. When you die, the beneficiary takes title, usually in a few weeks, without probate.

Because you name yourself as trustee of your own living trust, you keep control over the property while you're alive. You can easily change the title to the house, sell the house, or change the trust beneficiary.

To create a living trust, you must prepare and sign the trust document papers. They appoint you as trustee and set out the terms of the trust, including how you are to manage the property, that the trust is revocable, and when ownership should be transferred to the beneficiary. We recommend Nolo's *Quicken Legal Business Pro* (software), or *Plan Your Estate,* by Denis Clifford (Nolo), which contains a tear-out, fill-in living trust form with step-by-step instructions. Before putting your house into a trust, however, check with the lender to see if changing title triggers any due-on-sale provision (requiring full payment when ownership changes) of your mortgage.

If you decide to create a living trust but don't have it ready when you buy your house, take title in your name or, if you own the house with someone else, in your name and the other person's name. After you create the trust, transfer title to the house (if you're the sole owner), or your share of the house, to yourself as trustee of the trust. If you are married, you'll need your spouse's consent to transfer your share of community property. This is simple to do; see *Deeds for California Real Estate,* by Mary Randolph (Nolo).

CHAPTER

21

If Something Goes Wrong During Escrow

The likelihood of a major disaster befalling your purchase—such as the seller dying or an earthquake destroying the house—is slim. But it's possible that during escrow something will go wrong. A missing or incorrect loan document or last-minute title problems may simply delay closing a bit. More serious problems may jeopardize the whole deal. This chapter presents a brief overview of what may happen if your deal threatens to unravel. If you and the seller both agree to rescind the contract, there's no problem. Simply complete the Release of Real Estate Purchase Contract form in Chapter 18. If either of you wants to close the deal, however, you'll need quick help from an experienced real estate lawyer.

The Seller Backs Out

Your purchase agreement probably gives both you and the seller a number of outs—that is, legal excuses to drop out of the deal, such as if the other person fails to comply with a time limit or other obligation. If the seller backs out for one of these justifiable excuses, there's no breach of contract, and you can't really complain, much less sue for damages. We're not going to get into the whole panoply of justifiable reasons for the seller to back out. Some of these might be highly technical, and need lawyers and courts to sort them out.

But suppose a seller backs out of the deal after you have met or waived all contingencies simply because he or she doesn't want to sell the house or gets another offer that looks better. Isn't that a clear breach of contract? Yes, and your remedy is normally to mediate or arbitrate (an option in many standard real estate contracts) or sue, demanding that the seller sell you the house and pay you damages based on your out-of-pocket costs.

The Seller Refuses to Move Out

In rare circumstances, the seller may refuse to move out, even though the house is legally yours. This is a particular problem in areas with rent or eviction controls. To force a "holdover" seller from your property, you must follow the same procedure as a landlord uses to evict a tenant—and file an unlawful detainer lawsuit in superior court. You can do this even if your purchase contract includes a mediation or arbitration clause, providing unlawful detainers are listed as an exception to your dispute clause. See *The California Landlord's Law Book: Evictions,* by David Brown (Nolo), for step-by-step instructions and forms needed to file an eviction lawsuit in California.

CAUTION

If the seller has already moved out, keep an eye on the property. An obviously empty house can be a target for thieves and vandals. Now might be a good time to start getting to know your neighbors—ask them to watch for any suspicious activity. If you can, drive by the house regularly. Though chances are you won't catch a crime in progress, you might prevent one. You'll be making your presence felt and can deal with any obvious signs of your absence—such as a pizza flyer on the front door that would otherwise stay there for days.

You Back Out

If you refuse to go through with the deal without a good reason, the seller can pursue mediation, arbitration, or a lawsuit, requesting you pay damages. Damages aren't always easy to determine, however, because the seller has a duty to try to limit (mitigate, in legalese) losses by selling the house to someone else. To avoid arguing over the amount of the loss, most house purchase contracts provide a specific dollar figure (liquidated damages) for the seller's maximum damages if you breach the contract.

A liquidated damages clause means that the maximum amount the seller is entitled to is the stated amount. Disputes are often settled by the buyer and seller agreeing to allow the seller to keep part, but not all, of the deposit. Canny buyers know that sellers who are under pressure to find another buyer and transfer clear title want to get a deal-gone-bad behind them and are therefore often willing to compromise on the amount of the deposit they get to keep.

The Seller Dies

Technically, a contract to buy a house is enforceable even if the seller dies, because a deceased person's estate is responsible for fulfilling that person's lawful obligations. But in reality, the title insurance and/or escrow company will put on the brakes and call in their attorneys if the seller dies.

The executor of the seller's estate, and possibly the seller's inheritors, may want to get out of the deal. This could be a blessing in disguise, because after a seller dies, completing a house purchase transaction often becomes more complicated and time-consuming than when the seller was alive, especially if the house is part of an estate that must be probated. If the seller's inheritors do want out, insist that they reimburse you for any expenses you've thus far incurred.

If you and the inheritors want to proceed, be patient and sensitive. Try to determine whether the sale is likely to go through without difficulty. (Talking to an estate planning lawyer should help.) If settling the estate will be simple, the delay with the sale will probably be short. If settling the estate will be more complicated (for instance, the estate must be probated and 17 people claim the seller owed them money), consider discussing with the lawyer the best way to get out of the deal so that you can look for another house.

You Discover a Defect in the Property

If you feel that a seller knew about a defect—such as a basement that floods in a heavy rain—before the sale and failed to disclose it, contact the seller and the seller's broker and ask for money to correct the problem. If they turn down your request, and you can document that the defect was longstanding and should have been known to the seller, you have a good chance of going to court and recovering damages. You may sue both the seller and his or her broker in small claims court (up to $7,500). *Everybody's Guide to Small Claims Court in California*, by Ralph Warner (Nolo), shows how. If more money is involved or the situation is complicated, you'll need to obtain legal advice.

As long as the defect is disclosed, however, there is usually no legal liability. If the disclosure doesn't happen until late in escrow, however, you (the buyer) may have the right to get out of the deal or to be compensated. You may need to sue the seller or the title insurance company, depending on who was at fault. Again, you'll need legal advice for this type of situation. Your lawyer will want to refer to *Jue v. Smiser* (23 Cal. App. 4th (1994)), a case covering disclosure late in escrow.

The House Is Destroyed by Natural Disaster (Fire, Earthquake, Flood)

Destruction of the house is handled as follows: If you have either physical possession of, or legal title to, the property, you are responsible for its physical condition and insurance. Otherwise, the seller is responsible. Thus, the seller should make sure his or her homeowners' policy is in force until the close of escrow, at which moment your policy goes into effect.

If the house is flooded three days before escrow closes, the seller can pay for the repairs and deliver the property in the condition it was in before the flood. If you want out of the deal, however, simply refuse to grant an extension to the seller to make the repairs.

House-Hungry Martians Take Possession of the House

While we don't expect your deal to be threatened by extraterrestrials, we include this heading to remind you that in this weird and wacky world of ours, all sorts of unexpected events can frustrate even the best plans. If you suddenly find your house purchase threatened from a totally unexpected angle (for example, the state announces that construction of a new freeway running through the house's kitchen will begin in a month), see an experienced real estate lawyer pronto.

Finding a Lawyer

This chapter points out a few instances when an attorney's advice or services may be useful. Finding a good, reasonably priced lawyer is not always an easy task. If you just pick a name out of the phone book, you may get a lawyer who's not qualified to deal with your particular problem, one who will charge too much, or both. If you use the attorney who drew up your family will, you may end up with someone who knows nothing about real estate law.

As a general rule, experience is most important. The best way to find a lawyer who specializes in real estate law is through a trusted person who has had a satisfactory experience with one. Your agent may have some suggestions (unless, of course, your legal problem involves your agent).

The worst referral sources are:

- heavily advertised legal clinics, which are less likely to offer competitive rates for competent representation in this specialized area, and
- referral panels set up by local bar associations, which sometimes refer people to inexperienced practitioners who don't have enough clients and use the panel as a way of generating needed business.

Once you get a good referral, call the law offices that have been recommended and state your problem. Find out the hourly fee and cost of an initial visit. Most lawyers charge $200 to $450 an hour. If you feel the lawyer is qualified to handle your problem, make an appointment to discuss your situation.

Here are some things to look for in your first meeting:

- Will the lawyer answer all your questions about his or her fees, experience in real estate matters, and your particular legal problem? Stay away from lawyers who make you feel uncomfortable asking questions.
- Is the lawyer willing to answer your specific questions over the phone and charge you only for the brief amount of time the conversation lasted? If the lawyer won't give you any advice over the phone despite your invitation to bill you for it, find someone else.
- Does the lawyer represent sellers, too? Chances are that a lawyer who represents both buyers and sellers can advise you well on how to avoid many legal pitfalls of buying a house.

CAUTION

Attorney fees clauses. If your contract has an attorney fees provision, you are entitled to recover your attorney fees if you win a lawsuit based on the terms of that agreement. There's no guarantee, however, that a judge will award attorney fees equal to your attorney's actual bill, or that you will ultimately be able to collect the money from the seller.

Getting Your Deposit Back

If the deal falls through, you and the seller should sign a Release of Real Estate Purchase Contract form (see Chapter 18 for a sample). If one of you refuses to sign within 30 days following a written demand to do so from the other, the person who refuses to sign may be liable to the other for attorney fees and damages of three times the amount deposited in escrow—no more than $1,000 and no less than $100. (Civil Code § 1057.3.)

True Story

Felicity and Melinda: Earthquake Jitters

We had contracts to buy one house and sell our existing one. The buyers of the house we were selling had the house inspected and signed off. Then a big earthquake hit. Our house suffered no damage, but the buyers wanted to pay less, claiming that the earthquake had generally lowered real estate values. After much haggling, we agreed to a small reduction in price, provided they increase their deposit to $4,000 and sign that it was nonrefundable.

Three weeks later, on the day the buyers got notice of their loan approval, they backed out. The earthquake had scared them, and they changed their mind about living in California. Then they demanded that half of their nonrefundable deposit be refunded! A lawyer told us that going to binding arbitration or suing would be costly, risk clouding the title of the house, and prevent an easy sale to someone else. Nevertheless, we asked the lawyer to write a stiff letter demanding that we keep the full amount. As a result, the former buyers agreed to let us keep $3,000, which meant we ended up with $2,700 after our lawyer got his fee.

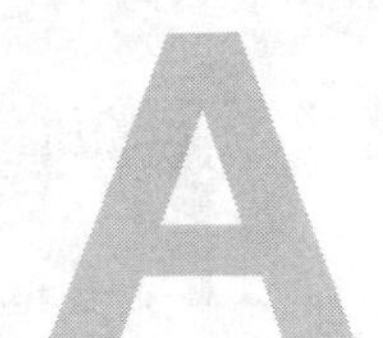

Welcome to California

This appendix is intended primarily for house purchasers who are new to California, moving from one part of the state to another, or first-time purchasers. There are a number of unique aspects to life on the Pacific coast—and to California in particular.

RESOURCE

California online. We list many California-specific websites throughout this section (and the entire book) on everything from home listings to crime to earthquake hazards to schools. Be sure to see Appendix B, Real Estate Websites, for a complete list organized by topic. We especially recommend the California Home Page at www.ca.gov.

Climate and Geography

Impressions of California are created by movie and television depictions of an endless summer. And why not? On New Year's Day, while you're snow-bound in the East or Midwest, the Rose Bowl is being broadcast from Pasadena, where the temperature is invariably 80 degrees. You're forgiven for your initial view of California.

But reality, even California-style, tends to come without a suntan in January. If you doubt this, trade your sunglasses for reading glasses and look at a map of the United States. Notice how far California stretches from top to bottom—a state of such varied latitude just can't be uniformly warm and sunny year-round. Sure, you might tan in January in San Diego on a particularly nice day, but tanning is the last thing you'd do in Crescent City, near the Oregon border, which is as far north as Boston and gets significantly more wintertime precipitation.

The key to understanding California climate is in the word "variety." If you doubt this, consider that the state holds the U.S. records for highest and lowest summer temperatures and for greatest annual snowfall. Much of the San Francisco Bay Area (called "northern" California, but really part of the middle coast) has a Mediterranean climate—temperate, dry summers and relatively mild, wet winters. Summers along the coast are kept cool by the high fog that rolls in at night—thus the remark attributed to Mark Twain, "The coldest winter I ever spent was a summer in San Francisco." Twain could have found all the summer he ever wanted just a few miles inland, though, where 100 degree temperatures abound.

To the far north, the coast is practically a rain forest, where California's famous redwoods thrive, and rainfall can exceed 100 inches a year. Inland, in the far north of the state, snow-capped Mount Shasta is often viewed as a symbol for the mountain regions of the state.

Most 14,000-foot peaks are in the Sierra Nevada mountain range, far to the south, and along the eastern side of the state. The Sierra not only is the source of much of the state's water, but also provides much of its power. Happily for all who love its spectacular natural beauty, it is within a reasonable drive of many of the state's population centers.

In southern California, the climate is semiarid; Los Angeles has dry, pleasant winters and warm summers, which attract flocks of people. Southeastern California is a desert (the best-known city is Palm Springs), inhabited by cacti and retired actors. It's within a few hours' drive of most of the southern part of the state.

Microclimates

In much of the state, especially in the San Francisco and Los Angeles areas, the local weatherperson's favorite word is "variable." The typical weather pattern, influenced by the topography near the coast, can change radically within just a few miles. Close to Los Angeles, in beachfront Santa Monica, the July high averages 75 degrees, but it heats up to 95 degrees in Canoga Park, just 15 miles north in the San Fernando Valley. Near San Francisco, Half Moon Bay on the coast averages a July high of 64 degrees, while 25 miles inland, in Walnut Creek, the average climbs to 87.

More locally still, the weather within one city's limits can change considerably from neighborhood to neighborhood: Summer in San Francisco's Sunset District, for instance, is far cooler and foggier than in the warmest neighborhood, the Mission, just a few miles to the east.

How close your house is to the coast is a big factor in determining the weather you'll be enjoying—or complaining about. Hills and valleys are also important: West-facing slopes generally get more rain and lower temperatures than east-facing ones. So, however sunny a weather picture a real estate broker paints for you, listen with a drop of skepticism. If you can, ask a local resident what the weather is like.

Average Precipitation and Temperatures Throughout the State

Location	Annual Precipitation (in.)	Temperatures (Fahrenheit)			
		January		July	
		Max.	Min.	Max.	Min.
Alturas	12.13	43.2°	18.1°	88.1°	43.8°
Bakersfield	6.49	56.3°	39.3°	96.9°	69.2°
Bishop	5.02	53.6°	22.4°	97.9°	55.7°
Blue Canyon	66.36	44.7°	32.9°	76.9°	58.3°
Eureka	38.10	54.0°	40.8°	63.3°	52.8°
Fresno	11.23	53.6°	38.4°	96.6°	66.1°
Imperial	3.02	69.0°	41.4°	75.2°	65.3°
Los Angeles	15.14	68.1°	48.5°	83.8°	64.6°
Paso Robles	14.71	61.4°	33.1°	91.3°	51.8°
Redding	33.52	55.4°	35.5°	98.5°	64.1°
Sacramento	17.93	53.8°	38.8°	92.4°	58.3°
San Diego	10.77	65.8°	49.7°	75.8°	65.9°
San Francisco	22.28	58.1°	46.4°	68.2°	54.4°
Susanville	13.44	40.8°	20.8°	88.4°	49.8°

Source: *California Statistical Abstract 2003* published by the Department of Finance. Averages are for the 30-year period from 1971 to 2000.

Natural Hazards

California still seems to be getting more than its share of natural disasters. The four major natural hazards you'll find in California are earthquakes, fires, floods, and droughts.

Earthquake

In truth, there have been, and likely will continue to be, some devastating earthquakes as well as many smaller ones in the next 50 years. And in a state where faults underlie the land like a capillary system and the most populated cities are on the coast, the area of highest fault activity, there are no areas where you are completely safe from earthquakes. (Take a look at the fault map on the following page.) While the odds of a quake shaking your home are unfortunately significant, you can take steps to minimize the risk of severe damage.

How Safe Is the Site?

Surprisingly, proximity to a major fault is not the primary factor that affects how well a house will hold up during an earthquake, according to seismic experts. Instead, other geologic and geographic factors should be examined, as should the structure of the house itself:

- **Avoid houses on unstable hillsides.** An unstable hillside is not a good place to be if an earthquake hits, because of the potential for landslides. In the San Francisco Bay Area, for example, Dr. Robert Uhrhammer of the University of California, Berkeley, Seismology Center, predicts that a sizable quake on the Hayward fault (one of the state's most dangerous), which runs through the Oakland and Berkeley hills on the east side of San Francisco Bay, will result in more homes being damaged from landslides than from shaking. The danger of a slide depends on the soil condition—rock is preferable to unconsolidated dirt. Flat, solid ground is even better.
- **The worst place for a house to be built is on fill.** Artificial fill is common along many California bays and rivers including, most notably, the San Francisco Bay. Some newer types of fill are sturdier than older ones. In a strong quake with a lot of vigorous shaking, older fill and bay mud may have a tendency to lose cohesiveness and liquefy. A house built on fill won't necessarily sink, but it could tilt.
- **Don't buy a house downstream from a dam.** Some dams in California will fail (leak or even break) in a really strong earthquake. This can sweep a whole town away in minutes.

A geologist or soils engineer can evaluate the site and give you an opinion on its safety. Seismic maps may also help you evaluate the earthquake hazards of a particular area. (See Resources: Earthquakes, below.)

How Safe Is the Structure?

Even more important than where a house is built is what it's made of. "Most wood frame houses won't suffer significant structural damage, even in a large earthquake with a lot of ground shaking," says Dr. Uhrhammer. Wood frame houses are quite flexible and, if properly secured to their foundations, will shake but not break. Dr. Uhrhammer says that masonry houses are significantly less earthquake resistant than wood frame houses. He describes an unreinforced brick house a few stories tall as "extremely dangerous."

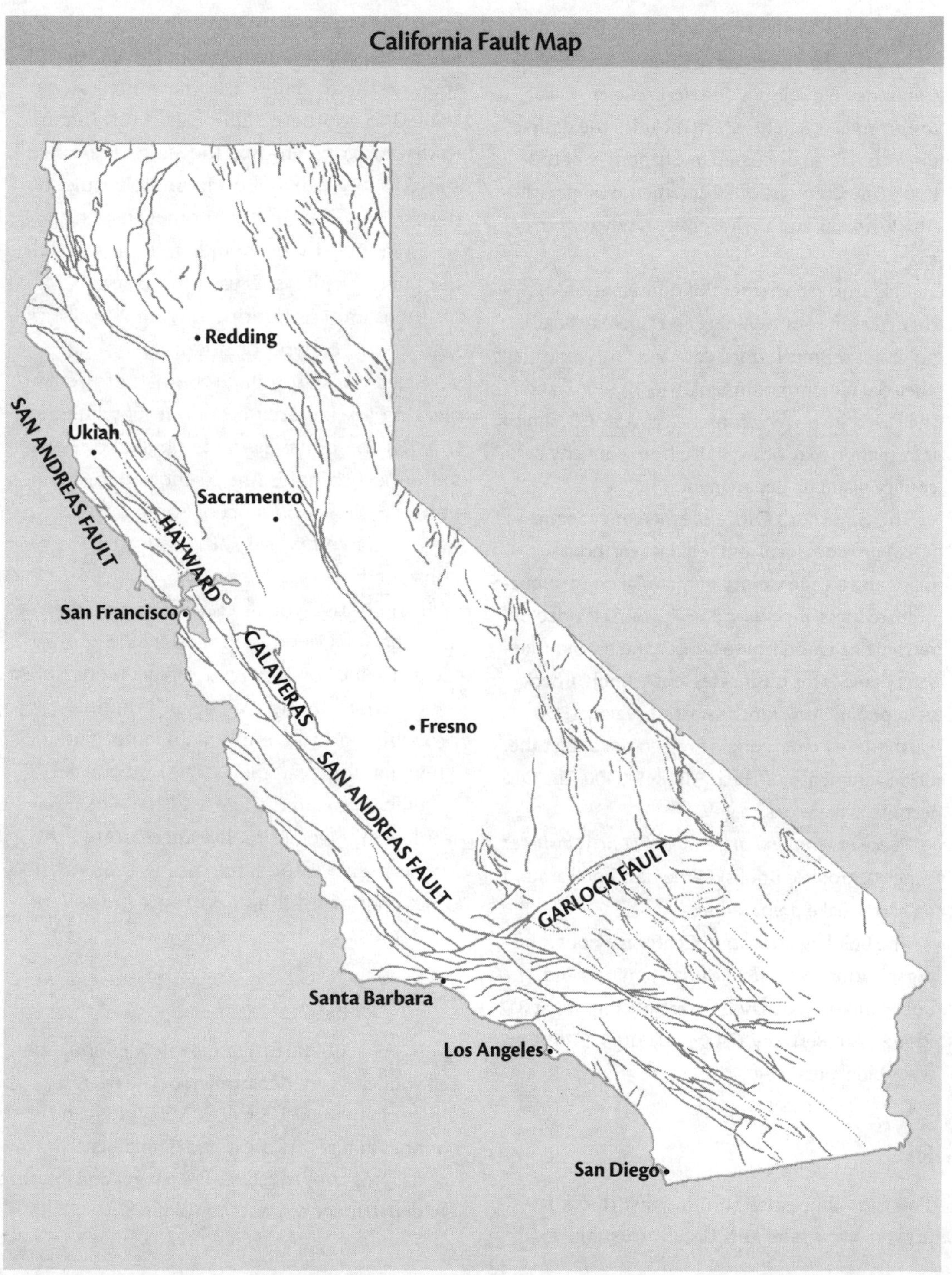
California Fault Map
Redding
Ukiah
Sacramento
San Francisco
Fresno
Santa Barbara
Los Angeles
San Diego
SAN ANDREAS FAULT
HAYWARD
CALAVERAS
SAN ANDREAS FAULT
GARLOCK FAULT

RESOURCE

Earthquakes. California Seismic Safety Commission publishes *The Homeowner's Guide to Earthquake Safety,* which includes the seismic disclosure form discussed in Chapter 19 of this book. The Commission's Sacramento office is at 916-263-5506, and their website is www.seismic.ca.gov.

California Department of Conservation, in particular the State Mining and Geology Board, publishes seismic hazard data and fault zone maps. Their Sacramento number is 916-322-1082, and their website is www.consrv.ca.gov/SMGB. Similar information may be available from your city or county planning department.

The Governor's Office of Emergency Services (OES) provides local and regional earthquake maps and a wide variety of material on earthquake preparedness, including a do-it-yourself video on retrofitting wood frame houses and earthquake safety guides for businesses and schools. Check your phone book for the nearest regional Earthquake Preparedness Project, or contact the OES Sacramento office at 916-845-8400. The OES website is www.oes.ca.gov.

Peace of Mind in Earthquake Country, by Peter Yanev (Chronicle Books), is the best book around on earthquake preparedness.

The Building Education Center is a nonprofit organization that offers all-day seminars and publications on earthquake retrofitting. It's at 812 Page Street, Berkeley, CA 94710, 510-525-7610, or www.bldgeductr.org.

Fire

The fires that pose the greatest threat to houses are grass and brush fires, most common in dry southern California, where large areas of parched brush and chaparral spark easily to flame. But these fires aren't limited to southern California. Fires begin in dry canyons all over the state. And once started, they can spread incredibly quickly, destroying thousands of homes, especially when fanned by hot winds that blow from the interior valleys toward the coast.

If you are considering buying a house near a wild canyon or hill area, look at whether you can reduce the risk of fire by clearing a wide area around it. Pay attention to what the house is made of; shake roofs and wood shingles are far more dangerous than tile roofs and stucco. Some cities have outlawed wood shingles for new construction.

If the house you're considering is in an area that has been identified as a high fire hazard zone, or is even a replacement house for one that burnt, any recent building probably had to comply with state standards. The roof, for example, should meet safety specifications, and there will have to be a minimum vegetation clearance around the house itself. (If the landscaping looks sparse, don't count on filling it in.) Ask the sellers for details.

RESOURCE

Wildfires. For fire safety information, call your city's fire department or the nearest Office of Emergency Services. Many cities and counties in high-risk areas have implemented special programs to reduce fire danger and improve fire department response to wildfires.

Flood

It hardly seems fair, but the same hills and canyons that make fires so hard to control in the summer are prone to dangerous floods and mudslides in the winter. The steep canyons in the San Gabriel mountains above Los Angeles are notorious for the torrents of water, mud, and boulders that have demolished many expensive homes over the years.

Houses by the ocean are also vulnerable to flood damage. Every year, Pacific storms combine with normal high tides to produce huge waves that roll over the beaches. The Russian and Sacramento rivers in northern California have flooded so often that locals know where the danger spots are. So, if you're considering buying a house near a stream or river, ask someone who has lived in the area for many years about floods. If you're told that the area flooded 40 years back or just last year, consider buying a bit higher up, because floods can recur at any time.

RESOURCE

Floods and landslides. The National Flood Insurance Program (NFIP) in Baltimore publishes hundreds of flood zone maps for California. For information on NFIP flood insurance policies, call 800-621-3362 or check the Federal Emergency Management Agency (FEMA) website at www.fema.gov/business/nfip.

The U.S. Geological Survey Earth Sciences Information Center in Menlo Park, 650-329-4309, can supply information about landslide susceptibility in California. Also, see www.usgs.gov to search for specific information online.

Drought

In the late 1980s, California, like much of the U.S., suffered the effects of a major drought, and many counties were on rationing. Smaller droughts are regular occurrences. As we proceed into the 2000s, much of California is either experiencing some level of drought or is at risk for drought. Climatologists say another multiyear drought may be on the way.

Rationing programs vary according to the severity of the drought. But they also vary depending on where you live—some water districts are harder hit than others.

Pollution

Like any other state, California has its environmental problems. Some make a place unpleasant; others make it unhealthy, especially if you're particularly sensitive to environmental contaminants.

Water Pollution

Many towns and cities in California get drinking water good enough to bottle and sell. That's because it comes from mountain river reservoirs. Other parts of the state are not so lucky. Southern California, Los Angeles included, must import most of its water, often from as far away as the Colorado River. The water is not as pure as mountain water, and tastes bad, too.

"Where does it come from?" is the most important question to ask in determining the quality of a water supply. In general, water from aboveground sources is good water.

Water pumped from ground aquifers can be just as good but can also be polluted with health-threatening substances such as toxic waste from industrial sources or agricultural chemicals. In a number of California areas, water quality isn't too different from that in developing countries. People who can afford to do so drink bottled water.

The key to determining water quality is to find out the source for a particular town. Often, one part of a county—Santa Clara, for example—will have excellent water piped in from the mountains, while a few miles away the water will be wretched.

RESOURCE

Water quality and water pollution. Ask the local water district where the water comes from. If it's pumped from the ground or comes from a river, demand information on recent water-quality tests.

The best source for candid information on all pollution is private environmental groups, such as Communities for a Better Environment (CBE) (www.cbecal.org). They do their own studies and can tell you if a known pollution problem exists in your neighborhood. CBE has offices in Oakland, 510-302-0430, and Huntington Park, 323-826-9771.

Ask your regional office of the State Water Resources Control Board about pollution (see the government pages of the phone book for the number), or check their main website at www.swrcb.ca.gov. Or try the Water Quality Information Line at 916-341-5455. These agencies, however, have limited information—they generally report only complaints received, unless a particular area has been tested recently. If so, ask for the results.

Toxic Waste

No one in his or her right mind would knowingly buy a house next door to a toxic waste dump. Unfortunately, the presence of toxic waste may not be obvious. Many toxic dumps are buried; other locations have yet to be disclosed. And some dumps may pose broader health threats if their contaminants leak into groundwater supplies.

A 1986 report by the California Legislature stated that all nine major toxic waste landfills in California leak, and that not one met state requirements to prevent leakage. Thousands of smaller waste landfills and underground storage tanks leak into the soil and water, resulting in almost 20% of California's major drinking water wells having been chemically polluted. Aquifers, which store water, are not naturally flushed. Once one becomes polluted, it stays that way. The situation is so bad that several communities in California whose aquifers became contaminated have been rendered uninhabitable.

RESOURCE

Toxic waste. Communities for a Better Environment (www.cbecal.org).

California Office of Environmental Protection, Department of Toxic Substance Control, 800-728-6942. This state agency maintains the Hazardous Waste and Substances Sites List of problem sites in California. (For more information, see www.dtsc.ca.gov.)

Environmental Defense Fund. This nonprofit organization provides information on toxic waste and environmental pollutants by community.

Check their informational website at www.scorecard.org.

Air Pollution

The air quality in California varies about as much as the weather, as the two are closely related. Residents breathe easier near the coast, where the air circulates regularly, keeping the smog from ever getting really thick.

Unfortunately, if you enjoy hot weather, learn to like polluted air. Anywhere the air sits still long enough to really warm up, pollution collects, particularly in the summer. Areas of the state east of the coastal range are blocked from the cleansing incursions of sea air. The Central Valley is often thick with smog, as are the San Gabriel and San Fernando valleys in southern California. Ditto the Livermore Valley, east of San Francisco, where a few years ago the development of a new town was blocked in part because air pollution was already dangerous.

Los Angeles has some of the most polluted air in the U.S. Despite efforts to convert to cleaner fuels, the situation is expected to worsen in coming years as more cars and industry fill the area. The Pacific winds blow much of L.A.'s smog inland to the rapidly developing Riverside and San Bernardino counties. L.A.'s coastal communities, such as Pacific Palisades, Santa Monica, Venice, and Palos Verdes, have relatively clean air, as well as the most expensive houses in the L.A. metropolitan area.

Many people consider air pollution more of a nuisance than a hazard, but recent studies show that airborne toxins pose a threat to anyone living near industry, including the "clean" computer industry. One survey linked exposure to air toxins with high cancer rates near Contra Costa County's petrochemical plants. If you're sensitive to air pollution, you'll want to move close to the coast or the Sierra foothills and avoid most areas in between, although there are still many rural parts of northern and central California where the air is relatively clean.

RESOURCE

Air pollution. Communities for a Better Environment (www.cbecal.org) does their own studies and can tell you if a known pollution problem exists in your neighborhood. CBE has offices in Oakland, 510-302-0430, and Huntington Park, 323-826-9771.

The Environmental Defense Fund provides information on toxic waste and environmental pollutants by community. Check their informational website at www.scorecard.org.

A local or regional air quality district such as Bay Area Air Quality Management District (415-749-5000, www.baaqmd.gov) and www.sparetheair.org; South Coast Air Quality Management District (800-288-7664, www.aqmd.gov); or San Joaquin Valley Air Pollution Control District (209-557-6400 in Modesto, 559-230-6000 in Fresno, and 661-326-6900 in Bakersfield, www.valleyair.org) will tell you more about the air where you live. A city manager's or mayor's office should be able to refer you to a specific air quality district, or check the Air and

Waste Management Association's website at www.awma.org for the nearest district.

Nuclear Plants

Atomically speaking, California is in better health than many other states. While four commercial nuclear power plants have been built, only two are operational—the Diablo Canyon plant in San Luis Obispo, 200 miles north of Los Angeles, and the San Onofre Nuclear Generating Station between Los Angeles and San Diego. Safety fears led to the close of the other two: the Humboldt Bay nuclear plant in Eureka and Rancho Seco near Sacramento. Many people believe it makes sense to avoid buying a house near any of the power plants, as serious safety questions have been raised about all four. These questions often center on whether the plants will withstand a strong earthquake, although operations problems (at the two up and working) also arise.

Even when a reactor is shut down, a hazard remains. At both of California's commercial nuclear power plants, spent fuel is stored in open containment ponds, awaiting the construction of a high-level waste repository. Should an earthquake occur before California gets around to building this repository, and should a containment pond crack and lose its water, the spent fuel could melt down and release radioactivity.

If you decide to live near a nuclear plant, a house to the north or west will be safer from possible releases of radioactivity than a house to the south or east, as winds in California blow toward the south and southeast 80% of the time.

RESOURCE

Nuclear plants. The Abalone Alliance informed people of the threats posed by nuclear power in California. Though disbanded in 1985, their archival website (www.energy-net.org) still has helpful information.

Schools

California has many excellent public schools —the problem is finding them. The solution is to look yourself, not to simply ask your real estate agent, "How are the schools around here?"

Since California's Proposition 13 cut taxes, schools have had less money. Some schools are in worse shape than others, but all have had to cut back programs, usually in sports, art, music, and drama. At some schools, where parent interest is high and financial resources available, parents pay to keep "nonessential" programs going.

Many people assume that the best schools are in the rich communities. This isn't always true. Money, by itself, doesn't guarantee good schools, although parents in prosperous areas (who themselves tend to have a relatively high level of education) usually take considerable interest in educating their children. But many middle class cities have excellent public schools too, because parents get involved.

To learn about average class size, course offerings, instructional practices, and available services, start by calling and visiting local schools and school districts. Obtain the *School Accountability Report Card* (or "SARC"), which each school must prepare annually. This report covers a range of important topics, including expenditures per student and types of services funded; class sizes and teaching loads; student achievement and progress toward meeting academic goals; assignment of teachers outside of their subject areas of competence; quality and currency of textbooks and instructional materials; availability of qualified personnel to provide counseling and other student support services; dropout rates; safety, cleanliness, and adequacy of school facilities; classroom discipline and climate for learning; teacher and staff training; and quality of school instruction and leadership. Each school is required to post its report on its website, which you can link to from the Department of Education's website www.cde.ca.gov (click "Testing and Accountability," then "Accountability," then "School Accountability Report Card").

Arrange to visit schools you're considering. Observe the atmosphere by sitting in on classes and talking to some parents or teachers. And look for locally produced publications such as a school newsletter or parent handbook.

The State Department of Education in Sacramento can also provide useful information. Student performance in California is measured by a series of standardized tests, known as "STAR" tests (Standardized Testing and Reporting). For information about these tests and how California's students are scoring, see the following website put up by the Standards and Assessments Office of the Department of Education: http://star.cde.ca.gov.

The Educational Demographics Unit provides much data for schools and districts, including enrollment figures, racial and ethnic information, language census data, and even dropout rates. Call them in Sacramento at 916-327-0219. The Department of Education's website is www.cde.ca.gov.

Check out local resources at public libraries. Look under "Schools" in the index of local newspapers at a public library for articles on how active the district PTA is and how well attended parent open houses are. Local civic groups, such as the League of Women Voters or PTA, often publish ratings of local schools. Ask a reference librarian for help finding these. If you're interested in private schools, ask for information on local guides, such as *McCormack's Guides,* discussed below.

Contact EdSource, a nonprofit resource center that distributes impartial statewide information. EdSource publishes numerous impartial pamphlets discussing school budgets and finances, the ramifications of state education legislation, demographics, and bilingual education. If EdSource doesn't have what you need, they can help you find it. Contact them in Mountain View at 650-917-9481 or at www.edsource.org.

RESOURCE

Check out online resources. Look in regional directories for a specific city or county, and then search the "schools" area for a particular school or district. Also, see The School Report, www.homefair.com (look in the left sidebar). This contains useful information on and maps of school districts throughout California. Another website offers detailed reports for a fee: School Match, www.schoolmatch.com. Also see the summaries of schools provided at www.greatschools.net (a nonprofit organization). Finally, be sure to check out websites that provide community and neighborhood (including school) information (listed in Chapter 6).

Traffic

In California cities, traffic has replaced weather as the favorite topic of conversation; as more people move here, traffic gets worse. In the San Francisco Bay Area, people in the North Bay and East Bay commonly arise before dawn and drive hours to reach major urban centers. Los Angeles has four of North America's five busiest freeways. Traffic typically crawls from morning to midnight.

Before you buy a house in California, figure out how you are going to get to work. Is driving reasonable? Will it still be in ten years? Don't assume you can jump in the car and turn the key. Sometimes in California, you *can't* always get there from here (at least not before 9:00 a.m.).

Consider the availability of public transportation. As traffic continues to worsen, rapid transit may be the only alternative. And, of course, if you live near your job, you can avoid a commute altogether. If you work in the city, a house there may cost more, but this extra cost is increasingly likely to balance against your commuting (and sometimes parking) costs. This is a popular approach in L.A., where people are "rediscovering" downtown and the advantages of living close to work.

RESOURCE

Transportation. Check the nearest office of the California Department of Transportation (Caltrans) for information on ride sharing and transportation planning, or call the state office. Call Caltrans at 916-654-5266, or check their website at www.dot.ca. gov. Also, city traffic departments may be of some help.

Crime

Crime always ranks high when people are asked about the social problems that most concern them. Indeed, in many areas neighbors are so concerned they have banded together to form crime prevention groups.

Picking an area that is reasonably safe is a major concern when purchasing a house, especially if you have children. Understand that a substantial percentage of the crime that occurs in any neighborhood is committed by people who live there—often teenagers and others who feel alienated, bored, or angry. There is no way to escape this type of crime except by taking home-security precautions and working with others as part of neighborhood groups designed to help local teenagers channel energy into healthier activities.

Still, it's sensible to be aware of a neighborhood's crime level when buying a house. Here are a few suggestions:

- Some cities have far less crime than others. The California Attorney General's Office publishes statewide statistics adjusted by population in *Crime in California*. It's available from the Criminal Justice Statistics Center in Sacramento at 916-227-3509 or online at http://ag.ca.gov/cjsc/pubs.htm.
- You can check on crime types and frequency with the local police department. Although they may not keep statistics on a block-by-block basis, you may be able to get numbers for the general neighborhood you are considering.
- Neighborhoods with active, effective neighborhood watch groups, where residents understand the importance of keeping their eyes on the street and maintaining good communication among neighbors, are usually much safer than those that remain unorganized.
- If you are seriously worried about crime, you may want to live in a community secured with walls and guards. But check with residents before you assume security is tight—some of these communities have become targets for burglars who easily evade lax security systems or unguarded front gates.
- Upscale suburban areas next to very poor ones are almost always targets for robbery and burglary. So before you buy, drive 20 blocks in every direction. Look for graffiti, broken windows, bars on doors, or boarded-up buildings. If you find yourself rolling up your window in your car, you'll likely need a burglar alarm and maybe bars on the windows at home.
- In California cities, neighborhood safety changes block to block, driven by many factors, most of which are invisible to newcomers. Ask long-time local residents in what areas they would feel safe walking the dog at 10:00 p.m. Then confirm what you hear by talking to patrol cops. Take any advice from a real estate agent with a grain of salt—they earn a commission regardless of how safe the neighborhood is.

Additional Information on California

For separate guides to many California counties, see *McCormack's Guides*. These annual publications provide a range of local information on schools (public and private), demographics, crime, weather, home prices, jobs, recreation, child and health care, and other topics of interest to newcomers, including profiles of individual cities. *McCormack's Guides* are available at many bookstores or at 800-222-3602, www.mccormacks.com.

California County Populations

In Alphabetical Order				In Order of Population			
County	Population	County	Population	County	Population	County	Population
Alameda	1,530,620	Orange	3,098,183	Los Angeles	10,294,280	El Dorado	178,689
Alpine	1,261	Placer	329,818	San Diego	3,120,088	Imperial	174,322
Amador	38,320	Plumas	20,891	Orange	3,098,183	Kings	153,268
Butte	219,101	Riverside	2,070,315	Riverside	2,070,315	Madera	149,916
Calaveras	45,950	Sacramento	1,415,117	San Bernardino	2,039,467	Napa	135,554
Colusa	21,945	San Benito	57,493	Santa Clara	1,820,176	Humboldt	132,364
Contra Costa	1,044,201	San Bernardino	2,039,467	Alameda	1,530,620	Nevada	99,587
Del Norte	29,207	San Diego	3,120,088	Sacramento	1,415,117	Sutter	95,516
El Dorado	178,689	San Francisco	817,537	Contra Costa	1,044,201	Mendocino	89,669
Fresno	923,052	San Joaquin	680,183	Fresno	923,052	Yuba	71,612
Glenn	28,018	San Luis Obispo	267,154	Ventura	826,550	Lake	63,821
Humboldt	132,364	San Mateo	734,453	San Francisco	817,537	Tehama	62,093
Imperial	174,322	Santa Barbara	425,710	Kern	809,903	San Benito	57,493
Inyo	18,253	Santa Clara	1,820,176	San Mateo	734,453	Tuolumne	56,910
Kern	809,903	Santa Cruz	265,183	San Joaquin	680,183	Calaveras	45,950
Kings	153,268	Shasta	181,380	Stanislaus	523,095	Siskiyou	45,695
Lake	63,821	Sierra	3,400	Sonoma	482,034	Amador	38,320
Lassen	36,223	Siskiyou	45,695	Tulare	430,974	Lassen	36,223
Los Angeles	10,294,280	Solano	423,970	Monterey	425,356	Del Norte	29,207
Madera	149,916	Sonoma	482,034	Solano	423,970	Glenn	28,018
Marin	256,310	Stanislaus	523,095	Santa Barbara	425,710	Colusa	21,945
Mariposa	18,356	Sutter	95,516	Placer	329,818	Plumas	20,891
Mendocino	89,669	Tehama	62,093	San Luis Obispo	267,154	Mariposa	18,356
Merced	252,554	Trinity	14,012	Santa Cruz	265,183	Inyo	18,253
Modoc	9,747	Tulare	430,974	Marin	256,310	Mono	14,055
Mono	14,055	Tuolumne	56,910	Merced	252,554	Trinity	14,012
Monterey	425,356	Ventura	826,550	Butte	219,101	Modoc	9,747
Napa	135,554	Yolo	197,530	Yolo	197,530	Sierra	3,400
Nevada	99,587	Yuba	71,612	Shasta	181,380	Alpine	1,261

Source: www.csac.counties.org

California County Map
OREGON
NEVADA
ARIZONA
MEXICO
Del Norte
Siskiyou
Modoc
Humboldt
Trinity
Shasta
Lassen
Tehama
Plumas
Mendocino
Glenn
Butte
Sierra
Nevada
Colusa
Yuba
Sutter
Lake
Placer
Sonoma
Napa
Yolo
El Dorado
Alpine
Sacra-
mento
Amador
Solano
Calaveras
Marin
Contra
Costa
San
Joaquin
Tuolumne
Mono
San Francisco
Alameda
Stanislaus
Mariposa
San Mateo
Santa
Clara
Merced
Madera
Santa Cruz
San Benito
Fresno
Inyo
Tulare
Monterey
Kings
San Luis
Obispo
Kern
San Bernardino
Santa Barbara
Ventura
Los Angeles
Orange
Riverside
San Diego
Imperial

APPENDIX

B

Real Estate Websites

There are hundreds of thousands of real-estate-related websites, with more added every day. That's a lot of surfing for home buyers! To make your online research easy, we've chosen the 100 or so websites of specific value to California homebuyers. Our list is organized in alphabetical order by topic, with reference to specific chapters for more information. This appendix also includes some general advice on doing real estate searches online, including how to find a California statute without setting foot in a law library.

Be sure to check Nolo's website at www.nolo.com for real estate calculators and other useful information and resources.

Top Real Estate Websites

From air pollution to title insurance, here are useful websites for California homebuyers.

Air Pollution (App. A)

Air and Waste Management Association: www.awma.org

Environmental Defense Fund: www.edf.org or www.scorecard.org

Asbestos Hazards and Inspections (Ch. 19)

American Lung Association: www.lungusa.org

California Department of Industrial Relations, Division of Occupational Safety and Health (Cal/OSHA): www.dir.ca.gov/dosh/Asbestos.html

Community and Relocation Information (Ch. 6)

California Home Page: www.ca.gov

HomeFair: www.homefair.com

Smarthomebuy: www.smarthomebuy.com

Sperling's Best Places: www.bestplaces.net

Also, see the real estate sections of newspapers. Websites are listed under *Homes for Sale.*

Comparable Sales Prices (Ch. 15)

HomeRadar.com: www.homeradar.com

Smarthomebuy: www.smarthomebuy.com

National Association of Realtors: www.realtor.com

Zillow: www.zillow.com

Contractors (Ch. 7 and 19)

Contractor's State License Board: www.cslb.ca.gov

Credit Bureaus and Reports (Ch. 2)

Equifax: www.equifax.com

Experian: www.experian.com

TransUnion: www.transunion.com

myFICO: www.myfico.com

Credit Counseling (Ch. 2)

National Foundation for Credit Counseling: www.nfcc.org

Myvesta.org: www.myvesta.org

Credit Scores (Ch. 2)

Fair Isaac: www.fairisaac.com or www.myfico.com

Crime (App. A)

California Attorney General's Office, Criminal Justice Statistics Center: http://ag.ca.gov/cjsc

Earthquakes and Seismic Hazards (Ch. 19 and App. A)

Seismic Safety Commission: www.seismic.ca.gov

Governor's Office of Emergency Services: www.oes.ca.gov

California Department of Conservation, State Mining, and Geology Board: www.consrv.ca.gov/SMGB

Escrow Companies (Ch. 18)

California Department of Corporations: www.corp.ca.gov

Floods (Ch. 19 and App. A)

Federal Emergency Management Agency (FEMA): www.fema.gov

U.S. Geological Survey: www.usgs.gov

Foreclosures (Ch. 3)

www.realtytrac.com

See **Government Loans** and websites of individual lenders.

Government Loans (Ch. 11)

Veterans Affairs (VA): www.va.gov

Federal Housing Administration (FHA): www.hud.gov/buying

California Housing Finance Agency (CHFA): www.calhfa.ca.gov

CalVet: www.cdva.ca.gov/calvet

Homes for Sale (Ch. 6 and 7)

California Living Network: http://ca.realtor.com

California Living Network's Spanish-language equivalent, Sucasa: www.sucasa.net

***Fresno Bee*:** www.fresnobee.com/realestate

HomeBuilder: www.move.com

***Los Angeles Times*:** www.latimes.com/classified/realestate

MSN Real Estate: www.realestate.msn.com

Owners' Network: www.owners.com

***Press-Enterprise* (Riverside):** www.pe.com/homes

Realtor.com: www.realtor.com

***San Diego Union-Tribune*:** www.realestate.signsonsandiego.com

***San Francisco Chronicle*:** www.sfgate.com/classifieds/homes

***San Jose Mercury News*:** www.mercurynews.com/real

Also, see websites of local papers, individual real estate brokers, and mortgage lenders.

Home Inspections (Ch. 7 and 19)

American Society of Housing Inspectors (ASHI): www.ashi.com

Contractor's State License Board: www.cslb.ca.gov

California Real Estate Inspection Association (CREIA): www.creia.org

Homeowners' Associations (Ch. 7)

Community Associations Institute: www.caionline.org

Homeowners' Insurance (Ch. 18 and 19)

California Department of Insurance: www.insurance.ca.gov

Insurance News Network: www.insure.com

Housing Discrimination (Ch. 6)

California Department of Fair Employment and Housing: www.dfeh.ca.gov

Lead Hazards, Inspections, and Disclosures (Ch. 19)

California Department of Health Services: www.dhs.ca.gov/childlead

National Lead Information Center: www.epa.gov/lead

Lenders (Complaints) (Ch. 13)

California Dept. of Real Estate: www.dre.ca.gov

California Dept. of Consumer Affairs: www.dca.ca.gov

Use a Web search engine such as Yahoo! to check out websites of individual lenders. Also sec *Mortgage Rates, Loans, and Calculators* to find online mortgage lenders.

Mortgage and Financial Calculators (Ch. 2, 3, 8, 9, and 13)

HomeFair: www.homefair.com

MortgageCalc: www.mortgagecalc.com

Yahoo! Real Estate: http://realestate.yahoo.com

Also, see websites listed under *Mortgage Rates, Loans, and Calculators,* and *Rent Versus Buy Decisions.*

Mortgage Rates, Loans, and Calculators (Ch. 2, 8, 9, and 13)

E-Loan: www.e-loan.com

Interest.com: www.interest.com

The Mortgage Superstore: www.infoloan.com

QuickenMortgage: www.quickenloans.com

LendingTree: www.lendingtree.com

MSN Real Estate: www.realestate.msn.com

HSH Associates: www.hsh.com (rates only)

Mortgagebot.com: www.mortgagebot.com

Mortgage-Net: www.mortgage-net.com

Nolo: www.nolo.com/calculators (calculators only)

Also, search for individual lenders, such as Bank of America, and see websites of *Homes for Sale,* including newspaper real estate sections online.

Moving Companies (Ch. 3 and App. C)

California Public Utilities Commission: www.cpuc.ca.gov

New Homes (Ch. 7)

HomeBuilder: www.move.com

Homeowners Against Deficient Dwellings: www.hadd.com

Homeowners for Better Building: www.hobb.org

J.D. Power Consumer Center: www.jdpower.com

Nuclear Plants (App. A)

Abalone Alliance: www.energy-net.org

Pest Control Inspections (Ch. 19)

California Structural Pest Control Board: www.pestboard.ca.gov

Radon (Ch. 19)

California Department of Health Services: www.cdph.ca.gov (search for "radon")

National Safety Council: www.nsc.org

Real Estate Agents and Brokers (Ch. 5 and 13)

California Association of Realtors: www.car.org

California Department of Real Estate: www.dre.ca.gov

HomeGain: www.homegain.com

Ira Serkes: www.berkeleyhomes.com

Council of Residential Specialists: www.crs.com

Real Estate Buyer's Agent Council: www.rebac.net

National Association of Realtors: www.realtor.com

Realty Locator: www.realtytimes.com

Real Estate Law (Ch. 5)

California Association of Realtors: www.car.org

California Department of Real Estate: www.dre.ca.gov

Refinancing Calculators (Ch. 9)

HomeFair: www.homefair.com

E-Loan: www.e-loan.com

Nolo: www.nolo.com/calculators

Remodeling (Ch. 3)

ImproveNet: www.improvenet.com

National Association of the Remodeling Industry: www.nari.org

Building Education Center: www.bldgeductr.org

Remodeling Online: www.remodeling.hw.net

Rent Versus Buy Decisions (Ch. 3)

HomeFair: www.homefair.com

E-Loan: www.e-loan.com

Yahoo! Real Estate: http://realestate.yahoo.com

Also, see other websites listed under *Mortgage Rates, Loans, and Calculators.*

Safe Drinking Water (App. A)

EPA Office of Ground Water and Safe Drinking Water: www.epa.gov/safewater

Communities for a Better Environment: www.cbecal.org

Schools (App. A)

Ed Source: www.edsource.org

The School Report: www.homefair.com/real-estate/school-reports

School Match: www.schoolmatch.com

Great Schools: www.greatschools.net

California State Department of Education: www.cde.ca.gov

Smart Home Buy: www.smarthomebuy.com

Also, see websites listed in *Community and Relocation Information.*

Secondary Mortgage Market (Ch. 2 and 4)

Fannie Mae: www.fanniemae.com

Freddie Mac: www.freddiemac.com

Tax Information (Ch. 4, 8, and 14)

IRS: www.irs.gov

State Franchise Tax Board: www.ftb.ca.gov

Title Insurance (Ch. 18)

California Land Title Association (CLTA): www.clta.org

American Land Title Association (ALTA): www.alta.org

Toxic Waste (App. A)

California Office of Environmental Protection, Dept. of Toxic Substance Controls: www.dtsc.ca.gov

Scorecard: www.scorecard.org

Transportation (App. A)

California Department of Transportation: www.dot.ca.gov

Water Pollution (App. A)

Communities for a Better Environment: www.cbecal.org

State Water Resources Control Board: www.swrcb.ca.gov

California Online

We don't want you to miss two special sites that have a lot of useful information for California homebuyers.

California Home Page: www.ca.gov. Every California homebuyer, especially those new to the state, should bookmark this site. It provides information on the Golden State—from schools and jobs to business and environmental protection programs. It's especially useful for tapping into state and government agencies, programs, and laws.

The California Association of Realtors (CAR): www.car.org. This site provides useful consumer information on its website, including updates on state and federal legislation; real estate listing information from nearly every Multiple Listing Service in California; median prices of California homes; and a directory of California Realtors®, including multilingual Realtors®.

General Real Estate Sites

If you can't find what you want on our top 100 list, here are some other useful suggestions for doing your online real estate search.

Realty Times: www.realtytimes.com. This is a great place to check out real estate information online. It provides real estate information and links nationwide. This site also has answers to common real estate questions, as does www.ourbroker.com, operated by real estate author Peter Miller.

The International Real Estate Digest (IRED): www.ired.com (provides links to 25,000 real estate websites throughout the world, primarily geared to real estate professionals).

For up-to-date real estate news, check out *Deadline News.com* by real estate writer Broderick Perkins, and *Inman News Features* at www.inman.com.

How to Find a California Statute Online

Using this book is a good way to educate yourself about the laws that affect the home-buying process. In some cases, you may want to read the exact California statute that we refer to in the text. This is easy to do online. Go to Nolo's home page at www.nolo.com. Click Site Map, then "State Statutes," then "California." There you'll find a list of statutes, also called codes, grouped by subject matter into 29 Titles (for example, the Civil Code, Business and Professions Code, and so on).

There are two ways to find statutes; both are free:

- If you know the subject matter of the code (for example, real estate agents), you can enter these "keywords" into the search box and you'll get a list of codes that include this phrase.
- You can also "browse" the codes by asking to see a Table of Contents for each Title. As you look down the list, you may see the statute that interests you.

The state's Legislative Counsel also maintains a free Web page with current legislative information, www.leginfo.ca.gov. You can read the text of any pending bill, the analyses prepared by assembly and senate members, voting records, and lists of sponsors. You can also ask to be notified via email any time there is legislative action on a bill that you want to follow.

RESOURCE

Legal research. *Legal Research: How to Find & Understand the Law,* by Stephen Elias and Susan Levinkind (Nolo). This book gives easy-to use, step-by-step instructions on finding legal information.

APPENDIX

C

Planning Your Move

In terms of stress, studies show that moving ranks right up there behind divorce and the death of a loved one. But, with intelligent planning, you can at least minimize this stress. The following will help you plan your move.

Tax-Deductible Moving Expenses and Costs of Sale

You may deduct job-related moving expenses—such as travel, transportation, and storage costs—from your gross income on your federal tax return if all of the following are true:

- Your move is within one year of starting your new job.
- The distance from your old home to your new job is at least 50 miles more than the distance from your old home to your old job.
- The distance from your new home to your new job is less than the distance from your old home to your new job; this test need not be met if your employer said moving was a condition of your employment, or if you'll spend less time or money on your new commute.
- You were fully employed for 39 weeks out of the year following the move; and, if you're self-employed, you also worked for 78 weeks out of the two years following the move.

You may also deduct certain costs of selling and/or buying a home such as points and other loan fees.

RESOURCE

Tax-deductible expenses. For information on tax-deductible moving expenses, see IRS Publication 521, *Moving Expenses.*

For tax rules that apply when you sell a house, see IRS Publication 523, *Selling Your Home.*

These publications and related forms are available by calling the IRS at 800-829-1040 or visiting its website, www.irs.gov.

Moving Checklist: Two Weeks Before Moving

Not all items on this list will apply to you. If you're moving within the same town, you probably won't have to transfer your kids to a new school or have your car serviced for travel. Just focus on the applicable items.

- ☐ Check with your childrens' new school about what records and transcripts are needed, and arrange for their transfer.
- ☐ Close or transfer bank and safe deposit box accounts.
- ☐ Cancel deliveries (newspaper, magazines (including alumni bulletins and nonprofit newsletters), diapers, laundry).
- ☐ Cancel utilities (gas, electric, cable, phone, water, garbage); transfer services (if possible) or arrange new services; request deposit refunds.
- ☐ Get recommendations for (or find in advance, especially if a medical condition needs regular attention) new doctors, dentist, and veterinarian; if possible, photocopy medical records to have with you.

- ☐ Get reference letters if you'll need to find a job.
- ☐ Cancel membership (and transfer membership, if relevant) in religious, civic, and athletic organizations.
- ☐ Have car serviced for travel.
- ☐ Buy travel insurance.
- ☐ Get maps.
- ☐ Line up storage facility.
- ☐ Arrange for moving pets, including a safe place for them to stay while the moving van is being loaded—a common time for animals to escape.
- ☐ Finalize arrangements with moving company. (Get bids and make preliminary arrangements weeks in advance.)
- ☐ Tell close friends and relatives your schedule.

RESOURCE

Moving companies. It's worth doing careful research before choosing a moving company. Complaints about them are skyrocketing. Customers report long delays, broken goods, and even having their possessions held "hostage" until an extra, unexpected cash payment is handed over. Ask friends for referrals, and get bids from at least three companies before choosing—while being wary of any exceptionally low bids. Also, check the state Public Utilities Commission's website, www.cpuc.ca.gov, for consumer information on choosing a moving company. Other good sources of information include the American Moving and Storage Association (a trade group, at www.moving.org) and the Web-based company Moving.com (www.moving.com).

Things to Remember While Packing

- ☐ Inventory your possessions before packing them, in case things get lost in the move. Take photos of the more valuable items.
- ☐ Label boxes on top and side—your name, new city, room of house, contents.
- ☐ Pack phone books.
- ☐ Assemble moving kit—hammer, screwdriver, pliers, tape, nails, tape measure, scissors, flashlight, cleansers, cleaning cloths, rubber gloves, garbage bags, lightbulbs, extension cords, step stool, mop, broom, pail, vacuum cleaner.
- ☐ Keep the basics handy—comfortable clothes, toiletries, towels, battery-powered alarm clock, disposable plates, cups and utensils, can opener, one pot, one pan, sponge, paper towels, toilet paper, plastic containers, toys for kids.
- ☐ Carry jewelry, extremely fragile items, currency, and important documents.
- ☐ Make other arrangements if moving company won't move antiques, art collections, crystal, other valuables, or plants.

TIP

How to pack a truck like a pro. If you're handling your own move, minimize damage to your possessions—and your spine—by first placing extra-long items such as mattresses and framed art works along the walls of the truck, then putting in the heaviest objects (always keeping appliances upright), then piling the lighter objects on top. Use some rope to tie the doors on your appliances and dressers, and rent some blanket-style furniture pads to protect surfaces.

Who Should Get Changes of Address

- ☐ Friends and relatives.
- ☐ Subscriptions.
- ☐ Government agencies you regularly deal with—VA, IRS, Social Security Administration, and so on.
- ☐ Charge and credit accounts.
- ☐ Installment debt—such as student loan or car loan.
- ☐ Frequent flyer programs.
- ☐ Brokers and mutual funds.
- ☐ Insurance agent/companies.
- ☐ Medical providers—if you'll be able to use them after moving.
- ☐ Catalogues you want to keep receiving.
- ☐ Charities you wish to continue donating to.
- ☐ Post office. (If you're trying to get off catalogue and other direct mailing lists, only have first-class mail forwarded. Give your new address to those catalogue companies on whose lists you want to remain, and don't forget to tell them not to trade or sell your name.)

Things to Do After Moving In

- ☐ Open bank accounts and safe deposit box account.
- ☐ Begin deliveries: newspaper, diapers, laundry.
- ☐ Register to vote.
- ☐ Change (or get new) driver's license.
- ☐ Change auto registration.
- ☐ Install new batteries in existing smoke detectors (and install any additionally needed smoke detectors); buy fire extinguisher.
- ☐ Hold party for your house scouts and moving helpers, and take yourself out for a congratulatory dinner!

APPENDIX

D

Forms

Explanations for the forms in this appendix can be found in Chapters 1 and 2.

Ideal House Profile

Upper price limit: ____________________

Maximum down payment: ____________________

Special financing needs: ____________________

	Must Have	Hope to Have
Neighborhood or location:		
School needs:		
Desired neighborhood features:		
Length of commute:		
Access to public transportation:		
Size of house:		
Number and type of rooms:		
Condition, age, and type of house:		
Type of yard and grounds:		

Absolute no ways:

____

____

House Priorities Worksheet

Date visited: ____________________ Price: $ ____________________

Address: ____

Contact: ____________________ Phone #: ____________________

Must have:

- ☐ ____________________
- ☐ ____________________
- ☐ ____________________
- ☐ ____________________
- ☐ ____________________
- ☐ ____________________
- ☐ ____________________
- ☐ ____________________
- ☐ ____________________
- ☐ ____________________
- ☐ ____________________
- ☐ ____________________

Hope to have:

- ☐ ____________________
- ☐ ____________________
- ☐ ____________________
- ☐ ____________________
- ☐ ____________________
- ☐ ____________________
- ☐ ____________________
- ☐ ____________________

Absolute no ways:

- ☐ ____________________
- ☐ ____________________
- ☐ ____________________

Comments about the particular house:

____

____

____

House Comparison Worksheet

House 1 ______________________________

House 2 ______________________________

House 3 ______________________________

House 4 ______________________________

	1	2	3	4
Must have:				
______________________________	__	__	__	__
______________________________	__	__	__	__
______________________________	__	__	__	__
______________________________	__	__	__	__
______________________________	__	__	__	__
______________________________	__	__	__	__
______________________________	__	__	__	__
______________________________	__	__	__	__
______________________________	__	__	__	__
______________________________	__	__	__	__
______________________________	__	__	__	__
______________________________	__	__	__	__
______________________________	__	__	__	__
Hope to have:				
______________________________	__	__	__	__
______________________________	__	__	__	__
______________________________	__	__	__	__
______________________________	__	__	__	__
______________________________	__	__	__	__
______________________________	__	__	__	__
______________________________	__	__	__	__
______________________________	__	__	__	__
Absolute no ways:	__	__	__	__
______________________________	__	__	__	__
______________________________	__	__	__	__
______________________________	__	__	__	__

Family Financial Statement

	Borrower	Coborrower
Name and address:		
Home phone number:		
Email address:		
Employer's name & address:		
Work phone number:		

WORKSHEET 1: INCOME AND EXPENSES

I. INCOME	Borrower ($)	Coborrower ($)	Total ($)
A. Monthly gross income			
1. Employment			
2. Public benefits			
3. Dividends			
4. Royalties			
5. Interest & other investment income			
6. Other (specify):			
B. Total monthly gross income			
II. MONTHLY EXPENSES			
A. Nonhousing			
1. Child care			
2. Clothing & personal expenses			
3. Food			
4. Insurance (auto, life, medical, & dental)			
5. Medical & dental care (not insurance)			
6. Taxes (nonhousing)			
7. Education			
8. Transportation			
9. Other (specify):			
B. Current housing			
1. Mortgage payment or rent			
2. Taxes			
3. Insurance			
4. Utilities			
C. Total monthly expenses			

WORKSHEET 2: ASSETS AND LIABILITIES

I. ASSETS (Cash or Market Value)	Borrower ($)	Coborrower ($)	Total ($)
A. Cash & cash equivalents			
1. Cash			
2. Deposits (list):			
B. Marketable securities			
1. Stocks & bonds (bid price)			
2. Other securities			
3. Mutual funds			
4. Life insurance			
5. Other (specify):			
C. Total cash & marketable securities			
D. Nonliquid assets			
1. Real estate			
2. Retirement funds			
3. Business			
4. Motor vehicles			
5. Other (specify):			
E. Total nonliquid assets			
F. Total all assets			
II. LIABILITIES			
A. Debts			
1. Real estate loans			
2. Student loans			
3. Motor vehicle loans			
4. Child or spousal support			
5. Personal loans			
6. Credit cards (specify):			
7. Other (specify):			
B. Total liabilities			
III. NET WORTH (Total assets minus total liabilities)			

Directions for Completing the Family Financial Statement

Top. Indicate the name(s), address(es), home phone number(s), email address(es), employer's name(s) and address(es), and work phone number(s) for yourself and any coborrower. A coborrower includes a spouse, partner, friend, or nonspouse relative with whom you are purchasing the house.

Worksheet 1: Income and Expenses

This worksheet shows you how much disposable income you have each month, a key fact in determining how big a mortgage you can realistically take on. In columns 1 and 2, you and any coborrower each list your monthly income and expenses. Total them in column 3.

IA. Monthly gross income. List your gross monthly income from all sources. Gross income means total income before amounts such as taxes, Social Security, or retirement contributions are withheld.

1. **Employment.** This is your base salary or wages plus any bonuses, tips, commissions, or overtime you regularly receive. If your income is irregular, take the average of the past 24 months. If you have more than one job, include your combined total.
2. **Public benefits.** Include income from Social Security, Disability, Temporary Assistance for Needy Families (TANF), Supplemental Security Income (SSI), and other public programs.
3. **Dividends.** Include all dividends from stocks, bonds, and similar investments.
4. **Royalties.** If you have continuing income from the sale (licensing) of books, music, software, inventions, or the like, list it here.
5. **Interest and other investment income.** Include interest received on savings or money market accounts, or as payments on rental property. If the source of the income has costs associated with it (such as the costs of owning rental property), include the net monthly profit received.
6. **Other.** Include payments from pensions, child or spousal support, or separate private maintenance income. Specify the source.

IB. Total monthly gross income. Total items 1–6. (This is the figure that lenders use to qualify you for mortgages.)

IIA. Monthly nonhousing expenses. List what you spend each month on items such as child care and clothing. These won't interest the lender as much as they are important to you in evaluating how much house you can afford. Here are some notes clarifying specific items:

2. **Clothing and personal expenses.** Include not only costs for your average monthly outlay on clothing, but your personal care (haircuts, shoe repairs, and toiletries) and personal fun (attending movies, buying DVDs and lottery tickets, and subscribing to newspapers). Also, include any regular personal loan payments.

3. **Food.** Include eating at restaurants, as well as at home.
7. **Education.** Include monthly payments for education loans here, plus educational payments such as your child's private school tuition.
8. **Transportation.** Include costs for both motor vehicle (include monthly car loan payments, but exclude insurance) and public transit. Include monthly upkeep for a vehicle and a reasonable amount for repairs.
9. **Other.** Specify such expenses as regular monthly credit card payments, charitable or religious donations, and savings deposits or child or spousal support payments.

IIB. Current housing expenses. If you currently own a home, list the mortgage and interest, taxes, and insurance. If you rent, include your monthly rent and renter's insurance (if any).

Also include utilities, such as gas, electricity, water, sewage, garbage, telephone, and cable service.

IIC. Total monthly expenses. Here, total your nonhousing and housing expenses.

Worksheet 2: Assets and Liabilities

I. Assets. In columns 1 and 2, you and any coborrower write down the cash or market value of the assets listed. Total them up in column 3.

A. **Cash and cash equivalents.** List your cash and items easily converted into cash. Deposits include checking accounts, savings accounts, money market accounts, and certificates of deposit (even if there is a withdrawal penalty).

B. **Marketable securities.** Here you list items like stocks and bonds that are regularly traded and that you can normally turn into cash fairly readily. List the cash surrender value of any life insurance policy. Include items such as a short-term loan you made to a friend under the category "Other."

C. **Total cash and marketable securities.** Add up items A and B.

D. **Nonliquid assets.** These are items not easily converted into cash.

1. **Real estate.** List the market value: the amount the property would sell for.
2. **Retirement funds.** Include public or private pensions and self-directed accounts (IRAs, Keoghs, or 401(k) plans). List the amount vested in the plan.
3. **Business.** If you own a business, list your equity in it (market value less the debts on the business). Many small businesses are difficult to sell, and therefore difficult to value, but do your best to estimate accurately.
4. **Motor vehicles.** List the current market value of any car, truck, RV, or motorcycle, even if you're still making payments. Check used car guides for the information. The *Kelley Blue Book*'s used car values can be accessed online at www.kbb.com.
5. **Other.** Include nontangible assets such as copyrights, patents, and trademarks; the current value of

long-term loans you've made to others; and any really valuable personal property such as expensive jewelry or electronic gear.

E. Total nonliquid assets. Total up items D1–5.

F. Total all assets. Total up items IC and IE.

IIA. Liabilities—Debts. In columns 1 and 2, you and any coborrower write the total balances remaining for your outstanding loans under their respective categories.

Under "Other," don't include monthly insurance payments or medical (noninsurance) payments, as these go on Worksheet 1, Section IIA, Monthly Expenses—Nonhousing. Do include stock pledges, lawyer's and accountant's bills, and the like.

IIB. Total Liabilities. Total the monthly payments and balances remaining for items 1–7.

III. Net Worth. Total of all assets minus total liabilities.

Index

D

E

F

M

N

Q

R

S

T

Get the Latest in the Law

Nolo's Legal Updater

We'll send you an email whenever a new edition of your book is published! Sign up at **www.nolo.com/legalupdater**.

Updates at Nolo.com

Check **www.nolo.com/update** to find recent changes in the law that affect the current edition of your book.

Nolo Customer Service

To make sure that this edition of the book is the most recent one, call us at **800-728-3555** and ask one of our friendly customer service representatives (7:00 am to 6:00 pm PST, weekdays only). Or find out at **www.nolo.com**.

4 Complete the Registration & Comment Card ...

... and we'll do the work for you! Just indicate your preferences below:

Registration & Comment Card

NAME DATE

ADDRESS

CITY STATE ZIP

PHONE EMAIL

COMMENTS

WAS THIS BOOK EASY TO USE? (VERY EASY) 5 4 3 2 1 (VERY DIFFICULT)

☐ Yes, you can quote me in future Nolo promotional materials. *Please include phone number above.*

☐ Yes, send me **Nolo's Legal Updater** via email when a new edition of this book is available.

Yes, I want to sign up for the following email newsletters:

- ☐ **NoloBriefs** (monthly)
- ☐ **Nolo's Special Offer** (monthly)
- ☐ **Nolo's BizBriefs** (monthly)
- ☐ **Every Landlord's Quarterly** (four times a year)

BHCA12

☐ Yes, you can give my contact info to carefully selected partners whose products may be of interest to me.

NOLO

Send to: **Nolo** 950 Parker Street Berkeley, CA 94710-9867, Fax: (800) 645-0895, or include all of the above information in an email to regcard@nolo.com with the subject line "BHCA12."